TRAINING AND CONDITIONING FOR
MMA

PROGRAMMING OF CHAMPIONS

Stéfane Beloni Correa Dielle Dias, PhD

Everton Bittar Oliveira, BS

André Geraldo Brauer Júnior, PhD

Pavel Vladimirovich Pashkin, MS

EDITORS

HUMAN KINETICS

Library of Congress Cataloging-in-Publication Data

Names: Dias, Stéfane Beloni Correa Dielle, 1980- editor.
Title: Training and conditioning for MMA : programming of champions /
  Stéfane Beloni Correa Dielle Dias, Everton Bittar Oliveira, André
  Geraldo Brauer, Pavel Vladimirovich Pashkin, editors.
Other titles: Teoria e prática do treinamento para MMA. English |
  Training and conditioning for mixed martial arts
Description: Champaign, IL : Human Kinetics, 2023. | "This book is a
  revised edition of Teoria e prática do treinamento para MMA, published
  in 2017 by Phorte Editora"--Title page verso. | Includes bibliographical
  references and index.
Identifiers: LCCN 2022013187 (print) | LCCN 2022013188 (ebook) | ISBN
  9781492598619 (paperback) | ISBN 9781492598626 (epub) | ISBN
  9781492598633 (pdf)
Subjects: LCSH: Mixed martial arts--Training. | BISAC: SPORTS & RECREATION
  / Martial Arts / General | SPORTS & RECREATION / Bodybuilding &
  Weightlifting
Classification: LCC GV1102.7.M59 T4613 2023 (print) | LCC GV1102.7.M59
  (ebook) | DDC 796.81071--dc23/eng/20220506
LC record available at https://lccn.loc.gov/2022013187
LC ebook record available at https://lccn.loc.gov/2022013188

ISBN: 978-1-4925-9861-9 (print)

This book is a revised edition of *Teoria e prática do treinamento para MMA*, published in 2017 by Phorte Editora.

The web addresses cited in this text were current as of February 2022, unless otherwise noted.

Senior Acquisitions Editor: Roger W. Earle; **Developmental Editor:** Laura Pulliam; **Managing Editor:** Hannah Werner; **Copyeditor:** Michelle Horn; **Indexer:** Rebecca L. McCorkle; **Permissions Manager:** Martha Gullo; **Senior Graphic Designer:** Sean Roosevelt; **Cover Designer:** Keri Evans; **Cover Design Specialist:** Susan Rothermel Allen; **Photograph (cover):** Al Bello/Zuffa LLC/Zuffa LLC via Getty Images; **Photographs (title page):** dmitr1ch / Adobe Stock; Taigi / Adobe Stock; dmitr1ch / Adobe Stock; **Photo Asset Manager:** Laura Fitch; **Photo Production Manager:** Jason Allen; **Senior Art Manager:** Kelly Hendren; **Illustrations:** © Human Kinetics, unless otherwise noted; **Printer:** Walsworth

Human Kinetics books are available at special discounts for bulk purchase. Special editions or book excerpts can also be created to specification. For details, contact the Special Sales Manager at Human Kinetics.

Printed in the United States of America   10 9 8 7 6 5 4 3 2 1

The paper in this book was manufactured using responsible forestry methods.

Human Kinetics
1607 N. Market Street
Champaign, IL 61820
USA

United States and International
Website: **US.HumanKinetics.com**
Email: info@hkusa.com
Phone: 1-800-747-4457

Canada
Website: **Canada.HumanKinetics.com**
Email: info@hkcanada.com

E8086

TRAINING AND CONDITIONING FOR

PROGRAMMING OF CHAMPIONS

To my wife, Francielle Dias, who has been my companion for over 20 years. Because she loves me, she moved to the United States and gave birth to my beautiful daughters, Lohana and Lauren, who inspired me to publish this latest work. To Jehovah God, for having given me such a beautiful family; my intelligent brother, Steeve, and his family; and my exemplary parents, Valdenir Dielle Dias (in memoriam) and Lucia Maria Beloni Correa. I love you all! Last, but not least, to my mentor, Dr. Victor N. Seluyanov (in memoriam), and to all my colleagues at Keiser University, students, and athletes who always inspire me to give my best every day.

Stéfane Beloni Correa Dielle Dias

First, I give thanks to God and to my family, who I love so much—in particular, my parents, Eólo de Oliveira and Maria de Lourdes Bittar Oliveira, and my brother, Cleverson Bittar Oliveira, for giving me all the support and backing I have needed throughout my life. I am eternally grateful to them. Next, my sincere thanks to all my friends and private students as well as American Top Team owner Dan Lambert, Marcus "Conan" Silveira, the coaches, staff, athletes (Amanda Nunes, Antônio "Bigfoot" Silva, Thiago Alves, Thiago Santos, Amanda Ribas, Junior Dos Santos, Alexandre Pantoja, Adriano Moraes, Edson Barboza, Marlon Moraes, Jussier Formiga, Marcos "Pezão" de Lima, Raush Manfio, Natan Schulte, Gleison Tibau, Pedro Munhoz, Philipe Lins, Joshua Silveira, Thiago Moisés, Glover Teixeira, Rodrigo "Ze Colmeia" Nascimento, Roan Carneiro, Rafael Dias, Rafael Rebello, Ana Frias, Junior Fernandes, and many others), and race car drivers (Oswaldo Negri Jr. and family, Matheus Leist and family, Lucas Kohl, James Egozi and family, Darren Keane, Reece Gold, Michael Auriemma, Glauber Granero, Gianluca Petecof, Lucas Fecury, Juan, Karla, and João Vergara) who have participated directly or indirectly in my career as a professional performance coach here in the United States.

Everton Bittar Oliveira

To my parents, for giving me the gift of life, for everything they have done to ensure that I can follow my professional career, and for all the values they have passed on to me. I am eternally grateful! To my beloved daughters, Isabele and Luana, who have taught me the real meaning of the word *love*. Because of you, I have become, and strive every day to be, a better human being. Because of you, I feel and understand what complete happiness is. Thank you for being in my life and for allowing me to perform the extremely important role of being your father!

To my colleagues: You are exemplary professionals from whom I learn on a daily basis.

To all my students: Without you, my profession would have no meaning. You are my main source of inspiration!

André Geraldo Brauer Júnior

This book is dedicated to all those who constantly seek knowledge. Enjoy the experience. My participation in this book comes from the desire to share with you my experience and the experience of my sporting family and my trainers. I express my thanks to my colleagues for being such a great team and to my family, who support me in all my efforts.

Pavel Vladimirovich Pashkin

CONTENTS

ACKNOWLEDGMENTS

We would like to start by thanking the entire staff of the American Top Team and, in particular, Dan Lambert and Marcus "Conan" Silveira, for providing the opportunity for all this to happen and for attaining the position that American Top Team occupies today as the best MMA team in the world! A significant part of this work was only possible with the help of Richie "Puma" Guerriero, Eddie "Primo" Miranda, and Ana Frias, along with the great trainers and masters: Ricardo Libório; Katel Kubis; Luciano "Macarrão" Santos; Dyah Davis and in memory of his father, Howard Davis Jr.; Steve Bruno; Ailton Barbosa; Steve Mocco; Marcos "Parrumpa" da Matta; Mike Thomas Brown; Thiago "Pitbull" Alves; and King Mo.

Immense credit goes to Juan Carlos Santana, the director of the Institute of Human Performance (IHP), for his readiness to provide assistance in developing various training circuits and models that appear in this book, and to our coauthors for their excellent work writing some of the best and most up-to-date content available today.

We are grateful to all our colleagues at Keiser University who strive so hard to put their students first at all times, thanks to the fine leadership and example of Dr. Arthur Keiser. The Exercise Science and Health and Human Performance programs were well organized, starting with Julie Snyder, Dr. John Hatten, and Dr. Ryan Fairall. Now the Exercise and Sport Science program is in full development under Dr. Jeff Williams' leadership. We would also like to thank Dr. David Hubbard, Dean Samuel Sparks, Dean Idanny Matos, Dean Linda Deturck, Dean Jerry Picott Jr., Professor Charla Girtman, and Brian Binkley for their huge efforts in making everything possible and ensuring that this book was published here in the United States of America.

We are also grateful to many other people who helped to keep the Orlando campus functioning properly, mainly with the great work of our campus president, Dr. Todd Harrison; administrative assistant Gladys Sanchez; Dennis Ferraro; Ann Marie Cooper and David Palmer from the student services department; our great computer specialist, Edwin Ayala; the staff of the registrar's office: Tami Weimer, Ricardo Perez, and Bryan Fisher; our librarian, Sarah Cruz Mendoza; and our security guard, Christopher Kogut. You are all amazing!

Without forgetting the teachers, coaches, fighters, and friends who have always supported us and who continue to play important roles in our careers, we thank Dr. Mary Jane Moore, Rachel Karpf, Antônio Eduardo Branco, Randy Barroso, Junior Fernandes, Saul Alencar, Jim Hartt, Gleison Tibau, Héctor Lombard, António "Bigfoot" Silva, Oswaldo Negri, Rafael Dias, Carlinhos "Vale-Tudo," Orlando Rasta, Ercilio Slaviero, Lucas Roveda, Augusto Slaviero, Dr. Howard Gelb and family, Nakia Geller, Isaac Geller, Dr. Shai Karpf, Dr. Parkash Bakhtiani, Donny Kent, Michael Gelfano, Gary Nocera, Mike Cauley, Marcio Pimentel, Daniel Dezan, Juliano Borges, Mauricio Kiel, Fabiano Paiva, Clovis Bevilaqua, Marco Aurelio Cota Jr., Cleyton Teixeira, Fabio Stremel, Vitaly Rybakov, Dr. Victoria Zaborova, Grigor Chilingaryan, Salim Kharkovsky, Egor Rubanov, Rio Santana, Rokaya Mikhailenko, Caleb Geller, Gonzalo Gutierrez, Devin Christie, Gabriel Rosa, Korey Folbrecht, Justin Cobb, Henrique Camboias, Carlos "Juninho" Ribeiro, Marcelo Alves, Eduardo Dezen, and all the athletes who offered to help demonstrate the exercises in this book. Last, but not least, thanks to all the staff from Human Kinetics, especially Roger Earle, Jason Muzinic, Laura Pulliam, and Hannah Werner, for all their hard work and patience to make this project happen. You guys are great!

PHOTO CREDITS

Chapter 1 opener photo courtesy of ONE Championship

Chapter 2 opener photo courtesy of International Brazilian Jiu-Jitsu Federation (IBJJF) and The Grapple Club

Chapter 3 opener photo courtesy of Natan "Russo" Schulte

Chapter 4 opener photo courtesy of Phil Lambert

Chapters 5 and 6 opener photos courtesy of Everton Bittar Oliveira

Figures 1.33, 2.07, 3.14, 3.16, 5.07-5.18, 5.26-5.27, 5.31-5.33, 5.35-5.89, 5.117-5.137, 5.139-5.153, 5.165-5.175, 5.182-5.199, 5.208-5.217, 5.223-5.260, 5.281-5.285, 5.324-5.332, 6.01, 6.05-6.12, 6.15-6.39 by Stéfane Beloni Correa Dielle Dias

Figures 2.01-2.02 courtesy of Raphael Giacomelli

Figures 3.02, 3.13, 3.15, 5.90-5.95 © Human Kinetics

Figures 3.03-3.06 with kind permission from http://prosportlab.com

Figures 3.08, 5.176-5.181 courtesy of Demetrius Borges

Figures 5.01-5.06, 5.19-5.25, 5.28-5.30, 5.34, 5.96-5.110, 5.154-5.159, 5.200-5.207, 5.218-5.222, 5.261-5.280 courtesy of Sarah Jaquemet

Figures 5.111-5.116 courtesy of Alexey Ivanov

Figures 5.160-5.164 courtesy of Darren Altman Photography

Figures 5.286-5.323, 6.02-6.03, 6.13-6.14 courtesy of Pavel Vladimirovich Pashkin

Figures 5.333-5.356 courtesy of Albina Rybakova

Figure 6.04 courtesy of Tone Ricardo Benevides Panassollo

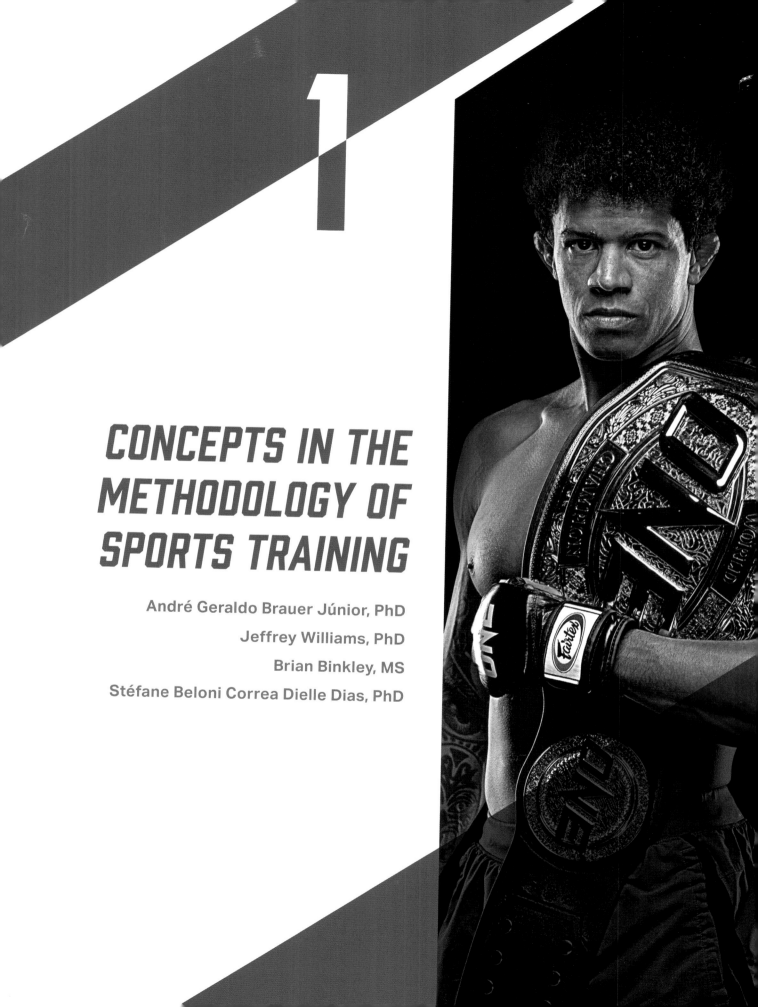

1

CONCEPTS IN THE METHODOLOGY OF SPORTS TRAINING

André Geraldo Brauer Júnior, PhD

Jeffrey Williams, PhD

Brian Binkley, MS

Stéfane Beloni Correa Dielle Dias, PhD

Periodization is the general and detailed planning of the time available for training according to established intermediate goals that respect scientific sports training principles (Matveev, 2008, 2001, 1991; Dantas, 2003; Tubino, 2003; Moreira, 2008; Mujika, 2018). The training process of periodization is creating a system of plans for different periods that follow a set of closely linked goals (Gomes, 2009; Matveev, 2001).

Accordingly, the training process structure should be part of a plan for achieving specific targets in preparation for the main competition established for the period, and the athlete is expected to reach their peak in sports performance (see figure 1.1) (Brauer, et al. 2019).

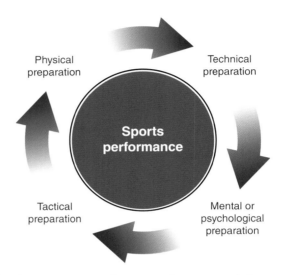

Figure 1.1 – Graphical representation of sports performance and the interdependence of its components.

Adapted by permission from A.G. Brauer Jr., R.M. Souza, S.L.F. Andrade, S.B.C.D. Dias, and T.F.F. Pimenta, *Esportes de Combate: A Ciência no Treinamento de Atletas de MMA* (Curitiba: Editora Juruá, 2019).

Sports performance is characterized by the athlete's state of optimal preparation to compete in competitions and is intimately connected to all the sports preparation components (physical, technical, tactical, and psychological). Sports performance is a long-term cyclical process and depends on three phases (Matveev, 2008, 2001), as seen in figure 1.2:

1. *Phase 1*, called *preparation* or *initial preparation*, is characterized by an increase in the athlete's functional capacity, improvements in physical and mental development, and the acquisition or reconstruction of motor skills.

2. *Phase 2* is characterized by stable sports performance and, in some cases, an improvement in certain components of it.

3. *Phase 3* is characterized by a temporary loss in sports performance but does not adversely affect the athlete's normal daily activities because the athlete is in active recovery.

According to Matveev (2008), in the sports preparation process, it is essential to understand the factors that influence preparation and the adaptation response dynamics of the different functional or organic systems of the athlete exposed to training stimuli. The sports preparation process leads to changes in their physical, technical, or tactical levels and psychological preparation and suggests it is important to observe the changes in several functional variables throughout the athlete's preparation to understand why the

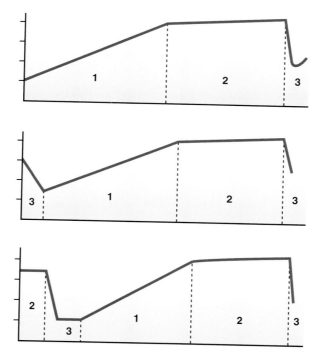

Figure 1.2 – Stages of sports performance development: 1 = preparation phase, 2 = stabilization phase, 3 = temporary loss phase.

Adapted by permission from A.G. Brauer Jr., R.M. Souza, S.L.F. Andrade, S.B.C.D. Dias, and T.F.F. Pimenta, *Esportes de Combate: A Ciência no Treinamento de Atletas de MMA* (Curitiba: Editora Juruá, 2019). Data from Matveev (2001).

adaptations occurred (i.e., what happened during the training process and the influence of its organization in the athlete's individual responses).

Observing the relationship between the preparation content and a change in the athlete's preparation level is possible by controlling the dynamics of the training load components (volume, intensity, and density) during the different preparation stages. This load control and changes in functional indicators during different preparation stages should be optimized by using different models of the training process structure, with the goal of getting the athlete fit (Brauer, et al. 2019).

Within this context, different models for organizing the athlete's preparation over the season have been discussed in specialized literature, but, as Issurin (2010) pointed out, it is more often as a professional report and in magazines for coaches than in scientific works.

From a scientific standpoint, little is known about the process for training fighters. Brauer and colleagues (2012) claimed that, among the research published between 1998 and 2012, only 5.8 percent was dedicated to studies on sports training in combat sports. This makes it difficult to establish precise relationships between sports results and the training process.

Moreira (2010) highlighted the following as possible explanations for this situation:

- Difficulty in accessing and reaching elite athletes.
- The prospect of advancing research in the real environment of these athletes is still challenging for those who focus on this area.
- Opportunities to experiment with different periodization models for high-performance athletes are few because trainers, athletes, and coaching staff resist doing the experiments.

These obstacles show, in part, that there is a gap between the scientific evidence and practice in the preparation of high-performance athletes in combat sports. This chapter will encourage reflection on questions about the training periodization for athletes in combat sports. We will discuss the periodization models that we believe are the most applicable to different combat sports.

Before presenting the periodization models themselves, we will review the sports training methodology concepts that will be used later to aid comprehension.

Overload Principle Applied to Sports Training

The concept of overload or physical load in sports training is related to the fact that physical exercise causes changes in body function versus its state at rest. Within this context, Matveev (2008, 1991) divided physical loads into two components: external and internal.

External Training Loads

These loads are the influence of the external environment on the body (i.e., all that is planned for the athlete to perform within a training session). The external load placed on an athlete during training is typically an objective measurement that can be monitored reliably and consists of various metrics, such as the weight or resistance used in a session (bar weight or band resistance), total volume performed over a session (sets × reps × weight), distance covered within a session (miles, kilometers, yards), and speed of an exercise being performed (plyometric push-up versus a standard push-up). It can often be monitored during training and competition, depending on the sport (Wallace, et al. 2009). To quantify it, we should know the intensity, volume, and density of the training load. The external training load is related to training quality, quantity, and periodization.

Intensity

Load intensity is defined by the magnitude of the influence of a certain physical exercise on the human body. Additionally, intensity determines which energy sources will be mobilized during the physical activity. It may be controlled by several variables: speed of locomotion (mph, km/h, or m/sec), complexity of coordination for technical or tactical actions, pace of execution (number of repetitions within a set time), magnitude of relative effort (percentage of personal best in a given exercise), resistance of the external environment (elevation, wind, water current, etc.), and psychological stress itself at different levels of competition.

Volume

Volume is determined by the duration of a physical exercise, the number of exercise sets, and the number of exercises in the training session or class (e.g., 10 minutes of warm-up, three minutes of shadow boxing in Muay Thai or in boxing, five minutes of fighting in jiu-jitsu, judo, or sambo). The following indicators may regulate volume: total time of execution of the exercise (minutes, hours), distance covered during the exercise (m, km, miles), total weight lifted (number of sets × number of repetitions × weight lifted in each repetition), and number of motor actions (technical and tactical).

Note that there is an inversely proportional relationship between intensity and volume. For example, a top-level athlete may be able to run one to two hours at 16 kilometers per hour (about 10 mph) but not more than 30 seconds at 30 kilometers per hour (about 18.75 mph) (see figure 1.3). Or, in resistance training, the higher the percentage of a repetition maximum (%1RM), the lower the number of repetitions possible (see figure 1.4). Therefore, we should not combine maximum volumes with maximum intensities in a single training session.

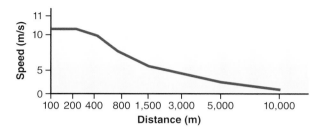

Figure 1.3 – Relationship between distance (volume) and speed (intensity) in 100-meter to 10,000-meter runs.

Adapted by permission from A.G. Brauer Jr., R.M. Souza, S.L.F. Andrade, S.B.C.D. Dias, and T.F.F. Pimenta, *Esportes de Combate: A Ciência no Treinamento de Atletas de MMA* (Curitiba: Editora Juruá, 2019). Data from Matveev (2008).

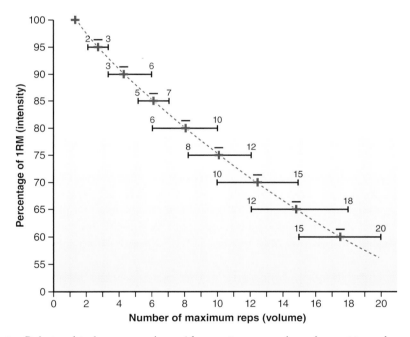

Figure 1.4 – Relationship between volume (the maximum number of repetitions that can be performed) and intensity (%1RM) in resistance training.

Adapted by permission from A.G. Brauer Jr., R.M. Souza, S.L.F. Andrade, S.B.C.D. Dias, and T.F.F. Pimenta, *Esportes de Combate: A Ciência no Treinamento de Atletas de MMA* (Curitiba: Editora Juruá, 2019). Data from Matveev (2008).

Density

The training load density is related to the rest between the training sets as well as between the separate training sessions. The nature of the rest breaks (active or passive) and their duration depend on the proposed objective. *Training density* typically refers to the volume (reps) performed over a given time or within a specific time. The training session density can be calculated based on the total number of repetitions within a specific time, and by either increasing total number of repetitions within the same amount of time or incrementally decreasing rest periods, the number of repetitions performed per minute in that session will effectively increase despite no change in total volume performed. For example, consider two athletes, one professional and another amateur. The professional executes the barbell bench press with 225 pounds (about 102 kg) and repeats this six times, finishes the first set and rests five minutes, does the second set and rests five minutes, and concludes with a third set (all with six repetitions).

On the other hand, the amateur, seeing the professional train, does practically the same workout and executes the barbell bench press with 225 pounds for three sets of six repetitions but rests 10 minutes instead of five minutes between each set. The training is apparently equal—intensity = 225 pounds, volume = 3 sets of 6 repetitions × 225 pounds = 4,050 pounds—but the training density is 50 percent lower for the amateur athlete compared to the professional athlete. Therefore, the fewer or shorter the rest breaks, the greater the training density.

Rest breaks between sets or different exercises in one training session are different from the breaks between training sessions, the former being shorter and more varied than the latter. Matveev (2008) classified the rests between sets of the same exercise and between exercises within a single training session as different types:

- *Ordinary*—The duration of this rest is sufficient for the body to normalize and execute the next set of exercises. The work capacity at the end of this rest is very close to initial levels and may be executed without compromising the quantity and quality of the work. The duration of ordinary rests and other types of rest is quite varied (from a few seconds in short-duration exercises to several minutes in long-duration and high-intensity exercises) and depends on several factors, such as the type of exercise and the level of the athlete. This kind of interval is used for training the physical qualities of strength, speed, and power, because these rests are designed to replenish the energy substrate (see figure 1.5). Verkhoshansky (1990) suggested that the rests for this kind of work be at least three or four minutes and may even reach eight minutes.

- *Tense or forced*—The duration of this rest is so short that the following exercise or set is executed with an incomplete recovery, with fatigue due to the previous exercise or set present. This kind of rest develops aerobic, anaerobic, and muscular endurance, where we may use the work–rest ratio to define the most appropriate rest breaks. The

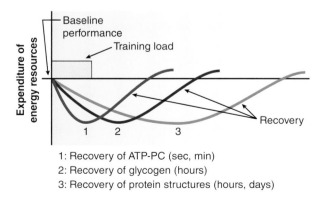

Figure 1.5 – Replenishment of different energy substrates according to time: 1 = recovery of ATP-PC (sec, min); 2 = glycogen recovery (hours); 3 = recovery of protein structures (hours, days).

Adapted by permission from A.G. Brauer Jr., R.M. Souza, S.L.F. Andrade, S.B.C.D. Dias, and T.F.F. Pimenta, *Esportes de Combate: A Ciência no Treinamento de Atletas de MMA* (Curitiba: Editora Juruá, 2019). Data from Suslov (1997).

main aim of rests with incomplete recovery is to partially remove metabolites formed during the sets. The following are some examples of how to use tense or forced rests.

- *Glycolytic endurance:* work–rest ratio of 1:3; volume is determined by mechanical efficiency. For example, an athlete performs repetitions of 30 seconds of running at maximum speed, so they should rest for approximately 90 seconds or more.
- *Intensive aerobic:* work–rest ratio of 1:0.25-0.5; is used in exercises ranging from 30 seconds to 2 minutes 30 seconds of work. For example, an athlete performs repetitions of 1 minute of running, so they should rest for approximately 15 seconds to 30 seconds.
- *Extensive aerobic:* is used in exercises ranging from 2 minutes 30 seconds to 10 minutes of work with a standard rest interval of 45 seconds to 1 minute and 30 seconds. For example, an athlete performs repetitions of 5 minutes of running and rests for approximately 1 minute and 30 seconds.

Compared with the rests used between sets or exercises, the rests between training sessions have a greater influence on recovery processes, a fact that should be considered when planning weekly training loads (see table 1.1).

Matveev (2008) distinguished between three types of intervals between training sessions:

- *Ordinary*—With this kind of rest between training sessions, the level of work capacity at the beginning of the next session returns to that seen at the beginning of the previous one.
- *Strict*—These rests are shorter than the ordinary ones. Using these rests yields a greater summation of the cumulative effects of the previous and subsequent sessions.
- *Supercompensatory*—This kind of rest is often used after a set of strict rests and occurs when the work capacity is greater than that of the previous training sessions. In sport science theory, supercompensation is the posttraining period during which the trained function or parameter has a higher performance capacity than it did before the training period (see figure 1.6).

Table 1.1 – Duration of Recovery Processes After Different Training Loads

Type	Influence on the autonomic nervous system	Influence on the neuromuscular system (peripheral)	Recovery time
Speed	Small	Large	24-36 hr
Speed endurance (alactic)	Large	Medium	Up to 48 hr
Maximum strength	Large	Maximum	48 hr
Speed or strength	Medium	Large	24-48 hr
Aerobic endurance	Maximum	Medium	48-72 hr
Endurance (glycolytic system)	Maximum	Medium	48-96 hr
Skills training or technical training	Small	Small	6 hr

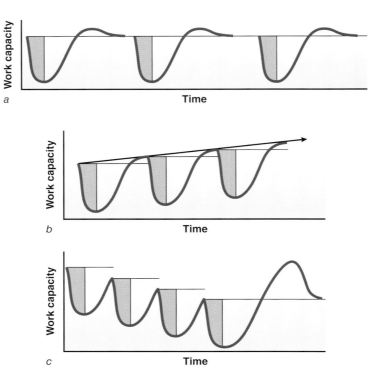

Figure 1.6 – Total effect of training loads in light of different rest intervals: (*a*) when the duration of rest is too long, the following load is executed after the supercompensation phase (without an increase in work capacity); (*b*) in executing the following load in the supercompensation phase, a gradual increase in work capacity is observed; (*c*) reduction in work capacity as a consequence of executing some loads without full recovery of the body, but after a sufficient rest, significant super-compensation occurs.

Adapted by permission from A.G. Brauer Jr., R.M. Souza, S.L.F. Andrade, S.B.C.D. Dias, and T.F.F. Pimenta, *Esportes de Combate: A Ciência no Treinamento de Atletas de MMA* (Curitiba: Editora Juruá, 2019).

Longer intervals than the supercompensatory intervals are not used, because large intervals between sessions result in the supercompensatory effect being lost, thus causing a decrease in the athlete's trainability and work capacity.

Internal Training Loads

These loads are characterized as being an acute body response to the influences of the external component (intensity, volume, and density). The magnitude of the internal training load will be responsible for expected chronic adaptations (supercompensation, see figure 1.6) and an increase in sports performance. Thus, the success of the training process depends on monitoring the internal training load.

The internal load can be controlled through several indicators, such as reaction time, heart rate, the speed of accumulation and quantity of blood lactate, respiratory rate and intensity, oxygen consumption, and blood pressure. However, most methods used for precise internal control require instruments often inaccessible to professionals who work with combat sports. For this reason, in sports practice, we can use simpler indicators, such as fatigue indicators (see table 1.2).

Another instrument widely used to control the internal training load is the rating of perceived exertion (RPE) as an indicator of intensity. With this approach, the athlete uses a numerical scale to rate the effort of an entire training session. The benefits of using the RPE for the session include the opportunity for the coaches to assess and compare the level of stress related to the different training components (Wallace, et al. 2009).

Use the protocol in this way: 30 minutes after the end of the training session, have the athlete answer the question "How intense was the training session?" The answer to the question is given using the scale shown in table 1.3.

Table 1.2 – Indicators of Fatigue Used to Control the Internal Training Load

Symptom	Light fatigue (light or moderate load)	Major fatigue (heavy or submaximal load)	Maximum fatigue (maximal load)
Athlete's concentration (focus)	Normal, without nervousness, attention under control during the demonstration of the exercises	Worsening of concentration, decreased capacity of differentiation, worsening of absorption of content	Significant decrease in attention, significant nervousness, delayed reaction speed
Coordination of movements	Correct execution (according to the level of the athlete)	Increase in number of errors, decrease in precision, feeling of insecurity	Large number of errors, major decrease in coordination
Perspiration	Little or average (in relation to ambient temperature and humidity)	Major perspiration above the waist (upper body)	Major perspiration all over the body
Skin color	Mild reddening	Strong reddening	Very strong reddening or unusual pallor

Adapted by permission from A.G. Brauer Jr., R.M. Souza, S.L.F. Andrade, S.B.C.D. Dias, and T.F.F. Pimenta, *Esportes de Combate: A Ciência no Treinamento de Atletas de MMA* (Curitiba: Editora Juruá, 2019). Data from Suslov (1997).

Table 1.3 – Sample Rating of Perceived Exertion (RPE) Scale

Rating	Description
1	Nothing at all (lying down)
2	Extremely little
3	Very easy
4	Easy (could do this all day)
5	Moderate
6	Somewhat hard (starting to feel it)
7	Hard
8	Very hard (making an effort to keep up)
9	Very, very hard
10	Maximum effort (can't go any further)

Reprinted by permission from D.H. Fukuda and K.L. Kendall, "Fitness Evaluation Protocols and Norms," in *NSCA's Essentials of Personal Training*, 3rd ed., edited by B.J. Schoenfeld and R.L. Snarr for the National Strength and Conditioning Association (Champaign, IL: Human Kinetics, 2022), 204.

Use the 30-minute interval so that light or intense activities performed at the end of the session do not interfere with the result. It is common, during the training session, for the RPE to be different from the one reported 30 minutes after the end of the training session, because it indicates the level of acute, momentaneous stress of a given exercise or pause (McGuigan, et al. 2008). The interval should not be much longer than 30 minutes so the athlete does not forget and adversely affect the subjective assessment of the training session intensity.

The RPE method combines the volume and intensity of the training session, assessing the magnitude of the internal load. The internal training load calculation, using the RPE of the session, consists of multiplying the RPE score by the total duration of the session expressed in minutes (including warm-up, cool-down, and pauses between exertion in the case of interval training). The product of the RPE (intensity) and the duration of the session (volume) is expressed in arbitrary units. For example, a training session with an RPE of 6 and a duration of 40 minutes would present a training load of 240 arbitrary units (see figure 1.7, Wednesday).

As Nakamura and colleagues (2010) stated, the RPE of the session may help construct training periodization curves or graphs, revealing the pattern of training loads over a preparation period. Comparing the external load (planned) and the internal load (actual), determined by the session RPE, is useful in the training process because it allows the training to be adjusted (Kelly and Coutts, 2007).

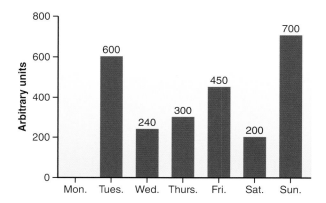

Figure 1.7 — Example of quantification of loads using the method of the RPE of the session.

Adapted by permission from A.G. Brauer Jr., R.M. Souza, S.L.F. Andrade, S.B.C.D. Dias, and T.F.F. Pimenta, *Esportes de Combate: A Ciência no Treinamento de Atletas de MMA* (Curitiba: Editora Juruá, 2019).

Modes of Training

Before we think about periodization in a broader sense, we need to know which kinds of exercise (modes of training) exert different effects on the athlete's body. Different exercises are prescribed for the fighter during preparation. Stop to think about the purpose each exercise serves. When should running, for example, be placed in the fighter's preparation? And in resistance training, should localized muscular endurance, hypertrophy, strength, or power be prioritized? Should sparring work be done every week?

With this in mind, we consider physical exercise classifications and some examples according to Matveev (2008) to better understand these and other questions relating to the exercise selection in different periods of the fighter's preparation.

General Preparation Exercises

The exercises selected in the general preparation part of the program are important because they create a foundation for the phases that follow. These exercises are related to varied physical qualities and are not directly related to the sports performance in the competitive activity. However, they indirectly affect the achievement of favorable results in sports activities. As Bompa (2003) mentioned, successful sports specialization in a given event largely depends on what the author called *multifaceted physical development*. Additionally, using only training fights (special preparation exercise) limits the athlete's capacities after an initial peak, and a lack of general preparation exercises for the fighter leads to inconsistent results and may hamper the fighter's progress.

The following are examples of goals geared toward general physical preparation: flexibility, aerobic endurance, general strength, localized muscular endurance, and predictable technical training, among others.

Table 1.4 shows examples of general preparation exercises performed in a circuit. The circuit should have two or three sets without any rest between the exercises (only the time spent in transition from one exercise to another) with 60 to 90 seconds of rest between the sets.

Table 1.4 – General Preparation Circuit for MMA Fighters

	Exercise	Reps or duration
1	Skipping rope	1 min
2	Body weight lunge	10 reps
3	Hang clean and push jerk	4-6 reps 60% of 1RM
4	Pull-up	8-10 reps
5	Dumbbell hang snatch	4-6 reps
6	Deadlift	6-8 reps 60% of 1RM
7	Medicine ball slam	6-8 reps
8	Medicine ball throw	6-8 reps
9	Kettlebell swing	10-12 reps
10	Plank	1 min

Specific Preparation Exercises

This is very similar to competition, because the elements of competition are what are trained. Examples include a bout of Muay Thai or boxing with restricted maneuver combinations. As another example, in judo, Brazilian jiu-jitsu, Greco-Roman wrestling, and sambo, use different positions with the training partner as the opponent and with the same intensity as what would occur in competition. As Gomes (2009) stated, these kinds of exercises are the main way to improve the athlete's performance, because they represent selective modeling of the different components of the competition activity.

We may highlight the following as examples of goals geared toward the specific preparation of the fighter: glycolytic endurance, power, unpredictable technical training, and the execution speed of specific movements, among others. In table 1.5, we present some examples of specific preparation exercises performed in the form of a circuit.

Table 1.5 – Specific Preparation Circuit for MMA Fighters

	Exercise	**Duration**
Round 1	Shadow boxing	50 sec
	Takedowns	50 sec
	Guard pass	50 sec
	Ground and pound	50 sec
	Arm lock with partner	50 sec
	Triangle	50 sec
Round 2	Kick heavy bag	50 sec
	Sprawls	50 sec
	Punch heavy bag	50 sec
	Kneeing in clinch	50 sec
	Elbows	50 sec
	Hip escape	50 sec
Round 3	Focus mitt	50 sec
	Throws	50 sec
	Kneeing in clinch	50 sec
	Sprawls	50 sec
	Bridge isometric exercises	50 sec
	Ground and pound	50 sec

The exercise is performed in a circuit format with three rounds of five minutes and one minute of rest between the rounds, with the exercises being performed at high intensity.

Competition Preparation Exercises

These exercises are carried out in a competition situation (see table 1.6), whether official or not, even under conditions of training (simulated combat). The competition exercises involve the athlete's overall motor skills according to the rules of the combat sport concerned. As an example, we may say "hard sparring" in Muay Thai, MMA, and boxing or a "fight" in jiu-jitsu, judo, or sambo.

Table 1.6 summarizes the main features of the general, specific, and competition exercises for a professional boxer. The exercise form relates to the biomechanics of the sports technique (motor movement), while the content relates to the physiological demands of the sport.

Competition exercises account for much less volume than the general and specific preparation, considering that the optimal number of competitions in combat sports should be lower compared with other sports (see table 1.7).

The optimal number of major competitions varies between 3 and 10 and may be even less in MMA, where the intervals between competitions are more than 20 days. Table 1.7 shows that between different sports, the number of competition days, annual competitions, and starts, fights, attempts, or games varies considerably. In martial art sports such as boxing, jiu-jitsu, Greco-Roman wrestling, and judo, the number of competitions

Table 1.6 – Examples of General, Specific, and Competition Exercises Used During a Professional Boxer's Training Camp

Group of exercises	Means	Pace of movement	Intensity (%) of maximum effort
General and specific preparation	Resistance bands exercises	Moderate pace	60
	Shadow boxing	Fast pace	70
	Jump roping	Fast pace	70
	Shadow boxing with partner	Fast pace with prolonged acceleration	75
	Jump roping	Fast pace with prolonged accelerations and double under skipping	75
With boxing equipment	Sandbags, water bags	Slow pace, work on some techniques	50
	Heavy bag against the wall	Moderate pace with brief accelerations	60
	Sandbag and water bag to train speed	Fast pace with accelerations	70
	Speed ball	Fast pace with accelerations or moderate pace	80
	Pad work with partner	Moderate pace with brief accelerations	80
	Hitting mitts with the coach	Fast pace with accelerations	85
Training fights	Training fight	Moderate pace	60
	Training fight	Fast pace (strong opponent)	70
Competition fights	Free combat	Fast pace (weak opponent)	90
	Free combat	Fast pace (strong opponent)	95
	Competition fight	Fast pace	100

Adapted by permission from A.G. Brauer Jr., R.M. Souza, S.L.F. Andrade, S.B.C.D. Dias, and T.F.F. Pimenta, *Esportes de Combate: A Ciência no Treinamento de Atletas de MMA* (Curitiba: Editora Juruá, 2019). Data from Platonov (2007).

Table 1.7 – Number of Competitions of Top-Level Athletes Annually

Type of sport	Total duration of all competitions in days	Number of competitions	Games, fights, attempts, starts
Short-distance running	30-50	20-30	45-60
Weightlifting	7-10	7-10	42-65
Boxing	15-25	5-8	15-25
Grappling	21-30	7-10	40-60
Greco-Roman	21-30	7-10	40-60
Judo	7-10	7-10	35-50

Adapted by permission from A.G. Brauer Jr., R.M. Souza, S.L.F. Andrade, S.B.C.D. Dias, and T.F.F. Pimenta, *Esportes de Combate: A Ciência no Treinamento de Atletas de MMA* (Curitiba: Editora Juruá, 2019). Data from Suslov (1997).

is lower compared to short-distance running, for example. This is mainly because the required rest interval between competitions or fights is longer due to the nature of the sport, which includes high impact and trauma. Table 1.8 shows differences in the competitive structure of various martial arts for top-level athletes in the annual period. These variations occur primarily due to sports regulations of different commissions and could differ according to the country (Brauer, et al. 2019).

Table 1.8 – Differences in the Competitive Structure of Various Martial Arts of Top-Level Athletes

Indicator	MMA	Wrestling	Judo	Professional boxing
Maximum duration of the contest (min)	15-25	6-7	5	36
Number of fights during the day	1-3	Up to 5	Up to 6 or 7	1
Total competition time (min)	17-29	6-30	30-35	47
Rest interval	1 min	30 sec	None	1 min
Number of attacks in the contest	Not determined	12-18	5-10	40-50

Adapted by permission from A.G. Brauer Jr., R.M. Souza, S.L.F. Andrade, S.B.C.D. Dias, and T.F.F. Pimenta, *Esportes de Combate: A Ciência no Treinamento de Atletas de MMA* (Curitiba: Editora Juruá, 2019). Data from Suslov (1997).

Traditional Periodization Methods

The traditional periodization model was publicized in the 1950s by Lev Pavlovich Matveev and became popular around the world. The classic periodization model uses a long preparation period with a relatively short competition period within which the main contests are concentrated, and adds a transition period to allow the athlete's body to recover. This type of periodization involves a system of simultaneous (within the same training unit or microcycle) and parallel (longer phases than preparation) load applications, allowing a series of training goals using loads with different functional orientations. This characteristic of dilution and simultaneity of the training loads within the classic periodization model has been widely criticized and has encouraged other coaches to propose other models. For Verkhoshansky and Lazarev (1989) and Issurin (2008, 2010), the simultaneous and competitive development of different goals (physical, technical, tactical training, etc.), and, consequently, of different physical qualities, is one of the key limitations of the classic model.

Despite this, we believe that the classic periodization model is appropriate for combat sports, especially those that involve few bouts during the year, such as MMA and boxing. This is mainly because fighters require a high degree of general physical preparation and because the competition period is only one or a few fights. As Dantas (2011 p. 490) said, "the impressive results achieved by the former Soviet Union by employing this model emphasize its efficacy for situations in which there are long periods of preparation for relatively short periods of competition."

Sports Periodization Fundamentals

The annual cycle, semiannual cycle, or cycles of many months of training are divided into separate periods (see figure 1.8). The annual cycle allows the athlete to see a long-term strategy implemented to achieve the overall goal of the training program within a year. Semiannual training breaks this down into six-month increments, potentially serving as a midpoint for reassessment to ensure the athlete is responding to training stimuli as planned. When the program is grouped together in two- to four-month cycles, it serves to incrementally prepare the athlete for future increased intensity within the training while limiting the risk for acute or chronic injury. The athlete's seasonal schedule dictates the training schedule format in order to allow both general and specific skills to be developed leading up to the closest competition event. The training program is divided into several cycles to allow the athlete to break down the overall program goal (i.e., increase athletic performance) and focus on certain metrics that influence the athlete's performance within specific sports. This process provides a systematic method to prepare the athlete physically (i.e., musculoskeletal system, nervous system) to adequately perform when increased metabolic and biomechanical demand via external load is placed on the athlete leading up to a competitive event.

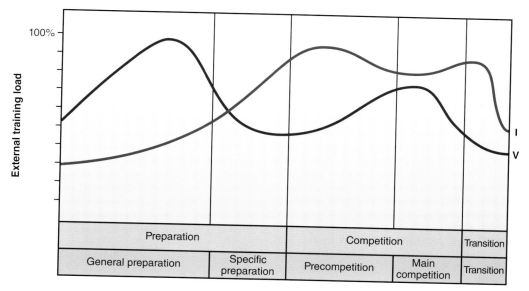

Figure 1.8 – Interdependence between volume (V) and intensity (I) under the classic periodization model.

Adapted from Matveev (2001) and Brauer et al. (2019).

General and Specific Preparatory Periods

The general and specific preparatory periods are the initial cycles of a periodization program.

- *General preparatory period (GPP):* According to Platonov (2008, 2007, 2004), the main objectives of the GPP are to increase the general physical preparation level, increase the capacity of the basic functional systems, develop technical and psychological qualities, and increase the capacity to withstand a significant number of large training loads. The volume of technical work is low in this period, assuming the athlete has mastered all the skill components of the sport and has been training systematically for several years. The main methodological characteristics of the GPP are the following:

- There is a predominance of volume over intensity.
- The general component of the training and physical preparation should be emphasized.
- It seeks to prepare for training.
- The athlete is not yet in a proper condition for competition.
- It lasts longer than the specific preparatory period.

- *Specific preparatory period (SPP)*: For Platonov (2008, 2007), training within the SPP is geared toward directly establishing sports performance and is achieved via an increase in the volume of specific preparatory exercises similar to those for competition. In this period, more intense fighting movements should be emphasized (sparring) and made as realistic as possible, with the exercises being as close as possible to the different situations found in competition. The sparring sessions should become more frequent in this period of preparation, with a duration and number of rounds similar to those of an official contest. The main methodological characteristics of the SPP are the following:

  - There is a predominance of intensity over volume.
  - The emphasis is on technical or tactical preparation.
  - The physical preparation should be highly specialized.
  - It seeks to prepare for competition.
  - The athlete is in an initial condition for competition.

Competition Period

The athlete should be at peak sports performance at competition time, beginning with eliminatory or qualifying competitions and ending with the main competition. In combat sports, the number of major competitions ranges from 3 to 10 (or less, as is the case with MMA), and the interval between competitions is normally more than 20 days. Thus, the competition period has the following characteristics:

- The target competition will take place in this period.
- The training volume is reduced.
- There is a predominance of technical and tactical preparation.
- The emphasis is on specific preparation.
- The goal should be to maintain sports performance until the end of the competition phase.

Transition Period

The transition period contributes to the athlete's physical and psychological recuperation. Its duration will depend on the structure of the annual cycle and may vary from three to eight weeks. The characteristics are the following:

- There should be a temporary loss of sports performance.
- Recovery should be predominantly active.
- Recreational activities should be included in this period.
- Volume and intensity are low, with the exclusion of high training loads.

Training Process Structures

For teaching purposes, we may divide the training process into three structures.

1. *Macrocycle, or macrostructure*—consisting of the major training cycles, semiannual, annual, Olympic, and multiyear
2. *Mesocycle, or mesostructure*—consisting of the stages of training involving a set of microcycles, as a rule two to six microcycles
3. *Microcycle, or microstructure*—consisting of separate training sessions and microcycles, lasting 2 to 14 days, with at least two phases: stimulation and recovery

Construction of a Macrocycle

The macrocycle is the largest training organization structure and is characterized by the fact that it develops peak performance. Its duration may be quarterly, semiannual, or annual, depending on the combat sport concerned and the fighter's experience level.

Construction of a Mesocycle

The mesocycle has a set of shorter cycles (microcycles) and is geared toward solving tasks in certain training periods. Normally, between two and six microcycles (weeks) compose each mesocycle. This will mainly depend on what is to be achieved in a given mesocycle. The essential feature of the mesocycle is a delayed effect of the training loads (chronic), which means that supercompensation occurs after a time of training load application. Therefore, mesocycles are used to control the cumulative effects of each set of microcycles, thus aiding the ratio between stimulus (training load) and recovery.

Next, we present the mesocycles most commonly used to prepare fighters. We include the respective training loads used as well as examples of composition for each of them.

- *Incorporation or introduction mesocycle:* This cycle should be used at the beginning of the season as well as after illnesses or trauma, and is roughly three to four weeks with moderate to low loads. General preparation exercises should predominate in this kind of mesocycle, and the total training load should begin low (50%-70% of the maximum total load that will be reached at the peak competition mesocycle) and increase progressively. A possible variation of the loads in the incorporation or introduction mesocycle (see figure 1.9) follows.

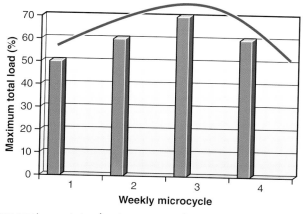

Figure 1.9 – Incorporation or introduction mesocycle.

Adapted by permission from A.G. Brauer Jr., R.M. Souza, S.L.F. Andrade, S.B.C.D. Dias, and T.F.F. Pimenta, *Esportes de Combate: A Ciência no Treinamento de Atletas de MMA* (Curitiba: Editora Juruá, 2019).

- *Development or basic mesocycle:* The main goal here is raising the athlete's physical aptitude levels through moderate to high loads (60%-80% of the maximum total load that will be reached at the peak competition mesocycle). This mesocycle consists of roughly four to six weeks and is mainly used in the first half of the general preparatory period. For the second half of the preparatory period, specific preparatory exercises should be predominantly used. According to the distribution of the loads, the development mesocycle may be classified as increasing or decreasing and oscillatory (see figures 1.10 and 1.11).

- *Stabilization mesocycle:* The main goal of this mesocycle is, after a set of increasing loads, to stabilize them, thus allowing the body to assimilate and adapt to the loads used. For this, the total training load should be slightly reduced, preferably using volume. This mesocycle consists of roughly two weeks of moderate-volume loads. In the stabilization mesocycle, competition and special preparation exercises should predominate.

- *Control mesocycle:* The main goal for this mesocycle is ensuring overall control over the efficiency of the development or basic mesocycles before gradually adapting the athlete to the demands of subsequent competition mesocycles. It is approxi-

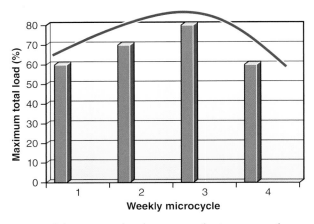

Figure 1.10 – Increasing and decreasing development or basic mesocycle.

Adapted by permission from A.G. Brauer Jr., R.M. Souza, S.L.F. Andrade, S.B.C.D. Dias, and T.F.F. Pimenta, *Esportes de Combate: A Ciência no Treinamento de Atletas de MMA* (Curitiba: Editora Juruá, 2019).

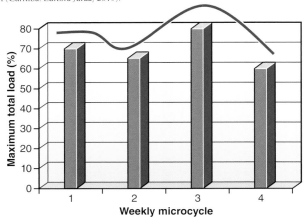

Figure 1.11 – Oscillatory development or basic mesocycle.

Adapted by permission from A.G. Brauer Jr., R.M. Souza, S.L.F. Andrade, S.B.C.D. Dias, and T.F.F. Pimenta, *Esportes de Combate: A Ciência no Treinamento de Atletas de MMA* (Curitiba: Editora Juruá, 2019).

mately two weeks long. The training may be combined with participation in minor competitions, with the goal being preparation or overall control of the athlete's training state.

- *Recovery mesocycle:* The main goal with this cycle is allowing the body to recover. The reduced loads offer a state of recovery and a potential boost to the athlete's performance. This mesocycle is roughly two to four weeks of light loads (30%-50% of the maximum total load that will be reached at the peak competition mesocycle). Recovery mesocycles are predominantly used in the transition period or after prolonged periods of maximum training loads and competition, in the tapering phase done in the weeks that precede the main competition.

- *Precompetition mesocycle:* The structure of this mesocycle will depend on the competition, and the goal is to create a competitive model reflecting factors that will interfere with performance, such as altitude, time, form of contest, and so on. The training should be as close as possible to all the conditions that the fighter will face in the competition. Additionally, it guarantees the immediate preparation of the athlete for the main competition of the macrocycle. Normally, it occurs four to six weeks before the main competition of the macrocycle.

- *Competition mesocycle:* This is the basis of the competition period, where the structure and content are determined by the specificity of the combat sport concerned, the preparation system chosen, and the competition schedule. Its duration will depend on the structure of the combat sport competition. Normally the competition mesocycle is four to six weeks. However, in MMA, this period may only be two weeks, considering that the athlete's competition period may only consist of one fight.

Construction of a Microcycle

A microcycle organizes the training focus during a consecutive series of training sessions. It can vary from 2 to 14 days. The sessions should connect to a broader process that seeks an optimal ratio between the training load and the athlete's recovery as well as the planned development of the stimuli on the different energy systems. Some points are essential in preparing the training microcycles, such as the athlete's lifestyle (diet, school hours, distance from home to the training center, etc.). For example, if an athlete is taking an online class from 10:00 a.m. to 12:00 p.m., instead of having a "regular" training session at the same time, they could do two small sessions, one from 8:30 a.m. to 9:30 a.m. and another one after school from 1:00 p.m. to 2:00 p.m. and still maintain the evening training session from 7:00 p.m. to 8:30 p.m. All those details factor in the cycle loads and their positioning within the mesocycles of the macrocycle. Therefore, it is important to consider the training cycle dynamics and foster positive adaptations in the athletes and, consequently, sufficient recovery for a new stimulus.

Table 1.9 and figures 1.12, 1.13, 1.14, 1.15, and 1.16 present the microcycle classifications and the respective loads of the maximum total load that will be reached at the peak competition mesocycle, as well as the dynamics of the distribution of training loads within each of them. This distribution allows the trainer or coach to more precisely see the training load dynamics within the microcycles.

- *Stabilizing microcycle:* The main goal of this microcycle is maintaining the stability of the athlete's preparedness. This type of microcycle normally follows the shock microcycle and stabilizes the changes occurring during those microcycles (see figure 1.12). Within the macrocycle structure, it generally appears after the most important competitions, at the beginning of the athlete's preparation, and when we need to allow the body to recover to a certain degree after a series of ordinary or shock microcycles.

Table 1.9 – Microcycle Classifications and Their Respective Loads of the Maximum Total Load Reached at Competition Mesocycle Peak

Microcycle	Intensity
Stabilizing	40%-60%
Ordinary	60%-80%
Shock	80%-100%
Precompetition	Based on the schedule
Control	Battery of performance tests or control competition
Competition	Main competition
Recovery	20%-40%

Adapted by permission from A.G. Brauer Jr., R.M. Souza, S.L.F. Andrade, S.B.C.D. Dias, and T.F.F. Pimenta, *Esportes de Combate: A Ciência no Treinamento de Atletas de MMA* (Curitiba: Editora Juruá, 2019).

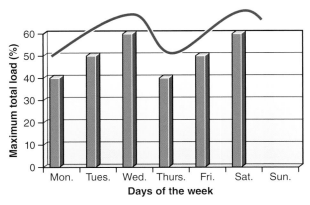

Figure 1.12 – Stabilizing microcycle.

Adapted by permission from A.G. Brauer Jr., R.M. Souza, S.L.F. Andrade, S.B.C.D. Dias, and T.F.F. Pimenta, *Esportes de Combate: A Ciência no Treinamento de Atletas de MMA* (Curitiba: Editora Juruá, 2019).

- *Ordinary microcycle:* This uses moderate or high loads, mainly due to the volume. Its main goal is to stimulate the adaptive processes of the athlete's body. Therefore, it is mainly used during the preparatory period (see figure 1.13).

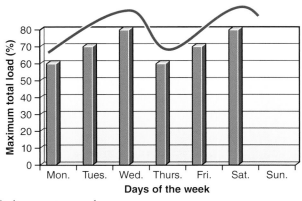

Figure 1.13 – Ordinary microcycle.

Adapted by permission from A.G. Brauer Jr., R.M. Souza, S.L.F. Andrade, S.B.C.D. Dias, and T.F.F. Pimenta, *Esportes de Combate: A Ciência no Treinamento de Atletas de MMA* (Curitiba: Editora Juruá, 2019).

- *Shock microcycle:* This microcycle employs maximal loads or loads close to maximal, which demands maximal mobilization of the body. It is primarily used from the second half of the preparatory period, when the specificity of the training increases, above all in the precompetition mesocycle (see figure 1.14).

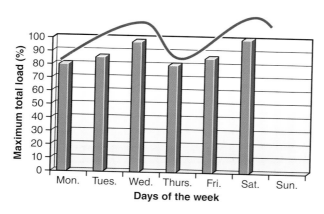

Figure 1.14 – Shock microcycle.

Adapted by permission from A.G. Brauer Jr., R.M. Souza, S.L.F. Andrade, S.B.C.D. Dias, and T.F.F. Pimenta, *Esportes de Combate: A Ciência no Treinamento de Atletas de MMA* (Curitiba: Editora Juruá, 2019).

- *Precompetition microcycle:* This microcycle employs moderate or heavy, but not maximal, loads. Its goal is to ensure an optimal preparation for the main competition, due to the mobilization of the athlete's potential capabilities accumulated in the preceding preparation process and adaptation to the specific conditions of these competitions. Its duration may be roughly 7 to 14 days, and it is used during the athlete's tapering period (Dias, et al. 2017) (see figure 1.15).

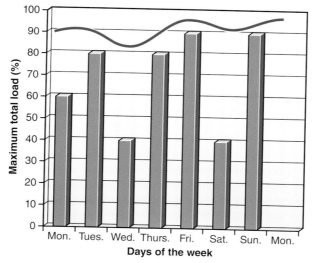

Figure 1.15 – Precompetition microcycle.

Adapted by permission from A.G. Brauer Jr., R.M. Souza, S.L.F. Andrade, S.B.C.D. Dias, and T.F.F. Pimenta, *Esportes de Combate: A Ciência no Treinamento de Atletas de MMA* (Curitiba: Editora Juruá, 2019).

- *Control microcycle:* This has the primary goal of assessing the athlete's preparation level at the end of a training stage. The training is combined with participation in control competitions, or testing protocols, which will analyze the efficiency of the preparation up to that point in time.
- *Competition microcycle:* The structure and duration of this microcycle is determined by competition regulations and by the specificity of the combat sport concerned.
- *Recovery microcycle:* This microcycle employs the lowest values of total training load, and its structure and content should lead the athlete to complete recovery. These cycles are used primarily in the transition period and after series of shock microcycles (see figure 1.16).

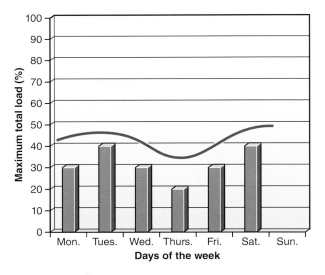

Figure 1.16 – Recovery microcycle.

Adapted by permission from A.G. Brauer Jr., R.M. Souza, S.L.F. Andrade, S.B.C.D. Dias, and T.F.F. Pimenta, *Esportes de Combate: A Ciência no Treinamento de Atletas de MMA* (Curitiba: Editora Juruá, 2019).

It is worth noting that the literature reports other microcycle types, but we believe that those mentioned in this book cover what is necessary to prepare athletes for combat sports.

Block Periodization

The increasing number of competitions, financial incentives, and the commercial nature of high-performance sports have resulted in changes in how an athlete is prepared. For example, in recent years, large organizations such as Bellator MMA and Professional Fighters League (PFL) incorporated the tournament format with several fights in a short amount of time, usually three to five fights in less than six months. This makes it impossible to use traditional periodization, which requires three to four months to get the athlete ready for one competition.

One way to solve these issues and fill the gaps in the classic periodization model is based on applying unidirectional or concentrated loads (training focused on only one physical component or capacity, such as power) in a given stage (block) of training, where there is a combined sequence of loads with different functional orientations (i.e., neuromuscular or cardiorespiratory training) distributed across time. There is also a concentrated volume of stimuli for specific preparation and a homogeneity of stimuli. Thus, the stimuli are specific and segmented into very well-defined blocks (Issurin, 2010). When doing this, there is a continual reduction in functional indicators followed by supercompensation. The general formation creates the foundation for recovering performance capacity after large-volume training loads.

Verkhoshansky presented this periodization model based on the application of unidirectional or concentrated loads. It demonstrates strong opposition to the pedagogical ideas and principles of classic periodization, especially the number of competitions in an annual cycle. Within the theories related to the organization of the sports training process, it is presented as a contemporary periodization model (Moreira, 2010). In this sense, we believe that this model may be adopted for athletes in combat sports who compete more often than just the major competitions or fights during the course of the annual cycle, but we stress that only more experienced athletes should primarily use periodization in blocks.

The mesocycle blocks form from three specialized types (Issurin, 2010): accumulation, transmutation, and realization (see table 1.10).

Table 1.10 – Mesocycles of the Block Periodization Model

Accumulation 2-6 weeks	Transmutation 2-4 weeks	Realization 2-3 weeks
Basic strength	Specific strength	Speed
Basic endurance	Specific endurance	Competitive training
General techniques	Specific techniques	Competitive techniques

Adapted by permission from A.G. Brauer Jr., R.M. Souza, S.L.F. Andrade, S.B.C.D. Dias, and T.F.F. Pimenta, *Esportes de Combate: A Ciência no Treinamento de Atletas de MMA* (Curitiba: Editora Juruá, 2019).

The accumulation mesocycle develops the fighter's general preparation, such as work geared toward cardiorespiratory fitness, muscle strength, flexibility, and basic coordination. This mesocycle has a relatively high volume and a reduction in workload intensity. Its duration may vary from two to six weeks (see table 1.11).

Table 1.11 – Characteristics of the Accumulation Mesocycle

Goals	Contents
■ Elevation of technical and physical potential ■ Accumulation of technical and motor skills that form the basis of the specific preparation ■ Increase the repertoire of technical elements	■ Training with high volume and moderate intensity: strength, aerobic endurance, basic technique, error correction

Adapted by permission from A.G. Brauer Jr., R.M. Souza, S.L.F. Andrade, S.B.C.D. Dias, and T.F.F. Pimenta, *Esportes de Combate: A Ciência no Treinamento de Atletas de MMA* (Curitiba: Editora Juruá, 2019).

The transmutation mesocycle is centered on the specific preparation of the sport, such as work geared toward specific endurance (aerobic or anaerobic/glycolytic), localized muscular endurance, and technical and tactical work in the most unpredictable manner possible. This is the most exhausting training mesocycle from the physiological standpoint and generally lasts from two to four weeks (see table 1.12).

Table 1.12 – Characteristics of the Transmutation Mesocycle

Goals	Contents
■ Transformation of the potential of the basic capabilities into specific preparation ■ To emphasize tolerance of fatigue and stability of technique	■ Training with an optimal volume and increased intensity ■ Training concentrating on strength and specific endurance

Adapted by permission from A.G. Brauer Jr., R.M. Souza, S.L.F. Andrade, S.B.C.D. Dias, and T.F.F. Pimenta, *Esportes de Combate: A Ciência no Treinamento de Atletas de MMA* (Curitiba: Editora Juruá, 2019).

The realization mesocycle is geared toward the athlete's recovery to achieve super-compensation (tapering) in the competition, which normally comes at the end of the macrocycle (see table 1.13).

Table 1.13 – Characteristics of the Realization Mesocycle

Goals	Contents
■ To achieve the best results, taking into account the possibilities of the preparation time ■ To use the motor and technical skills according to the specific competitive activity ■ Mobilization for competition	■ Adjustment of the competitive activity and competition exercises ■ Employment of exercises with maximal intensity ■ Training in a well-rested state ■ Participation in competitions

Adapted by permission from A.G. Brauer Jr., R.M. Souza, S.L.F. Andrade, S.B.C.D. Dias, and T.F.F. Pimenta, *Esportes de Combate: A Ciência no Treinamento de Atletas de MMA* (Curitiba: Editora Juruá, 2019).

Figure 1.17 presents two variations for organizing block periodization. Note that, even if the number of competitions is high, their importance should increase progressively during the course of the macrocycles (see figure 1.18).

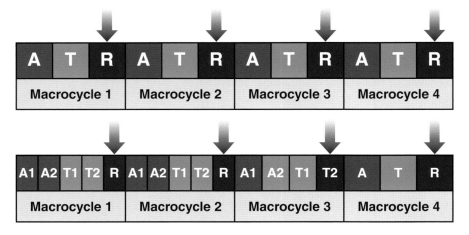

Figure 1.17 – Two variations in the organization of the block periodization model. The arrows represent the competitions.

A = accumulation; T = transmutation; R = realization.

Adapted by permission from A.G. Brauer Jr., R.M. Souza, S.L.F. Andrade, S.B.C.D. Dias, and T.F.F. Pimenta, *Esportes de Combate: A Ciência no Treinamento de Atletas de MMA* (Curitiba: Editora Juruá, 2019).

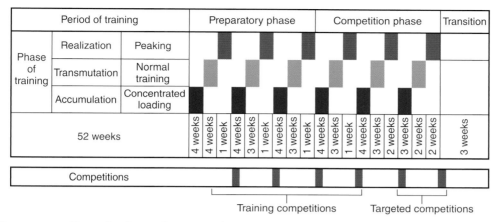

Figure 1.18 – Example of annual training plan.

Reprinted by permission from G.G. Haff and E.E. Haff, "Training Integration and Periodization," in *NSCA's Guide to Program Design*, edited for the National Strength and Conditioning Association by J.R. Hoffman (Champaign, IL: Human Kinetics, 2012), 241. Adapted from Issurin (2008a) and Issurin (2008b).

In table 1.14, we see some comparison between the classic and block periodization models. The main characteristics of the accumulation mesocycle are very similar to the general preparatory period in classic periodization, while the transmutation mesocycle is equivalent to the specific preparatory period and the realization mesocycle is equivalent to the competition period.

Table 1.14 – Comparison Between the Conventional or Classic and the Contemporary or Block Periodization Models

Main characteristics	Conventional or classic periodization	Contemporary or block periodization
Form of application of the training	Simultaneous, complex, and for various capacities	Consecutive and concentrated
Concentration of strength and aerobic endurance training	General preparatory period	Accumulation mesocycle
Concentration of power and power endurance training	Specific preparatory period and start of competition period	Transmutation mesocycle
Distribution of the competitions in the annual cycle	Competition period	Realization mesocycle
Volume of the exercises	Greater volume	Lesser volume

Adapted by permission from A.G. Brauer Jr., R.M. Souza, S.L.F. Andrade, S.B.C.D. Dias, and T.F.F. Pimenta, *Esportes de Combate: A Ciência no Treinamento de Atletas de MMA* (Curitiba: Editora Juruá, 2019).

Periodization Model Used at American Top Team

In training different athletes from the main team of American Top Team, the sports periodization models most commonly used are those marked with arrows in figure 1.19. There may be two or three performance peaks during the year. The difference between models B and C and the others is that they present short transition periods, and only at the end of the annual cycle do the athletes receive a longer transition period of two to four weeks.

Athletes on the grassroots team or minor events team do not have to follow these periodization models so strictly, given that their competitions are normally scheduled with short notice or leave little time for preparation (normally from six to eight weeks before the fight), requiring us to change our preparation system to an adapted version of model A. In this model, the athletes train for practically the whole year at between 60 percent and 80 percent of the maximum total load that will be reached at the peak competition mesocycle while waiting for a contract to fight. Athletes who are not professional but who would still like to use periodization could use model A as a guideline.

The way the human body adapts to stress similar to that of training, for example, was first described by Hans Selye. This response is called *general adaptation syndrome* (GAS), which, according to Selye, has three basic stages of stress response: (1) *alarm reaction*, which involves the initial shock of the stimulus on the system; (2) *resistance*, which involves the system adapting to the stimulus; and (3) *exhaustion*, in which recovery is inadequate, resulting in a weakening of the immune system. Figure 1.20 illustrates these three stages, and we may say that they help to explain scientifically the importance of periodizing training.

The *alarm reaction* (shock) stage is when the body initially responds to the training imposed on it. During this stage, muscle soreness, tension, and potential drops in performance may occur. The *resistance* (adaptation) stage is when the body adapts to the training.

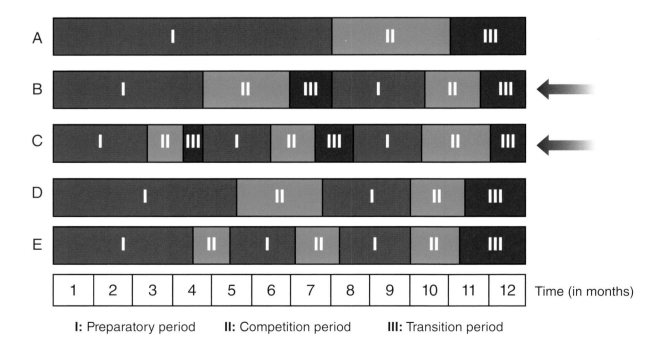

I: Preparatory period   **II:** Competition period   **III:** Transition period

Figure 1.19 − "Traditional" variants of annual periodization.
Source: Adapted from Dias and colleagues (2017).

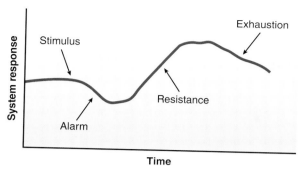

Figure 1.20 – Stages of GAS proposed by Hans Selye.
Adapted from Santana (2007).

In this phase, movement coordination may improve, and there is greater exercise tolerance, an increase in lean mass, and increased strength, among other benefits. In turn, *exhaustion* (fatigue) is the stage in which the body loses its capacity to respond to the training. Avoid exhaustion by using the periodization training principles, because otherwise the athlete may enter a state of *overtraining*, reducing their performance and increasing the risk of injuries or infections (Dias, et al. 2017; Mujika, et al. 2018).

Based on this information and various years of practical experience with top-level athletes, we will show some adaptations of these methods used by American Top Team.

Adapted Mesocycle

The traditional models, such as the example given in figure 1.21, state that the training loads should increase in intensity week to week. This is not wrong, but if we analyze it in greater detail, we will see that when we change the intensity, we are changing the stimulus imposed on the muscles. In other words, changes occur in the recruitment of muscle fibers with different thresholds (fast-twitch and slow-twitch fibers). In this model, the slow-twitch muscle fibers are trained for four weeks (microcycles 1, 2, 3, and 4), but the fast-twitch muscle fibers, which are the most important for short, explosive movements, are only trained for about two weeks: a portion of them in half of microcycle 2 and throughout microcycle 3. In the other weeks (microcycles 1 and 4), the low loads used do not allow the fast-twitch muscle fibers to reach their activation threshold. This reduces model effectiveness when compared to the model used by American Top Team.

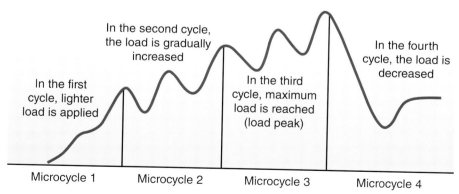

Figure 1.21 – Model 1: traditional mesocycle construction.
Source: Adapted from Matveev (2008).

Figure 1.22 shows that, in the first microcycle with low external resistances, according to the "size principle" Henneman initially proposed in the 1960s (Dias, et al. 2017), only low-threshold motor units and the muscle fibers that comprise that group are recruited. According to this principle, the greater the need to generate force, the more motor units will be recruited. This explains the importance of high intensities (70%-100% of the 1RM) to stimulate all the athlete's motor units and muscle fibers.

Under the periodization proposed in figure 1.23, the exercise intensity is always high, which stimulates the fibers to their maximum in all microcycles. Note that the volume changes in certain periods guarantee maintaining strength and aerobic endurance and has a low risk of chronic fatigue in the athletes' bodies (thereby avoiding Selye's exhaustion stage or an overtrained state). For every two weeks of intense, high-volume, strength-focused training, we have two weeks of a low volume of strength work and high volume of aerobic work (see figure 1.23), which creates a high level of combined intensity to maintain the athletes' trainability (see figure 1.24).

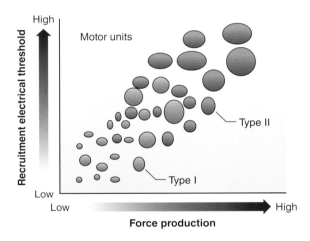

Figure 1.22 – Size principle.

Reprinted by permission from B. Schoenfeld, *Science and Development of Muscle Hypertrophy* (Champaign, IL: Human Kinetics, 2016), 6.

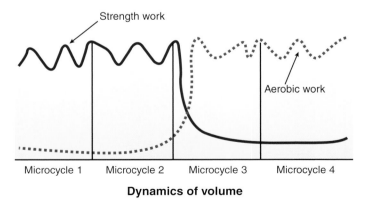

Figure 1.23 – Model 2: adapted mesocycle and the dynamics of volume.

Adapted from Seluianov, Dias & Andrade (2008).

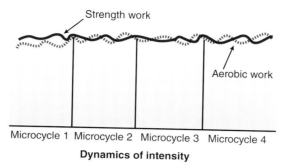

Figure 1.24 – Model 3: adapted mesocycle and the dynamics of intensity.
Adapted from Seluianov, Dias & Andrade (2008).

The intensity also changes slightly within the microcycles. The weekly microcycle has two or three peak strength loads interspersed with another two or three peak aerobic loads (see figure 1.24). In beginning athletes, we may use a basic, but very effective, combination. On Mondays, Wednesdays, and Fridays, the athlete performs resistance training exercises. On Tuesdays and Thursdays, they perform aerobic exercise of their choice (running, cycling, AirDyne, etc.) using the sprint method that chapter 2 will explain in detail. Saturday is for active recovery, and Sunday is a free day.

The intensity of these exercises is always high, but the volume may increase week by week until the third week, because in the fourth week, as a rule, we should give a week of high-intensity and low-volume active recovery. For example, we may reduce the number of sets of resistance training for each muscle group, which in the major groups varies from 6 to 12 sets per week, to 3 or even 1 set. In aerobic work, we may swap the formats (athletes who are running change to cycling, and vice versa, or reduce the volume of activity for that week). This guarantees the athletes constantly change the activities they perform, breaking the monotony and avoiding training plateaus.

To train top-level fighters, we need to work on strength (explosive strength and maximum strength, among others) and muscular endurance. For this, we may use the model in figure 1.23 because both physical capabilities should be developed to the maximum. The advantage of this system is that the body is overloaded in the two strength microcycles and "rests" in the other two aerobic microcycles without needing a recovery microcycle every three to four weeks and without entering a state of overtraining in the preparatory periods. The recovery microcycles only begin to become mandatory as we enter the competition period and immediately after the competitions (Dias, et al. 2017).

Adapted Microcycle

We should take care not to mix training with different priorities and training modes into a single training session (e.g., resistance training followed by aerobic training) because it reduces the training process effectiveness. However, if this combination is necessary because there is a lack of time, ensure that it is not done randomly so progress and results are not adversely affected even more.

To facilitate this combination, we present the following programs adapted from Russian professor and Olympic coach of various sports, Evgeny Borisovich Myakinchenko (see figure 1.25).

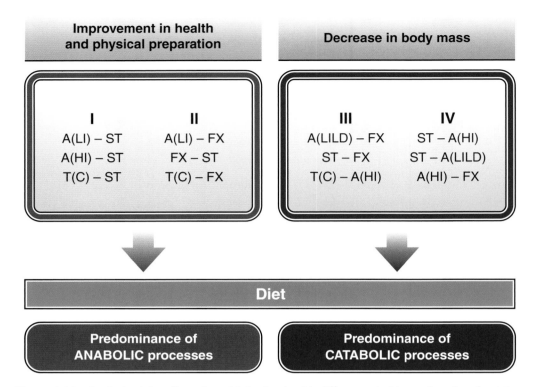

Figure 1.25 – Analysis of the effect of combining loads with different priorities and modes of training.

A(LI): low-intensity aerobic training; A(LILD): low-intensity and long-duration aerobic training; A(HI): high-intensity aerobic training; ST: strength training; FX: flexibility training; T(C): technical or skill work or activities high in coordination. Adapted from Dias, et al. (2017).

All combinations presented in numbers I and II of figure 1.25 improve health and the state of physical preparedness because anabolic processes predominate. This occurs because, in the combination of different training types, we always choose those of lesser intensity first or those that least tire our athletes' bodies yet serve to prepare them for the principal or most intense activities. When we finish training with resistance training exercises, we also have the predominance of anabolic processes due to the high level of hormones released (Dias, et al. 2017).

On the other hand, combining different training types, as shown in numbers III and IV, leads to a predominance of catabolic processes and a decrease in body mass. This is because of the increase in protein and hormonal catabolism that may occur when glycogen is depleted, a state that accompanies resistance training, for example. With muscle glycogen reduced, the prolonged execution or high intensity of aerobic exercises may catabolize lean muscle mass and increase the metabolism of steroid hormones present in the bloodstream, which consequently reduces the anabolic action of that training (Dias, et al. 2017).

Remember that there are cases in which it is necessary to increase the catabolic processes (even though this is not healthy and is not recommended in this book), such as an athlete losing weight to fulfill a contract in a weight division below their normal weight.

Amateur athletes may not be able to visit a gym more than three to five times a week. When this is the case, we, the coaches, can use the previous system shown in I or II in figure 1.25, minimizing catabolism by choosing the proper combination of exercises. The problem arises when an athlete wishes to engage in another activity shortly after an intense resistance training session. What should we do then?

In this case, we only have one option: a resource called the *mini snack*, which is nothing more than a light meal taken between two training sessions with different modes (see figure 1.26). This meal may be liquid (a protein shake, a meal replacement, or similar beverage) or solid (a protein bar, a piece of fruit, etc.) (Dias, et al. 2017).

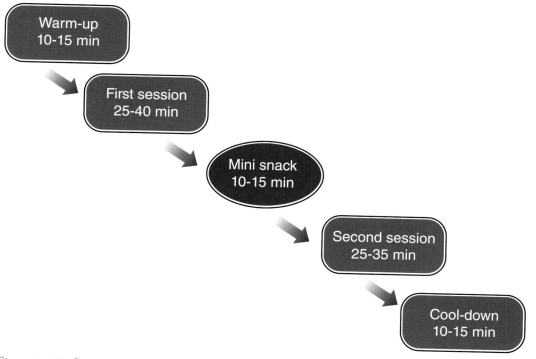

Figure 1.26 – Recommendation for the use and timing of a mini snack.

The difference in the content of the mini snack will depend on the athlete's goal. If it is to lose weight, we recommend avoiding sweet foods and the sugars present in many sports drinks, but we may suggest those that contain proteins (Dias, et al. 2017).

Adapted Macrocycle

Another important aspect various athletes in American Top Team use is the design and organization of the annual program. According to the current literature, there are many preparation phases and models, but in this book, we are going to describe the program that we use at American Top Team the most.

We may highlight five basic preparation phases (mesocycles): the initial conditioning phase (anatomical adaptation), hypertrophy phase, strength phase, power phase, and MMA circuit (power endurance) (Dias, et al. 2017). In each phase, we normally train for four weeks when we have sufficient time, but at the top level, the athletes fight on average every three months or less, which obliges us to shorten or remove some phases. For example, veteran UFC athlete Gleison Tibau does not perform a hypertrophy mesocycle, because he normally weighs 84 kilograms (185 lb), presenting between 8 percent and 10 percent body fat, and he fights in the 70 kilogram (155 lb) division. Accordingly, all his work is based on "getting the weight down," which is not at all easy because he is extremely strong and has practically no extra fat to burn.

As we can see, the annual program may vary according to each athlete and should always be designed backward. Thus, we note the date of the fight and count how many weeks we will have until the day we can start the training program. We then plan how many mesocycles will be performed and the priorities and duration of each one. On average, we need 12 weeks (three mesocycles of four weeks) to train an athlete and one final week to "make weight" and achieve supercompensation.

The time that remains between a given fight that has just taken place and the signing of the contract for the next fight is distributed less strictly. There are "only" six to eight sessions of training during the week, with most sessions focusing on the fighter's initial conditioning (anatomical adaptation). There is an emphasis on learning new techniques based on the athlete's deficiencies (Dias, et al. 2017).

An effective way to understand and justify the system we use in the periodization of our athletes is combining this model with the famous strength versus speed curve. The curve illustrates the inverse relationship that exists between strength and speed. In other words, the higher the load, the slower the movement, and the heavier the training, the slower the speed. Based on this concept, if we need to develop the physical quality of strength, we should train on the left side of the curve. To develop speed, we should stay on the right side. In figure 1.27, we can see the strength versus speed curve and the training zones.

Based on the strength versus speed curve, Dr. Joseph Signorile of the University of Miami developed a way to work all the phases of training: "Surfing the curve" was how he described figure 1.28, and according to Juan Carlos Santana from the Institute of Human Performance, this is the best way to understand and justify the correct use of training periodization.

To "surf the curve," we must start in the middle (initial conditioning), head upward and to the left to create muscle hypertrophy and develop strength, and then we gradually "surf" down the curve (toward the right) to work on power and speed.

The strength versus speed model explains how to divide the five phases of training, but, as mentioned, in the training program for athlete Gleison Tibau and other athletes of American Top Team, there is no desire to increase lean mass, because they normally

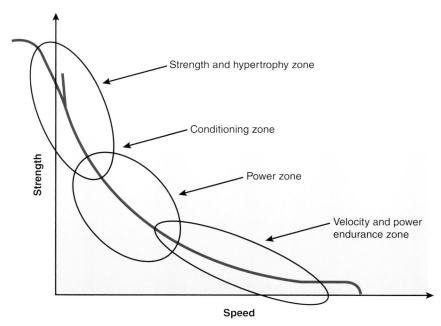

Figure 1.27 – Strength versus speed curve.

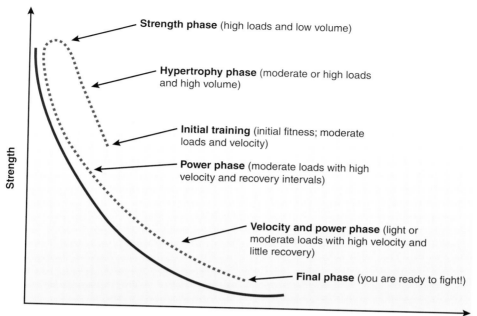

Figure 1.28 – Surfing the curve.
Adapted from Santana (2007).

fight in a division below their normal body weight. This obliges us to reduce the number of phases and remove the hypertrophy phase from the macrocycle. The total program ends up with 17 weeks, in which we use four weeks of training in each phase and the last week to make weight and achieve supercompensation.

During the design of the training program, some details need to be considered. Figure 1.29 shows the fluctuation of the work capacity during the day. The athletes' bodies adapt to the time at which the training is done. The athletes who train in accordance with model *a* respond better to physical work in the morning. The athletes who train under model *b* perform better at midday. Those who train under model *c* manage better physical performance in the afternoon, and athletes who train twice a day have two peaks of performance close to the hours at which the training is performed (model *d*).

This demonstrates the adaptability of the athletes' bodies to the time of the training and the importance of modeling the training program for the competition schedule. For example, athletes who compete in jiu-jitsu or grappling tournaments should prioritize their training in the mornings because those competitions begin early. By contrast, MMA fighters should train more intensely in the afternoon and evenings, because the events are normally held at night.

Another important aspect in the training program for professional MMA athletes is the periodization of sparring training for a team. The Russians adapted a periodization model, where instead of performing five rounds, it constantly uses a model of pyramids or waves (see figure 1.30). In the first week, they do five rounds; in the second week, six rounds; in the third week, peak training volume, if reached, is seven rounds. Note that a training session begins with an initial warm-up (roughly 15 minutes), followed by one round of shadow boxing plus four rounds of sparring. Under this adapted model, "extra" rounds are added in subsequent microcycles, with specific jiu-jitsu positions on the floor, wrestling starting with the back against the wall, and so on. After the third week, the cycle starts again with five, six, and seven rounds. American Top Team used this model for many years, and the results were excellent (Dias, et al. 2017).

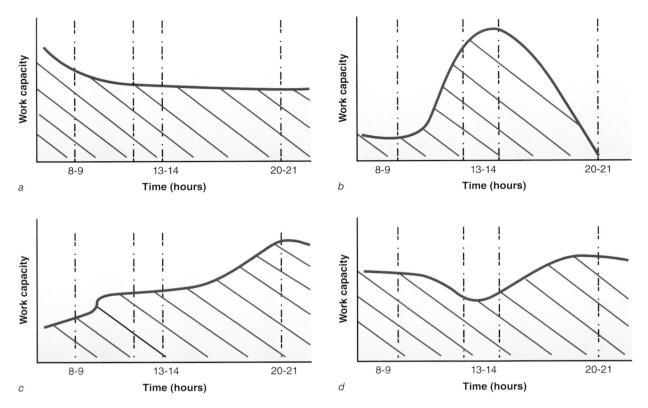

Figure 1.29 – Fluctuation of the work capacity during the day of the trained athletes: (*a*) in the morning, (*b*) at midday, (*c*) in the afternoon, and (*d*) in the morning and in the afternoon.

Adapted from Dias et al., 2017 based on Platonov (2007).

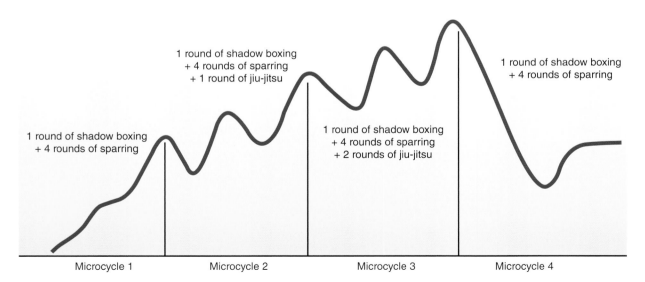

Figure 1.30 – Russian periodization model: construction of American Top Team–adapted mesocycle.

Figure 1.31 shows that within a microcycle, there are three peaks of intensity: Tuesday, Thursday, and Saturday. On the other days, the loads are moderate, and the training is more geared toward the technical and skill components.

Within a single session, figure 1.32 shows the changes in heart rate and lactate concentration based on the demand of an apparently equivalent activity. In the first situation, where the fighters threw a dummy with maximum possible effort (intensity), changes in heart rate and lactate concentration were not that pronounced. In the second situation, the athletes fought a control fight with the same duration as the first situation and experienced a greater physiological impact. Only in the third situation, an important actual fight, do we see that the athletes' heart rates and lactate concentrations significantly increased. So, why does this occur?

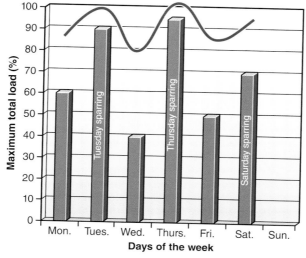

Figure 1.31 – Variations in the within-the-week training intensity of American Top Team fighters.

Adapted by permission from A.G. Brauer Jr., R.M. Souza, S.L.F. Andrade, S.B.C.D. Dias, and T.F.F. Pimenta, *Esportes de Combate: A Ciência no Treinamento de Atletas de MMA* (Curitiba: Editora Juruá, 2019).

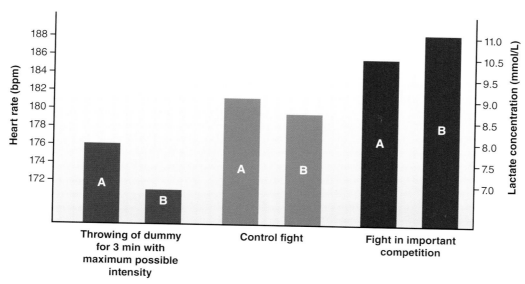

Figure 1.32 – Physiological responses of top-level fighters to three apparently equivalent activities: A = heart rate (bpm), B = lactate concentration (mmol/L).

Adapted from Dias et al., 2017 based on Platonov (2007).

One of the most significant factors contributing to these differences is the psychological influence that occurs with stress, because in the first situation, the athlete has full control over the activity. This does not happen when we face another athlete, whether in a control contest or an important fight.

Similar results occur in MMA, and to avoid an imbalance between training and fights, new athletes from other schools affiliated with American Top Team are brought in or they use a rotation system among the athletes to re-create the psychological effects of a real fight. The athletes do not train together all the time and are not "friends" in most cases, which increases the difficulty and intensity of the rounds.

When designing the training programs, we also cannot ignore that the same external load parameters do not always cause the same reaction in a given athlete, and even less so in athletes with different experience levels. As an example, we will show research data on the Polish athlete Mariusz Pudzianowski (five-time the World's Strongest Man champion) in his preparation for an MMA fight (see figure 1.33).

Figure 1.33 – Mariusz Pudzianowski in preparation for an MMA fight with his training partner and former Bellator champion, Attila Végh.

An identical external load parameter (in the example seen in figure 1.34, an 800-meter run in three minutes) can cause different internal reactions in a given athlete based on their stage of preparation. We can see that, during the initial stage of training, Pudzianowski's heart rate was between 180 beats per minute and 190 beats per minute, and this dropped as the competition grew closer, with the heart rate between 140 beats per minute and 150 beats per minute in the competition period (confirming the effect of adaptation to a given load).

With this in mind, an increase in the number of 800-meter runs or a reduction in the target time from 2 minutes 45 seconds to 2 minutes 30 seconds to increase the intensity of the exercise may be suggested. Note that Pudzianowski is a heavyweight weighing 125 kilograms (275 lb), which makes the 800-meter run even more difficult.

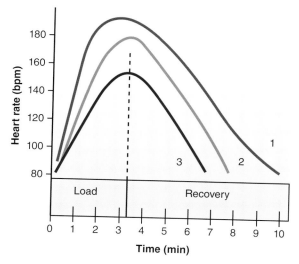

Figure 1.34 – Heart rate response of Mariusz Pudzianowski during and after a submaximal bout of exercise across three stages of training: 1 = first phase of preparation; 2 = second stage of preparation; 3 = competition period.

Source: Dias, et al. 2017.

Construction of a Training Session

Normally, a training session consists of three parts:

1. Introduction or preparation (warm-up)
2. Main part (workout)
3. Cool-down

Introduction or Preparation (Warm-Up)

In this part, we should organize the training (explain the goals and tasks of the training, decide which apparatus or equipment we will use, and motivate our athletes to train conscientiously). Next comes the warm-up, which serves to prepare the athlete's body for the main part of the training. In the warm-up, it is important to raise oxygen consumption to the aerobic threshold, roughly 110 to 130 beats per minute. To do this, aerobic exercises are (mainly) used, with the recruitment of major muscle groups (legs, chest, back) to activate the main physiological functions such as breathing, heart rate, increase in body temperature, among others. The tendons and ligaments warm up with the aid of stretching (Dias, et al. 2017).

When stretching, Dias and Oliveira (2013) recommended these principles:

- Warm up the muscles before stretching.
- Avoid sudden movements, because when the action of the muscle spindles is stimulated, the muscles contract, making stretching more difficult.
- Avoid asymmetric muscle activation (e.g., excessive stretching of one arm compared to the other).
- Stretching may be performed before and after the main part of the physical activity, according to the objective.

Stretching may last between 10 and 30 seconds and may be repeated between two and four times for each joint. The warm-up is divided into these categories:

- *General warm-up*, which has the objectives mentioned previously.
- *Specific warm-up*, in which the exercises should resemble as closely as possible the specific content of the training session or given sport.

This way, the (average) time spent on the warm-up will be between 10 and 20 minutes and may be a little more or less according to the environmental temperature or the complexity of the exercises chosen for the main part of the training session (Dias, et al. 2017).

Main Part (Workout)

In this part, the designed program should be prepared in accordance with the individual needs of the athlete. The specific training session objectives should be in accordance with the general annual plan of the practitioner (microcycles, mesocycles, and macrocycles). The athlete's current condition should be considered (health, state of preparation, etc.), as should the means and methods of training (Dias, et al. 2017).

Cool-Down

During the workout, anaerobic metabolism byproducts accumulate in the muscles and blood. So, in the final part of a training session, aerobic exercises should predominate. Approximately 5 to 15 minutes at the aerobic threshold (110-130 bpm) on a treadmill or stationary bicycle with a low intensity is enough to reduce the lactate level (acidity) to the point where recovery processes are accelerated. At the end of this work, we may also recommend approximately five minutes of relaxation and stretching to normalize breathing and heart rate (Dias, et al. 2017).

2

PROGRAM DESIGN

Sérgio Luiz Ferreira Andrade, PhD

Stéfane Beloni Correa Dielle Dias, PhD

Tim Crowley, BS

Diego de Castro e Silva Lacerda, MS

This chapter will address planning training programs based on updated scientific rationale and our years of professional experience. Although each variable will be presented in separate topics for clarity, they all interact in the training program framework. Moreover, because training adaptations are widely heterogenic, we acknowledge that multiple approaches elicit performance improvements. Hence, rather than propose radical changes, this chapter aims to help coaches broaden their training repertoires.

Principles of Resistance Training

Regardless of some new—and sometimes controversial—findings reported in scientific literature about resistance training, the training principles are always the cornerstone of any program design. Although the principles described in this chapter are the same postulated in the sports training literature, it is possible to revisit them within the context of resistance training.

Principle of Adaptation

The body can adjust itself to the conditions the surrounding environment imposes through multiple adaptation (from the Latin *ad* = more; *aptus* = appropriate, prepared) processes. However, the adjustments only occur if the stressor (e.g., exercise) causes a temporary disturbance in homeostasis. For example, eccentric actions are mechanically stressful to muscle fiber structure and cause microtrauma, mainly in the first weeks of training. However, over time, the systematic repetition of the harmful stimulus causes adaptations that make the muscle less susceptible to the microtrauma (Nosaka and Clarkson, 1995).

The physiological adaptations to training are reversible and should not be confused with the concept of evolutionary adaptation from the field of biology, because this refers to the permanent changes in a population (and not in an individual) over successive generations.

Adaptation is limited to the characteristics of each body, so the same training stimulus may lead to different responses even in the same individual. For example, an experienced, 60-year-old powerlifter (e.g., a masters athlete) may train the same way he trained when he was 30, but the magnitude of the responses will not be similar due to the influence of aging on the body.

Principle of Overload

If the stimulus is not stressful enough to induce adaptations, there will be no further gains (a plateau). For this reason, training must be adjusted so that the stress becomes progressively greater. In resistance training, a common way to apply progressive overload is by gradually increasing the load in each exercise over the long term. Indeed, despite increasing load being an almost intuitive overload strategy, it is important to emphasize that the overload does not refer to the weight being lifted itself but rather to the magnitude of the stress caused by the exercise on the body. For example, when doing deep squats, it is possible to increase the physiological overload of the muscles in comparison to partial squats, even though the training load is relatively lighter (Bloomquist, et al. 2013). Three approaches can be applied, either singularly or in combination to the principle of overload in resistance training (McArdle, et al. 2016):

1. Increase load or resistance
2. Increase repetition number
3. Increase speed of muscle action

Principle of Specificity

Any adaptations are specific to the training characteristics. For example, training sessions with loads of 90 percent 1RM are more efficient for increasing maximum strength in comparison to loads of 50 percent 1RM, because exercising with heavier loads is closer to the specific context of maximal strength.

Specificity also applies to the exercise performed, because each one requires learning different joint angles and speeds, as well as the characteristics of the equipment used (e.g., barbells, dumbbells, machines, cables). For example, the strength gains resulting from practicing the leg press are less transferrable to the barbell back squat, because they require different patterns of intermuscular coordination even though they work the same muscle groups (Carroll, et al. 2001).

Principle of Reversibility

Adaptations to training are not permanent. Complete discontinuation of the stimuli leads to a gradual reversal of the adaptations (detraining). For example, just two months of detraining are sufficient to cause a significant loss of strength. However, strength is a nonlinear physical capacity; therefore, some variability in strength is expected throughout the training course, even when training continuity is sustained. But this should not be confused with reversibility. Indeed, reversibility is only perceived if there is a constant strength loss over the long term, after several weeks without exercise, for example.

During detraining, the reversibility of hypertrophy (e.g., loss of muscle mass) is a slower process than that of strength loss. For example, after just a two-week break, significant strength losses might occur without loss of muscle mass (Staron, et al. 1991). This is because hypertrophy occurs via slower and more lasting local changes at the cellular level, such as an increase in the number of myonuclei. Studies conducted with rodents suggest that the nuclei added to the muscle fibers from hypertrophy remain intact after several months of detraining. Even though the detraining leads to a loss in cell size, the maintenance of the added myonuclei favors the magnitude of the protein biosynthesis and, consequently, the rapid recovery of cell volume during retraining (Gundersen, 2016).

Principle of Individuality

Genetic variability and factors related to quality of life (e.g., diet, sleep, stress) can explain the significant differences in individual responses to the same training method. Nevertheless, despite this variability, the physiological mechanisms that cause the adaptations are the same. Therefore, individuality does not mean that the adaptations follow an entirely unpredictable trend but rather that the scale of the effect varies widely. For example, it is possible to predict that an individual will achieve gains in strength after a few weeks of training, but it is impossible to accurately predict the magnitude of those gains. Hubal and colleagues (2005) conducted a multicenter study that analyzed gains in strength and muscle mass in 585 participants who trained the elbow flexors for 12 weeks. Comparing the individual gains at the end of the study, enormous variability was observed of between 0 percent and 250+ percent change in terms of gain in maximum strength.

Even though the supposed "ideal training" may lead to an athlete achieving full potential, each individual has genetically determined limits that will be reached with different relative rates of progress when compared to other athletes.

Resistance Training for Strength and Muscle Hypertrophy

Resistance exercise may help athletes in different sports to increase strength and muscle mass, when necessary. For fighters, increasing strength is essential as a basis for increasing power. Likewise, one study has shown that resistance training is a relatively more effective strategy in preventing injuries when compared to other types of intervention, such as stretching and proprioception training (Laursen, et al. 2014). However, considering that resistance training itself is a stress-inducing physiological stimulus, a good training program should be designed to interfere as little as possible with a fighter's performance.

Relationship Between Strength and Hypertrophy

Strength is the ability to produce movement against resistance. Strength also stabilizes joints—the ability to remain in a certain position during an exercise, such as the strength required to stabilize the spine during deadlifts and back squats. In that case, the role of strength is to prevent unwanted movement. Muscle hypertrophy is an increase in the size of muscle cells, which leads to an increase in muscle volume. Unlike strength, hypertrophy is a local morphological adaptation of the muscle cells and therefore is unrelated to a specific movement or task. For example, muscle hypertrophy can be obtained even with isometric training (i.e., no joint movement) (Kubo, et al. 2006). Furthermore, noticeable muscle hypertrophy can be obtained in cyclists, rowers, and sprinters, regardless of whether they lift weights (Hug, et al. 2006).

Strength and muscle hypertrophy appear to be less closely related than traditionally suggested in conventional literature on sports training. For example, it is believed that, during the first four to six weeks of training, most gains in strength are attributable to neural adaptations and that, thereafter, additional increases would only be possible with an increase in muscle mass.

By contrast, more recent studies suggest that hypertrophy is not directly related to strength. In one study, Mattocks and colleagues (2017) divided untrained men into two groups who worked on the bench press and leg extension machine for eight weeks. One group only performed the 1RM test twice a week for both exercises while the other group followed a "hypertrophic" protocol of four sets of 8 to 12 RM. The results were a similar strength increase for both groups, but hypertrophy only occurred in the group that trained longer. Another study of the same group trained experienced subjects with a unilateral protocol in which one arm only performed the 1RM test for the biceps curl during each session while the other arm performed the test followed by a "hypertrophic" protocol of three sets of 70 percent 1RM. After 21 days, the increases in strength were similar, although hypertrophy only occurred in the arm that was subjected to a greater training volume.

Contrary to the hypothesis that muscle hypertrophy would be necessary to elicit further strength gains after the initial neural adaptations, Zourdos and colleagues (2016) showed significant increases in back squat 1RM in competitive weightlifters with no changes in muscle size after 37 days of training. In another study, Bickel and colleagues (2011) showed that 32 weeks of detraining in young subjects reverted the increases in muscle fiber cross-sectional area (CSA) to baseline levels, whereas the strength gains remained elevated. The authors suggested that this finding was due to the monthly 1RM tests performed throughout the detraining period, which could have maintained the neural adaptations necessary to produce force. These findings suggest that strength is highly dependent on specific neural adaptations to the movement performed and that, although hypertrophy and strength are concomitant, one does not necessarily cause the other. Indeed, in practice, it is notable that some Olympic weightlifters in the lighter categories (e.g., up to 67 kg or 147 lb) can lift almost three times their own bodyweight, whereas some bodybuilders who are more than 100 kilograms (220 lb or more) are much weaker, pound for pound.

That said, it is known in the literature that increases in muscle CSA is a determinant of or at least related to force production capabilities, and improving CSA could enhance force production. An increase in a fighter's muscle mass may undermine their ability to make weight for their weight division. Even though this concern is legitimate, it is important to stress that hypertrophy training also promotes a reduction in body fat when nutrition is controlled (Paoli, et al. 2015), which may make the gains and losses in muscle and fat, respectively, cancel each other out on the scale. Moreover, for fighters in heavier categories, hypertrophy itself may offer greater advantages—for example, a heavier bodyweight may be more stable when clinch fighting during stand-up or ground fighting or make it harder to be taken down.

Training Volume

Considerable evidence shows that the training volume does not need to be high to produce increases in strength and hypertrophy. This is especially important for the multicomponent structure used to train fighters, because for them, resistance training is just another resource, not the priority. The portion of training spent on resistance training should thus be controlled so that it is sufficient to induce the desired adaptations (e.g., strength or hypertrophy) without undermining the fighter's recovery for their specific training or to make weight successfully.

The training volume geared toward hypertrophy should take into account the total number of weekly sets intended for each muscle group. A common error is to think only of the number of sets per exercise, without considering how many exercises are performed for the same muscle group and what the weekly frequency of the training sessions will be. For example, if a training session consists of four sets of back squats, leg presses, and leg extensions, repeated twice a week, 24 sets per week should be considered for the quadriceps. Therefore, an excessive number of sets may be unnecessary and, worse still, counterproductive if there is insufficient recovery.

In a study by Schoenfeld and colleagues (2019), resistance trained subjects were randomly assigned to one of three experimental groups that performed low-, moderate-, and high-volume training. The training routine targeted all major muscle groups and consisted of three weekly nonconsecutive, full-body workouts with six and nine sets for the low-volume group, 18 and 27 sets for the moderate-volume group, and 30 and 45 sets for the high-volume group in the upper and lower body, respectively. The results showed significantly greater hypertrophy in three of the four muscles measured in the high-volume training group after eight weeks. The authors suggested a graded dose-response relationship between training volume and muscle growth, with greater gains attained with higher volumes. However, one should be cautious in extrapolating these findings when designing a fighter's training program. In that study, the subjects refrained from any other type of high-intensity training (e.g., interval training, power training, etc.), which is not comparable to the reality of a fighter's weekly routine. This is important because in the study by Schoenfeld and colleagues (2019), all sets were carried out to failure, which in the "real world" context of a fighter's weekly training routine would be very taxing to the neuromuscular system and could compromise recovery when using high-volume training protocols (e.g., 45 sets to failure for the quadriceps).

A classic study frequently cited to support a lower number of weekly sets per muscle group was published in 1997 by Karl Ostrowski and colleagues. This study divided men into training groups that performed 3, 6, or 12 weekly sets per muscle group for 10 weeks. The participants had between one and four years of training experience and were expected to be able to lift at least 100 percent and 130 percent of their bodyweight when doing bench presses and back squats, respectively. The results showed that three weekly sets per muscle group led to a similar increase in hypertrophy when compared to 6 or 12 weekly sets.

By contrast, a meta-analysis published by Schoenfeld and colleagues (2017) suggested that gains in hypertrophy are dose-dependent, whereby at least 10 weekly sets per muscle group would be necessary to induce maximum hypertrophy. However, other researchers have questioned the reliability of the meta-analyses for suggesting training volumes, because they generally include studies with highly heterogeneous protocols (e.g., different weekly frequencies, different muscle groups, different training histories, different loads), to ensure a more consistent comparison (Arruda, et al. 2017). Furthermore, even if a greater number of sets would elicit relatively more hypertrophy (than fewer sets), in practice, the relevance of a larger muscle mass for a fighter's performance is questionable. Also, a higher volume of resistance training could be counterproductive to a fighter's ability to fully recover between training sessions or competitions.

Repetition Duration

The speed of execution of a training exercise corresponds to the speed of linear movement for the equipment (barbell, dumbbell, machine, etc.) or angular movement of a joint (e.g., elbow, knee). However, in practice, these movements can only be measured using specific instruments. Thus, a more feasible alternative is to control the execution speed by controlling the repetition duration—mentally counting the duration (in seconds) of the concentric and eccentric phases of each repetition. This time may also be called *tempo*. For example, a tempo of 4010 means a four-second eccentric phase, a one-second concentric phase, and no pause in the transition between phases.

The tempo the repetitions are performed should also be considered in the stimulus-recovery relationship. In a study, Hackney and colleagues (2008) investigated recovery after a training session with eight sets of 6RM for each muscle group in university athletes with and without resistance training experience. The exercises were performed with three seconds of emphasis on the eccentric phase in each repetition. The results showed that muscle damage markers and delayed onset pain remained high for up to 48 hours after the training, even in subjects experienced in training. This is especially important in individuals with no previous resistance training experience.

For example, Sayers and Clarkson (2001) demonstrated in untrained subjects that maximal eccentric actions with a three-second duration led to 50 percent to 60 percent losses in maximum voluntary contraction capacity and took several weeks to fully recover from. Additionally, Flann and colleagues (2011) demonstrated that the muscle damage (microtrauma) caused by eccentric contractions does not lead to a proportional effect in hypertrophy. In that study, two groups were subjected to 12 weeks of exclusively eccentric training, with one group having trained previously for four weeks to minimize muscle damage, whereas the other group started training with no pretraining protocol. Despite the considerable difference in the quantity of muscle damage between the groups, there was a similar increase in the volume of the quadriceps (i.e., a higher amount of muscle damage did not produce greater anabolic stimulus).

Therefore, resistance training designed for fighters should have a limited eccentric component to avoid performance interference. In addition to producing strength, muscle damage is also associated with delayed onset muscle soreness, pain, and a temporary reduction in range of motion. This may compromise the performance of fighters in specific training (fighting), primarily when more than two resistance training sessions are held per week. To prevent excessive muscle damage, a tempo of 1010 or 2010 may be most appropriate for training fighters.

Training Intensity for Hypertrophy

For several decades, hypertrophy training was based on the assumption that the loads should be high to maximize results. Indeed, the American College of Sports Medicine exercise prescription suggested loads of at least 70 percent of 1RM (ACSM, 2009) for hypertrophy. It is possible that this paradigm has been widely accepted due to the interpretation that lifting heavy weights will result in proportionally large and strong muscles. Indeed, there is evidence of muscle cell adaptations to high mechanical stress levels (Tidball, 2005; Goodman, 2014). This physiological response of a tissue to stimuli of a mechanical nature (e.g., tension in the muscles or compression in the bones) is called *mechanotransduction* (Martineau and Gardiner, 2001). Studies in animal models demonstrate that when muscle fibers are maintained in a stretched position, the muscle adapts, increasing its protein content and strengthening its structure, even in the absence of exercise (James, et al. 1995; James, et al. 1997; Cox, et al. 2000).

Although hypertrophy training is traditionally performed with relatively heavy loads (e.g., above 70 percent 1RM), various studies have shown that much lighter loads may give similar results. Lasevicius and colleagues (2018) divided untrained men into groups that trained dumbbell biceps curls and leg presses with three sets until failure with loads of 20 percent, 40 percent, 60 percent, and 80 percent 1RM, for 12 weeks. Similar increases in hypertrophy were demonstrated with loads of 40 percent, 60 percent, and 80 percent 1RM.

Another study divided university students who had been training from between 1.5 and 9 years into two groups: one group trained with three sets of 8 to12 RM, while the other group trained with 25 to 35 RM. After eight weeks, similar increases in hypertrophy were observed (Schoenfeld, et al. 2015). Other studies have also demonstrated that training intensity does not predict hypertrophy magnitude (Ogasawara, et al. 2013; Mitchell, et al. 2012; Barcelos, et al. 2015). Indeed, performing sets closer to concentric failure appears to be a more important factor than the amount of weight being lifted, because the magnitude of muscle hypertrophy will be similar regardless of the training intensity. The physiological rationale for this finding is the central nervous system increasing recruitment of motor units to cope with fatigue as the lifter is still trying to perform one more repetition (i.e., until concentric failure). Therefore, because more motor units are recruited, more muscle fibers are stimulated.

There is no question that training intensity itself is of little relevance to hypertrophy magnitude, provided that the highest possible number of motor units are recruited. Therefore, because there is no ideal number of repetitions or amount of weight to be lifted for hypertrophy, fighters may achieve similar results through a wide range of repetitions, such as 5 to 15 RM.

Rest Periods

There is no consensus about the most efficient rest periods between sets for hypertrophy. Some authors suggest that this rest should be approximately one minute, based on studies that investigated the acute responses of testosterone and growth hormone (GH) released during training (De Salles, et al. 2010). This suggestion is controversial, because there is little evidence that acute elevations in GH caused by exercise have a major relevance in the signaling of muscle hypertrophy (West and Phillips, 2010).

A very short rest period may interfere with performance during training by preventing the performance of the desired range of repetitions for each set. For example: Rests shorter than one minute between maximal sets above 10RM cause greater metabolic stress during training than rests of three minutes do. This is from an acute increase in the concentration of H^+ ions and a drop in glycogenolysis, which temporarily reduces contraction capacity (Spriet, et al. 1989). Additionally, the accumulation of intracellular inorganic phosphate from the anaerobic energy system appears to inhibit the release of calcium by the sarcoplasmic reticulum (Westerblad, et al. 2002). For this reason, rests of at least 90 seconds appear to be necessary to allow recovery when the training protocol leads to glycolytic lactate buildup (Glaister, et al. 2005).

For how rest periods between sets affect chronic adaptations, some studies have shown greater increases in maximal strength with rests of three to five minutes (De Salles, et al. 2010). However, it appears that for muscle hypertrophy, the amount of rest between sets has less relevance. In one study, Ahtiainen and colleagues (2005) showed no differences in hypertrophy after six months of training with rests of two and five minutes. DeSouza and colleagues (2010) investigated the effect of shorter rests, in which trained men were subjected to eight weeks of training with a constant or decreasing rest between the sets. In that study, both groups began training with the same rest of two minutes between sets. From the third week, the group with the constant rest continued resting for two minutes, while the group with the decreasing rest trained with rests that grew gradually shorter each week, until they reached 30 seconds in the final week. The results showed similar increases in the cross-sectional area of the arm and the thigh.

Therefore, it appears that rest between sets should be controlled primarily according to the intended training load. For example, for a range of 5 to 8RM, rests of three to five minutes are required to partially reestablish phosphocreatine reserves and maintain strength. If the range of repetitions is higher (e.g., 12-15RM), the loads are lighter and therefore rests of one to two minutes may be sufficient and not interfere in work capacity.

Resistance Training for Power

Power is defined as the amount of work divided by time or the amount of force multiplied by the velocity of that force. Power is in high demand for fighters, principally because the capacity to produce a certain amount of strength with maximum speed is more important than producing maximum strength slowly. Like strength, power is highly specific to the task concerned, such as jumping, pushing, or pulling. However, the training-induced increase in power seems to occur from specific adaptations that are not observed from training for maximal strength, such as increased exploitation of energy generated in the muscles by the stretch-shortening cycle, the rate of force development (RFD), and the rigidity (stiffness) of the musculotendinous unit.

Repetition Duration

In power training, it is essential to execute the concentric phase of repetitions as fast as possible and explosively. The eccentric phase should only be slow enough to maintain control over the equipment (e.g., dumbbells) without pauses in the eccentric-concentric transition. For example, an execution tempo of 10X1 in power training means lowering the bar in one second and immediately pushing it explosively (X), maintaining a brief pause of one second at the end of the concentric phase to ensure stability in the exercise before the next repetition (King, 1998).

Because the movement speed should be kept high during the set, a loss of speed in relation to the first repetition is the first sign that the set should be discontinued. Unlike training for hypertrophy, in which fatigue may even be desirable (even with light loads), in power training, fatigue should be minimized because an increase in fatigue prevents the movement from being performed at maximum speed.

Training Intensity for Power

To produce high-speed movements, it is suggested that the weight lifted for power should be 30 percent to 60 percent 1RM—well below the load normally used in training for maximum strength (above 85% 1RM). Indeed, loads heavier than 60 percent 1RM may acutely interfere in the capacity to produce the concentric phase with maximum speed, an important factor in power training. For example, with a load of 95 percent 1RM in the bench press, the speed produced tends to be low, regardless of the intention for producing an explosive movement.

Loads should be adjusted according to the number of desired repetitions. After multiple consecutive repetitions, fatigue prevents a high rate of force development. For example, loads such as 30 percent 1RM may be used if the aim is to complete approximately six to seven repetitions at maximum speed. However, if the aim is to perform one or two repetitions, a load of 60 percent 1RM is more appropriate. In both cases, the set should be discontinued before the person starts to lose speed and well before concentric failure.

Resistance training alone should not be viewed as an isolated strategy for power improvement, because it only forms an adaptational basis that increases the neuromuscular system's ability to activate agonist muscles as fast as possible. Indeed, although other training strategies such as plyometrics (e.g., jumping and throwing) are also effective for power, the highest specificity to enhance punching and kicking performance will obviously come from practicing throwing punches and kicks by themselves with little or no external mass besides boxing wraps and gloves added to the arms or shin pads for the legs. It is important to replicate a fighter's technical training, and it may be more beneficial to train power at similar loads, because they will normally be exposed during MMA training or competition. For more about the details and variations of power training, see chapter 5.

Training Volume

Unlike hypertrophy training, in power training, performance during the sets demands the capacity to sustain high speed in each repetition. Therefore, an excessive number of sets, repetitions, and exercises may cause fatigue to accumulate during training, acutely interfering in work capacity. For this reason, a limit of one to three sets per exercise is recommended but do no more than five sets per muscle group in the same training session. This way, a muscle group may be trained with 10 weekly sets, for example, divided into two sessions per week of five sets each.

Care should be taken not to exceed the training volume if the training sessions take place more frequently, such as three or four times a week. In this case, the total number of weekly sets per muscle group should be reorganized (e.g., 4 + 4 + 2 sets in three weekly training sessions). Additionally, because power training is highly specific, the exercises should be reduced to the minimum necessary to achieve transfer for the demands of the sport. Thus, single-joint exercises on machines, such as the leg extension machine, pec deck fly, and shoulder fly should be avoided, while standing multijoint exercises such as deadlifts and squats are preferable, especially with its concentric action performed as quickly as possible (explosively).

Rest Periods

Due to its short, explosive characteristics, power training predominantly demands reserves from the ATP-PC system. As the depletion of high-energy phosphates occurs in a few seconds of maximum effort, it makes sense that the power sets should have a short duration and long rests, such as four to five minutes. Indeed, Harris and colleagues (1976) demonstrated that it takes over four minutes to resynthesize most ATP-PC reserves in the quadriceps after a dynamic exhaustive exercise.

In addition to long rests between sets, high work capacity is maintained by the cluster method, in which brief pauses of 10 to 30 seconds are taken between blocks of a few repetitions within each set. Under the cluster method, the pause is taken during the set. Physiologically, this is based on two potential mechanisms: One takes advantage of the "rapid component" of partial resynthesis of ATP-PC just enough to minimize the fatigue accumulation that occurs with multiple successive repetitions (traditional method); the other takes advantage of *post-activation potentiation*, which consists of increasing the contractile capacity of the muscle after previous, high-intensity contractions.

One example of a cluster in the deadlift is performing a set of eight repetitions in four blocks of two repetitions, separated by a 20-second pause. The repetitions should be performed with the maximum speed possible in the concentric phase, following the same logic as mentioned in the Training Intensity for Power section.

High-Intensity Interval Training

High-intensity interval training (HIIT) involves short, intense intervals with rest or active recovery. HIIT is an effective and time-efficient training method for conditioned athletes. There are several ways to design an HIIT training session. By manipulating training variables such as intensity, volume, rest intervals, and types of training, you can target specific energy systems and create endless variations of interval sessions. This can help the coach or trainer to prepare athletes to arrive in the ring healthy and ready for competition.

Research has found that HIIT may be more effective in developing aerobic fitness than moderate continuous aerobic training and is more time efficient than aerobic exertion sustained for longer periods. Research done at Cal State University showed that athletes doing HIIT self-selected higher power outputs than those the researchers imposed. This led to a higher level of enjoyment by the self-selected group and better performance (Kellogg, et al. 2019).

Several variables are used to create high-intensity intervals: intensity, exercise mode, number of reps, number of sets, rest interval between intervals, rest interval between sets, interval duration, and rest interval duration. Manipulating these variables will allow the coach to create the proper workouts and progressions to allow the athlete to reach peak performance. We can put these intervals into three general categories: $\dot{V}O_2$max intervals, power intervals, and high-resistance intervals.

Types of HIIT

Several interval formats can be used to create interval training sessions. These can be based on speed or velocity, power output, or resistance training. Each has a specific purpose and outcome that the coach or trainer can implement to maximize the athlete's training.

$\dot{V}O_2$max Intervals

$\dot{V}O_2$max intervals are generally two to five minutes long at maximal sustainable intensity. This can be determined by conducting laboratory tests or doing a five- to six-minute time trial, which will give an estimate of maximal heart rate, velocity at $\dot{V}O_2$max for running, or watts at $\dot{V}O_2$max for cycling. The recovery for these exertions should be equal to the work interval or until the athlete is ready to execute another interval. These are difficult intervals and should not be done more than twice a week with several days of recovery between each of them.

A $\dot{V}O_2$max sample workout would be: 5 × 3 minutes at maximum speed with a three-minute or longer rest interval or until heart rate (HR) recovers to 60 percent of max HR.

Power Intervals

Power intervals are best done with equipment that will measure power outputs. Today, many bikes, rowers, swim ergometers, and other high-end machines come equipped with power output devices. This allows the coach and athlete to know when to end a session due to fatigue. These intervals are generally executed with a 1:1 work–rest ratio. This type of training was popularized by French physiologist Veronique Billat's work on velocity at $\dot{V}O_2$max (Billat, et al. 1996). Interval durations can range from 15 seconds to 3 minutes in length. Intensities for these intervals are max sustainable watts, speed, and so on. Recoveries are equal to the work interval or longer.

To conduct this workout and find the max sustainable power and speed, note the speed or power for the third interval. From this speed or power subtract 5 percent. In subsequent intervals, if speed or power drops below this 5 percent figure, the workout is over. The workout goal is to accumulate time at max sustainable power or speed. Here is an example of the bike session using power intervals: 12 × 1-minute power intervals with a one-minute recovery between each interval. If interval 3 is executed at 300 watts, subtract 5 percent, which gives you 285 watts. If interval 10 is executed at 275 watts, this signifies fatigue, and the workout is concluded.

This can provide an added motivator for athletes to push as hard as they can to achieve as many intervals as possible. Using fatigue as an indicator for when to end the workout ensures that the athlete does not dig too deep and provides a way to measure progress.

High-Resistance Interval Training

High-resistance interval training (HRIT) can be done in the weight room using specific types of resistance training formats or outdoors with exercises such as hill sprint repetitions of varying lengths and inclines. These workouts train fast-twitch muscle fibers and allow for repeated high-powered exertion and lactate tolerance.

Some examples of HRIT are the following:

- Compound movements combining two or more exercises done back-to-back for multiple repetitions followed by a rest interval are commonly done with a barbell or dumbbells using the same load for each exercise.

  Example: 3 × (1 rep of the deadlift, 1 rep of the hang clean, 1 rep of the push press) = 9 total reps followed by a two- to four-minute rest interval.

- Complexes are generally higher repetitions where the athlete performs a set of repetitions and then moves directly into the next movement with no rest. The rest interval is taken after each exercise is completed. Just like compound movements, the same load is used throughout the entire set.

    Example: 4 reps of the deadlift, 4 reps of the hang clean, 4 reps of the push press = 12 total reps followed by a two- to four-minute rest interval.

- Clusters allow high intensity and high repetitions by inserting a short rest interval between each subset.

    An example using a Romanian deadlift (RDL): 5 × (2 reps + 10 sec rest). The result is 10 repetitions with an intensity higher than the athlete could do for one set of 10 reps. The short rest allows the athlete to reset and maintain a high intensity.

There is an infinite number of combinations that can be used to create high-intensity resistance workouts to help develop power endurance, lactate tolerance, and work capacity.

There are forms of HRIT that do not require barbells or dumbbells, such as hill sprints, which can be done on a treadmill with a steep incline or drive sled if a suitable hill is not readily available. Executing 10- to 30-second hill sprints with a walk-back recovery will develop lower-body power as well as high conditioning levels. Drive sleds, prowlers, and tire pulls are suitable replacements for hill sprints for those who do not have hills or treadmills available. Medicine balls can also be effectively used in HRIT for the upper body.

Periodization of HIIT

HIIT can be sport-specific or energy system–specific. There are times it is important to do HIIT that is highly specific to the sport of MMA, such as sparring, heavy-bag training, mat drills, and so on. At other times, there may be a focus on energy system–specific HIIT. The ability to control and monitor output with data is valuable to ensure the proper intensity level is executed and to know when to stop the session due to fatigue. The following equipment will allow for the testing and monitoring of athletes' output.

Lower-Body Emphasis

Motor-driven exercise bike

Treadmill

Keiser runner

Hill sprint

Drive sled

Upper-Body Emphasis

Rowing machine

Ski ergometer

Vasa ergometer

Full-Body Emphasis

Air-driven bike (AirDyne, Assault)

Versa climber

Designing HIIT Sessions

There are many ways to design HIIT sessions. The coach or trainer is only limited by equipment availability, their creativity, and the specific energy system to be developed. It is important to do these intervals at a very high intensity but allow for proper recovery, both within the workout and after it to not create an overtraining scenario by attempting to do too many sessions per week. By combining MMA-specific workouts along with HIIT workouts where intensity can be measured accurately, athletes can be properly trained and tapered for optimal performance.

New Russian Concept of Training

This section is based on the extensive work of Professor Emeritus and Russian scientist Victor Nikolaevich Seluyanov. He developed hundreds of international champions and several world and Olympic champions in different sports, including boxing, judo, MMA, wrestling, sambo, combat sambo, karate, taekwondo, grappling, and others. Professor Nikolaevich is the founder of the ProSportLab in Russia.

The main goal of the laboratory is to conduct fundamental and applied scientific research in biological cybernetics, physical education, health and human performance, and sports. In professional sports, the laboratory provides scientific and methodological support, training, and consulting for sports teams, coaches, and professional athletes as well as comprehensive testing, control, and assessment of athletes' physical fitness, training plan development, and participation in the training process.

Methods to Hypertrophy Muscle Fibers Through Hyperplasia

Muscle is composed of muscle fibers (cells) that are stimulated by physical exercise. Resistance training directed toward increasing muscle strength leads to hypertrophy of the muscle fibers, which is reflected by an increase in the mass of the muscle groups stimulated during the training. At least two factors are involved in the development of this hypertrophy:

1. *Direct mechanical influence*—mechanical tension, using external physical loads (Schoenfeld, 2016)

2. *Products of tissue metabolism abundant in the muscle groups worked*—metabolic stress (Schoenfeld, 2016; Kraemer, et al. 1995; Ahtiainen, et al. 2003; Häkkinen, et al. 2003)

To increase the traction force of the muscle fibers, it is essential to reach myofibril hyperplasia (which is an increase in the number of myofibrils) and muscle hypertrophy. This process arises during the acceleration of protein biosynthesis and in the face of the precedent rates of protein decomposition (Dias, et al. 2017; Hoeger and Hoeger, 2014; Seluianov, et al. 2008).

Several research projects found in the scientific literature demonstrate four main factors affecting the acceleration of protein biosynthesis in the cell.

1. Amino acid reserves in the cell—amino acids in the cell accumulate after ingestion of foods rich in proteins (Jäger, et al. 2017; Dias, et al. 2017; Seluianov, et al. 2008)

2. High concentration of anabolic hormones in the blood as a result of psychological tension or intense training (Dias, et al. 2017; Holloszy, 1975; Schantz, 1986; Seluianov, et al. 2008)

3. High concentration of free creatine in muscle fibers (Dias, et al. 2017; Walker, 1979; Volkov, et al. 1983), which also occurs when we maintain the muscle under tension for more time (Cintineo, et al. 2018; Howe, et al. 2017)

4. High concentration of hydrogen ions (Schoenfeld, 2016; Seluianov, et al. 2008; Dias, et al. 2017)

The second, third, and fourth factors are directly linked to training exercise content. The synthesis mechanism of organelles in the cell, especially the myofibril, may be described in the following way: During physical exercise, ATP energy is expended in the formation of actin-myosin connections and the execution of mechanical work. ATP resynthesis occurs thanks to phosphocreatine reserves. The appearance of free creatine activates all metabolic pathways, which are linked to the formation of ATP (glycolysis in the cytoplasm and aerobic oxidation in different mitochondria like myofibrils and those found in the nucleus and in sarcoplasmic reticulum membranes).

It is known that strength exercises damage cell membranes, confirmed by an increase in creatine kinase (CK) activity in the blood 15 to 20 hours after high-intensity resistance training (Vinogradova, et al. 2013). In fast-twitch muscle fibers, muscle lactate dehydrogenase predominates, and this is why the pyruvate that forms during anaerobic glycolysis basically transforms into lactate. During this process in the cell, hydrogen ions accumulate. The power output of the glycolysis is lower than that of ATP expenditure, so in the cell, free creatine, hydrogen ions, lactate, and ADP start to accumulate (Dias, et al. 2017; Seluianov, 2001; Seluianov, 1996).

In addition to determining the contractive characteristics in energy metabolism regulation, when free creatine accumulates in the sarcoplasmic space, it serves as endogenous stimulation potential, which excites protein biosynthesis in the skeletal muscles (Walker, 1979; Volkov, et al. 1983). There is a close relationship between contractile protein content and creatine content. Free creatine visibly influences the synthesis of messenger RNA (mRNA), which is a single-stranded RNA molecule that is complementary to one of the DNA strands of a gene.

The mRNA is an RNA version of the gene that leaves the cell nucleus and moves to the cytoplasm where proteins are made. During protein synthesis, an organelle called a *ribosome* moves along the mRNA, reads its base sequence, and uses the genetic code to translate each three-base triplet, or codon, into its corresponding amino acid. Thus mRNA can be used in transcribing the nuclei of the muscle fibers. It can also activate the nuclei of the mitochondria that begin to produce ATP, which is used for DNA transcription (Walker, 1979).

It is supposed that the increase in hydrogen ion concentration causes the labilization of the membrane (an increase in the size of the pores in the membranes, making it easier for the hormones to penetrate the cell), activates enzyme actions, and facilitates the hormonal access to hereditary information in DNA molecules. In response to the simultaneous increase in creatine and hydrogen ion concentrations, mRNA is formed. The life cycle of mRNA is short: a few seconds during the execution of strength exercises but five minutes during rests (Viru, 1981). After that, mRNA molecules degrade. After high-intensity resistance training, the mRNA content of the myostatin continually falls for 22 hours after recovery (Vinogradova, et al. 2013).

Theoretical analysis shows that while strength exercises are performed to failure, such as, for example, 10 squats (with barbell) with an execution time for each squat of three to five seconds, the exercise has a duration of approximately 30 to 50 seconds. During this time, a cyclical process occurs in the muscles. Therefore, full execution of the exercise (concentric and eccentric parts of the movement with the barbell) over one to two seconds is due to ATP reserves; during a two- to three-second pause, when the muscles become relatively inactive (the load is distributed along the entire spinal column and the legs), ATP resynthesis occurs from phosphocreatine reserves, which is resynthesized due to aerobic processes in the oxidative muscle fibers (slow-twitch muscle fibers) and anaerobic glycolysis in the glycolytic muscle fibers (fast-twitch muscle fibers). Because the output of the aerobic and glycolytic processes is substantially lower than the speed of ATP expenditure, phosphocreatine reserves gradually run out and continuation of the exercise at the given output becomes impossible, starting the process of failure. At the same time, with the anaerobic glycolysis development in the muscles, lactate and hydrogen ions accumulate (Sapega, et al. 1987).

As they accumulate, hydrogen ions start to damage the structure of the protein molecules, leading to changes in enzyme activity, labilization of the membrane, and easy hormone access to DNA. Excessive accumulation or an increase in the duration of the acid actions, even though they are not in large concentrations, may lead to serious damage. After this, part of the destroyed molecules must be eliminated (Salminen, et al. 1984). The free radicals that emerge can cause fragmentation of the mitochondrial enzymes, which occurs more intensely during low pH levels (i.e., with high acidity in the cell) and influences the lysosomes. These, in turn, participate in free radical production in catabolic reactions. Salminen and colleagues (1984) conducted research with rats that showed intense (glycolytic) running causes major necrotic changes and increases the activity of lysosomal enzymes by four to five times.

In humans, the joint action of the hydrogen ions and free creatine leads to activation of mRNA synthesis. It is known that creatine is present in the muscle fibers during the exercise and for 30 to 60 seconds after it, while the resynthesis of phosphocreatine occurs (Volkov, 1990). Thus, in a set of any exercise to failure, the athlete gains approximately one minute of pure effective time with accelerated protein synthesis, when mRNA formation occurs in the active muscles. During the training with multiple sets with short rest between the sets, the amount of mRNA accumulated will increase but with a simultaneous increase in the concentration of hydrogen ions. Therefore, a contradiction emerges: We could stimulate more muscle damage (catabolism) than the stimulation of protein synthesis (anabolism), and that is not optimal for performance and could delay the adaptation process of the athletes (Seluianov, et al. 1990).

To avoid this problem, perform sets with long rest intervals between them or break up the training into two or three parts during the day, with a small number of sets in each training session. The latter training program has been used by some Olympic weightlifters in recent years. Indeed, if we analyze the data obtained in Fry's (2004) review, Olympic weightlifters and powerlifters have more hypertrophied glycolytic (fast-twitch) muscle fibers than slow-twitch muscle fibers. This contrasts bodybuilders, who have a nearly proportional ratio of hypertrophied slow- and fast-twitch muscle fibers. Both Olympic weightlifters and powerlifters routinely train with loads exceeding 90 percent 1RM and with longer rest intervals, but bodybuilders perform a larger number of repetitions and take shorter rest intervals between sets (favoring muscle acidification and metabolic stress) and more varied loads below 80 percent 1RM.

Doubts about the rest between resistance training days are linked to the speed of mRNA realization in the cell organelles, especially the myofibrils. It is known that mRNA by itself only decomposes in the first 10 minutes after exercise (Viru, 1981). However, its basic formation structures are 70 percent to 80 percent synthesized in the organelles over four to seven days. Research data may also be presented (Seluianov, 1996) in which it is demonstrated that, after resistance training, urea concentration in the blood in the morning while fasting for three to four days is below the usual level, which shows the predominance of synthesis (anabolism) over degradations (catabolism).

The rationale stemming from resistance training is based on several theoretical assumptions, but its veracity may only be demonstrated by practical experience. That which works for one athlete may not always be the best training for another.

It should be clear that the oxidative (slow-twitch) and glycolytic (fast-twitch) muscle fibers should be trained using different exercises and different methods.

Hypertrophy of Glycolytic Muscle Fibers Through Hyperplasia

To activate fast-twitch (glycolytic) muscle fibers, it is essential to execute exercises with maximal or near maximal intensity, because, according to the size principle (see figure 1.22, page 28) initially proposed by Henneman and colleagues (1965), when exercises are performed with low external resistances, only low-threshold motor units and the muscle fibers that comprise that group are recruited. According to this principle, the greater the need to generate force, the more motor units will be recruited. This explains the importance of heavy loads (70%-100% of maximal training intensity) to stimulate all the athletes' motor units and muscle fibers.

If muscle contraction is combined with relaxation, this training will not interrupt blood circulation and the effects of the exercise will be directed to fast-twitch muscle fibers. Popov and colleagues (2006) proved this through research conducted using biopsies.

Seluianov (1996) researched the reaction of the body during exercise with an intensity of 85 percent performed as barbell back squats with an execution time for each squat of five seconds, a rest of five seconds (between the repetitions), and repetitions until failure.

As a result, the evaluated person managed to do four to five repetitions in a set. Phosphocreatine reserves in the muscles fell by up to 60 percent. After this, a three-minute recovery period was given with active rest, which allowed the consumption of one liter to two liters of oxygen per minute. For three minutes, lactate concentration in the blood remained practically unchanged, phosphocreatine was almost totally resynthesized, but maximal power at that time was only 70 percent of peak power. Prolonging the active rest to six minutes allowed an increase in power of up to 75 percent and with 10 minutes of active rest, up to 85 percent. At 10 minutes, the concentration of lactate fell to 4.5 mmol/L. The maximum concentration of lactate was observed from two to four minutes of recovery, with the value standing at 6.9 mmol/L.

Exercises with 85 percent intensity do not lead to a significant dissociation of phosphocreatine. To increase the resistance training effectiveness for muscle-fiber hypertrophy, it is essential to increase the number of repetitions in the sets and to reduce the load of the exercises. This conclusion is consistent with data from experiments on methods of muscle hypertrophy that other researchers have proposed (Schoenfeld, 2016; Zatsiorsky, 1970; Hartmann and Tünnemann, 1989).

Vinogradova and colleagues (2013) found that high-intensity resistance training (80% RM) increased the 1RM value by 34 percent, whereas the cross-sectional area of the vastus lateralis muscle increased by 23 percent in type II (glycolytic) fibers and 9.4 percent in type I (oxidative) fibers. This likely occurs because the high-intensity working of the muscle causes more reactions in type II muscle fibers, and this may be explained by the greater activation of the mTORC1 and ERK1/2 signaling pathways that control protein biosynthesis (Schoenfeld, 2016).

Sarsania and colleagues (1990) researched long-term adaptive processes and demonstrated that, when the exercise intensity is 85 percent, the duration of the resistance training changes by 1 to 20 minutes. For example, the athlete can perform from 1 to 15 sets until fatigue of a certain movement, and the rest between training sessions is one to seven days for full recovery. This research showed how muscle mass changed during 20 training microcycles. An analysis of the findings showed that an increase in the number of rest days reduces training cycle effectiveness with a given intensity and duration. Increasing the duration of the training by 1 to 20 minutes (useful time that allows the formation of mRNA) increases training cycle effectiveness.

However, under these conditions, hormone metabolism increases, with the speed of hormone elimination exceeding the speed of synthesis, and the concentration of hormones in the body starts to fall (this occurs when the coaches do not correctly schedule training periods, and athletes constantly train with high volume and intensity). The reduction in hormone concentration (production) to below normal levels leads to Selye's general adaptation syndrome (exhaustion of the body), a reduction in the intensity of the synthesis of myofibrils, mitochondria, and the organ cells of the endocrine and immunological systems. The latter situation increases the potential for disease. Hence, the decrease in immunity increases the risk of falling ill. Consequently, the high intensity and duration of the training may substantially increase the synthesis of different structures in the cells, but at the same time, this may be why an athlete will become ill and experience phenomena linked to overtraining. This conclusion is consistent with the opinion of specialists and is reflected in phrases such as "forcing the sports performance" and "cumulative negative effect of training."

To minimize this negative effect and preserve the effectiveness of resistance training, the following variation may be proposed for planning the weekly training cycle. Let us suppose that on the first day of the microcycle, development training focused on creating stimulus in the body to stimulate gains is performed. It uses heavy loads and moderate to high training volume for a certain muscle group—for example, barbell back squats with loads of 80 percent to 90 percent of 1RM executed until failure (the exercise having a duration of 40 to 60 seconds). Over the course of the exercise and in the recovery period of 60 seconds, active formation of mRNA should occur in the muscle fibers.

Therefore, the useful time of a set is 1 minute 30 seconds to 2 minutes with accelerated protein synthesis in the active muscles. To achieve this, perform 6 to 10 sets per muscle group per week, which is 12 to 20 minutes of useful work (Seluianov, 1996; Schoenfeld, 2016). Work with high intensity as described above causes a significant release of hormones into the blood. The increase in hormone concentration persists over the course of two to three days, which stimulates protein synthesis (anabolism). On the fourth day, the hormone concentration goes back to normal.

This is why it is essential to perform another resistance training session for toning (training designed to maintain previous gains), not only for the formation of mRNA but also to increase hormone concentration in the blood during the course of the following two days of recovery. This maintains the intensity of the myofibrils synthesis after development training. These toning training sessions should be high intensity to stimulate the release of hormones into the bloodstream but should not have a high volume (half of or even less the volume of the development training), so as not to cause an increase in hormone metabolism (reduction or exhaustion) in the athlete's body (Seluianov, et al. 2008).

Research with this training variation has shown that, in six microcycles, the mass of myofibrils grew on average by 7 percent and the mass of mitochondria decreased by 14 percent. The mass of endocrine glands initially had a tendency to grow (10 days), after which they had a tendency to reduce and, on day 42, they returned to normal. Consequently, the proposed microcycle is effective. However, it cannot be used for longer than six weeks in a row, because in the future, signs of exhaustion or overtraining may appear. So, to reach the maximal effect of training, it is essential to observe the following series of conditions:

- The exercise should be performed with maximal or near maximal intensity and loads above 60 percent RM.

- The exercise should be performed until failure, or rather, until exhaustion of phosphocreatine reserves and the formation of high concentrations of free creatine.

- The rest intervals should be longer, 5 to 10 minutes, with five minutes of active rest for exercise performances that have outputs at the aerobic threshold level (usually, heart rate of between 110-130 bpm). This significantly accelerates the reduction of the concentration of lactic acid and hydrogen ions. With 10 minutes of relatively inactive rest, the resynthesis of phosphocreatine occurs mainly during anaerobic glycolysis with accumulation in the fast-twitch muscle fibers of hydrogen ions and lactate. The number of sets in the training should be five to seven with passive rest and 10 to 15 with active rest.

- The number of training sessions per day should be one or two or more, depending on the intensity and level and training of the athlete.

- For training sessions per week, after a training session with maximum volume for each muscle group, the training session may be repeated only after 7 to 10 days, precisely the time required for myofibril synthesis in muscle fibers (Seluianov, 2001).

To better illustrate this, we may follow these recommendations from Seluianov and our colleagues at ProSportLab in Russia:

Hypertrophy of Glycolytic Muscle Fibers Through Hyperplasia

Objective
To increase the number of myofibrils, strength, and the speed of contraction of the glycolytic muscle fibers (GMF).

Training parameters
- *Muscle contraction intensity:* 60 percent to 100 percent of 1RM
- *Duration:* 20 to 40 seconds to failure, with two additional forced repetitions
- *Rest:* 5 to 10 minutes, until minimal concentration of hydrogen ions
- *Number of sets per muscle group:* for toning, one to three sets; for development, 6 to 10 sets
- *Number of training sessions per week:* for toning, three to seven sessions; for development, one session

Factors that stimulate hyperplasia in the muscle fibers include:
- Protein (of animal origin: 2-3 g/kg of bodyweight)
- Hormones (GH, testosterone), as a result of physical stress
- *Free creatine:* activates metabolism in the cell
- *Hydrogen ions:* an optimal concentration ensures the labilization of the membranes (dilatation of the pores of the membranes, which, in turn, facilitates the penetration of hormones into the cells)

The experimental confirmation of theoretical effectiveness of the development variant of resistance training proposed above can be found in many publications from 1970 onward (Zatsiorsky, 1970; Platonov, 2004, 1997, 1988, 1986; Hartmann and Tünnemann, 1989). When performing resistance exercise with near maximal intensity, respiration will be affected, so systolic blood pressure normally increases. For example, among top-level weightlifters, systolic blood pressure increases even before training by up to 150 mmHg, and with forced hyperventilation while lifting, systolic blood pressure rises to 200 mmHg to 250 mmHg (Kotsa, 1986, 1982). In the first minute after lifting the weight, systolic blood pressure reaches between 150 and 180 mmHg, mean arterial pressure increases, and diastolic blood pressure may rise or fall (Vorobiov, 1977). These data serve as a warning to health professionals about the risks of these resistance training methods and their use in the elderly, those with high blood pressure, nonathletes, or people exercising to improve their health, fitness, and appearance.

Hypertrophy of Oxidative Muscle Fibers Through Hyperplasia (Isoton Method)

The hypertrophy method for slow-twitch, oxidative muscle fibers (OMF) by hyperplasia of the myofibrils is similar to the method described previously for glycolytic muscle fibers (Seluianov, et al. 2008; Dias, et al. 2017). The main difference is related to exercise performance, which occurs without relaxing the activated muscles and with reduced movement range (partial range of motion) and angles of greater tension (static-dynamic method, a methodology patented in Russia as *Isoton*). Controlled ischemia of the extremities (arms and legs) potentiates hormonal responses during resistance training and aerobic exercise (Takarada, et al. 2000; Sundberg, 1994; Viru, et al. 1998).

In this case, the constantly contracted muscle fibers compress the capillaries (Kotsa, 1982) and cause vascular occlusion (interruption of blood circulation) in the muscle groups used to perform the exercise. The reduction in blood circulation leads to hypoxia of the muscle fibers, so anaerobic glycolysis intensifies in the oxidative (type I) muscle fibers, and lactate and hydrogen ions accumulate. This training method and these conditions can be created by working against the force of gravity with elastic bands, free weights, or specific resistance training machines (Dias, et al. 2017).

To facilitate learning, we will show an example of the Isoton training method. Performing the barbell back squat (see figure 2.1), the athlete executes the complete movement, squatting down until the hips are below the knees during the eccentric phase, then pushing back up to a position of 100 to 110 degrees in the knee joint (knee flexion) during the concentric phase, without allowing the working muscles to relax (partial range of motion). The athlete then repeats the motion immediately for another repetition.

Figure 2.1 – Carlos "Cachorrão" Eduardo performing the barbell back squat using the Isoton method. In this exercise, we mainly work the quadriceps femoris, gluteal muscles, hip adductors, erector spinae muscles, abdominal muscles, and hamstrings (Delavier, 2011).

The exercise intensity is chosen so that only oxidative muscle fibers (slow-twitch) are recruited. The duration of the exercise should not exceed 60 seconds; otherwise, the hydrogen ion accumulation may exceed the optimal concentration essential for protein biosynthesis activation (Dias, et al. 2017). To increase the time that free creatine and hydrogen ions remain in oxidative muscle fibers, it is essential to perform the exercise as a superset, where the first set should not be performed until failure (approximately 30 seconds), followed by recovery for 30 seconds.

Thus, the sets are repeated three to six times in a superset format (with all the sets in the same exercise), after which a long rest is taken and another muscle group is exercised. This superset approach is mostly used in bodybuilding and consists of free creatine and hydrogen ions being present in oxidative muscle fibers during the exercises as well as in the recovery (rest). Consequently, the total action time (that stimulates anabolism) of the factors (free creatine and hydrogen ions) causes mRNA to form, significantly increasing protein biosynthesis. Vinogradova and colleagues (2013) demonstrated this in a study, where they observed differences in the area occupied by the type I (oxidative) fibers, which was increased (hypertrophy) by 18 percent using the static-dynamic training method (Isoton).

It is important to stress that the increase in protein biosynthesis in oxidative fibers is better exploited at the end of the training session and, preferably, at the end of the afternoon or in the evening, given that a large amount of GH (growth hormone) is normally released before sleep. To confirm the increase in GH (growth hormone) being stimulated by training oxidative (type I) fibers, we may consider McCall and colleagues (2000), who claimed that an increase in GH concentration is related to the activity of type Ia sensory fibers.

Popov and colleagues (2006) compared two groups: group I, using the classic method of resistance training (dynamic training method, including full range of motion), and group II, using the static-dynamic (Isoton with partial range of motion) method for seven weeks. They found a significant increase in GH synthesis in group II (Isoton). There was also an increase of IGF-1 (a principal mediator of the anabolic effects of GH, secreted both systemically by the liver cells and autocrinally in the skeletal muscle fiber during highly contractile activities). These data were not found in group I (in which there was no significant change). In addition, the authors observed greater acute concentrations of GH in the blood postexercise in group II, though the mechanical effects exerted by the muscle fibers were significantly less than in group I (who used the classic resistance training method using higher loads).

Therefore, in response to resistance training, protein molecules form. If a long resistance training session is performed with a high consumption of oxygen (for example, a long run on a treadmill), then with the exhaustion of glycogen reserves, the proteins may be more intensely metabolized with greater amounts of catabolism. In the end, this will reduce the effect of the resistance training program. To better illustrate the planning of the training under a static-dynamic Isoton method, we may look at the following recommendations from Seluianov and our colleagues at ProSportLab in Russia:

Hypertrophy of Oxidative Muscle Fibers Through Hyperplasia

Objective

To increase the number of myofibrils, strength, and speed of contraction of the oxidative muscle fibers (OMF).

Training parameters

- *Intensity:* 10 percent to 60 percent of the repetition maximum (RM)
- *Duration:* 30 to 60 seconds of contraction in each superset (until failure caused by muscle pain with two additional forced repetitions)
- *Rest between supersets:* 30 to 45 seconds
- *Number of supersets:* three to six
- *Rest between the sets of supersets:* 5 to 10 minutes (the rest should be active)
- *Number of sets:* for toning, one to three sets; for development, 4 to 10 sets
- *Number of daily training sessions:* one, two, or more
- *Number of training sessions per week:* for toning, three to seven sessions; for development, the exercise is repeated after three to seven days for each muscle group

Factors that stimulate hyperplasia in the muscle fibers include:

- Protein (of animal origin: 2-3 g/kg of bodyweight)
- Hormones (GH, testosterone), as a result of physical stress
- *Free creatine:* activates metabolism in the cell
- *Hydrogen ions:* an optimal concentration ensures the labilization of the membranes (dilatation of the pores of the membranes, which, in turn, facilitates the penetration of hormones into the cells)

In figure 2.2, we show the barbell bent-over row to build the back muscles. Note in the photos that the muscles are under tension the whole time with a partial range of motion. In this exercise, we develop the latissimus dorsi muscles, the teres major muscle, the posterior deltoid, the flexors of the forearm (biceps brachii, brachialis, brachioradialis), and during the approximation of the scapulae, the rhomboids, and the trapezius (Delavier, 2011). For more details about how to design a specific training session with the Isoton method, please read the proposed model in chapter 5 of this book.

Figure 2.2 – Carlos "Cachorrão" Eduardo performing the barbell bent-over row using the Isoton method.

Methods to Increase the Number of Myofibrillar Mitochondria Through Hyperplasia

One aerobic training objective is developing mitochondria in the muscle fibers. The mitochondrial protein synthesizes itself between 85 percent and 95 percent in the cytoplasm, and only 5 percent to 15 percent of the protein content constitutes the product of the mitochondrial translation itself (Lusikov, 1980; Seluianov, 1996).

The proteins synthesized in mitochondrial ribosomes bind themselves to the internal mitochondrial membrane. The external membrane and the space between the membrane and the matrix complete themselves with proteins that were produced in the cytoplasmic ribosomes. The thickening of the mitochondria constitutes one of the causes of their degradation. This thickening of the mitochondria (Lusikov, 1980; Schmeling, 1985; Fridén, et al. 1988; Gollnick, 1986) may occur due to disturbances in the transformation of energy in relation to the hydrogen ions. It is supposed that exhausting the internal reserves of ATP mitochondria causes the mitochondria to thicken, which leads to the breakage of the external membrane and the widening of the components in the space between the membranes. Mitochondria formation in the cell is controlled based on the principle of selection by function criteria. According to this principle, mitochondrial structures are concentrated in such a way that they cannot effectively transform energy, eliminating themselves during mitochondrial differentiation (Lusikov, 1980).

One natural factor that leads to destruction of mitochondria is hypoxia, which happens during the first few days of spending time in medium- or high-altitude regions when performing high-intensity training and affects anerobic metabolism. Under a lack of oxygen, indices of capillarization of skeletal muscle decline, causing intercellular swelling, disturbances to the contractile apparatus (myofibril), destructive and degenerative changes to the mitochondria, sarcoplasmic reticulum enlargement, and a sudden reduction in glycogen content (Schmeling, 1985). This explains the need to stay at the high-altitude location for several days, normally more than 10, before the athletes begin to feel the positive effects of the altitude as an improvement in their aerobic endurance (Suslov, 1997).

Glycolytic training with high intensity and acidity exhibits an effect similar to that of altitude, damaging and potentially eliminating the mitochondria instead of stimulating their synthesis (Seluianov, et al. 2008; Dias, et al. 2017). The overall position of multiple experiments allows us to make the following generalizations:

- Mitochondria are the energy stations of the cell, supplying ATP as a result of aerobic metabolism.
- Synthesis exceeds decomposition of the mitochondria in the case of their intense functioning (oxidative phosphorylation).
- Mitochondria tend to form in areas of the cell where there is a demand for intense energy supply (ATP).
- Damage of mitochondrial structures occurs under conditions of intense functioning of the cell using anaerobic metabolism, causing significant or prolonged accumulation (under conditions of high altitude) of hydrogen ions in the cell and in the body.

When considering these tendencies, a method of aerobic preparation for the muscles may be drawn up. Each skeletal muscle may be divided into three parts:

1. Muscle fibers involved in regular activity, which are activated continually during human life (oxidative muscle fibers—type I)

2. Muscle fibers that are activated only under conditions of training with average tension of the muscles (intermediate muscle fibers—type IIa)

3. Rarely used muscle fibers, which are called upon to work only under conditions of maximum effort, for example, during jumping or sprinting (glycolytic muscle fibers—type IIx)

Muscle fibers that are regularly recruited (oxidative muscle fibers) achieve their maximum degree of aerobic conditioning when all the myofibrils involve themselves with the mitochondrial system, so that forming new mitochondrial structures becomes impossible. This phenomenon is demonstrated by cardiac muscle fibers (Hoppeler, 1987; Seluianov and Sarsania, 1991). The cardiac muscle fiber hypertrophy is not accompanied by an increased concentration of the aerobic metabolism enzymes. Indirectly, this standpoint confirms many studies focusing on the influence of aerobic training performed with a power output at the aerobic threshold (Aulik, 1990; Zatsiorsky, 1970; Karpman, et al. 1974; Karpman, et al. 1978). All these studies convincingly demonstrate that training at the aerobic threshold does not improve performance in highly conditioned athletes (Seluianov, et al. 2008; Dias, et al. 2017).

Consequently, to increase the aerobic capacity of the oxidative muscle fibers, it is essential to create the basic structure in the muscle fiber, like new myofibrils. After that, next to the new myofibrils, new mitochondrial systems are formed. If we agree with these methods for increasing aerobic capacity, then the increase in strength (hyperplasia of the myofibrils) of the oxidative muscle fibers must lead to an increase in the consumption of oxygen at the aerobic and anaerobic thresholds (Dias, et al. 2017).

For an effective increase in $\dot{V}O_2$max or oxygen consumption at the anaerobic threshold, scientific literature and experienced coaches usually suggest two training methods: 1) continuous exercises at the anaerobic threshold level, or 2) repeated training intervals at the level of the $\dot{V}O_2$max. In this case, not only are oxidative muscle fibers recruited but also high-threshold muscle fibers in which there are few mitochondria. The increase in output demands the recruitment of all the high-threshold motor units in the muscle fibers in which anaerobic glycolysis predominates, which leads to acidity in the fast-twitch, type IIx (glycolytic) muscle fibers and subsequent acidity in the oxidative muscle fibers and blood. The higher acidity of the glycolytic muscle fibers and the intermediate muscle fibers (fast-twitch, type IIa) could lead to damaging changes in the mitochondria, reducing aerobic training effectiveness (Dias, et al. 2017).

One argument against increasing the aerobic capacities of oxidative muscle fibers due to an increase in the strength and power of the myofibrils is the idea that, with the increase in muscle fiber size (hypertrophy), the process of oxygen diffusion to the center of the muscle fiber is inhibited. However, Gayeski and colleagues (1986) showed that pO_2 had no correlation with the diameter of the muscle fibers. The minimum pO_2 is not observed in the center of the muscle fibers. These experimental data reproduce well the models that consider the facilitated diffusion of oxygen inside the muscle fibers throughout the myoglobin (Stroeve, 1982). Consequently, the size of muscle fibers does not pose any difficulty for increasing the aerobic capacity of oxidative muscle fibers (Dias, et al. 2017).

To achieve optimal aerobic preparation, observe the following optimal conditions:

- *Intensity*: normally does not exceed the power output of the anaerobic threshold when performed for a prolonged time
- *Volume*: 5 to 20 minutes, given that longer durations may lead to significant acidity of the blood and of the intermediate muscle fibers, in the event of exceeding the power output of the anaerobic threshold level

- *Rest interval*: 2 to 10 minutes is essential for preventing the body from potentially becoming acidic
- *Training duration*: the maximum number of repetitions in the training is limited to glycogen reserves in the active muscles (approximately 60-90 minutes of pure training time)
- *Training frequency*: training with maximum volume is repeated after two to three days; in other words, after the resynthesis of glycogen within the muscles with the appropriate replacement of carbohydrates, as described in chapter 4

Seluianov and our colleagues at ProSportLab in Russia also suggested the following training methods to stimulate the hyperplasia of mitochondria in fast-twitch type IIx (glycolytic muscle fibers or GMF) fibers.

Methods of Mitochondrial Hyperplasia in Glycolytic Muscle Fibers

Objective
To increase the quantity of mitochondria of the glycolytic muscle fibers (GMF) to increase the work capacity of the active muscle fibers.

Training parameters
- *Muscle contraction intensity:* 60 percent to 100 percent of maximum effort
- *Duration (sets and repetitions):* 3 to 40 seconds, until local fatigue. Examples: a 5- to 10-second sprint, multiple jumps (10), push-ups (10)
- *Rest interval:* 45 seconds to 5 minutes, given the minimal concentration of hydrogen ions
- *Number of repetitions (sets)*: for toning, 10 sets; for development, 20 to 40 sets
- *Number of training sessions per week:* for toning, two to three sessions; for development, five to seven sessions

Factors that stimulate hyperplasia of the mitochondria in the muscle fibers include:
- Muscle fibers activity
- Protein (2 g/kg of bodyweight)
- Hormones, as a result of physical stress
- The presence of oxygen
- Minimum concentration of hydrogen ions in the muscle fibers

Another highly effective aerobic preparation model follows. Recently, this methodology has been employed in training numerous high-level Russian athletes, mainly in cyclic sports, in which the demand for muscular endurance is very high (Dias, et al. 2017). In the cyclic exercises, the methodology consists of each muscle contraction being performed with near maximal intensity, but the average power output of the exercises should not exceed the power output of the anaerobic threshold, as demonstrated in figure 2.3 under the sprint method. In this case, all, or almost all, muscle fibers are activated. However, thanks to the planning of the rest or muscle recovery period, the extraction of metabolism byproducts from anaerobic glycolysis can be fully guaranteed.

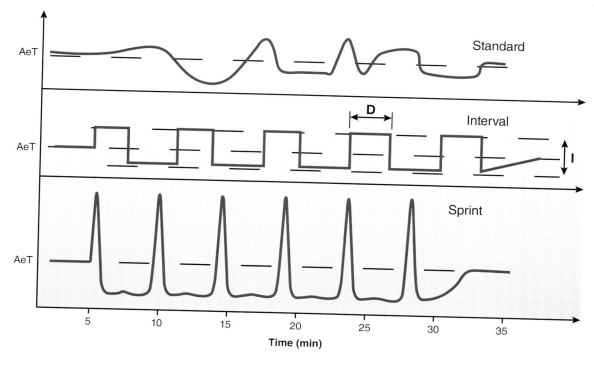

Figure 2.3 – Methods of aerobic interval training. The higher the value of intensity (I), the higher the load on the muscles for a given heart rate, and the longer the duration (D), the greater the chance of overstraining the heart. AeT = aerobic threshold.

The sprint method is highly effective but should only be used by highly trained exercisers or athletes, given that the greater the intensity, the greater the load on the muscles for a given heart rate. We should also ensure that the duration of the stimuli is not very long, because this increases the chance of overloading the heart and a possible sports-related sudden cardiac arrest from training.

For this reason, for beginners, we normally recommend the "standard" interval aerobic training method so that the exerciser can reduce the stimuli (e.g., the speed of a run or the workload on a bicycle) or even stop for a few moments, if necessary. As the months go by, we will increase the difficulty and efficiency of aerobic exercise using the interval method, in which the stimuli and rests are already well organized. Finally, we arrive at the sprint method, which has been widely applied with various elite athletes of American Top Team due to its high degree of efficiency and the reduction in total time spent doing the activity. The effectiveness of this method to improve muscular endurance and the number of mitochondria in the muscle fibers (in arbitrary units), is demonstrated by Dudley and colleagues (1982) and through Maksimov and colleagues (2011) and Seluianov (1996), which confirm these findings.

Figure 2.4 shows the influences of intensity and duration of aerobic exercise on muscle adaptation. The training programs vary from moderate to very intense. Note that continuous runs with an intensity of 40 percent of $\dot{V}O_2$max (letter A) only manage to maintain the initial content (level) of mitochondria in trained subjects and did not serve as stimulus for new gains in performance or muscular endurance. Only with intensities greater than 50 percent of $\dot{V}O_2$max (letters B, C, and D) do gains in performance start to become significant, and it is worth mentioning that the maximum gains of muscle fiber mitochondria occur with exercises performed at 100 percent of $\dot{V}O_2$max (letter E).

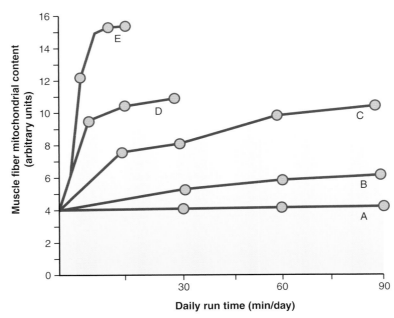

Figure 2.4 − Influences of intensity and duration of aerobic exercise on muscle adaptation. The training programs have the following intensities: A = 40% of $\dot{V}O_2$max; B = 50% of $\dot{V}O_2$max; C = 70% of $\dot{V}O_2$max; D = 85% of $\dot{V}O_2$max; and E = 100% of $\dot{V}O_2$max.

Adapted from Dudley and colleagues (1982).

Another advantage of training with the high-intensity sprint method is that it requires much less time (a few minutes a day) compared to the continuous low-intensity training method and offers results that exceed by 200 percent the results achieved with low-intensity training at 40 percent of $\dot{V}O_2$max (letter A), for example. The high-intensity sprint method is used closer to the competition, after the preparatory mesocycle that incorporates other (less intense) methods of aerobic training.

It is clear from the literature that the muscles need to be recruited during the exercise so that they may adapt to the training program. Muscles (or muscle fibers from a certain muscle region) not involved in the exercise will not adapt (Holloszy, 1967).

Another important aspect of the training is the course of time for adaptations to the training and detraining in the mitochondrial content of the muscle fibers (Booth, 1977). Note in figure 2.5 that it takes approximately four to five weeks of training to double the mitochondrial volume in a certain muscle group, and a kind of plateau occurs from the fifth week (Terjung, 1979). However, in the study by Booth (1977), almost 50 percent of the increase in mitochondrial content was lost with just one unit of time (one week) of detraining (a), and all the adaptation was lost after five weeks of detraining (inactivity). Also, it is necessary to train for four weeks (b) to resume the adaptation that was lost in the first week of detraining (Booth, 1977). Based on this and other information, we should advise our athletes never to be totally inactive for more than three or four days to prevent the risk of delaying the training process, with considerable losses in performance.

Even those who seek to lose weight should prioritize high-intensity, short-duration exercises combined with low-intensity and longer-duration aerobic exercise to increase the metabolic rate and possibly accelerate the mobilization and release of fatty acids into the blood by up to eight times, so that this fat also serves to supply energy to the muscles at an increased rate, leading to a leaner athlete (Guyton and Hall, 1997).

Karlsson and colleagues (1981) studied exercise with near maximal power of muscle contraction at a slow pace. It was shown that exercise with four maximal contractions per

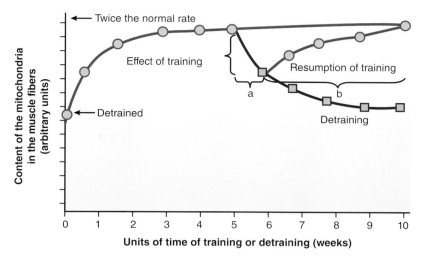

Figure 2.5 — Course of time for adaptations to training and detraining in the mitochondrial content of the muscle fibers.
Adapted from Booth (1977).

minute causes a reduction in the concentration of ATP by 20 percent and phosphocreatine by 40 percent. The concentration of lactate in muscles increased by up to 4.5 mmol/L. During exercise, the energy came from the endogenous glycogen of the oxidative and glycolytic muscle fibers. Notably, other researchers have also shown the positive effects of interval training on athletic performance (Alekseev, 1981; Volkov, 1990; Cheetham, et al. 1986; Holmyard, et al. 1988; Jacobs, et al. 1983; Thorstensson, et al. 1975).

An increase in aerobic capacity may occur based on an increase in the strength of the oxidative muscle fibers and may be achieved with static-dynamic exercises (Isoton method) for hyperplasia of the myofibrils in the oxidative muscle fibers. At the same time, this may trigger the processes to guarantee new myofibrils with subsequent new mitochondria (see figure 2.6). This proposal is confirmed by the results of the experiments Sarsania and colleagues (1982) conducted.

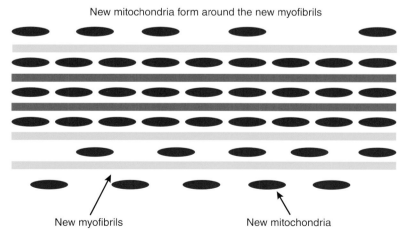

Figure 2.6 — Hyperplasia of the mitochondria in the oxidative muscle fibers (OMF).
Adapted from Seluianov and colleagues (2008).

Volunteer students from the Russian State University of Physical Culture, Sports, Youth and Tourism (GTSOLIFK) were separated into two groups: experimental and control. The two groups performed the same strength exercise program with muscle tension of 60 percent of 1RM. The exercises were performed in a circuit with the extensor and flexor muscles of the arm, extensors of the leg, extensors of the spine, and the abdominal muscles. In each set, the load was slowly lifted ten times. The last two repetitions, the exercises were performed with clear local fatigue but not to failure. Each subject performed three full cycles (circuits).

In a week, three training sessions were completed, and the subjects trained for four weeks. In the experimental group (eight people), the anabolic hormone Retabolil (nandrolone decanoate) was administered, either an ampule of 1 milliliter of intramuscular oily solution once every seven days for those weighing up to 154 pounds (70 kg) or 1 milliliter every five days for people weighing over 154 pounds (70 kg), or Neurobol at 0.18 milligrams per kilogram of bodyweight (therapeutic dose). In the control group, a placebo was administered in the form of a vitamin complex. Before and after the experiment, all the subjects took anthropometric and functional tests and a gradual test on a stationary bicycle with measurement of oxygen consumption.

In the control group, positive changes occurred in all indices, but they were not as great as in the experimental group. The anabolic hormone (experimental group) accelerated the anabolic processes, which allowed significant statistical differences to be reported in all the indices recorded. The results were:

- Strength increased in all the muscle groups by 25 percent, which constituted 2 percent in each session. When the resistance training took place without the anabolic hormone, the average growth was 1 percent to 1.2 percent per training session. Lean mass increased by 3.55 kilograms (8 lb).

- Total fat fell by 0.88 kilograms (2 lb). Physical stress stimulates the release of hormones from the pituitary gland and activates the sympathetic nervous system. Adrenaline, noradrenaline, as well as testosterone and somatotropin stimulate the release of fatty acids from their deposits into the blood. The concentration of the hormones increases and remains in body tissues for one to two days, which increases the basal metabolic rate and the use of fatty acids from their deposits for heart function, respiratory muscles, and synthesis processes in the skeletal muscles.

- Oxygen consumption ($\dot{V}O_2$max) increased by 0.231 milliliters, and the power output with a pulse of 170 beats per minute increased by 22.7 watts per minute. The increase in oxygen consumption ($\dot{V}O_2$max) and the power output of the PWC-170 test confirmed the stated proposal, insofar as, with an increase in the strength of oxidative muscle fibers (i.e., an increase in the number of their myofibrils), morphological conditions were created for the growth of all that is essential for cell organelle activity (symmorphosis theory). For this reason, the sarcoplasmic reticulum and the mitochondria increase. The latter changes were shown in the form of an increase in $\dot{V}O_2$max and the power output of the PWC-170 test (Seluianov, 2001).

Thus, the static-dynamic exercises (in the format of the Isoton method) are an effective way of reinforcing the synthesis process in skeletal muscles. Another study conducted by Popov and colleagues (2006) using biopsies also proved the effectiveness of the static-dynamic exercises in promoting an increase in the size of the oxidative muscle fibers.

Therapeutic doses of anabolic hormones significantly intensify anabolic processes that accelerate the effectiveness of the prepared variants of the training process, but it is considered doping in most sports, with possible suspension ranging from two to four years. That is why we strongly recommend the Isoton method to stimulate the metabolism of proteins and fats and to increase the aerobic capacity of the slow muscle fibers (Seluianov, et al. 1991; Dias, et al. 2017).

The range of changes resulting from the Isoton training method provides a basis for the supposition regarding how highly effective these exercises are in the physical preparation of fighters and other athletes who require muscular endurance.

Methods of Training the Heart Muscle

The cardiac output of blood in the circulatory system is determined by stroke volume and heart rate. The heart rate reaches its limit at magnitudes of 190 to 220 beats per minute, or more. The stroke volume grows until the heart rate reaches 120 to 130 beats per minute, after which increases in stroke volume, as a rule, stabilize, and subsequently, may fall (Seluianov, et al. 2008).

The stroke volume of the heart is a factor in the increase in the cardiac output of the blood in the circulatory system, which is determined by the dilatation of the ventricle and myocardium hypertrophy. Myocardium hypertrophy is reached thanks to the acceleration of protein biosynthesis in its fibers (i.e., the hyperplasia of the myofibrils). On this basis, the mitochondrial network grows (theory of symmorphosis) (Carpenter and Karpati, 1984). To intensify myofibril synthesis, it is essential to create the following in the myocardium fibers:

- Amino acid reserves
- A natural increase in the concentration of anabolic hormones
- A high concentration of free creatine
- An increased concentration of hydrogen ions

To create these conditions, start anaerobic glycolysis in the myocardium fibers. In some animal experiments, a state of anaerobic glycolysis is reached through simple pressure of the coronary arteries (narrowing). As a result, the heart muscle experiences hypoxia and anaerobic glycolysis occurs inside, with hypertrophy of the heart reaching 80 percent after five days (Meerson, 1965, 1975, 1981).

In humans or animals, hypoxia occurs when a state of diastolic dysfunction is reached. This occurs when maximal cardiac contraction rates are reached, when diastolic time falls so much that the heart muscle cannot totally relax. As a result, a hypoxic state occurs. Consequently, we have a high concentration of free creatine and an increased concentration of hydrogen ions in the cardiac muscle cells.

An analysis of the above mechanism of hypertrophy of myocardium fibers leads to formulating the rules of this method (interval training method), which Seluianov and colleagues (2011, 2008) perfected. The rules of the method of hypertrophy of the heart muscle are:

- *Intensity:* The exercise is performed with a power output above $\dot{V}O_2$max and with a maximum total training duration of 4 to 10 minutes.
- *Duration of the exercise:* The duration is 60 to 120 seconds. Care should be taken to ensure that the maximum heart rate is kept at that maximum only between 30 and 60 seconds to avoid increasing the chance of overloading the heart and possible sports-related sudden cardiac arrest from training.
- *Rest interval:* This interval is 120 to 180 seconds, until resumption of a heart rate of 120 beats per minute.

- *Number of repetitions:* The repetitions are 30 to 40 accelerations or 60 to 90 minutes of pure exercise time, the limit being linked to the glycogen reserves in skeletal muscles.
- *Frequency:* The training is repeated four to seven days after a training session at maximum duration or volume.

To confirm that this rationale is correct, we will present data from Nikityuk and Talko (1991). These results were obtained in experiments with rats. For the experiments, three groups were formed: *control* (C), *experimental-1* (E-1), and *experimental-2* (E-2). The rats in the experimental groups ran daily. In group E-1, they initially ran slowly, but toward the end of the experiment, the speed increased by 30 percent and the duration went from 55 to 65 minutes. In group E-2, from the outset, the run was executed at maximum speed and for maximum duration. The results demonstrated that in group E-1, the greatest changes occurred at the subcellular level: The number of mitochondria increased significantly, but their size decreased in relation to the myofibrils. The size of the cell and the nucleus did not change, and the structure of the connective tissues remained transparent, which, as proposed, allows the potential dilatation of the heart.

In group E-2, changes occurred rapidly: The mass of the heart increased and the relationship between the mitochondria and myofibrils was disrupted, as was the size of the cell and of the nucleus. It appears that the elastic characteristics of the myocardium were reduced. In the vessels, similar processes occurred: Some animals became overtrained, and the relationship between the sizes of the cytoplasm and the nucleus of the cell of the smooth muscle tissue of the vessels was disrupted. Consequently, inappropriate daily loads lead to dystrophy of myocardium fibers and cells of the vessels, which are found solely at the subcellular level.

Indirectly, the results of an analogue training session (six times a week, for seven weeks, at an intensity of 85%-90% of maximum oxygen consumption [$\dot{V}O_2max$] for 40-55 minutes) were judged by Cox and colleagues (1986). During the seven weeks, the $\dot{V}O_2max$ increased by 32 percent (the subjects were not athletes), the size of the left ventricle at the end-diastole increased from 4.96 centimeters to up to 5.13 centimeters (2 in.), and the thickness of the interventricular septum increased by between 11 percent and 15 percent. Related to the activity of all myocardium fibers during each systole, the heart muscle was always at the maximum of its functional capacity—there is a maximal relationship of myofibrils to mitochondria. This relationship is linked to the following phenomena:

- After the training interval, the myofibrils in myocardium fibers grow, and new myofibrils become covered with new mitochondria.
- The detraining process occurs very slowly.

For example, in 1990, researcher Giovanna (apud Seluianov, et al. 2008) studied, among other athletes, seven boxers aged between 40 and 60 years who were engaged in professional sport for 16 years and had not trained for over 10 years. Their echocardiograms showed signs of hypertrophy in the left ventricle and disruptions in conductibility. The echocardiogram confirmed these data: heart mass was 332 ± 90 grams (12 ± 3 oz), whereas for persons of the same age who had not trained, it was 220 ± 27 grams (8 ± 1 oz). To achieve dilatation of the left ventricle, it is necessary to perform the exercises with a heart rate of 120 to 150 beats per minute when the maximum stroke volume of the heart is reached. The duration of these training sessions may take hours, and when this is the case, this task may be successful with the introduction of two to three daily training sessions.

Methods of Directing Adipose Tissue Activity

Adipose tissue consists of cells (adipocytes). In humans, we differentiate between subcutaneous, intramuscular, perirenal, and abdominal adipose tissue.

According to Seluianov and colleagues (2008), the mobilization of the fats from deposits (adipocytes) is caused by a set of hormones. The series of consequent processes occurs in the following manner:

1. Transformation of the triglycerides into fatty acids inside the adipocytes
2. Release of the fatty acids and entry into the bloodstream
3. Delivery of fatty acids into the bloodstream for different organs and tissues (the intense metabolism of the fat goes to the heart, diaphragm, and active oxidative muscle fibers, because they contain a large quantity of mitochondria)

The hormones that activate the mobilization of lipids of the adipose tissue are epinephrine (adrenaline), norepinephrine (noradrenaline), steroids, and hormones from the pituitary gland. Consequently, psychological tension (intense exercise) causes the release of hormones into the bloodstream and through the adrenal glands (adrenaline and noradrenaline), constituting the basic cause of the activation of the lipid metabolism. The hormones from the adrenal glands interrelate with the enzyme adenylyl cyclase present in the membranes of many cells. This leads the cell to form cyclic AMP with the consequent activation of the processes of synthesis of mRNA and lipolysis. Lipolysis substantially intensifies during physical exercise. It appears that the release of noradrenaline from the terminal nerve of the sympathetic nervous system leads to the supplementary stimulation of biochemical processes, with greater formation of cyclic AMP in the adipocytes. Its speed of formation substantially increases with the acidity of the cell, with insufficient output of the metabolic pathways and the guarantee of resynthesis of ATP (Maksimov, et al. 2011; Seluianov, et al. 2011).

Thus, physical exercise performed with major psychological tension (intense exercise) until clear local muscle fatigue (acidity) must be the most effective for intensifying fatty acid release from the lipid deposits in the activated muscles, always in combination with a rational, organized diet. As a practical example of this, we may analyze the results of WWE champion and professional MMA athlete Bobby Lashley (see figure 2.7), who, with a reduced amount of aerobic exercise on a treadmill and stationary bicycle (less than

Figure 2.7 – MMA athlete Bobby Lashley.

15 percent of the total training volume) and who performs most training with intense strength exercises and specific fighting exercises, has an entire year with around 6 percent to 10 percent body fat. This contradicts many coaches, who overvalue the importance of aerobic exercise to lose weight and body fat.

Guyton and Hall (1997) also agreed with our position, and wrote the following paragraph in their book:

> *Probably, the most notable increase that occurs in the use of fat is that observed during intense exercise. This results almost entirely from the release of epinephrine and norepinephrine by the adrenal medulla during exercise, during sympathetic stimulation. These two hormones directly activate the triacylglycerol lipase, which is present in abundance in the adipose cells, causing the rapid degradation of the triglycerides and the mobilization of fatty acids. Sometimes, the concentration of free fatty acids in the blood increases by up to eight times, such that the use of these fatty acids by the muscles as a source of energy also rises correspondingly.* (p. 786)

Heat Acclimation

Heat acclimation can be an effective training tool for athletes preparing to train or compete in hot, humid environments. Most combat sports athletes will make weight using sweating methods from heat, and heat acclimation can help better prepare the athlete for the sweating involved in the weight cut. By using heat acclimation training protocols, athletes can have a competitive advantage in warm environments as well as when competing in cooler weather (Lorenzo, et al. 2010).

There are two main categories of heat training: *direct* or *active acclimation* (inducing heat stress within the training session), and *indirect* or *passive acclimation* (inducing heat stress using passive modalities). This section will outline heat acclimation factors that will allow you to better understand how to use this information for improved performance.

Characteristics of heat training include the following:

- Training in heat increases blood plasma volume and cardiovascular fitness.
- Heat acclimation decreases core temperature over time.
- Heat acclimation may provide similar benefits to altitude training.
- In hot, humid environments, the heart rate can be up to 10 beats per minute higher for the same perceived effort, making heart rate monitoring less accurate.
- Heatstroke generally occurs at core temperatures of 103 to 106 degrees Fahrenheit (39-41 degrees Celsius). Trained distance runners can reach up to 105 degrees Fahrenheit (40 degrees Celsius) without harm.
- Environment accounts for 80 percent to 90 percent of heat loss in hot or dry environments.
- Training needs to induce a 1 degree increase in core temperature for effective heat acclimation.
- Biggest improvements occur in dry heat. Effects may be minimal in humidity due to reduced evaporation.
- Gastric emptying of fluids is approximately 1 liter (1 qt) per hour, but well-trained athletes can lose up to 2 liters (2 qt) per hour.

There are two major strategies for heat acclimation: active and passive. This can be accomplished by increasing the tolerance to heat over time or by shocking the body to adapt to high heat stress. The shock method can be dangerous to the athlete, so it should be avoided or used with extreme caution.

Active strategies involve getting your heat stress during your training sessions. This method can include the following:

- Executing harder or quality sessions earlier in the day when it is cooler, and keeping easy sessions in the heat for later in the day.
- Using a thermometer to monitor core temperature during and after training sessions. This allows athletes to reach optimal heat stress by raising core temperature 1 degree Fahrenheit above average but not exceeding 104 degrees Fahrenheit (40 degrees Celsius), which could lead to heatstroke. A handheld unit that can measure core temperature in the ear or via a forehead scan has proven to be effective.
- Taking core temperature measurements during simulated competition can help with competition strategy, pacing, and hydration strategies.

Passive strategies are implemented outside of training to induce a thermic effect for heat acclimation. This can be especially effective for athletes training in a cold climate who will be traveling and competing in a hot, humid environment.

- After a quality training session when the core temperature is elevated, immerse in a hot tub until core temperature reaches 104 degrees Fahrenheit (40 degrees Celsius). This should be done gradually. Exposure time can build up to 40 minutes.
- In the final 10 to 14 days before traveling to a warm climate, use a steam room or sauna and increase exposure gradually. Do this on quality training days, not recovery days.

Once heat acclimation has been achieved, additional strategies can be implemented before competition in hot or humid conditions.

- Precool with an ice vest before competition. This may reduce core temperature during warm-up. Others say it has a psychological effect, but both have proven to be effective.
- Keep warm-ups short to prevent an excessive rise in core temperature.
- Slushies made with sports drinks reduce core temperature before, during, and after competition in the heat.

A well-designed training plan that includes heat acclimation can be of physical and psychological benefit to the athlete. This allows for better knowledge of how athletes can perform optimally while maintaining the health and safety of the athlete. Since it has been shown that heat acclimation can offer performance benefits at cooler temperatures, there is no reason not to include this in an athlete's yearly training plan.

3

PHYSICAL ASSESSMENT OF THE FIGHTER

Vitaly Rybakov, PhD

Ryan Fairall, PhD

Stéfane Beloni Correa Dielle Dias, PhD

André Geraldo Brauer Júnior, PhD

João Carlos Alves Bueno, MS

Guilherme Ferreira, MS

Rokaya Mikhailenko, MS

Diego de Castro e Silva Lacerda, MS

Assessing the fighter is essential for creating a targeted training process. With proper information about the fighter's physical abilities, it is possible to compare their performance with that of other fighters (Franchini, et al. 2007; Fujise, et al. 1998) and with reference values for different forms of combat (Arruga, et al. 2003), and to check changes in the preparation level during training (Franchini, et al. 2011; Paiva, 2009).

Because assessing these athletes is not common practice, only a few publications cover this subject (Siqueido, 2010; Schick, et al. 2010; Marinho, et al. 2011; Bueno, et al. 2022). *A Cross-Sectional Performance Analysis and Projection of the UFC Athlete: Volume 2* (2021) is one of the most contemporary and comprehensive collections of performance data for MMA. Most of the tests generally assess the athlete's physical preparation (cardiorespiratory and neuromuscular or musculoskeletal fitness), as in the judo example in table 3.1. Although other tests assess the athlete's special physical preparation (Paiva, 2009), they still require scientific validation and, therefore, their interpretation remains inconclusive.

What should we assess in a fighter? In combat sports, athletes need to maintain high-intensity exertion for different periods of time, depending on the specific sport concerned. Motor actions such as punches, kicks, knees, and striking techniques are combined with very brief moments of rest or less-intense activity and, in some sports, there is a short break between *rounds*. This means that the fighter requires good cardiorespiratory fitness (power and aerobic capacity) and neuromuscular fitness (strength, speed, power, and localized muscular endurance) (Bueno, et al. 2022). Good cardiorespiratory fitness allows the athlete to maintain the high intensity of motor actions during the entire contest period and to recover more quickly in the less-intense periods of the fight and the breaks between *rounds* (Alm, et al. 2013). On the other hand, neuromuscular fitness is essential for executing the different motor actions and maneuvers found in different combat sports.

To correctly plan the athlete's training process, the assessment must consist of the following three stages (Tristschler, 2003):

1. *Diagnostic assessment* should be carried out at the beginning of the training program. It should analyze the strengths and weaknesses in the athlete's preparation, assist in the planning of tasks, and help form more homogenous training groups.

2. *Formative assessment* indicates the athlete's progress during the training process. It reveals what needs correction. It should be constantly performed—daily, if possible.

Table 3.1 – Normative Values of Adult Judokas at National Level

Tests	≤70 kg (154 lb)	>70 kg (154 lb)
1,600 m (1,750 yd) run (minutes, seconds)	6 min 19 sec to 5 min 57 sec	6 min 50 sec to 6 min 44 sec
Pull-ups (quantity)	13-19	10-14
Pull-ups (10 reps in seconds)	13.9-11.6	14-10
Push-ups on the floor (10 times in seconds)	7.4-6.3	7.8-6.9
Grip strength (kg)	50-61	60-70
Standing triple jump (cm)	654-687 (257-270 in.)	673-702 (265-276 in.)
Suicide running drill 4 × 10 m (in seconds)	10.8-10.6	11.8-11.5
Number of judo throws (ippon seoi nage technique) with 3 partners in 180 seconds	66-68	56-60

Source: Suslov (1997).

3. *Summative assessment* is the sum of all the assessments carried out during training before a competition or fight camp. Its goal is to obtain an overview of the athlete's progress; the results are compared with national and international standards or other preestablished benchmarks. It also analyzes results achieved in competition.

In this chapter, tests will be presented to assess body composition and the fighter's general and special physical preparation. The testing protocols will be described and commented on, and where there is literature, reference values will be presented for rating the athletes.

Body Composition

Body composition is the study of the components of the body and their relative proportions to describe the percentages of fat mass (subcutaneous and visceral), bone, water, and muscle in human bodies (ACSM, 2014). Making weight to compete in a desired weight class or weight division is an essential component of combat sports. Strength and conditioning regimens, nutrition, hydration status, and training volume all contribute to an ideal body composition, and to track this, we can use various assessment tools. There are benefits and drawbacks to the many different techniques, methods, and instruments used to measure body composition. In this chapter we will discuss two of the most widely used and available methods: one clinical evaluation and one field assessment.

Dual-Energy X-Ray Absorptiometry

Dual-energy X-ray absorptiometry (DXA) is a laboratory assessment with a very low standard error of estimate (SEE) of ±1.8% (ACSM, 2014). DXA measurement is beneficial because it evaluates regional body fat proportions, not only lean muscle tissue and fat (ACSM, 2014). This method also provides the individual's bone mineral density and visceral fat. However, one drawback could be the high cost; it will also require a clinical visit and may not be accessible in every city or even all countries.

In figure 3.1*a*, you see data obtained during a DXA scan of one of our athletes. Each body segment is measured and assessed to create a total bone mineral density (BMD) score. Figure 3.1*b* demonstrates how the body composition changes during a training camp. In this example, the athlete's body fat decreased around 20 pounds (9 kg, black line) while fat free mass increased nearly 10 pounds (4.5 kg, magenta line) between November 2019 and the end of January 2020.

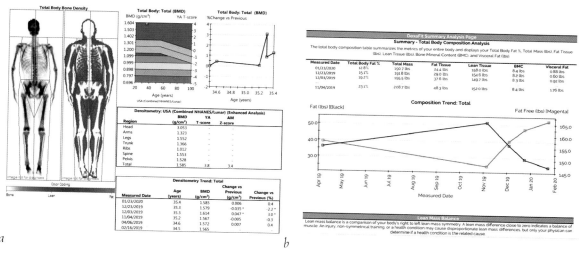

Figure 3.1 — A body composition report from a total body dual-energy X-ray absorptiometry scan.

Data from DexaFit.

Skinfold Measurements

Skinfold measurements are some of the most common methods for determining body composition, yet they must be performed correctly to limit the errors that come from the rater or the equipment. Preferably, a recorder will be present while the rater measures the subject (Norton, 2018). Skinfold measurement is used to estimate body fat percentage and is based on the assumption that the total amount of body fat is proportional to the amount of subcutaneous fat (ACSM, 2014). Skinfold measurements can be used regularly to create comparative data, keeping in mind a few cautions and considerations. First, the caliper used for taking the measurement needs to be of good quality so it applies the proper amount of force to pinch the fold.

The process of skinfold measurement is:

1. Place the thumb and index finger about three inches (7 cm) apart and pull the skin from the muscle.

2. The measurement scale should be facing the rater.

3. Wait one or two seconds and maintain the skin pinch while reading the caliper.

4. Take all measurements three times (you may measure three times and average all three if within 1 mm or exclude a measurement if it is more than 1 mm different from the other two to enhance accuracy) and from the right side of the body, being careful to use the correct anatomical landmarks.

5. Take all measurements before going back to the same site to take the second reading to allow the skin to recover.

6. Make sure the same rater is used for the same individual every time to increase accuracy of comparative data (ACSM, 2014).

For each site measured, the average value of the multiple measures is used (Norton, 2018). Measurements need to be taken at the appropriate landmark (see figure 3.2). All measurements are taken on the right side of the body with the subject standing upright. Use the following procedures (McGuigan, 2016):

- *Chest or pectoral-diagonal fold:* half the distance between the anterior axillary line and the nipple (men) or one-third of the distance between the anterior axillary line and the nipple (women; not pictured)

- *Thigh-vertical fold:* on the anterior midline of the thigh, midway between the proximal border of the patella and the inguinal crease (hip)

- *Abdominal-vertical fold:* two centimeters (1 in.) to the right side of the umbilicus

- *Triceps-vertical fold:* on the posterior midline of the upper arm, halfway between the acromion and olecranon processes, with the arm held freely to the side of the body

- *Suprailiac-diagonal fold:* in line with the natural angle of the iliac crest taken in the anterior axillary line immediately superior to the iliac crest (not pictured)

- *Midaxillary-vertical fold:* on the midaxillary line at the level of the xiphoid process of the sternum

- *Subscapular-diagonal fold (at a 45-degree angle):* one to two centimeters (0.5 to 1 in.) below the inferior angle of the scapula

- *Calf-vertical fold:* at the maximum circumference of the calf on the midline of its medial border

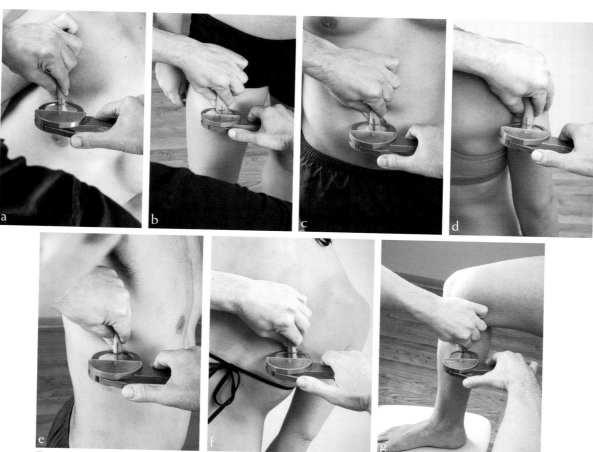

Figure 3.2 — Standardized skinfold sites and the anatomical landmarks: (*a*) chest or pectoral-diagonal fold (men); (*b*) thigh-vertical fold; (*c*) abdominal-vertical fold; (*d*) triceps-vertical fold; (*e*) midaxillary-vertical fold; (*f*) subscapular-diagonal fold; and (*g*) calf-vertical fold.

Table 3.2 presents the formulas for using skinfold measurements to estimate body fat percentage. The quality of the measurement will greatly affect the outcome and success of subsequent interventions. Therefore, it is extremely important that proper protocol be followed (Schuindt and Vieira, 2020).

Fighters typically need a very lean body composition; exceptions may be seen in the heavyweight and super heavyweight divisions. The UFC Performance Institute (2021) recommends that at the start of fight camp, men have 9 percent to 16 percent body fat (BF) and women 16 percent to 26 percent; mid fight camp should be 7 percent to 14 percent for men, 14 percent to 24 percent for women. At weigh-in or fight, it should be 5 percent to 12 percent for men, 12 percent to 22 percent for women. Off-season (not in fight camp), it should be <18 percent men and <28 percent women. This off-season weight is called a fighter's *walk-around weight*, which is still lean when we compare to normative data (see table 3.3). Making weight is essential to a fighter's ability to perform, so following healthy guidelines to manage body composition, decreasing BF gradually, and maintaining a healthy walk-around weight (not gaining too much) help negate the negative effects of cutting weight during camp and allow the athlete to perform optimally.

The UFC Performance Institute states that there is an increased risk of body image distortion and eating disorders for athletes in weight-restricted sports. Therefore, we want

Table 3.2 – Skinfold Prediction Equations

SKF sites	Population	Equation	Ref
Σ7SKF (chest + abdomen + thigh + triceps + subscapular + suprailiac + midaxillary)	Black or Hispanic women, 18-55 years	$Db (g \cdot cc^{-1}) = 1.0970 - 0.00046971$ (Σ7SKF) $+ 0.00000056$ (Σ7SKF)$^2 -$ 0.00012828 (age)	[1]
	Black men or male athletes, 18-61 years	$Db (g \cdot cc^{-1}) = 1.1120 - 0.00043499$ (Σ7SKF) $+ 0.00000055$ (Σ7SKF)$^2 -$ 0.00028826 (age)	[2]
Σ4SKF (triceps + anterior suprailiac + abdomen + thigh)	Female athletes, 18-29 years	$Db (g \cdot cc^{-1}) = 1.096095 - 0.0006952$ (Σ4SKF) $+ 0.0000011$ (Σ4SKF)$^2 -$ 0.0000714 (age)	[1]
Σ3SKF (triceps + suprailiac + thigh)	White or anorexic women, 18-55 years	$Db (g \cdot cc^{-1}) = 1.0994921 - 0.0009929$ (Σ3SKF) $+ 0.0000023$ (Σ3SKF)$^2 -$ 0.0001392 (age)	[1]
Σ3SKF (chest + abdomen + thigh)	White men, 18-61 years	$Db (g \cdot cc^{-1}) = 1.109380 - 0.0008267$ (Σ3SKF) $+ 0.0000016$ (Σ3SKF)$^2 -$ 0.0002574 (age)	[2]
Σ3SKF (abdomen + thigh + triceps)	Black or white collegiate athletes, 18-34 years	%BF $= 8.997 + 0.2468$ (Σ3SKF) $- 6.343$ (sex[a]) $- 1.998$ (race[b])	[3]
Σ2SKF (triceps + calf)	Black or white boys, 6-17 years	%BF $= 0.735$ (Σ2SKF) $+ 1.2$	[4]
	Black or white girls, 6-17 years	%BF $= 0.610$ (Σ2SKF) $+ 5.1$	

ΣSKF = sum of skinfolds (mm). Use population-specific conversion formulas to calculate %BF (percent body fat) from Db (body density).

[a]Male athletes = 1; female athletes = 0.

[b]Black athletes = 1; white athletes = 0.

[1] Jackson et al., 1980. Generalized equations for predicting body density of women. *MSSE* 12: 175-182. [2] Jackson and Pollock. 1978. Generalized equations for predicting body density of men. *Brit J Nutr* 40: 497-504. [3] Evans et al. 2005. Skinfold prediction equation for athletes developed using a four-component model. *MSSE* 37: 2006-2011. [4] Slaughter et al.1988. Skinfold equations for estimation of body fatness in children and youth. *Hum Biol* 60: 709-723.

to have a clear picture of both body weight and the lean muscle mass to body fat ratio. Rapid weight loss measures ("cutting weight") can be unsafe for the athlete, and even deadly. Coaches and trainers need to discourage unhealthy weight loss practices and be knowledgeable about and encourage healthy weight loss methods.

For example, to combat unhealthy and rapid weight loss, changes in the regulations for college wrestlers in the United States, such as weekly weight loss limits and changes to the weight classes, have been made. These measures, along with prohibiting and discouraging methods for rapid weight loss, such as extreme hot environments and sweatsuits, were shown to be effective in the collegiate wrestling population at minimizing unhealthy weight loss (Jetton, et al. 2013). Maintaining body composition that does not demand extreme weight loss measures before competition is both a short- and long-term advantage to the athlete.

Table 3.3 – Norms for Percent Body Fat in Males and Females

Male rating	Age (years)					
	18-25	**26-35**	**36-45**	**46-55**	**56-65**	**66+**
Excellent	3-7	4-10	5-13	8-16	11-17	12-18
Good	8-10	11-13	15-17	17-19	19-21	19-20
Above Average	11-12	14-16	18-20	20-22	22-23	21-22
Average	13-15	17-19	21-22	23-24	24-25	23-24
Below Average	16-18	20-22	23-25	25-27	26-27	25-26
Poor	19-21	23-26	26-28	28-30	28-29	27-29
Very Poor	23-35	27-38	29-39	31-40	31-40	30-39
Female rating	**18-25**	**26-35**	**36-45**	**46-55**	**56-65**	**66+**
Excellent	9-17	7-16	9-18	12-21	12-22	11-20
Good	18-19	18-20	19-22	23-25	24-26	22-25
Above Average	20-21	21-22	23-25	26-28	27-29	26-28
Average	22-23	23-25	26-28	29-30	30-32	29-31
Below Average	24-26	26-28	29-31	31-33	33-35	32-34
Poor	27-30	29-32	32-35	34-37	36-38	35-37
Very Poor	32-43	34-46	37-47	39-50	39-49	38-45

Reprinted by permission from J.R. Morrow, D.P. Mood, J.G. Disch, and M. Kang, *Measurement and Evaluation in Human Performance*, 5th ed. (Champaign, IL: Human Kinetics, 2016), 208. Data from L. Golding (ed.), *YMCA Fitness Testing and Assessment Manual*, 4th ed. (Champaign, IL: Human Kinetics, 2000).

Metabolic and Cardiorespiratory Fitness: Laboratory Testing

One of the most used indicators of cardiorespiratory fitness in sport to assess and prescribe training is maximal aerobic power, which can be assessed using maximal oxygen uptake ($\dot{V}O_2$max). A good cardiorespiratory fitness level is essential for fighters because a large proportion of the energy used during a contest comes from the aerobic system (Dias, et al. 2017). Therefore, field and laboratory protocols will be described below for assessing different cardiorespiratory parameters essential to determining and controlling the training process.

To strategically plan the training process, it is necessary to understand the restrictions on the MMA fighter's physical preparation. Assessments conducted under laboratory conditions allow a more precise analysis of the cardiorespiratory and other systems than field testing. According to Maksimov and colleagues (2011), the indicators that provide the most information about the functional condition of combat athletes are:

- Aerobic threshold, which determines the capacity of oxidative muscle fibers
- Quantity of oxygen consumed or power at the anaerobic threshold, which may take into account the mitochondrial mass of active muscles
- Volume of maximal oxygen uptake ($\dot{V}O_2$max) or power at the level of maximal oxygen uptake, which is a complete indicator of the MMA fighter's work capacity and from which the aerobic capacity of the active muscles, myocardium, and respiratory system may be evaluated

- Maximum alactic power criteria to evaluate the mass of myofibrils in the active muscles of MMA fighters

Stationary Bicycle Tests

Two functional or exertion tests on the lower body may be performed on a stationary bicycle. The progressive test determines power and oxygen consumption at the aerobic and anaerobic thresholds and maximal oxygen uptake during the work of the lower body. The sprint test determines maximum alactic power and evaluates the power of the lower-body muscles.

- *Progressive test:* The progressive test is best performed on a stationary bicycle that allows a given power to be maintained regardless of the rotations (e.g., the Monark 839, Ergoline Ergoselect 200, an ergometer by the brand Lode, or similar equipment). The test can also be performed on other ergometers (i.e., mechanical ergometers like Monark 828 E, Monark 894, and Monark 874), maintaining a combination of power work and pedal rotation. To perform the progressive test, a gas analysis apparatus is required (e.g., Cortex MetaLyser3B, MetaSoft, or similar equipment) to determine oxygen consumption, respiratory quotient, respiratory ventilation, intensity, and frequency. It is also necessary to monitor heart rate (using a heart rate monitor) to determine the frequency of heart contractions. It is also possible to determine lactate concentration in the blood by using a lactate meter (e.g., Lactate Scout).

The progressive test is performed with a gradual increase in load on the lower body on an ergometer set at 75 pedal rotations per minute until pedal velocity decreases. The process is started with a power of 35 watts and increases by 35 watts every two to four minutes. For athletes with poor functional conditioning, the recommendation is to start the test with a power of 20 watts and increase it by 20 watts every two minutes. The external respiration parameters are evaluated during the entire test with the gas analysis apparatus (see figure 3.3). Heart rate is evaluated with a heart rate monitor. At the end of each level, it is possible to measure the lactate with a lactate meter by using a drop of blood from the finger or earlobe. After the test, the person being evaluated should continue pedaling on the ergometer with a minimum load and without the gas analysis apparatus until fully recovered, which is usually when the heart rate is <120 beats per minute and the person can speak normally.

Figure 3.3 – Progressive bicycle testing being conducted at ProSportLab-Russia.

■ *Sprint test:* The sprint test determines the maximum alactic power and evaluates the speed-strength ability of the leg muscles in MMA athletes. The test needs to be performed on a stationary bicycle that targets maximum power and can be set up to 2,000 to 2,500 watts, such as the Monark 894 or Monark 874 mechanical ergometers or similar equipment. Likewise, electromagnetic ergometers made by Lode, or comparable equipment, may be used.

Maximum alactic power is determined on the stationary bicycle by measuring the force in Newtons and revolutions per minute (RPM) reached during acceleration. The load is applied to the athlete during the test in the following manner: 0.09 × body weight in kilograms. For example, if the athlete weighs 80 kilograms (176 lb), 0.09 × 80 = 7.2 kilograms (15.87 lb). The evaluated person starts pedaling, increasing the pace progressively. At the same time, the load is gradually increased. When the pace reaches 90 to 100 rotations per minute, the athlete receives a command and a specific maximum load for the test is established. Immediately after, the athlete should pedal as fast as possible so that between five and seven seconds later, they reach 130 to 150 rotations per minute. As soon as the pace starts to slow, the test is discontinued. From this, the maximum result for pace and power is established, and from that the maximum alactic power is determined. If the person fails to reach or exceeds the pace established, then after three to five minutes, the test is performed again, decreasing or increasing the load. For example, if the pace was below 130 rotations per minute, then the load is decreased; if the pace was above 150 rotations per minute, then the load is increased. After the end of the test, the athlete should continue pedaling on the ergometer using a minimal load until full recovery.

Arm Ergometer Tests

Functional or exertion tests of the upper body are performed using arm ergometers on which it is possible to perform various tests. The progressive test determines the power and oxygen consumption at the aerobic threshold, anaerobic threshold, and maximal oxygen uptake during the work of the upper body. The sprint test determines maximum alactic power and evaluates the strength capacity of the upper-body muscles of MMA athletes.

■ *Progressive test:* The progressive test is best performed on an arm bike ergometer that allows a given power to be maintained regardless of the rotations, such as the Monark 831, Ergoline Ergoselect 400 (see figure 3.4), an arm ergometer by Lode, or similar equipment.

Figure 3.4 – Progressive arm ergometer testing being conducted at ProSportLab-Russia.

The test can be performed on other arm ergometers (e.g., the Monark 891, Monark 881, and others), maintaining a combination of power work and arm rotation. To perform the progressive test, a gas analysis apparatus is required (e.g., Cortex MetaLyser3B, MetaSoft, or similar equipment) to determine oxygen consumption, respiratory quotient, respiratory ventilation, intensity, and frequency. It is also necessary to monitor the heart rate (using a heart rate monitor) to determine the frequency of heart contractions. It is also possible to determine the concentration of lactate in the blood with a lactate meter (e.g., Lactate Scout).

The progressive test uses the same protocol described previously for the lower-body cycle test with a gradual increase in load on the arm ergometer set at 75 pedal rotations per minute until the pedal velocity decreases. After the test, the person being evaluated should continue pedaling on the arm ergometer with a minimum load and without the gas analysis apparatus until full recovery.

- *Sprint test*: The sprint test determines the maximum alactic power and evaluates speed-strength ability of the upper-body muscles in MMA athletes. The test needs to be performed on an arm bike with maximum power (1,500-2,000 watts), such as the Monark 891 or Monark 881 (see figure 3.5) mechanical ergometers or similar equipment. Likewise, electromagnetic ergometers made by Lode, or comparable equipment, may be used.

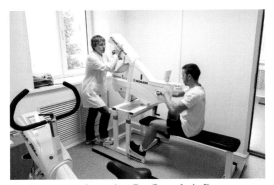

Figure 3.5 – Sprint arm test being conducted at ProSportLab-Russia.

Maximum alactic power is determined on the arm ergometer by measuring the force in Newtons and maximum pace (RPM) reached during acceleration. The test uses the same protocol described previously for the lower body. After the test, the athlete should continue pedaling on the ergometer using a minimal load until full recovery.

Treadmill Test

Functional tests on the treadmill are performed progressively to determine the oxygen consumption at the aerobic threshold, anaerobic threshold, and maximal oxygen uptake ($\dot{V}O_2$max). As with the tests on the stationary bicycle and arm ergometer, a gas analysis apparatus is required (e.g., Cortex MetaLyser3B, MetaSoft, or similar equipment) to determine oxygen consumption, respiratory quotient, respiratory ventilation, intensity, and frequency. It is also necessary to monitor the heart rate (using a heart rate monitor) to determine the frequency of heart contractions. It is also possible to determine the concentration of lactate in the blood with a lactate meter (e.g., Lactate Scout).

Before beginning the test, a three-minute warm-up is performed at a velocity of six to seven kilometers per hour (4 mph) with a 1 percent incline. The progressive test is performed on the treadmill with a 1 percent incline. The initial velocity of the test is eight kilometers per hour (5 mph or 2.2 mps) for athletes in good physical condition and seven kilometers per hour (4 mph or 1.9 mps) for athletes in poor physical condition. Every two minutes, the velocity is increased by one kilometer per hour (0.62 mph or 0.3 mps). The external respiration parameters are evaluated during the entire test with the gas analysis apparatus (see figure 3.6), and heart rate is evaluated with a heart rate monitor. At the end of each level, it is possible to measure the lactate with a lactate meter using a drop of blood from the finger or earlobe. After performance of the test, it is recommended that the person being evaluated should continue running at a velocity of six to seven kilometers per hour (4 mph) or walking at a lower speed until full recovery.

Figure 3.6 – Treadmill test being conducted at ProSportLab-Russia.

Aerobic and Anaerobic Threshold Testing

The tests to evaluate the anaerobic and aerobic thresholds use a stationary bicycle, arm bike, and treadmill, as explained in detail in the preceding sections. According to Maksimov and colleagues (2011), the aerobic and anaerobic threshold values are the most informative indicators for evaluating the functional condition of an MMA fighter. The aerobic threshold (also called VT1) represents the strength of the oxidative muscle fibers demonstrated in the aerobic system of energy supply, as well as the quantity of oxygen consumed. In VT1, the VO_2 and carbon dioxide production (VCO2) increase proportionally, while HCO_3^- acts to buffer lactic acid concentration in blood (Del Coso, et al. 2009); this intensity is ideal for high-volume low-intensity exercise (Stöggl and Sperlich, 2014).

The concept of anaerobic threshold or lactate threshold (also called VT2) was introduced to define when metabolic acidosis and the associated changes in gas exchange in the lungs occur during exercise. To explain it in another way, during incremental exercise, at a certain intensity, there is a nonlinear, steep increase in ventilation, called *ventilatory anaerobic threshold* (VT); a nonlinear increase in blood lactate concentration, called *lactate threshold*; a nonlinear increase in CO2 production; an increase in end tidal oxygen; an increase in CO2 production; and an arterial lactate level of 4 mm/L, called *onset of blood lactate accumulation* (OBLA), according to Ghosh (2004). The magnitude of $\dot{V}O_2$max, or power at the level of $\dot{V}O_2$max, represents an integral indicator of an MMA fighter's work capacity that may show the aerobic capacity of the active muscles, myocardium, and respiratory system (Seluianov, et al. 2008).

During the progressive test on the stationary bicycle, arm ergometer, or treadmill, muscle fibers are gradually recruited. Initially, oxidative muscle fibers, which work in the face of fatty acid oxidation, are recruited. In this period, a respiratory quotient of between 0.77 and 0.85 is typically observed, as well as a linear relationship between heart rate (HR) and power (bike/arm ergometer) or speed (treadmill). After the recruitment of all the oxidative muscle fibers, the work of the intermediate muscle fibers begins, in which the resynthesis of ATP and phosphocreatine (PCr) molecules occurs due to oxidative phosphorylation and anaerobic glycolysis. An accumulation of anaerobic glycolysis byproducts—hydrogen ions, lactate, and carbon dioxide (CO_2)—begins in the blood and stimulates heart activity and the respiratory organs. This moment is the aerobic threshold, and with this, the strength of the oxidative muscle fibers can be evaluated (Maksimov, et al. 2011).

The first abrupt change in the pulmonary ventilation chart corresponds to the aerobic ventilatory threshold (VT1) (see figure 3.7). The second abrupt change in the pulmonary ventilation chart corresponds to the anaerobic ventilatory threshold (VT2), which coincides with lactate accumulation in the blood at a level of 4 mmol/L, characterizing the boundary between the lactate production and its consumption. When the respiratory quotient equals 1.0, the proportion of CO_2 emitted and the velocity of its use is balanced. An additional increase in load results in an increase in the concentration of CO_2 in the air exhaled and in the concentration of lactate in the blood, and as a result the respiratory quotient may exceed 1.20. After the appearance of the anaerobic threshold, glycolytic muscle fibers are recruited. After muscle fiber reserves are depleted, there is a real decrease in power. The athlete cannot maintain speed, and the test is discontinued.

The aerobic and anaerobic thresholds, as well as $\dot{V}O_2$max, are better evaluated by oxygen consumption and work output in relation to bodyweight. In top-level MMA fighters, oxygen consumption at the anaerobic threshold should be between 47 and 50 milliliters per minute per kilogram for tests on the stationary bicycle and between 42 and 45 milliliters per minute per kilogram on the arm ergometer. The work output at the level of the aerobic threshold is 3.6 to 3.75 watts per kilogram for tests on the stationary bicycle, and 2.4 to 2.6 watts per kilogram for tests on the arm ergometer.

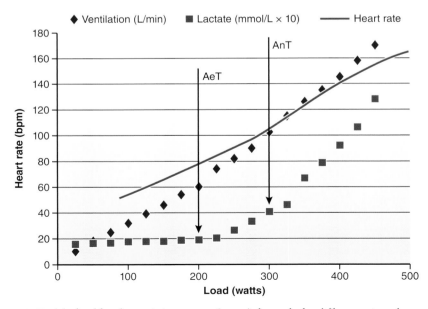

Figure 3.7 – Method for determining power (watts) through the difference in pulmonary ventilation and lactate concentration in the capillary blood in the progressive test of leg muscles on a stationary bicycle. AeT = aerobic threshold or VT1; AnT = anaerobic threshold or VT2.

Maximal oxygen uptake should be between 60 and 70 milliliters per minute per kilogram for tests on the stationary bicycle and treadmill and between 50 and 55 milliliters per minute per kilogram on the arm ergometer. The work output at the $\dot{V}O_2$max level should be between 4.6 and 5.0 watts per kilogram for tests on a stationary bicycle, and 3.0 and 3.3 watts per kilogram for the arm ergometer. These $\dot{V}O_2$max levels are the highest results that we were able to test in UFC fighters of lighter-weight categories (e.g., lighter fighters will generally have higher relative $\dot{V}O_2$max than heavier fighters do).

Maximum Alactic Power

The speed-strength ability in MMA fighters is determined by maximum alactic power, which may be used to evaluate myofibril mass and ATPase activity in the fighters' active muscle fibers. Maximum alactic power is evaluated in a max effort sprint test on the stationary bicycle and arm ergometer, because at this time, the energy sources in the muscles are represented by ATP and phosphocreatine (PCr) molecules. If the test is performed again, the changes will only occur if there is an increase in the number of myofibrils, given that the activity of the ATPase of the myosin is a hereditary factor (Maksimov, et al. 2011).

Properly controlling maximum alactic power enables indirect evaluation of the level of speed-strength ability preparation in the athletes' muscles or the quantity of myofibrils in the active muscles under evaluation. A description for how to perform the sprint test on the stationary bicycle and the arm ergometer appears earlier in this chapter.

Maximum alactic power is best evaluated according to the athlete's body mass. In top-level MMA athletes, maximum alactic power in tests performed on the stationary bicycle should be between 16 and 17 watts per kilogram, and in the tests performed on the arm ergometer, it should be between 15 and 16 watts per kilogram.

Metabolic and Cardiorespiratory Fitness: Field Testing

In many instances, laboratory testing is not realistic or feasible due to the equipment and space required to perform the testing. Therefore, field tests may be needed to assess fitness measures among fighters.

Velocity at $\dot{V}O_2$max and Maximal Time at $v\dot{V}O_2$max

The phrase *velocity at $\dot{V}O_2$max* and the abbreviation $v\dot{V}O_2$max combines $\dot{V}O_2$max and running economy into a single factor that can identify aerobic differences between various runners or runner categories. The time to exhaustion (TLim) at $v\dot{V}O_2$max is reproducible in an athlete, but there is a great variability among individuals with a low coefficient of variation for $v\dot{V}O_2$max. However, the minimal velocity that elicits $\dot{V}O_2$max and the TLim at this velocity appear to convey valuable information when analyzing aerobic endurance performance (Billat, et al. 1996).

$v\dot{V}O_2$max, the fastest velocity achieved in a progressive test, is a measure widely used today to prescribe aerobic training, whether on a treadmill, track, or field (Billat, 2001). The test consists of a warm-up for two or three minutes at an initial velocity of six kilometers per hour (4 mph). This velocity may be changed at the behest of the person evaluated. After the warm-up, the treadmill should be adjusted to 8.5 kilometers per hour (5 mph) for the first stage of two minutes of the progressive test. Every two minutes, the velocity should be increased by one kilometer per hour (0.62 mph) until the athlete gives up. Once the

$v\dot{V}O_2$max has been identified, the equation Billat and Koralsztein (1996) proposed is used to calculate maximal aerobic consumption ($\dot{V}O_2$max), in relative values ($mL \cdot kg^{-1} \cdot min^{-1}$), as follows:

$$\dot{V}O_2\text{max} = 2.209 + 3.163 \times v\dot{V}O_2\text{max} + 0.000525542 \times v\dot{V}O_2\text{max}$$

The time limit test (TLim) on the $v\dot{V}O_2$max should also be conducted. For its determination, the person should warm up for five minutes. After that, the velocity should be adjusted to the $v\dot{V}O_2$max achieved in the previous test. From this point, the run should begin, and the time spent running should be recorded until the evaluated person gives up voluntarily. The TLim is recorded in seconds (Farzad, et al. 2011).

Léger Test (Beep Test)

The Léger test offers many advantages for evaluating aerobic endurance, because it is easy to administer and cheap, and the results are easily recorded by only one marker. Furthermore, there is the option to evaluate many athletes simultaneously. The test has the following characteristics:

- This is a "suicide drill" test. The subjects must run from one side to the other of a marked space of 20 meters (22 yd) at a pace determined by a sound recording. At each signal, the evaluated person must have crossed a dotted line marked two meters (2 yd) from the 20-meter line. The recording gradually gets faster, and the evaluated person's running must keep up with the changes in pace.

- The running speed increases 0.5 kilometer per hour (0.31 mph) every minute, starting at a velocity of 8.5 kilometers per hour (5 mph). The test ends when the subject twice fails to reach the dotted line before the audible alarm sounds or when they give up due to fatigue. The number of runs completed (corresponding velocities are shown in table 3.4) will be used to predict $\dot{V}O_2$max using the following equations and table 3.5 to rank the athlete's aerobic power. Ideally MMA fighters should maintain their $\dot{V}O_2$max in the "Good" category during the whole year and try to reach "Excellent" level during the competition phase.

For individuals between 6 and 18 years old:

$$\dot{V}O_2\text{max } (mL \cdot kg^{-1} \cdot min^{-1}) = 31.025 + 3.238 \times X - 3.248 \times Y + 0.1536 \times X \times Y$$

For individuals over 18 years old:

$$\dot{V}O_2\text{max } (mL \cdot kg^{-1} \cdot min^{-1}) = -24.4 + 6.0 \times X$$

Where: X = maximum velocity reached in the test (km/h) and Y = age (to nearest year) in years

Tests Specific to Fighters

The specific tests for fighters simultaneously evaluate different physical qualities and motor and technical skills. They are important for planning the training process because they resemble as closely as possible the different situations of competition.

Table 3.4 – Velocities Corresponding to the Number of Runs in the Léger Test

Number of runs	Stage	Maximum velocity (km/h)
1-6	1	8.5
7-14	2	9.0
15-22	3	9.5
23-30	4	10.0
31-38	5	10.5
39-47	6	11.0
48-56	7	11.5
57-66	8	12.0
67-76	9	12.5
77-86	10	13.0
87-97	11	13.5
98-108	12	14.0
109-120	13	14.5
121-132	14	15.0
133-144	15	15.5
145-157	16	16.0
158-170	17	16.5
171-184	18	17.0

Source: Léger and colleagues, 1988.

Table 3.5 – Classification of Aerobic Power Based on $\dot{V}O_2$max (mL·kg^{-1}·min^{-1})

Age	Very poor	Poor	Average	Good	Excellent
Women					
20-29	<24	24-30	31-37	38-48	≥49
30-39	<20	20-27	28-33	34-44	≥45
40-49	<17	17-23	24-30	31-41	≥42
50-59	<15	15-20	21-27	28-37	≥38
60-69	<13	13-17	18-23	24-34	≥35
Men					
20-29	<25	25-33	34-42	43-52	≥53
30-39	<23	23-30	31-38	39-48	≥49
40-49	<20	20-26	27-35	36-44	≥45
50-59	<18	18-24	25-33	34-42	≥43
60-69	<16	16-22	23-30	31-40	≥41

Source: National Ergometric Council (1995).

Special Judo Fitness Test

The special judo fitness test (SJFT) aims to indirectly evaluate the aerobic and anaerobic capabilities of judo athletes. Although there are no studies on fighters in other martial arts, we believe it is possible to apply it to fights involving throwing, such as wrestling, sambo, and jiu-jitsu, among others (i.e., change the ippon to a double-leg takedown). The test consists of positioning two athletes from the same weight division six meters (6.5 yd) from each other.

The test should be performed in three stages: 15 seconds, 30 seconds, and 30 seconds, with a rest of 10 seconds between the stages. During all the periods, after the evaluator gives a signal, the athlete should apply the throwing technique *ippon seoi nage* (e.g., shoulder throw) as many times as possible in the stipulated time. The number of throws performed in each stage should be summed and an index calculated, per the following formula:

$$\text{Index} = \frac{\text{final heart rate (bpm)} + \text{heart rate 1 minute after the end of the test (bpm)}}{\text{total number of throws}}$$

The value of the index should be the lowest possible, thus indicating better performance in the test (see table 3.6).

Table 3.6 – Classification Norms for the Special Judo Fitness Test

Classification	Total of throws	HR immediately after (bpm)	HR 1 min after (bpm)	Index
Excellent	≥29	≤173	≤143	≤11.73
Good	27-28	174-184	144-161	11.74-13.03
Average	26	185-187	162-165	13.04-13.94
Poor	25	188-195	166-174	13.95-14.84
Very poor	≤24	≥196	≥175	≥14.85

n = 141. HR = heart rate.

Reprinted by permission from E. Franchini, F. Boscolo Del Vecchio, and S. Sterkowicz, "A Special Judo Fitness Test Classificatory Table," *Archives of Budo* 5 (2009), 127-129.

Frequency of Speed Kick Test

The frequency of speed kick test (FSKT) was designed to evaluate alactic anaerobic capacity. The athlete should be 90 centimeters (about 35 in.) from a heavy punch bag, with the bag set at 110 centimeters (about 43 in.) up from the floor (Villani, et al. 2004). For 10 seconds, they should perform the highest number of kicks possible using the *bandal tchagui* technique (e.g., middle kick), alternating right and left legs. To perform the FSKT, each athlete is placed in front of the heavy bag. On command, the athlete should perform the maximal number of kicks possible while maintaining good technique. The total number of kicks determines test performance. For reference, MMA athletes should complete between 15 and 20 kicks, with the higher numbers during the competition phase (da Silva Santos, et al. 2015; da Silva Santos and Franchini, 2016).

Paiva and Del Vecchio Test

The Paiva and Del Vecchio test was developed by Brazilian coaches Leandro Paiva and Fabrício Boscolo Del Vecchio and is designed to evaluate the specific resistance to fatigue of MMA athletes. The tests consist of a simulation of three exercises specific to this sport (see figure 3.8):

1. *First exercise*: This exercise needs a training partner with similar body mass or who competes in the same weight division as the person being evaluated. From a standing position, the athlete should perform a *tackle* movement, lifting their training partner but not throwing them. The athlete should perform the highest number of tackles possible in 20 seconds. The rest interval will be 10 seconds between the first and the second exercise.

2. *Second exercise*: Straddling a sandbag, heavy bag, or punching dummy on the floor, the athlete should use the straight punch technique, simulating a "ground and pound." The person being evaluated should perform the highest number of punches possible in 20 seconds. The rest interval will be 20 seconds between the second and the third exercise.

3. *Third exercise*: Starting in a standing position, the athlete should perform the highest number of straight punches possible on the sandbag or hanging heavy bag in 20 seconds.

Figure 3.8 – An example of a first, second, and third exercise for the Paiva and Del Vecchio test.

Three sequences of the exercises described above should be performed, and between the end of the first sequence and the beginning of the second, the athlete should rest for 10 seconds. Between the end of the second sequence and the beginning of the third, a rest interval of 20 seconds should be given. The data are analyzed in the following manner:

1. *Step 1*: The number of maneuvers in each exercise in the three sequences is noted, summing the total number of maneuvers in each sequence.

2. *Step 2*: The sum of the maneuvers in the first sequence is considered the maximum level.

3. *Step 3*: The number of maneuvers in the second and third sequences are summed and divided by two to obtain the mean.

4. *Step 4*: The fighter's index of specific resistance to fatigue (FISRF) is calculated according to the following equation:

$$\text{FISRF} = \frac{\text{mean of the number of maneuvers in the second and third sequences}}{\text{number of maneuvers in the first sequence}}$$

Table 3.7 shows an example of the calculation.

Table 3.7 – Example of Calculations for the Paiva and Del Vecchio Test

First exercise		Second exercise		Third exercise		Sum
1st sequence	10 tackles	1st sequence	18 straights	1st sequence	17 straights	45 maneuvers
2nd sequence	9 tackles	2nd sequence	16 straights	2nd sequence	15 straights	40 maneuvers
3rd sequence	8 tackles	3rd sequence	15 straights	3rd sequence	12 straights	35 maneuvers

$$0.83 = \frac{(40 \text{ maneuvers} + 35 \text{ maneuvers}) \div 2}{45 \text{ maneuvers}}$$

The closer the FISRF gets to 1, the greater the athlete's specific resistance. The athlete may be classified using table 3.8.

Table 3.8 – FISRF Classifications

Low	Result between 0 and 0.5
Moderate	Result between 0.51 and 0.8
High	Above 0.81

Source: Paiva (2009).

Neuromuscular-Musculoskeletal Fitness

Neuromuscular-musculoskeletal fitness is intimately related to the physiological condition of the central nervous system and the skeletal muscles (Tritschler, 2003). The physical qualities that form this condition are maximum force, velocity, power, localized muscular endurance, and flexibility. *Maximum force* corresponds to the highest possible force that the individual can demonstrate using a muscle or muscle group under a voluntary maximum muscle contraction (1RM) against resistance. *Velocity* allows the body to cover a given distance or carry out a given number of motor actions in the shortest possible span of time or to react to a given stimulus in the shortest possible time. *Power* is the product of force times velocity. *Localized muscular endurance* is the capacity to maintain submaximal levels of muscle contraction for a long time. *Flexibility* is the voluntary execution of a movement at maximum angular amplitude, in a joint or a set of joints (Dantas, 2005). In the following sections, we will present some indirect tests for MMA athletes.

Running Test of 50 Meters

These tests are designed to measure travel speed. Two evaluators and one stopwatch are required. Take the values in table 3.9 as a reference for the results obtained. MMA fighters could use the results of novice sprinters for reference. The protocol should use the following guidelines (Matsudo, 1987):

- Running area measuring over 50 meters (54 yd)
- 50 meters (54 yd) marked out between start and finish line (see figure 3.9)
- Standing start
- Commands: "Ready" and "Go" (Evaluator 1)
- Evaluator 1 on the start line (lowers arm on "go") and Evaluator 2 on the finish line (starts and stops the stopwatch)

Table 3.9 – Normative Values for the 50-Meter (54 yd) Sprint Test

	Poor (sec)	Average (sec)	Good (sec)	Very good (sec)	Excellent (sec)
Experienced sprinters	5.7	5.6	5.5	5.4	<5.4
Novice sprinters	6.1	6.0	5.9	5.8	<5.8

Source: Matsudo (1987).

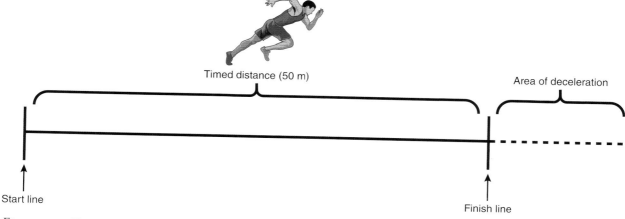

Timed distance (50 m)

Area of deceleration

Start line

Finish line

Figure 3.9 – Execution of the 50-meter (54 yd) sprint test.

Medicine Ball Throw Test

The objective is to indirectly measure the power of the upper body. The following equipment is required: one three-kilogram (7 lb) medicine ball, a wall, adhesive tape, string, and a tape measure. The protocol should use the following guidelines:

- The tape measure is fixed to the floor perpendicularly to the wall. The end of the tape measure is fixed next to the wall.

- The athlete should sit with their knees extended, legs together, and back flush to the wall. The medicine ball is held to the chest with the elbows bent. At the signal of the evaluator, the person evaluated should throw the ball (chest pass) as far as possible, keeping their back against the wall (see figure 3.10). The distance of the throw will be recorded from the end of the tape measure to where the ball touched the ground for the first time. The ball should be thrown twice, with the best result being recorded. The distance should be recorded in centimeters to one decimal place. In table 3.10, we may observe reference values for ranking the person evaluated.

Figure 3.10 – Body position for the medicine ball throw test.

Table 3.10 – Normative Values for the Medicine Ball Throw Test

	Males	Females
Advanced	≥763	≥428
Intermediate advanced	611-762	367-427
Intermediate	367-610	214-366
Advanced beginner	275-366	123-213
Beginner	0-274	0-122

Source: Johnson and Nelson (1979) and Marins and Giannichi (1998).

Vertical Jump Test

To perform this test, a smooth surface (wall) is required with a height of at least three meters (3 yd), marked every two centimeters (1 in.) with chalk lines. The person evaluated stands next to the surface, and with their hand covered in chalk, marks the highest point they can reach without jumping. Then, they should jump and touch the highest point they are able to (see figure 3.11). The knees may be bent and the arms swung to give impetus. The result will be given in centimeters or inches. Subtract the value recorded without jumping from the value achieved in the jump. See table 3.11 for the reference values.

Figure 3.11 – Execution of the vertical jump test.

Table 3.11 – Normative Values for the Vertical Jump Test

	Age	Nonathletes (cm)	Athletes (cm)
Male	15-20	42.1 ± 6.9 (16.57 ± 2.72 in.)	45.1 ± 8.0 (17.75 ± 3.15 in.)
	21-30	45.6 ± 7.2 (17.95 ± 2.83 in.)	49.9 ± 8.4 (19.65 ± 3.31 in.)
	31-40	40.9 ± 7.8 (16.10 ± 3.07 in.)	45.8 ± 8.2 (18.03 ± 3.23 in.)
	41-50	37.3 ± 7.9 (14.69 ± 3.11 in.)	42.0 ± 7.6 (16.54 ± 2.99 in.)
	>50	30.9 ± 7.2 (12.17 ± 2.83 in.)	35.6 ± 8.6 (14.02 ± 3.39 in.)
Female	15-20	33.1 ± 6.0 (13.03 ± 2.36 in.)	32.3 ± 5.8 (12.72 ± 2.28 in.)
	21-30	32.4 ± 6.2 (12.76 ± 2.44 in.)	33.1 ± 6.2 (13.03 ± 2.44 in.)
	31-40	28.4 ± 6.0 (11.18 ± 2.36 in.)	30.7 ± 6.0 (12.09 ± 2.36 in.)
	41-50	27.2 ± 6.0 (10.71 ± 2.36 in.)	27.5 ± 5.4 (10.83 ± 2.13 in.)
	>50	21.2 ± 5.9 (8.35 ± 2.32 in.)	22.4 ± 5.0 (8.82 ± 1.97 in.)

Source: Suslov (1997).

Horizontal Jump Test

To perform this test, adhesive tape and a tape measure are required. The evaluated person should start in a standing position behind the start line and jump the longest possible horizontal distance (see figure 3.12). The tape measure will be extended on the floor from the start line, between the evaluated person's feet. The lower body may be flexed and the arms swung to give impetus. The result is given in meters or yards, from the start line to the evaluated person's heel. See table 3.12 for normative values.

Figure 3.12 – Execution of the horizontal jump test.

Table 3.12 – Normative Values for the Horizontal Jump Test

	Age	Excellent (m)	Very good (m)	Good (m)	Average (m)	Poor (m)
Male	11-12	≥2.10 (2.30 yd)	2.09-2.00 (2.29-2.19 yd)	1.99-1.90 (2.18-2.08 yd)	1.89-1.80 (2.07-1.97 yd)	≤1.79 (1.96 yd)
	13-14	≥2.46 (2.69 yd)	2.45-2.32 (2.67-2.53 yd)	2.31-2.21 (2.52-2.41 yd)	2.20-2.07 (2.40-2.26 yd)	≤2.06 (2.25 yd)
	15-16	≥2.71 (2.96 yd)	2.70-2.57 (2.95-2.81 yd)	2.56-2.43 (2.79-2.65 yd)	2.42-2.29 (2.64-2.50 yd)	≤2.28 (2.49 yd)
	Adult, elite	≥3.0 (3.28 yd)	2.99-2.80 (3.26-3.06 yd)	2.79-2.70 (3.05-2.95 yd)	2.69-2.60 (2.94-2.84 yd)	≤2.59 (2.83 yd)
Female	11-12	≥2.02 (2.20 yd)	2.01-1.94 (2.19-2.12 yd)	1.93-1.86 (2.11-2.03 yd)	1.85-1.78 (2.02-1.94 yd)	≤1.77 (1.93 yd)
	13-14	≥2.07 (2.26 yd)	2.06-1.96 (2.25-2.14 yd)	1.95-1.88 (2.13-2.05 yd)	1.87-1.83 (2.04-2.00 yd)	≤1.82 (1.99 yd)
	15-16	≥2.13 (2.33 yd)	2.12-2.06 (2.31-2.25 yd)	2.05-1.99 (2.24-2.17 yd)	1.98-1.92 (2.16-2.09 yd)	≤1.91 (2.08 yd)
	Adult, elite	≥2.7 (2.95 yd)	2.69-2.60 (2.94-2.84 yd)	2.59-2.50 (2.83-2.73 yd)	2.49-2.40 (2.72-2.62 yd)	≤2.20 (2.40 yd)

Adapted from Suslov (1997) and Fukuda (2019).

One Repetition Maximum Testing

One repetition maximum (1RM) testing refers to the quantity of load (kg or lb) voluntarily moved in a dynamic movement to measure maximum dynamic concentric strength. Before beginning the test, it is crucial that the person carrying out the test be familiar with both the test and the potential results. Determine in advance what results are expected—such as the possible velocities of muscular action—and which muscular structures may boost or interfere with the results—such as muscle length–tension relationships based on anatomical configurations. Specificity also has relevance during 1RM testing because each muscle group tested will have different capabilities depending on the specific requirements of the test methodology.

The individual should perform a three- to five-minute warm-up involving the major muscle groups. Next, they should execute 8 to 10 repetitions of a set of specific warm-ups at approximately 50 percent of the proposed 1RM value, followed by another set of three repetitions at 70 percent of the estimated value of 1RM. Progressively increase resistance by 2.5 to 20 kilograms (4-44 lb) until the subject cannot complete the selected repetition of the movement.

The first increases in load should be made uniformly and at established intervals so that at least two individual sets occur between the warm-up sets of three repetitions and the estimated value of 1RM. During the concentric failure attempt, the load used should be the last attempt in which maximum voluntary exertion occurred, without assistance and with appropriate technique. The time estimated for the pause between the sets is at least three, and no more than five, minutes. Determine the 1RM within four trials. All repetitions should be performed at the same speed of movement and range of motion to ensure consistency between attempts.

Multiple Repetition Testing

Another way to calculate 1RM is with the multiple repetition test, because although the direct 1RM test is the most used and mentioned in the literature, it may be influenced by numerous factors, given that it demands a high degree of concentration and prior knowledge of the techniques, among other important characteristics. Additionally, exertions with maximal intensities may generate high stress levels in the muscles, bones, and ligaments. The multiple repetition protocol consists of:

1. General warm-up with low-intensity aerobic exercise for 5 to 10 minutes. This may be performed on a treadmill, bicycle, or elliptical trainer.

2. One or two sets of specific warm-up exercises with a progressive increase in the weight to be lifted (approximately 50% of the maximum possible), with 6 to 10 repetitions without any failure in the execution of the movement.

3. An execution of 7 to 10 maximum repetitions, using the following equation (Brzycki, 1993):

$$1RM = (100 \times \text{weight lifted}) \div (102.78 - [2.78 \times \text{number of repetitions performed}])$$

Here is an example of the calculation where a person lifts 60 kilograms (132 lb) a total of 10 times.

$$1RM = (100 \times 60) \div (102.78 - [2.78 \times 10]) = 80 \text{ kg}$$

The 1RM test can be performed with any muscle group and can be tested using either machines or free weights. Usually, coaches prefer to use the bench press as a general measure of upper-body strength, the bench pull exercise for the back muscles, and the barbell back squat for lower-body strength.

Free-Weight Bench Press Testing

The free-weight bench press involves using a barbell and a bench with uprights. Lying on a horizontal bench, the person's buttocks, shoulders, and head should be firmly on the bench and their feet flat on the ground (see figure 3.13*a*). The person should hold the barbell with an overhand grip at a distance greater than shoulder width. During execution, the person should inhale and lower the barbell to the chest with a controlled movement, and after brief contact, push the barbell upward by extending the arms while exhaling. At the end of the set, rack the bar back in the uprights (see figures 3.13*b-d*) (Baechle and Earle, 2020).

Follow the same standardized procedures described to determine the 1RM within four trials. All repetitions should be performed at the same speed of movement and range of motion to ensure consistency between attempts. Elite male fighters should have a relative bench press greater than 1.2 pounds per pound of body weight (Bueno, et al. 2022). Elite female fighters should be able to bench press at least 0.9 pounds per pound of body weight (Gochioco, et al. 2011).

Lopez-Laval and colleagues (2020) studied the relationship between bench press strength and punch performance in male professional boxers and showed that coaches can use the bench press exercise with high loads (i.e., 80% 1RM) because this could be a reliable predictor of performance during specific punching action.

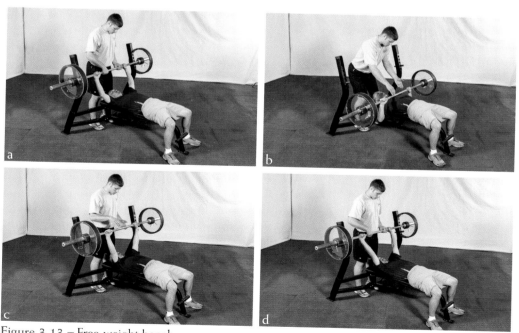

Figure 3.13 – Free-weight bench press.

Bench Pull Testing

As the primary objective, this test aims to measure the horizontal pulling force of the upper body. A horizontal bench with adjustable height, a barbell and collar clips, and weight plates are needed to conduct the test. Adjust the height of the bench so that the individual to be evaluated can hold the barbell without it meeting the floor. Elite male fighters should have a relative bench pull greater than 1 pound per pound of body weight. Elite female fighters should be able to bench pull at least 0.9 pounds per pound of body weight (Naka, et al. 2021).

Lying in a prone position, with the arms extended next to the bench, the individual to be evaluated should pick up, hold, and pull the barbell until it touches the underside of the bench, at a tempo of one repetition every two seconds (see figure 3.14). The elbows should remain pointing outward during the time in which the chest will need to be stationary and in contact with the bench. During the test, only the arms and shoulders may move, while the rest of the body (head, torso, and legs) remains immobile.

Incorrect execution should not be counted. Common errors include the following:

- Changing the chosen position of the feet or head (choose a position and maintain it)
- Flexion or extension of the hips or changing the position of the torso
- Not bringing the barbell to the underside of the bench
- Significantly changing the manner with which the barbell is directed during the warm-up considering the exaggerated use of scapular abduction or adduction
- Not complying with the suggested tempo of execution

Figure 3.14 – Bench pull.

Barbell Back Squat Test

One of the most widely used exercises in training gyms for users who wish to increase their strength, regardless of gender or age, the free squat with barbell offers an excellent indicator of lower-body strength. However, for these values to be representative and comparable, familiarization with the appropriate technique is necessary to avoid common errors involving the angles of the hips and knees and the alignment of the back. A squat rack, Olympic barbell, weight plates, and collar clips are needed to perform the test. Elite male MMA fighters should have a relative back squat greater than 1.6 pounds per pound of body weight (Bueno, et al. 2022). Elite female MMA fighters should be able to squat more than 1.1 pounds per pound of body weight (Gochioco, et al. 2011).

Follow the same standardized procedures described above to determine the 1RM within four trials. All repetitions should be performed at the same speed of movement and range of motion to ensure consistency between attempts.

To perform the barbell back squat test, some precautions should be taken to ensure safety and prevent potential injuries over the course of the test. The hand grip should be slightly wider than shoulder width; the barbell should be behind and above the shoulders, roughly five centimeters (2 in.) below the top of the trapezius muscle; and the feet should be slightly apart, with the heels pointing in the direction of the anterior superior iliac spine and may be turned outward at an angle of 30 degrees. The barbell may then be removed from its rack or stand. Keeping the feet pointing outward and roughly shoulder-width apart, bend the knees and the hips, as if sitting down on a bench. During the whole movement, keep the shins perpendicular to the floor and the core contracted. The head and eyes should be focused on a fixed point in front of the lifter (see figure 3.15) (Baechle and Earle, 2020). Table 3.13 presents reference values for athletes.

Precautions to be taken include the following:

In the standing phase:

- Keep the chest and the head up, while the load (kg or lb) is properly distributed on the base of the heels.
- Keep the abdominal and gluteal muscles contracted.
- Inhale deeply to maintain the intrathoracic pressure.

In the descent and lift phases:

- Squat slowly.
- When the thighs are horizontal to the floor, straighten the legs and lift the torso to return to the initial position.
- During the return from the low phase to the standing phase, avoid excessive extension (hyperextension) of the knees.

In the bottom phase:

- The hamstrings should be at least parallel to the floor.
- Avoid internal rotation of the knees or ankles.

Figure 3.15 – Barbell back squat.

Table 3.13 – Reference Values for the Barbell Back Squat Test

	Men	**Women**
Excellent	>150% of bodyweight	>110% of bodyweight
Good	100%-125% of bodyweight	90%-110% of bodyweight
Average	Bodyweight	70%-90% of bodyweight
Fair	75%-100% of bodyweight	50%-70% of bodyweight
Poor	<75% of bodyweight	<50% of bodyweight

Reprinted by permission from T. Howley, *Complete Conditioning for Lacrosse* (Champaign, IL: Human Kinetics, 2016), 20.

Pull-Up Testing

The pull-up fatigue test is used to provide data about the muscular endurance of the upper body during a pull-up. For its application, a rigid horizontal bar is required, suspended and fixed at a height sufficient to allow the person evaluated to hang, the arms completely extended, while ensuring that the feet do not touch the ground.

In front of the suspended bar, extend the arms above the head (with the hands pronated), wider than shoulder-width apart. The evaluated person should raise their body to a point at which the chin passes the bar, subsequently returning to the starting position with the arms extended (see figure 3.16).

Figure 3.16 – Pull-up.

Valid pull-ups consist of continuous movements, with the chin passing above the bar. Abrupt movements, swinging the body, kicking the air, or bending the legs render the pull-up invalid. The final value (maximum number of pull-ups) performed until concentric failure (i.e., the chin cannot pass the bar) will be considered.

YMCA Bench Press Test

The YMCA bench press test assesses muscular endurance by standardizing repetitions of the bench press exercise (see figure 3.13 on page 95) at a specific tempo. In this test, the total value of the barbell with the weight plates should be 80 pounds (36.4 kg) for men and 35 pounds (15.9 kg) for women. A metronome set at 60 beats per minute is used. The athlete performs the highest number of repetitions possible without losing the up-down movement rhythm of the metronome or using incorrect technique and at the end notes down the total number of repetitions successfully completed. Normative data for the YMCA bench press test are presented in table 3.14. As an example, numbers above 50 repetitions are considered satisfactory for athletes, and above 65, excellent.

Table 3.14 – YMCA Bench Press Test Fitness Categories

| | Age (years) | | | | | |
| | 18-25 | | 26-35 | | 36-45 | |
Sex	M	W	M	W	M	W
Excellent	64	66	61	62	55	57
	44	42	41	40	36	33
Good	41	38	37	34	32	30
	34	30	30	29	26	26
Above average	33	28	29	28	25	24
	29	25	26	24	22	21
Average	28	22	24	22	21	20
	24	20	21	18	18	16
Below average	22	18	20	17	17	14
	20	16	17	14	14	12
Poor	17	13	16	13	12	10
	13	9	12	9	9	6
Very poor	<10	6	9	6	6	4

M = men; W = women.

Data from Golding (2000).

Velocity

In recent years, the exponential growth in combat sports means the need to understand and quantify physical performance beyond scientific laboratories has become commonplace. New portable wireless technologies have facilitated this because they allow physical actions to be controlled and monitored in a practical environment.

Velocity-based training (VBT) assesses and assigns the intensity of a given movement by calculating displacement and time through the monitoring of bar or body speeds. Usually, this test uses a wireless inertial sensor that has an accelerometer and a gyroscope and can be connected via Bluetooth, providing measures of movement and acceleration (i.e., an increase in speed in m/s^2) of the barbell. The sensor was developed for application in resistance training and provides instantaneous kinematic feedback about the current performance of the exercises. Just affix the device to the forearm, waist, or barbell to obtain data on velocity during movements with free weights or bodyweight. From this, estimates of peak and mean velocity—important markers for training strength, power, and velocity—may be easily accessed via a smartphone or tablet app. For more information, consult *Velocity-Based Training* by Nunzio Signore (2022).

Mean velocity is the velocity of the entire concentric, or ascending, part of the exercise. This measurement is relevant for typical strength exercises such as the squat, bench press, deadlift, and so on. There are two main reasons for this: First, mean velocity represents the subject's capacity throughout the entire range of motion better than peak velocity. Second, the mean velocity during the concentric phase decreases linearly with an increase in the load, thus facilitating an analysis of trends in an athlete's strength levels (Jidovtseff, et al. 2011). To limit muscle damage and improve recovery while maintaining strength and power, mean velocity loss should be limited to 20 percent for squats and 30 percent for upper-body exercises (Baker, 2018).

Peak velocity, in turn, is the highest value recorded in any part of the movement during the concentric phase of the lift. It is relevant for power exercises, which involve higher velocities or allow acceleration until the end of the range of movement. Some examples are the variations of Olympic weightlifting (hang power clean, power snatch, etc.), and variations of resistance training exercises with lighter loads, such as jump squats, bench press, clean and jerks on the Smith Machine, and so on. In table 3.15, we may observe peak velocity values in the jump squat for national- and international-level MMA athletes.

To maximize the adaptations to power training, Baker (2018) recommended limiting velocity loss for power exercises such as Olympic lifts, jumps, and clean and jerks to 10 percent for most sessions and 5 percent for tapering phases. For squat jump exercises, the peak velocity should be maintained between 1.5 and 2.5 meters per second for optimum performance (see figure 3.17).

Table 3.15 – Peak Velocity Values in the Jump Squat for National- and International-Level MMA Athletes

	Jump squat with a dowel rod on the shoulders	Peak velocity		
		+50% BWT	+75% BWT	+100% BWT
International	3.77 m/sec	2.50 m/sec	2.15 m/sec	1.86 m/sec
National	3.29 m/sec	2.34 m/sec	2.01 m/sec	1.74 m/sec

BWT: body weight training

Adapted from James et al. (2016).

A cheaper alternative, but not as accurate, to VBT is using a smartphone application, such as BarSense or Iron Path. With BarSense, we may analyze the velocity (both peak and mean) of the barbell to better understand what happens during the movement, and we may also analyze the trajectory of the barbell as the exercise is performed. Figure 3.18 shows both sets of data (trajectory of the barbell, the red line on the left; velocity values, the blue line on the right) provided by BarSense.

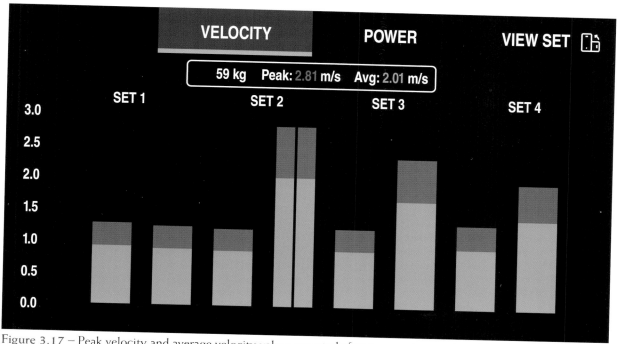

Figure 3.17 – Peak velocity and average velocity values reported after an exercise monitored by the PUSHBand.
Data from PushBand.

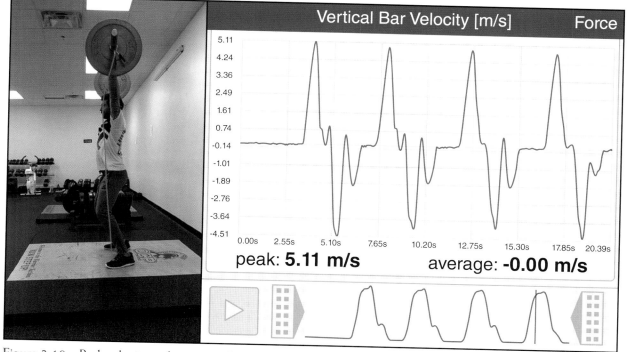

Figure 3.18 – Peak velocity and average velocity values reported after an exercise monitored by BarSense.
Data from BarSense.

Flexibility

The Flexitest evaluates flexibility and has numerous advantages over other methods reported in the literature, mainly due to its practicality and speed of application and due to the quality of the information obtained (Araújo, 1986). The method consists of measuring and evaluating passive and active mobility of 20 joint movements (36, if we consider the two sides of the body), including the ankle, knee, hip, torso, wrist, elbow, and shoulder joints. Eight movements are performed in the lower body, three in the trunk, and the other nine in the upper body. Each movement is measured on an ascending, discontinuous scale of whole numbers from 0 to 4, giving a total of five possible values. Measurements are taken via the slow execution of the movement until the maximum range of motion has been reached. Then the evaluation chart and the maximum range of motion achieved by the evaluator are compared. The point of maximum range of motion is detected easily by the major mechanical resistance to continuing the movement or by when the person evaluated reports discomfort. Perform the Flexitest by following the images in figure 3.19 and then refer to the reference scores in table 3.16.

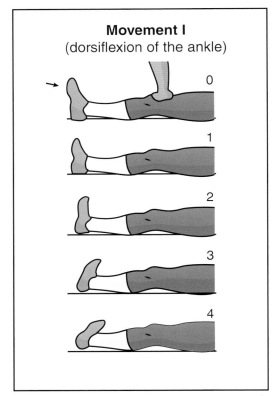

Figure 3.19a – Flexitest evaluation: movement I.

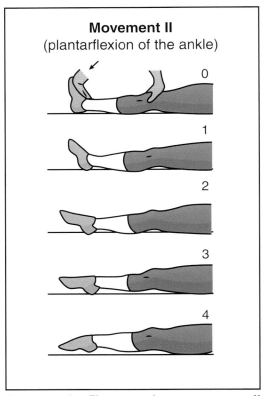

Figure 3.19b – Flexitest evaluation: movement II.

Movement III
(flexion of the knee)

Figure 3.19c – Flexitest evaluation: movement III.

Movement IV
(extension of the knee)

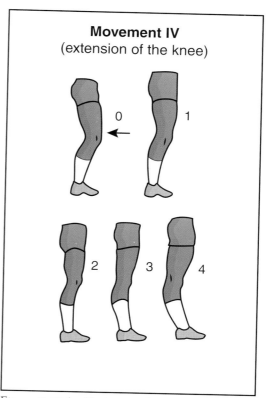

Figure 3.19d – Flexitest evaluation: movement IV.

Movement V
(flexion of the hip)

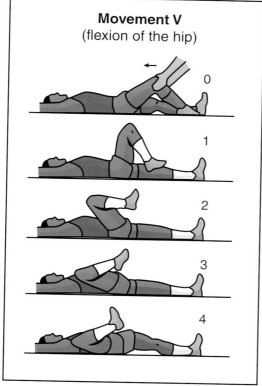

Figure 3.19e – Flexitest evaluation: movement V.

Movement VI
(extension of the hip)

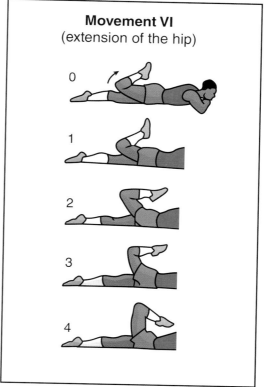

Figure 3.19f – Flexitest evaluation: movement VI.

Movement VII
(adduction of the hip)

Figure 3.19g – Flexitest evaluation: movement VII.

Movement VIII
(abduction of the hip)

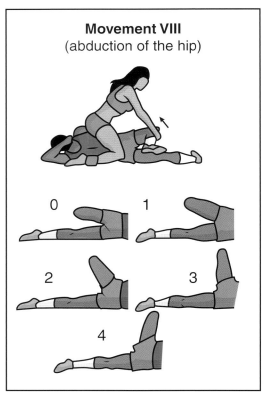

Figure 3.19h – Flexitest evaluation: movement VIII.

Movement IX
(flexion of the torso)

Figure 3.19i – Flexitest evaluation: movement IX.

Movement X
(extension of the torso)

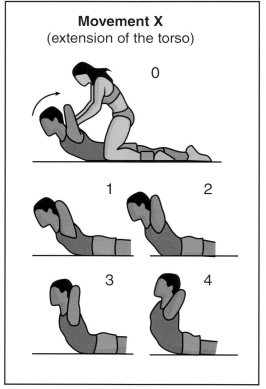

Figure 3.19j – Flexitest evaluation: movement X.

Figure 3.19k – Flexitest evaluation: movement XI.

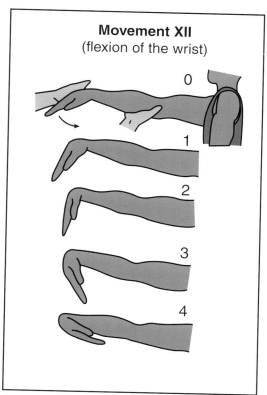

Figure 3.19l – Flexitest evaluation: movement XII.

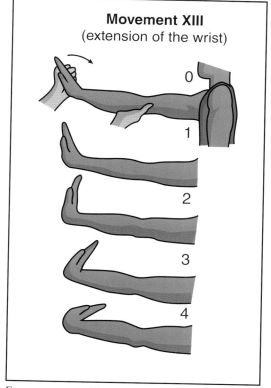

Figure 3.19m – Flexitest evaluation: movement XIII.

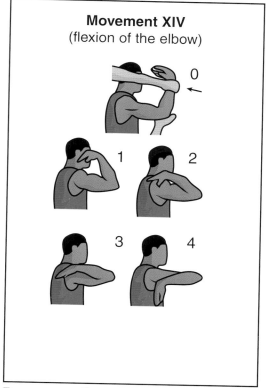

Figure 3.19n – Flexitest evaluation: movement XIV.

Movement XV
(extension of the elbow)

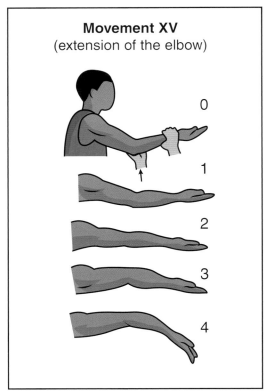

Figure 3.19o – Flexitest evaluation: movement XV.

Movement XVI
(posterior adduction from
180° abduction in the shoulder)

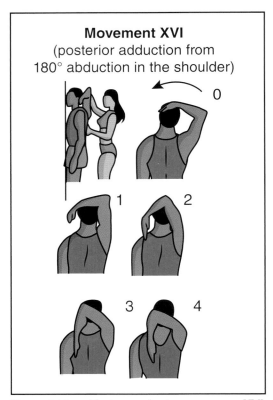

Figure 3.19p – Flexitest evaluation: movement XVI.

Movement XVII
(extension + posterior
abduction of the shoulder)

Figure 3.19q – Flexitest evaluation: movement XVII.

Movement XVIII
(posterior extension of the shoulder)

Figure 3.19r – Flexitest evaluation: movement XVIII.

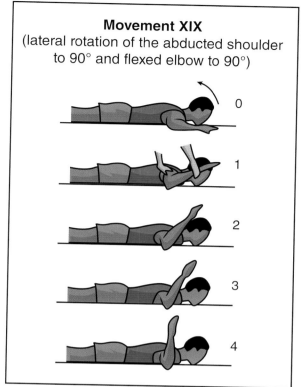

Figure 3.19s – Flexitest evaluation: movement XIX.

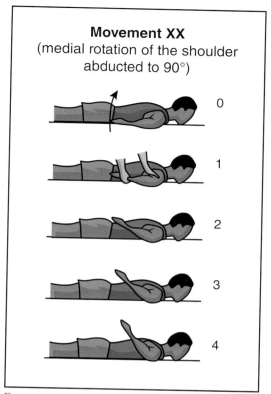

Figure 3.19t – Flexitest evaluation: movement XX.

Table 3.16 – Flexitest Classifications

Scoring	Classification in terms of flexibility
<20	Very poor (ankylosis)
21-30	Poor
31-40	Lower average
41-50	Upper average
51-60	Considerable
>60	Very considerable (hypermobility)

Source: Araújo (1986).

It should be stressed that, regardless of the test or battery of tests chosen, coaches and athletes should keep notes with the results of control tests and physical evaluations. This is important to create an athlete's baseline, so future changes could be perceived with accuracy in the development of a given physical capability, and the aspects of training that should be improved could also be identified.

4

THE IMPORTANCE OF NUTRITION IN HIGH-LEVEL TRAINING

Eduardo Poloni Silveira, MD

Rokaya Mikhailenko, MS

Stéfane Beloni Correa Dielle Dias, PhD

Victoria Zaborova, MD

The importance of good nutrition for combat sports is not a recent idea, especially considering the weight divisions and weight-cutting requirements for competition in modern times. The Greek physician Hippocrates, who was born around 400 BC and is considered by many to be one of the most important figures in the history of health and medicine, formulated the following phrase: "Let food be thy medicine and medicine be thy food." Currently, eating well is more important than ever, given that at least 4 in every 10 causes of death in the United States can be related to poor nutrition.

The impact of good nutrition on people who engage in physical activity is undeniable, even more so in top-level athletes. In recent decades, research in the sports nutrition field has produced an impressive volume of information, making it increasingly difficult to properly filter the evidence published to achieve good results in a practical application. According to the American College of Sports Medicine, Academy of Nutrition and Dietetics, and Dietitians of Canada (Thomas, et. al 2016), certain concepts should be considered in our new understanding of sports nutrition, especially the following:

- Nutritional objectives and demands are not static. The different phases of the athlete's training and competitions should be considered.

- Nutritional plans should be customized according to the event, competition type, performance objectives, barriers encountered, dietary preferences, and responses to interventions.

- The achievement of an ideal body composition for performance is an important objective, and different training phases should be considered. Also, avoid practices that result in a very low energy availability or other health risks.

- The timing of nutrient distribution over the day should be considered over generic daily guidelines.

- Nutrition for competition should employ specific strategies to reduce or slow factors that may lead to fatigue during the event, considering the environment and type of competition as well as the individual peculiarities of the athlete.

- Evidence indicates that the brain can perceive the presence of carbohydrates (and potentially other nutrients) in the oral cavity, improving perceptions of well-being and levels of effort. Thus, the ingestion of fluids, foods, or alternative strategies like carbohydrate mouth rinses during short events may offer a metabolic advantage in central pathways linked to performance.

- A rational approach should be used for prescribing supplements and sports foods, using high-level published evidence with a good cost–benefit relationship for the athlete and avoiding potential damage resulting from adverse reactions or contamination.

In this chapter, we will highlight the importance of a combined effort by coaches, exercise science professionals, doctors, and nutritionists to achieve maximum results in combat sports.

According to Platonov (2007), the current training and competition loads place maximum demands on the athlete's functional systems, further increasing the role of rational diet and supplements to optimize sports performance and the effective course of recovery and adaptive processes.

The substances that the body receives with foods, or in the form of supplements, may be divided as follows:

- Products whose action ensures the regeneration of the structures used during training and competition
- Vitamins and minerals

- Substances that stimulate hematopoiesis (production of red blood cells)
- Substances that aid the recovery of energy resources and increase resilience in the face of stress (products that contain amino acids, glucose, phosphorous, etc.)

Energy

During sports activities, energy (caloric) demands increase substantially, and total daily expenditure may reach, and even exceed, 6,000 to 7,000 calories per day during periods of high-volume training in some sports (e.g., cycling or endurance events) (De Vries and Housh, 1994).

Table 4.1 shows energy expenditure per kilogram of body weight in relation to the respective sport activity. The expenditure in athletes whose activity involves aerobic endurance is twice or more greater than that of athletes in other sports activities.

Since mixed martial arts is so variable in terms of fighting styles and physical effort, little specific data are available about energy expenditure in high-level combat sports athletes; therefore, data provided by studies on other martial arts (e.g., judo) could be extrapolated to estimate the energy cost of MMA practice.

Experiments with fighters and runners demonstrate that maintaining an energy imbalance for a prolonged period leads to not only a reduction in fat but also the loss of mass from other tissues. A rapid reduction in body mass caused by a reduction in the body's water component is often accompanied by a loss of glycogen reserves and may result in a drop in performance.

Table 4.1 – Expenditure in Elite Athletes in Different Sport Activities

Sports activity	Sex	Mean energy expenditure (kJ/kg/day)	Mean caloric expenditure (kcal/kg/day)
Cycling (Tour de France)	M	347	82.9
Triathlon	M	272	65.0
Swimming	M	221	52.8
Swimming	F	200	47.8
Rowing	M	189	45.2
Rowing	F	186	44.5
Bodybuilding	M	157	37.5
Bodybuilding	F	110	26.3
Judo	M	177	42.3
Judo	F	157	37.5
Gymnastics	F	207	49.5
American football	M	192	45.9
Ice hockey	M	181	43.3
Ice hockey	F	145	34.7

The athletes analyzed in the research were top-level athletes, including medalists in European championships, world championships, and Olympic Games. The evaluation of energy expenditure was performed using data on food consumption for four to seven days. 1 kilocalorie = 4.184 joules, 1 kilogram = 2.205 pounds.
Source: Van Erp-Baart and colleagues (1989).

Maintaining a chronic energy deficit also has multiple negative repercussions for health, such as hormonal changes (e.g., a drop in testosterone levels in diets with severe fat restrictions) and immunological changes, as well as various negative effects on the athlete's performance. Thus, it is important to understand the concept of energy availability (EA) (Loucks, 2004), which represents the energy required for the body to carry out all its functions after subtracting the energy cost of the exercise. It is calculated using the following formula:

$$\text{energy availability (EA)} = (\text{energy intake [EI]} - \text{exercise energy expenditure [EEE]}) / \text{fat free mass (FFM)}$$

expressed in kcal/kg FFM/day (Thomas, et al. 2016).

As an example calculation, consider an athlete weighing 65 kilograms (143 lb), with 20 percent body fat (consequently with 80% fat free mass, i.e., 52 kg [114 lb] FFM), 800 kcal/day exercise energy expenditure and following a 2,500 kcal per day diet:

$$EA = (EI - EEE) / FFM$$

$$EA = (2{,}500 \text{ kcal/day} - 800 \text{ kcal/day}) / 52 \text{ kg}$$

$$EA = 32.7 \text{ kcal/kg FFM/day}$$

It is estimated that an EA below 30 kcal per kilogram FFM per day significantly increases health risks associated with low energy availability, representing a condition called *relative energy deficiency in sport*, or RED-S (Mountjoy, et al. 2018). The potentially negative effects of RED-S on performance are illustrated in table 4.2. Although this occurs in both sexes, it is more prevalent in women; therefore, even greater attention should be given to female athletes, a category of growing importance in MMA.

It would be outside the scope of this chapter to discuss the details of the strategies for losing and regaining weight for competition, but in certain situations, like in weight cutting, an energy deficit may be temporarily recommended. On the other hand, in sports in which body weight marks the division between categories in competitions, such as in MMA, appropriate nutritional management of the athlete is essential, because it guarantees adequate energy stores and minimizes the risks to health and performance.

Table 4.2 – Impact of Relative Energy Deficiency in Sport (RED-S) on Performance

Decreased muscle strength	Irritability	Decreased coordination
Decreased glycogen stores	Increased injury risk	Impaired judgment
Depression	Decreased training response	Decreased concentration

Adapted from Mountjoy et al. (2018).

Carbohydrates

Researchers demonstrated the importance of the synthesis process in building muscles over 50 years ago. Christienssen (1960) convincingly demonstrated that to exhibit high aerobic endurance levels it is essential to maintain a diet rich in carbohydrates and to ingest them mainly during long-duration physical exercises. Hermansen (1981) demonstrated the role of glycogen reserves found in the muscle tissues in the athlete's work capacity.

Carbohydrates contain carbon, hydrogen, and oxygen in such a proportion that a carbon atom binds to a water molecule ($C–H_2O$). As a result, the structural formula of glucose (monosaccharide) has the form $C_6H_{12}O_6$. Carbohydrates can be divided into simple (e.g., table sugar) and complex (e.g., starch). Glycogen is a glucose polymer, so it is a complex carbohydrate that works as a main energy source for sports activities. It is found in the liver, the muscles, and other tissues. If a person has a mass of 70 kilograms (154 lb), then the liver (1.8 kg) can contain 70 grams to 135 grams of glycogen, and the muscles from 300 grams to 900 grams of this same energy reserve.

Glycogen from the liver is essential to forming glucose as an energy source for the central nervous system (brain), blood cells, and kidney cells. Glycogen from the muscles may be transformed into glucose, but it cannot directly enter the bloodstream and be used for the work of other tissues. However, during exercises with a power output close to the anaerobic threshold, lactate is formed, which enters the bloodstream, transforms into pyruvate in the tissues, and is used by the mitochondria as an energy source (Katch, et al. 2011).

Carbohydrates During Physical Exercise

Muscle glycogen initially transforms into a glucose 1-phosphate molecule under the action of phosphorylase, which then transforms into glucose 6-phosphate. This substance is a common point (general) for the start of glycolysis, an essential step for energy production through the conversion of glucose to pyruvate. Glycolysis ends with pyruvate formation, which may reach the mitochondria, and in the Krebs cycle, it is subject to oxidative phosphorylation. In this case, when the mitochondria in muscle fibers and cardiac lactate dehydrogenase are insufficient, the surplus pyruvate may transform into lactate. Glycolysis is accompanied by a useful energetic result: 1 mol of glucose supplies 2 to 3 mols of adenosine triphosphate (ATP), an organic compound that releases energy from the breakdown of its chemical bonds. When pyruvate arrives at the mitochondrion, 36 to 37 more moles of ATP are formed. The mitochondria use one liter (1 qt) of oxygen to form 5.05 kcal of energy (21.1 kJ) during carbohydrate oxidation.

According to Seluianov and colleagues (2008), during exercise with a maximal or submaximal intensity (80%-100% of maximal aerobic capacity, or $\dot{V}O_2$max), for example, during sprints, the phosphagens (ATP, phosphocreatine) degrade, and this is used as the energy for movement. During the recovery period, resynthesis occurs due to glycolysis. As a result, in glycolytic muscle fibers, lactate and hydrogen ions accumulate, with consequent muscle acidosis, which is one of the principal factors that leads to a sensation of peripheral fatigue.

Carbohydrate reserves (glycogen) during an exercise are usually sufficient to prevent fatigue, but during multiple repetitions, which is a frequent occurrence in training or in competitions, fatigue may occur due to insufficient glycogen in the muscle fibers. In accordance with the increase in volume or intensity of the exercises executed, the use of glycogen reserves in the oxidative muscle fibers is impaired, leading to the anaerobic glycolysis system generating energy. During exercises with an intensity of 60 percent to 85 percent $\dot{V}O_2$max (anaerobic threshold level), a greater expenditure of glycogen in intermediate muscle fibers is observed; and the slow-twitch (oxidative) muscle fibers receive energy in the form of lactate, which forms in active muscle fibers. For example, muscle glycogen during cycling is mainly exhausted in the quadriceps, but in running, it is exhausted in the gastrocnemius and soleus muscles.

A diet with a higher carbohydrate content increases the respiratory quotient (the amount of CO_2 produced versus O_2 used by the body) during exercise at a power output below the anaerobic threshold. The higher respiratory quotient is related to a greater metabolic oxidation of carbohydrates, with a consequently smaller contribution of fat to provide energy.

Although diets low in carbohydrates and rich in fats have been demonstrated to have positive effects in terms of increasing lipolysis (i.e., fat breakdown), recurring evidence indicates that greater carbohydrate ingestion may increase the duration an athlete can exercise at certain power outputs when compared to a high-fat diet (Christienssen, 1960; Gollnick, 1986; Gollnick, et al. 1974). Thus, a low-carb, high-fat diet may not offer advantages in prolonged exercise and may even impair performance in high-intensity training (Burke and Kiens, 2006). See table 4.3 for recommendations for daily carbohydrate ingestion based on training intensity.

Table 4.3 – Recommendations for Daily Carbohydrate Ingestion in Sport

Intensity of training	Carbohydrate targets based on bodyweight
Light (e.g., low-intensity drilling)	3-5 g/kg/day
Moderate	5-7 g/kg/day
High (e.g., high-intensity sparring sessions)	6-10 g/kg/day
Very high	8-12 g/kg/day

Adapted from Burke et al. (2011).

Glycogen Resynthesis

The exhaustion of glycogen reserves from exercise occurs mainly after aerobic exercises that last over 90 minutes, with variations depending on the individual's muscle reserve, the intensity and exercise duration, and the athlete's aerobic capacity (Hawley, et al. 1997). Glycogen resynthesis may occur from noncarbohydrate sources (lactate, glycerol, pyruvate, alanine) in the absence of carbohydrate availability through a process called *gluconeogenesis* or directly from glucose when ingesting carbohydrates, a reaction called *glycogenesis*.

The energy expenditure during training and competitions may be such that during nighttime rest, when ingesting food is not possible, total resynthesis may not occur. Thus, for example, to guarantee a high work capacity for cyclists in multiple daily races, carbohydrate-rich foods should be ingested on the eve of the competition as well as during it (Seluianov, 2001). Moreover, it has been demonstrated that consuming a small amount of easily digestible food (e.g., cereals) 30 minutes before the competition or intense training session starts (De Vries and Housh, 1994) may also contribute to providing glucose for training.

Factors that influence the intensity of recovery of glycogen reserves after heavy training and competition include the following:

- Type and absorption speed of the carbohydrate ingested
- Degree of glycogen reserve depletion
- Timing and frequency of carbohydrate consumption after training
- Coingestion with other nutrients, such as proteins

Table 4.4 shows current strategies for acute carbohydrate supplementation, correlated with frequent situations in combat sports.

In high-intensity exercises sustained for periods of 45 to 75 minutes, which is common in preparation for combat sport competitions, carbohydrate ingestion should be staggered during the training session. Liquid form is usually the most practical, but the solution concentration should not exceed 8 percent (e.g., 40 g of dextrose diluted in 500 mL of water) to avoid nausea or other symptoms of gastrointestinal discomfort, which is common in strenuous exertion. The "mouth rinse" technique that can be accomplished by rinsing the mouth with a carbohydrate solution for 5 to 10 seconds (and then swallowing or spitting out) during the training session has also proved effective in athletes who cannot tolerate ingesting it during exercise (Burke, et al. 2011). This technique could be useful in the last weeks of training camp during the weight-cutting phase, for example.

When devising the athlete's ideal diet, consider the net weight of different foods. This allows the daily diet to be balanced, taking into account not only the energy value and the relationship of the different food groups but also their volume, an important factor for effectively planning the training load and competition (Platonov, 2007, 2004). Thus, it may be useful to ingest carbohydrates in liquid form to facilitate a greater intake of this nutrient with a lower risk of gastrointestinal discomfort while rehydrating. Table 4.5 illustrates variations in the carbohydrate content of foods habitually ingested.

Table 4.4 – Strategies for Carbohydrate Fueling in Sport

Strategy	Quantity of carbohydrates based on body-weight	Potential applications in MMA
Fueling up	7-12 g/kg in 24 hours	Preparation for competition or key training session
Speedy refueling (2 intense sessions with an interval between them of less than 8 hours)	1-1.2 g/kg/hour for the first 4 hours, after that, resume habitual carbohydrate requirements	Physical conditioning in the morning and sparring in the afternoon

Adapted from Burke et al. (2011) with MMA applications added by author.

Table 4.5 – Approximate Food Quantities That Provide 50 Grams of Easily Consumable Carbohydrate

Group	Product	Quantity (in g)	Quantity (in oz)
Grains	Whole wheat bread	200	7
	White bread	120	4.2
	Rye bread	104	3.6
	Whole-grain rice	196	6.9
	White rice	169	5.9
	Popcorn	60	2.1
	Spaghetti and other pasta	200	7
	Oatmeal (without hulls)	69	2.4
Fruits	Raisin	80	2.8
	Banana	260	9.1
	Grape	320	11.2
	Orange	50	1.8
	Apple	400	14
Sugars	Glucose	50	1.8
	Honey	70	2.5
	Sucrose	50	1.8
	Fructose	50	1.8

Source: Adapted from Platonov (2007, 2004).

Protein

For a long time, it was believed that protein metabolism was not related to energy production during exertion. However, studies have demonstrated that 5 percent to 15 percent of energy during exercise comes from protein sources. Anaerobic exercise is less dependent on the energy production using protein sources than prolonged aerobic exercise is. As an example, during intense resistance training, only 5 percent of energy comes from proteins, while during prolonged aerobic exercise, the catabolism of proteins to generate energy may reach 10 percent to 15 percent (Williams, 1992). Additionally, the lower the glycogen reserves in the muscles, the more proteins will be used for energy production (Lemon and Mullin, 1980).

The protein requirements and quantities in athletes' diets have been discussed for over 100 years. Proteins constitute around 15 percent of body mass, with the protein turnover of skeletal muscles being approximately 2 percent per day. The human body may synthesize proteins from amino acids generated endogenously or via the degradation of the protein ingested in food (exogenously). Some amino acids are considered essential (histidine, isoleucine, leucine, lysine, methionine, phenylalanine, threonine, tryptophan, valine) and need to be consumed through food. Leucine is the main amino acid that stimulates protein biosynthesis pathways (Garlick, 2005).

The following are recommendations for protein ingestion and exercise (Jager, et al. 2017):

- Daily protein ingestion should be between 1.4 and 2 grams per kilogram of body weight to achieve a positive protein balance and to build or maintain muscle mass. Note that this value is significantly above the recommended daily allowance (RDA) of 0.8 grams per kilogram per day.

- Studies have indicated that higher consumption (>3 g/kg/day) may have some benefit for body composition for resistance-trained individuals, especially in situations of caloric deficit, but the results are not yet conclusive.

- Although controversial, it is recommended that total daily protein be divided into portions ingested every three or four hours and contain proteins with high biological value in a dose of 0.25 grams per kilogram of body weight per serving, or an absolute dose of 20 to 40 grams of protein per serving.

- In addition to having a balanced distribution of essential amino acids, a good-quality protein should contain 0.7 grams to 3 grams of leucine per dose.

- The ideal period for protein ingestion should take into account the individual's tolerance and routine. Muscle synthesis is optimized by protein ingestion close to the time of the exercise, but anabolic signaling may last for more than 24 hours after the training session. Therefore, it is important to schedule meals according to the training routine of the athlete and guarantee protein intake spread over the course of the day.

- Data indicate ingesting slowly absorbed protein (e.g., casein protein) before sleep may also be a valid strategy for building muscle.

Ideally, the athlete should choose good-quality proteins and, when possible, associate their meals with training times so that they may ingest them from natural sources during the day (i.e., eating some type of meat for lunch after training). Good-quality protein supplements may also be helpful, depending on the individual's routine and training schedule, both due to their practicality and the rapid digestibility and high biological value of certain proteins. An athlete should check that the brand chosen is reputable to ensure that the product has the quantity of nutrients described on the label, is free from potential contaminants, and is not a doping risk. Protein food supplements are generally based on whey protein, which has high biological value and excellent digestibility, with a standard dose typically containing 25 grams of protein.

To illustrate some options for foods that provide 25 grams of protein to athletes' bodies, see table 4.6.

Table 4.6 – Approximate Food Quantities That Provide 25 Grams of Protein

Product	Quantity (in g)	Quantity (in oz)
Grilled chicken	80	2.8
Grilled lean beef	90	3.2
Roast pork	90	3.2
Turkey	90	3.2
Grilled salmon	100	3.5
Shrimp	120	4.2
Low-fat cottage cheese	200	7
Whole eggs (boiled or scrambled)	200	7
Greek yogurt	300	10.5

Data from USDA National Nutrient Database for Standard Reference, Legacy Release (Haytowitz et al., 2019).

Fat

Fats (lipids) are an important metabolic energy substrate and plasmatic triglycerides are the main lipidic energy sources.

Subcutaneous fat is the adipose tissue under the skin and consists of adipocytes, which contain the highest energy reserve. Part of this fat is found on the abdominal surface and between the muscles. The speed of free fatty acid mobilization (esterification) from adipose tissue depends on lipolysis speed, the transport of these free fatty acids to the blood, and the re-esterification (absorption) of adipocytes (Seluianov, et al. 2008).

Research has shown that when a person is exercising aerobically, glycerol concentration in the blood grows three to six times. Lipolysis is activated by catecholamines, glucagon, growth hormone, adrenocorticotropic hormone, and many other chemical mediators. Catecholamines are the most effective lipolysis stimulators compared to their physiological concentration in the bloodstream. They include alpha-adrenergic inhibitors and beta-adrenergic stimulators, which have an influence on lipolysis speed by altering adenylyl cyclase activity. Adenylyl cyclase is an enzyme that catalyzes ATP transformation in cyclic AMP, a molecule that acts as a second messenger in a cascade of events that culminate in a cellular response.

Insulin is the most effective lipolysis inhibitor, and its blood concentration may be reduced by activating the central nervous system during physical exertion (Bjorntorp, 1991). Thus, muscle activity causes a rise in lipolysis in adipose tissues due to an increase in beta-adrenergic activity.

The transport of free fatty acids in blood plasma is mostly carried out by albumin and conducted actively by the muscle fibers. With the increase in the activation of these fibers, free fatty acid transport accelerates regardless of its concentration in the blood.

According to Seluianov (2001), even at a power output of 30 percent $\dot{V}O_2$max, there is already an increase in plasma-free fatty acids. The principal source of free fatty acids is triglycerides, and exogenous free fatty acids participate in triglyceride granule formation. The direct oxidation pathway of free fatty acids is possible, but its role as an energy source is nonexistent. In situations of continuous muscle contractions—for example, during unilateral knee extension—the role of plasma triglycerides in the muscles in action is minimal (Lemon and Mullin, 1980; Tarnopolsky, et al. 1992).

Thus, it may be proposed that intramuscular triglyceride reserves constitute the basic energy source from free fatty acids during low-intensity muscle activity.

Vitamins

Vitamins are essential micronutrients found in minimal quantities in natural food sources. They are organic compounds; are different from fats, carbohydrates, and proteins; and are indispensable for maintaining normal body function. The body does not synthesize them in quantities adequate to satisfy daily physiological needs so they must be ingested via food, except vitamin D, whose active form may be synthesized from exposure to the sun. Vitamins may be divided, according to their solubility, into *water-soluble vitamins* (thiamine, riboflavin, ascorbic acid, pyridoxine, niacin, pantothenic acid, biotin, folate, cobalamin, among others) or *fat-soluble vitamins* (A, D, E, and K) (Mahan, et al. 2008).

Studies about the role of vitamins in improving physical performance are contradictory. For example, Powers and colleagues (2010) related the reduction of certain positive adaptations to training to the supplementation of antioxidant vitamins (mainly vitamin C and vitamin E). This may be due to a moderate increase in free radicals as a result of exercise being one of the main drivers for these positive training adaptations to occur.

If supplementing with vitamins, consider that temporarily using water-soluble vitamins (vitamin C and vitamin B complexes) in doses above the daily requirements is generally not toxic to the body, given that any excess is eliminated when urinating. By contrast, ingesting very high doses of fat-soluble vitamins over a long time, especially vitamin A and vitamin D, is potentially toxic and may negatively influence the athlete's health (Nielsen, 1992).

The importance of vitamin D in athletes has been extensively studied, given how often vitamin D is deficient in athletes. Inadequate vitamin D levels in athletes is related to immunological changes, such as repeated respiratory infections, impaired muscle recovery, and even an increased risk of stress fractures in more extreme cases (Sikora-Klak, et al. 2018). Vitamin D blood levels appropriate for health are above 30 ng/mL, and the continuous consumption of at least 2,000 UI/day is generally sufficient to avoid any drop in these levels in the winter months in athletes (Farrokhyar, et al. 2017). However, higher doses may be necessary to correct significant deficiencies. Studies have pointed to the potential benefits of vitamin D in improving parameters related to sport, such as the hypertrophy of type II muscle fibers, which produce fast muscle contraction and power, and it is speculated that levels around 50 ng/mL may be related to "peak neuromuscular performance" (Cannell, et al. 2009).

Tables 4.7 and 4.8 illustrate the different vitamins and their functions in the bodies of healthy adults.

Table 4.7 – Fat-Soluble Vitamins and Their Functions in the Body

Vitamins	Main functions	Main sources
A (retinol)	Protein synthesis, immune system function, increase in glycogen content in the liver and muscles, scavenging of free radicals (antioxidant), and important for eye health	Egg yolk, milk, butter, margarine, cheese, oranges, fruits, and dark-green vegetables
D	Promote the absorption and use of calcium and phosphorous, bone metabolism, important for muscle contractions, and immune system function	Fortified and whole dairy products and egg yolk (often, diet is not as important as exposure to the sun)
E (tocopherol)	Antioxidant action that prevents lesions to the cell membrane, increased resistance to hypoxia, increase in glycogen in the muscles and liver, and stimulation of muscle contractions	Vegetable oils and their products, chestnuts, eggs, milk, and fish
K	Aids the formation of certain proteins, especially those related to blood coagulation, cofactor in amino acid metabolism, and important for bone health	Green leafy vegetables and tea

Source: Powers and Howley (2000) and Platonov (2007).

Table 4.8 – Water-Soluble Vitamins and Their Functions in the Body

Vitamins	Main functions	Main sources
Thiamine (B_1)	Coenzyme essential for energy metabolism, regulates the functions of the central nervous system and the circulatory and digestive systems, and important for DNA and RNA synthesis	Pork, vegetables, peanuts, dried fruits, and egg yolk
Riboflavin (B_2)	Participation in energy production, assimilation and synthesis of proteins and fats, and important for red blood cell production and iron metabolism	Yeast and byproducts, eggs (yolk), milk, cheese, grains, meat, fish, and beans
Niacin (B_3)	Coenzyme used in energy metabolism and important for lipid synthesis and DNA repair	Chestnuts, meat; pro-vitamin B_3 (tryptophan) is found in bananas and in most proteins
Pyridoxine (B_6)	Extraction of glucose from glycogen, involved in gluconeogenesis from amino acids, and participation in the synthesis of compound proteins and neurotransmitters	Meat, vegetables, wheat, and protein-rich foods in general
Folic acid (B_9)	Ensures red blood cell production, important for amino acid metabolism, and coenzyme used in the metabolism of DNA and RNA	Green vegetables, orange juice, chestnuts, legumes, grains, potatoes, and liver
Cobalamin (B_{12})	Maintenance and stimulation of red blood cell synthesis, regulation of protein biosynthesis, stimulation of the extraction of energy from carbohydrates, and important for the health of the nervous system	Fish, milk products, and animal products
Pantothenic acid (B_5)	Coenzyme used in energy extraction from carbohydrates and fatty acids	Animal products, grains; pantothenic acid is widely distributed in foods
Ascorbic acid (C)	Functions in collagen synthesis, antioxidant, assists in detoxification, increases iron absorption, and aids the immune system	Fruits and vegetables, broccoli, cabbage, melon, cauliflower, citric fruits, kiwi, and strawberries

Source: Powers and Howley (2000) and Platonov (2007).

Minerals

Minerals or trace elements are essential micronutrients necessary to maintain normal cell function. They cannot be synthesized by the body and are bound to other compounds in human tissue. When we speak of minerals, we must remember that their proper ingestion is one of the most important guarantees of complete recovery in synthesis, regulatory, and energy functions for athletes after intense training and competitions.

According to Platonov (2007), minerals are important not only for the recovery of water and salt balance, nerve conductivity, and cell electrolytes but also for the blood, enzymatic loading, assimilating vitamins, and immunological resistance, among other physiological functions.

In states of mineral deficiency, supplements may help to improve energy production, reduce tiredness, maintain bone mineral density, and participate as cofactors in many metabolic reactions (Clarkson, 1991).

Minerals may be divided into *macrominerals* (substances that are conserved in the body in not less than 0.01% of total body mass) and *microminerals* (they constitute only 0.001% or less of total body mass). Common macrominerals include calcium, magnesium, potassium, sodium, sulfur, and chlorine, and common microminerals include iron, zinc, copper, selenium, and cobalt (Dias, et al. 2017; Seluianov, et al. 2008).

Calcium is essential for building bone tissue and plays an important role in muscle contraction, among other physiological functions. With adequate calcium levels in the diet and good blood vitamin D levels, the risk of bone tissue density problems may also be prevented (Thompson and Manore, 2013).

Magnesium is a cofactor in energy metabolism enzymes, supports muscle and nerve cell functions, and is found in bone tissue. For example, magnesium deficiency may result in muscle weakness and may lead to muscle spasms (Lee, et al. 2017).

Phosphorus is a crucial part of the composition of bone, ATP, nucleotides, and enzymes. A high concentration of phosphorus in blood plasma allows a high concentration of ATP and phosphocreatine (PCr) to be maintained in the cells. Because phosphocreatine is a main energy source during the first seconds of high-intensity efforts, phosphorous is essential for energy production (Seluianov, 2001).

Selenium acts as an antioxidant in combination with vitamin E and reduces peroxide oxidation in the cell membrane with intense exercise, an important step for maintaining muscle function and recovery (Thompson and Manore, 2013).

Iron is an indispensable element of myoglobin and hemoglobin and is essential for proper oxygen transport. In addition to the risk of iron-deficiency anemia, the consequences of a lack of iron have been extensively studied in athletes over recent years. Evidence indicates that iron deficiency may be associated with the following negative effects on performance, among others (Lee, et al. 2017):

- Impaired aerobic capacity ($\dot{V}O_2$max and $\dot{V}O_2$peak)
- Reduced energy efficiency
- Reduced daily training volume
- Shorter time to exhaustion

Table 4.9 illustrates the role of the main minerals and their functions in the bodies of healthy adults.

Table 4.9 – Minerals and Their Functions

Minerals	Main functions	Main sources
Calcium	Muscle contraction, formation of bones and teeth, blood coagulation, and nerve transmission	Milk products, dark-green vegetables, and legumes
Phosphorus	Formation of ATP for energy production; separation of oxygen from erythrocytes, making aerobic metabolism possible; a component of coenzymes; and bone formation	Milk, cheeses, red meat, chicken, and grains
Magnesium	Muscle contraction, metabolism of glucose of the muscle cells for energy production, and participates in wound healing	Whole-grain bread, cereals, leafy green vegetables, and grains
Sulfur	Component of cartilage, tendons, and proteins; participates in liver detoxification	Amino acids with sulfur from dietary proteins
Sodium	Regulation of body fluid balance and hydration and conservation of the excitability of nerve and muscle tissue allowing normal muscle contractions	Salt, fish (saltwater), cold meats, and cheese
Potassium	Regulation of body fluid balance and hydration and essential for energy production and nerve function	Fish, meat, milk, vegetables, and fruits
Chloride	Plays a role in the acid–base balance and important for digestion through participation in gastric acid formation	Same as sodium
Iron	Transports oxygen via the erythrocytes, which is used by the muscle cells	Eggs, lean meat, green vegetables, and legumes
Iodine	Component of thyroid hormones	Fish, seafood, dairy products, and iodized salt
Zinc	Component of several enzymes and positively influences the immune and endocrine systems	Red meat, seafood, and grains

Source: Platonov (2007) and Powers and Howley (2000).

Ergogenic Aids

Ergogenic aids are nothing more than substances or phenomena that potentially improve athletes' performance. Ergogenic aids may include foods, nutritional supplements, drugs, warm-up exercises, hypnosis, stress control, doping, and oxygen inhalation, among others (Powers and Howley, 2000). In this chapter, we will concentrate on nutritional supplements as ergogenic aids.

According to Garthe and Maughan (2018), nutritional supplementation is a widespread practice, mainly among professional athletes, with studies indicating a prevalence ranging from 47 percent to 100 percent. The main reasons related to their use are listed in figure 4.1.

In table 4.10, we may observe, for example, a summary of some supplements that have been used by American Top Team athletes in recent years and the effects suggested by their manufacturers. It is worth remembering that many supplements have not been tested or had their efficacy proven by solid scientific research (Dias, et al. 2017).

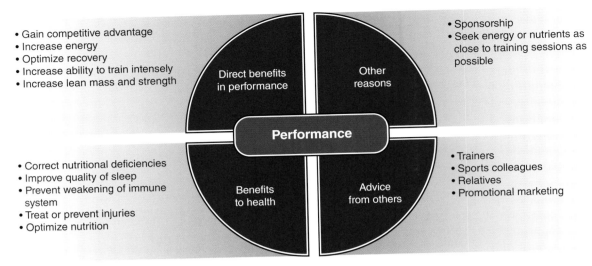

Figure 4.1 – Frequent reasons athletes use supplements.

Adapted by permission from I. Garthe and R.J. Maughan, "Athletes and Supplements: Prevalence and Perspectives," *International Journal of Sport Nutrition and Exercise Metabolism* 28, no. 2 (2018): 126-138.

Table 4.10 – Examples of Supplements Used by American Top Team Athletes

Nutritional supplement	Purported ergogenic effects
Protein supplements	Provide an adequate quantity of proteins to aid muscle growth and weight gain
Arginine, lysine, ornithine	Stimulate the release of growth hormones and insulin; promote muscle growth
Creatine	Increases phosphocreatine in the muscle; increases energy and stimulates muscle growth
Vitamin B_{12}	Increases DNA synthesis; increases muscle growth
Antioxidant vitamins: C and E	Prevent muscle lesions due to undesired oxidative processes after high-intensity training
Supplements mixing carbohydrates and protein in a 4:1 proportion	Accelerate recovery after intense training
Medium-chain triglycerides	Increase thermal effect; promote fat loss
Caffeine	Improves performance at muscle level; stimulates the CNS; increases the use of fats
Nitric oxide	Supplement based on nitric oxide that increases blood flow and helps increase resistance

Adapted from Dias et al. (2017).

Creatine

Creatine is a nonprotein nitrogen compound synthesized in the liver, kidneys, and pancreas from arginine, glycine, and methionine. It is one of the substances essential to cellular energy production. In addition to the endogenous production of creatine (1-2 g/day), it is ingested when consuming proteins of animal origin, such as fish, beef, and pork (Walker, 1979).

The enzyme creatine phosphokinase participates in phosphocreatine degradation to creatine and inorganic phosphate, during which energy is released. Consequently, creatine maintains cellular activity and muscle contraction, especially in high-intensity exertion. Other possible functions have been attributed to creatine, such as the antioxidant effect, buffering, and an increase in the expression of genes linked to growth factors, among others (Rawson and Persky, 2007). Figure 4.2 summarizes the possible effects of creatine supplementation.

Figure 4.2 – Possible Effects of Creatine Supplementation

- Increase in maximum isometric force
- Increase in performance during single and repeated bouts of high-intensity exercise <150 seconds, with greater effect in exercise <30 seconds
- Improvement in adaptive responses to training, with increases in lean mass and force
- Reduction in delayed onset muscle soreness (DOMS)
- Improvement in cognitive function, especially in situations of extreme fatigue and sleep deprivation
- Reduction in damage and improvement in recovery from traumatic brain injury

Adapted from Maughan et al. (2018).

Numerous studies have demonstrated the benefits of creatine supplementation in improving performance during short-burst, high-intensity exercise. As a result, athletes have used creatine for many years in various sports activities. Considering the metabolic demands of an MMA fighter (high intensity and power), it may be said that this supplement has potential benefits in the sport. Of the few studies on creatine supplementation in combat sports participants, one study (Campbell, et al. 2011) is of particular interest. It was conducted with judokas using a protocol of one week of loading (5.5 g 4x/day) followed by one week of maintenance (5.5 g 1x/day). The findings showed an improvement in peak power output (up 12%) and average power output (up 10.8%) in ergometry of the upper body in the supplemented group over the control group. It was observed that creatine use may lead to an increase in body weight of 1 to 2 kilograms (2-4 lb) shortly after the "loading" week (Kreider, et al. 2017); therefore, this effect should be taken into account for athletes who compete near the upper limits of their weight division.

Around 95 percent of the body's creatine is stored in skeletal muscles, with habitual saturation of the reserves of between 60 percent and 80 percent. Therefore, supplementation during the "loading" phase (0.3 g/kg/day, or usually 20-30 g/day, divided into 4 daily doses for 5-7 days) may lead to a 20 percent increase in creatine reserves (Greenhaff, 1995). Various protocols for creatine use have been tested, but classic loading (5 g 4x/day for 5-7 days) with subsequent maintenance (3-5 g/day) still offers the best evidence of effectiveness, especially if ingested with carbohydrates or carbohydrates and protein. Urinary creatine loss is around 2 grams per day, meaning that, after the supplementation period, creatine reserves can take four to six weeks to return to baseline levels (Kreider, et al. 2017).

In some circles, the belief persists that creatine may have toxic effects on the liver and kidneys; however, many studies over the last 20 years have demonstrated its safety, even in continued use for up to five years (Castell, et al. 2015). Currently, creatine supplementation does not violate the doping regulations of the main athletic organizations, and its use is permitted.

Caffeine

Caffeine has been recognized for centuries as a stimulant for increasing alertness and attention and has been used as an ergogenic resource in sport for many decades. Its main mechanism is blocking adenosine receptors in the central nervous system and in other tissues (Fredholm, et al. 1999), as well as increasing the secretion of beta-endorphins (Grossman and Sutton, 1985). Many studies have sought to establish ideal doses and have documented effects on various aspects of sports performance, as described in figure 4.3.

Figure 4.3 – Possible Effects of Caffeine Supplementation

- Improvement in capacity for endurance (e.g., time to fatigue) in activities lasting 5 to 150 minutes
- Increase in average power output and peak power output during anaerobic activities of 1 to 2 minutes
- Evidence of a positive impact on changes in immunity from a training session (activation of lymphocytes, mitigation of the fall in neutrophils)
- Increase in fat mobilization from adipose tissue and muscle tissue
- Increase in adrenaline
- Lower perception of exertion intensity
- Increase in resynthesis of glycogen posttraining (when ingested with carbohydrates)

Adapted from Maughan et al. (2018), Burke (2008), and Goldstein et al. (2010).

After caffeine is ingested and absorbed into the gastrointestinal tract, blood levels rise 15 to 45 minutes after consumption. Its circulating concentration falls by 50 percent to 75 percent three to six hours after consumption. The doses most used for potential benefit in sport are around 3 to 6 milligrams per kilogram—for example, 210 to 420 milligrams per dose for an athlete weighing 70 kilograms (154 lb). For purposes of comparison, a cup of espresso contains around 100 milligrams of caffeine. While doses near the lower limit of the usual range (3 mg/kg) demonstrate a positive impact on various performance aspects, higher doses such as those up to 9 milligrams per kilogram do not result in greater benefit and can be related to a higher incidence of adverse reactions, such as nausea, insomnia, agitation, and anxiety, which could result in a drop in the athlete's performance (Burke, 2008).

The effects of caffeine on muscle power output offer conflicting results, with some research showing null benefits on muscle strength (Goldstein, et al. 2010). Similarly there is also a lack of quality evidence regarding its use as an ergogenic aid in combat sports. López-González and colleagues (2018) conducted a systematic review of caffeine supplementation in combat sports and highlighted the possible benefit of reducing reaction time and improving the efficacy of glycolysis pathways related to anaerobic activity. Diaz-Lara and colleagues (2016) evaluated using 3 milligrams per kilogram of caffeine 60 minutes before simulated combat in jiu-jitsu athletes, with the supplemented group showing improvements in grip strength, static lift, and number of bench press repetitions.

Meanwhile, a study conducted with athletes in simulated taekwondo combat (5 mg/kg caffeine 50 minutes before simulated combat) revealed an improvement in reaction time (Santos, et al. 2014). On the other hand, research conducted with MMA athletes using doses of 5 milligrams per kilogram of caffeine 60 minutes before three sets of 15 seconds of punching demonstrated no improvement in punch performance (de Azevedo, et al. 2019).

Thus, caffeine may be considered a useful ergogenic resource at certain stages of a fighter's training cycle, such as endurance work and aerobic training, but further studies are needed to evaluate its real impact in combat situations, bearing in mind individual variations in sensitivity to caffeine.

β-Alanine

Beta-alanine (β-alanine) is an amino acid produced endogenously in the liver or ingested in food sources such as beef or chicken. Under normal conditions (i.e., not supplementing with β-alanine), it does not possess significant ergogenic properties. It is, however, essential for carnosine synthesis, a dipeptide composed of β-alanine and L-histidine, which is one of the main intracellular buffers, particularly in muscle tissue. Since the first studies in humans published after 2006, evidence consistently points to the benefits of β-alanine supplementation for some performance aspects (Trexler, et al. 2015).

In high-intensity training, sustained exertion results in an increase of muscular lactic acid and a consequent elevation in H^+ (hydrogen ions) and acidosis, one of the most important mechanisms of peripheral muscle fatigue. This effect occurs mostly in movements highly dependent on type II muscle fiber contraction, such as in throws, sprawls, and takedown attempts in MMA (Campbell, et al. 2011). Thus, β-alanine supplementation was shown to increase carnosine concentrations, consequently improving the efficacy of the buffering of muscular acidosis. This is the main mechanism through which β-alanine supplementation in sustained high-intensity training would be justified (Saunders, et al. 2017). Figure 4.4 summarizes the possible effects of β-alanine supplementation.

Figure 4.4 – Possible Effects of β-Alanine Supplementation

- Increase in time to exhaustion in high-intensity exercises >60 seconds
- Mitigation of neuromuscular fatigue, mainly in older individuals
- Potential increase in anaerobic threshold
- Benefit absent or modest in long-duration aerobic exercise (>25 minutes)
- Evidence of being related to an increase in tolerance of training volume, without documented effect on gains in strength to date

Adapted from Maughan et al. (2018) and Trexler et al. (2015).

The main application of β-alanine supplementation would be in high-intensity training, especially in tasks lasting 0.5 to 10 minutes and maximal exercises ≥30 seconds, separated by intervals of about three minutes (Saunders, et al. 2017). This kind of exertion is similar to rounds in MMA competition. The main protocols for β-alanine use indicate a better effect in supplementation of 4 to 6 grams per day (or approximately 65 mg/kg/day) divided into doses, for example, from 0.8 to 1.6 grams every three or four hours (to reduce the tingling associated with its ingestion). Its supplementation ideally should be maintained for 10 to 12 weeks to optimize muscular reserves of carnosine (Maughan, et al. 2018).

To date, few studies on combat sports have been published. Donovan and colleagues (2012) evaluated 16 amateur boxers with around six years of experience, divided into a placebo group (P) and a group (S) supplemented with 1.5 grams of β-alanine four times a day for four weeks. The simulated contest consisted of three three-minute rounds, the first two minutes and 50 seconds of standardized punching followed by 10 seconds of maximal-output punching. During the 10-second maximal-output period, the S group exhibited an improvement in a mean punch force of 20 kilograms ± 1.01 kilograms against 1 kilogram ± 1 kilogram for group P, and punch frequency of 5 ± 4 punches for the supplemented group against –2 ± 3 punches for the placebo group.

de Andrade Kratz and colleagues (2017) studied the effects of β-alanine supplementation on 23 top-level judokas divided into a placebo group and a group supplemented with 6.4 grams per day for four weeks. The performance was evaluated after a five-minute simulated fight with three bouts of the special judo fitness test, resulting in an increase in the number of throws per set and total number of throws in the supplemented group, without any change in these variables in the placebo group. Thus, the evidence indicates that β-alanine supplementation in combat sports is related to possible benefits in performance.

Sodium Bicarbonate

Sodium bicarbonate ($NaHCO_3$) has the capacity to increase pH and the concentration of extracellular HCO_3, contributing to increased intracellular buffering capacity through an efflux of H^+ and lactate from exerted muscle cells. Its effects have been extensively documented, mostly with a dose of 0.3 grams per kilogram of body weight used before training (Maughan, et al. 2018), as illustrated in figure 4.5.

Figure 4.5 – Possible Effects of Sodium Bicarbonate Supplementation

- Increase in performance (±2%) in high-intensity activities lasting one to seven minutes
- Increase in capacity to perform repeated sprints or prolonged intermittent exercises
- Increase in capacity to perform sprints during aerobic endurance exercises
- Benefit absent or modest in exercises lasting more than 10 minutes

Adapted from Maughan et al. (2018), Thomas, Erdman, and Burke (2016), and Castell, Stear, and Burke (2015).

For combat sports, Siegler and Hirscher (2010) evaluated amateur boxers during a simulated competition consisting of two sparring sessions of four rounds lasting three minutes, separated by a one-minute rest. The group supplemented with sodium bicarbonate (dose of 0.3 g/kg of body weight) saw a significant increase in punches landed and thrown (an increase in punch efficacy). Lopes-Silva and colleagues (2018) concluded that a sodium bicarbonate dose of 0.3 grams per kilogram of body weight ingested 90 minutes before three rounds lasting two minutes separated by one minute of passive recovery increased the glycolytic metabolism and performance of taekwondo athletes in simulated combat. On the other hand, doses less than 0.1 grams per kilogram of body weight consumed for 10 days did not demonstrate significant benefits in the dummy-throw test in wrestlers, although their Wingate time to peak power was shorter. This study concluded that the lower dose may have been insufficient to improve anaerobic power output and performance in wrestling (Durkalec-Michalski, et al. 2017).

The main protocol for sodium bicarbonate use is with a dose of 0.2 to 0.4 grams per kilogram of body weight consumed between 60 and 150 minutes before exercise. Due to the high prevalence of gastrointestinal symptoms, such as nausea and diarrhea when ingested "in bolus" (at once), alternative strategies have also shown positive results, such as coingestion with carbohydrates (approximately 1.5 g/kg of body weight) or splitting the dose in the hours preceding training. Given the high demand of glycolysis pathways and the repetition of intense, short-duration exertion in MMA fights, sodium bicarbonate supplementation in combat athletes may potentially be useful when gastrointestinal tolerance is properly monitored.

Nitrate

Duncan and colleagues (1995) demonstrated that nitrate ingestion, which is mainly found in leafy vegetables (e.g., spinach, kale) and in beetroot, results in an increase in nitrate production in saliva, with a consequent increase in nitric oxide (NO) production. Nitric oxide is a potent vasodilator and may positively affect performance in exercise through improved muscle fiber oxygenation, including fast-twitch (type II) muscle (Bailey, et al. 2015). It also increases muscular blood flow and mitochondrial efficacy (Bailey, et al. 2010), among other effects, as described in figure 4.6.

Figure 4.6 – Possible Effects of Nitrate Supplementation

- Increase in exercise tolerance
- Increase of 4 percent to 25 percent in time to exhaustion at set power output
- Increase in type II muscle fiber oxygenation
- Conflicting evidence in exercises having a duration <12 minutes

Adapted from Maughan et al. (2018), Thomas, Erdman, and Burke (2016), and Bailey et al. (2015).

In addition to the benefits demonstrated in longer training sessions, evidence points to a smaller effect in highly trained athletes (Jones, 2014). Doses that demonstrated the best immediate effect on performance were between 310 and 560 milligrams of nitrate (e.g., beetroot juice) ingested approximately two to three hours before exercise (Hoon, et al. 2014).

HMB

In recent years, a new supplement called HMB (beta-hydroxy beta-methylbutyrate) has appeared, with its use becoming widespread since 1995. Used by several athletes from American Top Team, it is a metabolite of the amino acid leucine (Seluianov, 2001; Dias, et al. 2017). The two most common forms are calcium-HMB and a free acid form of HMB, the proposed effect being to improve recovery and lower muscular catabolism, with supposed benefits in force, power, and muscle hypertrophy (Wilson, et al. 2013a).

Some mechanisms related to its action have been proposed, such as the stimulus of protein biosynthesis pathways through mTOR (a protein essential for muscle hypertrophy) activation and satellite cell differentiation, catabolic pathway attenuation through IGF-1 (a factor important for muscle development and fat oxidation) stimulation, and ubiquitin ligase (an enzyme related to muscle catabolism) inhibition (Wilson, et al. 2013b), with the proposed effects summarized in figure 4.7.

Figure 4.7 – Possible Effects of HMB Supplementation

- Reduction in muscle damage from exercise and improvement of muscle recovery
- Positive impact on force, power, and muscle hypertrophy
- Greater reduction of fat mass when used with a program of structured exercises
- Potential improvement in aerobic capacity

Adapted from Wilson, Fitschen, Campbell, et al. (2013).

Some studies on HMB have demonstrated exciting results. For example, Nissen and colleagues (1996) conducted a study in which 41 participants were divided into three groups with the ingestion of 0 grams, 1.5 grams, and 3 grams per day of HMB for three weeks. In the group that did not ingest the HMB, lean body mass increased by 0.4 kilograms (0.88 lb). In the second group (1.5 g/day of HMB), the increase was 0.8 kilograms (1.8 lb), and in the third group (3 g/day of HMB), the increase in lean mass was 1.3 kilograms (3 lb). Strength increased in the first group by 8 percent, in the second by 13 percent (1.5 g/day of HMB), and in the third by 18 percent (3 g/day of HMB). In another study, athletes who ingested HMB (3 g/day) and creatine monohydrate performed five hours per week of resistance training and three hours per week of sprint exercises over the course of 28 days. An increase in strength and sprinting speed of 13 percent was demonstrated (Seluianov, et al. 2008).

Seluianov (2001) conducted a study in which over two weeks, eight cyclists ingested different preparations: 3 grams per day of HMB, or 3 grams per day of leucine, or 3 grams per day of placebo. At the beginning and end of each period, analyses were carried out. $\dot{V}O_2$max and maximum lactate concentration in the blood were measured. During the HMB ingestion, a rise in $\dot{V}O_2$max of 0.18 liters per minute was observed; in the other cases, the differences were questionable.

For combat sports, Durkalec-Michalski and colleagues (2017) recently evaluated 42 highly trained athletes from judo, Brazilian jiu-jitsu, and wrestling for 12 weeks. The participants were randomized into a placebo (P) group and a supplemented (S) group taking 3 grams per day of HMB in calcium form. Body composition, aerobic and anaerobic capacities, and hormonal and creatine kinase levels were evaluated during the experiment. Compared to the P group, the S group increased significantly in lean mass, with a simultaneous reduction in fat mass. They also showed improvements in time taken to reach ventilatory threshold (VT), power at VT, and heart rate at VT, as well as peak anaerobic power, mean power, maximum speed, and postexercise lactate concentrations. Due to the improvement in those parameters, the authors concluded that HMB use would be justified in combat sports.

There are no reports of significant adverse reactions to HMB, and the most common protocol is 3 grams of HMB per day, consumed close to the training session, with a probable increase in efficacy if ingested for at least two weeks (Wilson, et al. 2013a).

Final Considerations on Nutritional Supplements in Sports

External pressures, industry marketing, and a thirst for performance improvements may lead a fighter to waste financial resources and put their health at risk by using ineffective products or banned substances. Supplement contamination is a reality, and a review indicated that the contamination rate of nutritional supplements sold in various countries may range from 12 percent to up to 58 percent (Martinez-Sanz, et al. 2017). It is thus crucial to stress that ingesting banned substances, even if inadvertently, is considered a breach of anti-doping law and may incur the same penalties as voluntary doping.

The trainer, coach, doctor, and nutritionist who accompany the athlete must know the supplements the individual uses in all phases of the training cycle and offer guidance about the efficacy of their use and monitor potential adverse reactions. Suspend supplementation when there is no evidence of benefit or when there is a potential risk to health by supplement contamination. Conscious and informed decisions should be made regarding nutritional supplementation with athletes.

5

METHODS OF TRAINING FOR MMA

Stéfane Beloni Correa Dielle Dias, PhD

Everton Bittar Oliveira, BS

Pavel Vladimirovich Pashkin, MS

Jeffrey Williams, PhD

Brian Binkley, MS

Fabio da Silva Ferreira Vieira, PhD

Rokaya Mikhailenko, MS

Vitaly Rybakov, PhD

Grigor Chilingaryan, BS

We begin this chapter with body weight training because it is the basis for more advanced training, teaches motion mechanics, and fosters body awareness during movement. Conventional environments such as an indoor gym with free weights and other resistance training equipment and other nonconventional environments like various outdoor settings will be covered in this chapter. We will demonstrate how to begin and how to advance body weight training in almost any environment conducive to the training function. Finally, we will discuss why removing the athlete from a conventional environment can be beneficial because it introduces unpredictability, an inherent element in MMA.

This chapter connects the theory described in previous chapters and puts it into practice. Throughout the chapter, we will show various training programs that could organize training variables over a specific time. These are based on more than 20 years of experience working with high-level athletes who achieved peak performance and became world champions in the most prestigious combat sporting events, including Ultimate Fighting Championship (UFC), Bellator MMA, Rizin Fighting Federation, ONE Championship, M-1 Global, ADCC Submission Fighting World Championship, Bare Knuckle Fighting Championship, IBJJF World Jiu-Jitsu Championship, among others.

Body Weight Training

Body weight training consists of performing various exercises to recruit specific muscle groups to enhance performance, typically in a calisthenic manner. But it can be done with traditional movements like push-ups, pull-ups, squats, lunge variations, and so on. Using body weight training diversifies an athlete's training opportunities because it does not require special equipment, has been shown to be effective in enhancing muscular strength and endurance in various settings, and can be performed almost anywhere at nearly any time. This makes it a valuable tool, especially for athletes who might not have access to specific equipment while traveling to competitions. The relative intensity of the exercises is low because body weight serves as the main source of resistance. Low intensity allows training to enhance or maintain specific performance metrics, such as muscular strength, power, and endurance. It also allows metabolic conditioning to be performed with a low risk for injury.

Body weight training is important because it promotes core stability, which means the athlete can be better equipped to withstand blows. It also allows them to throw punches more effectively and with greater precision, accuracy, and power. Good positioning of a fighter's center mass during competition enhances the ability to efficiently shoot for and defend takedowns and move from their feet to the ground, a critical aspect in combat sports, especially those involving grappling such as MMA. Body weight training promotes a fully balanced athlete who can more easily move their own mass.

Indoor Body Weight Training

Generally, training in an indoor environment is understood to be in a gym or sports club environment—a specific location to train. However, to avoid a psychological plateau or monotony, any space can be used to develop training functions, as the following situations illustrate.

General warm-up exercises include aerobic exercises, such as skipping rope (see figure 5.1a), shadow boxing exercises in front of a mirror (see figure 5.1b), stretching exercises, or repetitions of movements specific to the style of fighting.

Biomechanics is the study of the mechanical laws relating to the movement or structure of living organisms. Before an athlete interacts with an opponent by punching, they must master their own movements, which begins with stabilization, locomotion, and muscle action. The athlete first balances and then moves, culminating in attacks. From this perspective, as a starting point to movement, proprioception is extremely important.

Proprioception is the perception or awareness of the position and movement of the body. Using body weight itself is crucial to developing proprioception, and exercises that require strength and stability may be used. In figure 5.2, veteran UFC fighter Gleison Tibau demonstrates a proprioceptive movement on a gel X-PAD.

To perform this movement, stand on one leg with the foot pointing straight ahead. The knee of the other leg is slightly flexed. The arms are extended for balance or kept at the sides. Weight is centered over the ball of the foot, the upper body is erect, and the head is facing forward. Lower to a squat position, keeping the knee of the supporting leg centered over the ball of the foot. Start with shallow squats and increase them, getting closer to the ground. At the end of the movement, the arms and body lean forward to simulate a takedown technique.

Using an X-PAD makes the exercise unstable and harder than a single-leg squat on a stable surface, so proprioceptors are stimulated. This exercise mainly works the quadriceps and gluteal muscles. Other muscles involved include the hamstrings, calves, and core muscles. Complete 2 to 4 sets of 8 to 10 repetitions of the single-leg squat on each side.

Figure 5.1 – Gleison Tibau warms up with (*a*) jump rope and (*b*) shadow boxing, both of which are aerobic exercises specific to his sport.

Figure 5.2 – Single-leg squat exercise for proprioception on the X-PAD.

One body weight exercise important for the general physical preparation of an athlete is the push-up. Begin facedown on the ground, the arms under the shoulders to support the body, hands usually shoulder-width apart, and feet touching or slightly apart. Inhale and flex the elbows to bring the chest close to the ground (avoid arching the low back). Push back up to complete the arm extension, exhaling at the end of the movement. This exercise is great for the pectoralis major and triceps brachii (Delavier, 2010). Complete 2 to 4 sets of 15 to 50 repetitions with body weight.

This exercise may be performed on the floor or, as demonstrated by athlete Deivison "Dragon" Ribeiro in figure 5.3, with support for the hands, allowing a greater range of movement.

Normally, during the rest between push-ups, an athlete can perform various abdominal exercises. Figures 5.4 through 5.6 demonstrate three variations of increasing difficulty. We recommend inhaling before the exercise and exhaling at the end of the movement. These exercises work the rectus abdominis and, to a lesser degree, the external oblique and the flexor muscles of the hip (iliopsoas, rectus femoris, and tensor fasciae latae). Rotating the torso focuses some of the effort on the internal and external obliques (Delavier, 2010). Complete 2 to 4 sets of 30 to 50 repetitions per exercise.

Figure 5.3 – Push-up with hand supports.

Figure 5.4 – Abdominals at the end of the round.

Figure 5.5 – Abdominals at the end of the circuit.

Figure 5.6 – Auxiliary exercise with a ball to strengthen the core.

Within the indoor training environment, group training maintains athletes' physical fitness and is widely used by gyms like American Top Team. This work is normally performed twice a week outside competition. When an athlete signs a contract for a fight, the coaches separate them from the group training to begin specific training (Dias, et al. 2017).

The group training is three to five rounds (or circuits) lasting five minutes each. The sets vary during the training and are composed of exercise rounds that work the whole body, such as sprawls (a variation of the burpee) and squats while carrying a partner. Specific "ground and pound" rounds are also worked on using rubber dummies. Following is the sequence of circuits normally used.

First Round: The first round includes a warm-up with moderate running in a group and dynamic stretching for 10 to 15 minutes (see figure 5.7).

Figure 5.7 – Athletes from the American Top Team warming up.

Second Round: The second round involves intervals of sprints and walking (serving as active rest) for 5 to 10 minutes (see figure 5.8).

Figure 5.8 – Group sprint.

Third Round: The third round is more specific, with fighting movements and techniques (e.g., punches, knee lifts, and sprawls). The round starts with knee lift exercises and punching in line (see figure 5.9a). Next, exercises are performed related to the sprawl (a movement characteristic of defense against takedown attempts) (see figures 5.9b-c). The sequence finishes with takedowns with resistance created by tensioners or elastic bands attached to the waist (see figure 5.9d). Remember that, in this round, the exercises are dynamic and overload the whole body.

Figure 5.9 – Fighting movements and techniques for the third round of training.

Fourth Round: In the fourth round, exercises are performed in pairs, with the team divided by weight division for partner squats and a second movement called the *turquesa*, which is a characteristic rotational wrestling movement. The main objective of the partner squat is to increase the strength and muscular endurance of the lower-body muscles (see figures 5.10a-b). It begins with one athlete standing with their legs slightly wider than hip width and carefully lifting their partner onto their shoulders in a "fireman's carry" position. The exercise of carrying a person whose weight distribution is uneven (compared to a barbell) requires additional abdominal stabilization and mimics the uneven forces encountered during competition. In the turquesa, the athlete holds their partner at waist level perpendicular to their own body and proceeds to swing their partner over their shoulder, continuing the angular momentum of the swing until their partner achieves the perpendicular position on the opposite side. The rotation of the partner around the working athlete is continuous for the set (in a movement similar to a windshield wiper). This compound exercise works the muscles of the whole body, but the objective of the vertical lift and rotational movement is strengthening the lumbar region and upper body to prepare the athlete for the necessary movements and forces specific to combat sports (see figures 5.10c-d). The sets are executed for 30 seconds each, totaling 2 to 5 sets of each movement, and a rest of 2 to 3 minutes between each set.

Figure 5.10 – Demonstration in pairs of partner squat and turquesa.

Fifth Round: The fifth round consists of alternated ground and pound (see figure 5.11*a*) and abdominal strengthening (see figure 5.11*b*) exercises. The sets vary from 1 to 2 minutes of ground and pound with 30 seconds of varied abdominals (ABS).

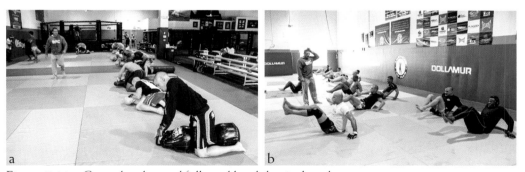

Figure 5.11 – Ground and pound followed by abdominal work.

Table 5.1 presents an indoor body weight training program based on indoor exercises.

Table 5.1 – Indoor Body Weight Training Program

	Week 1	Week 2	Week 3	Week 4
First round				
Running + stretching	10 min	10 min	15 min	15 min
Second round				
Sprints + active recovery	2 runs over 30 m	3 runs over 30 m	4 runs over 30 m	5 runs over 30 m
Third round				
Sprawls + punches + takedowns	6 sprawls + 4 takedowns	8 sprawls + 6 takedowns	10 sprawls + 8 takedowns	12 sprawls + 10 takedowns
Fourth round				
Partner squats + turquesas	2 squats + 2 turquesas	3 squats + 3 turquesas	4 squats + 4 turquesas	5 squats + 5 turquesas
Fifth round				
Ground and pound + abs	2 × 1 min ground and pound + 30 sec abs	2 × 1 min 30 sec ground and pound + 30 sec abs	2 × 1 min 45 sec ground and pound + 30 sec abs	2 × 2 min ground and pound + 30 sec abs

Outdoor Body Weight Training

MMA athletes do many hours of highly intense and exhausting training routines to prepare for competition. Sometimes during training, athletes feel suffocated by the same training environment and are mentally stressed from spending so much time inside the gym. One solution is to remove the fighters from the conventional training environment and take them outdoors.

Outdoor training aims to recruit the muscles of the entire body and stimulate strength, reaction time, speed, agility, and balance, among many other physical qualities essential for fighting. In these instances, the terrain chosen to perform the activities influences the load on the athletes (Dias, et al. 2017; Dias and Oliveira, 2013). To demonstrate an intense training session on the beach, we invited three former athletes from Bellator MMA (USA): Ailton Barbosa, Cristiano "Soldado" Souza, and Deivison "Dragon" Ribeiro.

Warm-Up

The warm-up consists of shadow boxing for 5 minutes. After warming up, the athletes stand facing each other and practice takedowns with their partners (see figure 5.12). They repeat this between 8 and 14 times.

a   b   c

Figure 5.12 – Cristiano Souza begins the takedown by lifting Ailton Barbosa to head height. Next, they reverse their positions.

Russian Kettlebell Full Swing

Stand in front of the kettlebell with the feet parallel and shoulder-width apart. Flexing the hips and knees while keeping the spine in a neutral position, reach down and grasp the kettlebell with both hands. The upper body is parallel to the floor and the knees are slightly flexed. Forcefully swing the kettlebell back between the legs and quickly reverse the direction with an explosive hip extension, swinging the kettlebell out to chest level so the hips and knees are extended and the person is standing upright. Finish the exercise with full flexion, the arms above the head. This movement engages the whole body and requires using muscles that stabilize the spine (core muscles). Perform 2 to 3 sets of 15 to 20 repetitions with a kettlebell weighing 20 to 40 pounds (9-18 kg) (see figure 5.13).

a   b   c

Figure 5.13 – Russian kettlebell full swing.

Kettlebell Snatch

Follow the same postural pattern as in the Russian kettlebell full swing, with the difference being that this must be done unilaterally. Place a kettlebell on the floor directly under the hips. The shoulders should be a "proud chest" position. Hinge at the hips to grasp the kettlebell with the right hand. The wrist should be slightly flexed. Explosively extend the hips and pull the kettlebell up, keeping it close to the body. As it passes head level, allow the kettlebell to rotate around the forearm and punch through at the top. Lower the kettlebell slowly to the starting position. Unravel the kettlebell back to the ground and repeat.

It is important to avoid rounding the back when picking up the kettlebell. Use a loose grip to avoid cutting the hands or calluses. Keep the kettlebell close to the body throughout the entire movement (see figure 5.14). Perform 2 to 3 sets of 10 repetitions on each side using a kettlebell weighing 20 to 40 pounds (9-18 kg).

Figure 5.14 – Kettlebell snatch.

Medicine Ball Throw Followed by 30-Meter (33 yd) Shuttle

Squat slightly and lean forward, pick up the ball (weighing 10-20 lb [4-9 kg]), and raise it to chest height. Throw the medicine ball forward, run at high speed to the ball, and throw it again, completing a 30-meter (33 yd) shuttle—that is, 60 meters (66 yd) total including the return trip (see figure 5.15). This exercise works various muscles in a dynamic, high-speed fashion. Perform this exercise for 2 or 3 sets with a rest of 1 minute between sets.

Figure 5.15 – Medicine ball throw followed by a run.

Wheelbarrow

One athlete holds the legs of the other athlete, who has their hands on the ground (see figure 5.16). They should run 30 meters (33 yd), changing places for the return journey, with active rest (shadow boxing) of 1 minute. Repeat this 2 or 3 times. This exercise requires balance, strength, and agility and works the legs, arms, and core.

Figure 5.16 – Wheelbarrow with Deivison Ribeiro and Ailton Barbosa.

30-Meter (33 yd) Runs

Perform 2 to 5 sets of 30-meter (33 yd) runs at maximum speed and with active rest of 1 minute (see figure 5.17).

Figure 5.17 – 30-meter (33 yd) run with Ailton and Cristiano.

Fireman's Lift Race

One athlete carries the other 30 meters (33 yd) to the end of the course (see figure 5.18). At this point, they change places before returning. Normally 1 to 4 sets are performed.

Figure 5.18 – Deivison running with Ailton in a fireman's lift.

Aerobic Run

The workout concludes with a 15- to 30-minute aerobic run. The recommended training should be performed once or twice a week.

Physical exercise in hot environments, such as training on the beach, may lead to hyperthermia (an increase of body temperature above normal ranges) and, in extreme cases, may lead to death. Therefore, if this kind of training is done without the aid of a medical professional, do the following (Dias, et al. 2017):

- Ingest fluids before exercise (300-500 mL).
- Ingest water or a sports drink with 6 percent carbohydrates and electrolytes, in an amount of around 100 mL to 300 mL (3-7 fl oz) for every 15 to 30 minutes of intense exercise.
- For exercise lasting less than 1 hour, the only replenishment should be water. When the activity lasts over 1 hour, drinks should also contain sodium, chloride, and carbohydrates.
- Cold drinks are absorbed more quickly than warm drinks.

- It is necessary to expose the body surface to the maximum extent possible to stimulate evaporation. Choose clothing made from light fabrics, such as cotton, that conduct the sweat to the surface for evaporation.
- In the event of dizziness, cramps due to the heat (very common in the calves), pallor, or an internal temperature exceeding 104 degrees Fahrenheit (40 degrees Celsius), stop all activity immediately and seek medical attention.

Table 5.2 presents an example of an outdoor body weight training program based on the previous outdoor exercises.

Table 5.2 – Outdoor Body Weight Training Program

	Week 1	Week 2	Week 3	Week 4
1. Tackle exercises with partner	× 8	× 10	× 12	× 14
2. Russian kettlebell full swing	2 × 15	2 × 20	3 × 15	3 × 20
3. Kettlebell snatch	2 × 10	2 × 10	3 × 10	3 × 10
4. Medicine ball throw + sprint (60 m [66 yd])	× 2	× 2	× 3	× 3
5. Wheelbarrow with partner (30 m [33 yd])	× 2	× 2	× 3	× 3
6. Sprints (30 m [33 yd])	× 2	× 3	× 4	× 5
7. Fireman's carry exercise with partner	× 1	× 2	× 3	× 4

Resistance Training

Muscle strength and power are required in different forms and magnitudes during sports activities. Among them, the literature highlights sprints, kicks, throws, punches, jumps, and direction changes. In MMA athletes, special attention should be given to isometric strength (Souza-Junior, et al. 2015). MMA fighters need to develop high levels of strength and power for success (UFC, 2021).

Traditional Resistance Training (Anatomical Adaptation)

Traditional or general resistance training is one of the most efficient methods for promoting increases in muscle strength. General resistance training usually involves using free weights and weight machines common in the gym setting (Souza-Junior, et al. 2015).

In the beginning of a training program, after a period of rest or low-intensity training, it is important to perform a training sequence to activate the main parts of the body, according to Bompa (2002). Therefore, using an anatomical adaptation (AA) phase is recommended, remembering the body's need for time to adapt to a new training stimulus.

The main function of the AA phase is to provide a process for strengthening tendons, ligaments, and muscle tissues, enabling the athlete to go on to the more intense phase of training injury-free (Brauer, et al. 2019; Bompa, 2004). In this first phase of the training process, we invited current ONE-FC champion Adriano Moraes; World Extreme Cagefighting (WEC) and UFC veteran Rafael Dias; and UFC, Bellator, and Strikeforce veteran

Shawn Jordan to demonstrate the best way to execute exercises that correctly develop anatomical adaptation.

Normally, an AA phase lasts 2 to 4 weeks, and before performing the training, always start with a short warm-up ranging from 5 to 15 minutes (Dias, et al. 2017).

Choose exercises that recruit all muscle groups. The choice of training loads and volume are also important factors, given that we are seeking to load the athlete's body gradually. At this stage, we normally use light or moderate loads and perform 1 to 3 sets per muscle group with between 15 and 20 repetitions.

Skipping Rope Warm-Up

Warm up by skipping rope. This movement is an excellent exercise in the world of fighting because it mobilizes the arms and legs in a movement coordinated with small jumps. The jumps may be performed with the feet together (see figure 5.19) or alternating from one foot to the other.

Figure 5.19 – Skipping rope.

Barbell Deadlift

This exercise has a high degree of difficulty because the athlete needs to control their posture when performing it (stabilization of the core). Using an Olympic bar to perform the movement, face the barbell with the legs slightly apart and abdominal muscles contracted. Flex the knees until the thighs are almost parallel to the floor. Use an over-under (alternated) grip on the bar with the hands slightly more than shoulder-width apart. Inhale, hold the breath, contract the core muscles, and lift the bar by extending the legs and allowing the bar to slide up the shins. When the bar reaches the knees, extend the torso while extending the knees. Stand upright with the arms straight down at the sides, exhaling at the end of the movement (see figure 5.20). This exercise works many muscles and is effective for developing lumbosacral and trapezius muscles. It also intensively works the gluteal muscles and quadriceps (Delavier, 2010).

Figure 5.20 – Barbell deadlift.

Barbell Bench Press

This traditional exercise uses a barbell and a bench with uprights. Lie on a horizontal bench so that the buttocks, shoulders, and head are firmly positioned on the bench and the feet are flat on the ground. Use an overhand grip at a distance greater than shoulder width. During execution, inhale and lower the barbell, flexing the elbows to the chest with a controlled movement. After brief contact, push the barbell upward, extending the arms and exhaling at the end of the effort (Baechle and Earle, 2020). This exercise engages the complete pectoralis major muscle, pectoralis minor, anterior deltoid, serratus anterior, coracobrachialis, and triceps brachii (Delavier, 2010). Perform an eccentric action in its initial lowering phase and a concentric contraction in its lifting or return phase (see figure 5.21).

Figure 5.21 – Barbell bench press.

One-Arm Dumbbell Row

Kneel one leg on a free bench. Support the other leg against the side of the bench and rest one hand on the bench to align the upper body so that the exercise may be performed safely (see figure 5.22). Inhale and lift the upper arm and elbow of the arm holding the dumbbell as high as possible, keeping it next to the body with the elbow flexed. Exhale at the end of the movement. This exercise works the latissimus dorsi, teres major, posterior deltoid, and, at the end of the movement, the trapezius and rhomboids. The forearm flexors (biceps brachii, brachialis, and brachioradialis) are also stimulated (Delavier, 2010).

Figure 5.22 – One-arm dumbbell row.

Lateral Dumbbell Raise

Stand with a straight back, legs slightly apart, and arms hanging next to the body. Hold a dumbbell in each hand. Raise the arms to horizontal (shoulder height), keeping the elbows slightly flexed. Then return to the initial position (see figure 5.23). This exercise works the deltoid muscles (anterior, middle, and posterior deltoid) but mainly the middle deltoid (Delavier, 2010).

Figure 5.23 – Lateral dumbbell raise.

EzBar Biceps Curl

The EzBar biceps curl is a variation of the barbell curl. The bar shape minimizes wrist tension. Considered a basic exercise where the action is to flex the elbow, it can be performed in a standing position with the legs parallel or with a staggered stance (see figure 5.24). Grasp the EzBar with the palms facing forward and thumbs pointing laterally. The torso and shoulder joints should be aligned (with the shoulder blades pulled in toward each other). Using heavy loads for this exercise is not recommended at this stage, because the torso may move too much when lifting the weight. The abdominal and spinal muscles stabilize the exercise. Inhale and raise the bar by flexing the elbows. Exhale at the end of the movement. This exercise mainly contracts the biceps brachii, brachialis, and, to a lesser degree, the brachioradialis, pronator teres, and wrist flexor group (Delavier, 2010).

Figure 5.24 – EzBar biceps curl.

EzBar Lying Triceps Extension

Begin by lying in a supine position, holding the bar with an overhand grip and the arms extended (see figure 5.25a). Inhale and lower the bar to the forehead or until it has passed head level (eccentric phase) (see figure 5.25b), then return it to the starting position, extending the arms fully (concentric phase). Exhale at the end of the movement. Using an EzBar helps prevent excessive strain at the wrists. This exercise is important for the triceps brachii muscles (medial head, lateral head, and long head).

Figure 5.25 – EzBar lying triceps extension.

Leg Extension

Sit on the equipment, grasping the handles to hold the torso immobile. Flex the knees and place the ankles under the ankle pads (see figure 5.26). Inhale and extend the legs until they are horizontal. If there is an injury limitation, the coach should control the angle at which the exercise is performed. Exhale at the end of the movement. This is a great exercise for isolating the quadriceps (rectus femoris, vastus lateralis, vastus medialis, and vastus intermedius).

Figure 5.26 – Leg extension.

Lying Leg Curl

Lie facedown on the machine. Grasp the handles, extend both legs, and position the ankles under the ankle pads (see figure 5.27). Inhale and flex both knees at the same time, trying to touch the gluteal muscles with the heels. Exhale at the end of the effort and return to the initial position in a controlled manner (Delavier, 2010). This exercise works the hamstring group (semitendinosus; biceps femoris, long head; semimembranosus; and biceps femoris, short head) and gastrocnemius (medial head and lateral head).

Figure 5.27 – Lying leg curl.

Alternate Front Arm Raise

Stand with the feet slightly apart. Hold the dumbbells with an overhand grip as they rest to the sides of the body. Inhale and alternate raising the dumbbells with a straight arm to the front to shoulder height (see figure 5.28). Exhale at the end of the effort. This exercise may be executed with a pronated, supinated, or neutral grip. This exercise uses mainly the anterior deltoid and, to a lesser degree, the middle and posterior deltoid (Delavier, 2010).

Figure 5.28 – Alternate front arm raise.

Leg Raise

In this abdominal exercise, the athlete supports themselves with the arms extended (straight arms) on the apparatus (see figure 5.29a). Inhale and raise the knees to the chest to contract the abdominal core (see figure 5.29b). Exhale at the end of the movement. The action of the abdominal muscles and hip flexors, mainly the iliopsoas, are essential to the performance of this movement. This exercise also works the rectus femoris, tensor fasciae latae, and, to a lesser degree, the internal and external obliques. It intensely works the lower part of the rectus abdominis (Delavier, 2010).

Figure 5.29 — Leg raise.

Back Extension

Lie facedown on a Roman chair and place the ankles under the roller pads. This exercise could be performed on a machine or on the floor; in figure 5.30, it is performed using a Roman chair. With the torso flexed forward, extend back to horizontal, raise the head, and continue into a light hyperextension by arching the lumbar spine. This exercise mainly develops the group of paraspinal erectors of the spine (iliocostalis, longissimus thoracis, spinalis thoracis, splenius, and semispinalis capitis), quadratus lumborum, and, to a lesser degree, the gluteus maximus and the hamstrings, except for the short head of the biceps femoris (Delavier, 2010).

Figure 5.30 — Back extension.

Based on the practical application of this program over several years for elite athletes, we know the anatomical adaptation program is necessary for athletes to aid longevity and reduce injuries. Plan the training on a case-by-case basis, choosing the exercises according to the needs of the athlete and the volume and intensity used in this phase. This training program may be implemented one to three times a week, with at least one day of rest between sessions (Dias, et al. 2017). Table 5.3 includes two training programs for the anatomical adaptation phase.

Table 5.3 – Two Anatomical Adaptation Phase Programs

	Week 1	Week 2	Week 3	Week 4
Training A				
1. Barbell deadlift	1 × 15	2 × 20	3 × 15	3 × 20
2. Barbell bench press	1 × 15	1 × 20	2 × 15	3 × 15
3. One-arm dumbbell row	1 × 15	1 × 20	2 × 15	3 × 15
4. Lateral dumbbell raise	1 × 15	1 × 20	2 × 15	3 × 15
5. Alternate front arm raise	1 × 15	1 × 20	2 × 15	3 × 15
6. Leg raise	2 × 25	3 × 25	2 × 30	3 × 30
7. Back extension	2 × 15	2 × 15	3 × 15	3 × 15
Training B				
1. Barbell bench press	1 × 15	2 × 20	3 × 15	3 × 20
2. Leg extension	2 × 15	2 × 20	3 × 15	3 × 20
3. Lying leg curl	2 × 15	2 × 20	3 × 15	3 × 20
4. EzBar biceps curl	1 × 15	1 × 20	2 × 15	2 × 20
5. EzBar lying triceps extension	1 × 15	1 × 20	2 × 15	2 × 20
6. Abdominals	2 × 25	3 × 25	2 × 30	3 × 30
7. Back extension	2 × 15	2 × 15	3 × 15	3 × 15

Maximum Training for Strength (Total Body)

Strength is the ability of the neuromuscular system to produce internal tension to overcome an external load (Sutton, 2022). Resistance training is excellent for building muscle strength and, to a lesser extent, muscular endurance (ACSM, 2012). Strength improves when sufficient tension is applied in the muscle fibers and their contractile proteins. Muscle contraction involves different cellular proteins and energy production systems in a complex process. As a result, we have the slippage of actin myofilaments over myosin, developing tension and making the muscle contract. For maximum strength gains to occur, it is important to use loads greater than 60 percent of 1RM (Dias, et al. 2017). To optimize these maximum muscle strength gains, Fleck and Kraemer (2004) recommended using loads of 75 percent to 90 percent of one repetition maximum (1RM).

Muscle contractions may be divided into the following:

- *Reflexive contraction*—involuntary muscle movement due to reflexes
- *Tonic contraction*—contractions maintained even when the muscle is "relaxed" and helps maintain posture—for example, of the neck—and tonus of the fingers

- *Isotonic contraction,* further divided into the following:
  - *Concentric contraction*—muscle contraction in which the muscles contract during the generation of force
  - *Isometric contraction*—the muscle generates force without changing length but with a greater tension than tonic contraction
  - *Eccentric action*—when the muscle lengthens because the contractile force is less than the resistive force (Haff and Triplett, 2016)

To improve maximum strength, the muscular system must be progressively overloaded by an increase in load, repetitions, or sets. The most prominent adaptations for resistance training include increases in muscle strength and muscle volume, a condition called *hypertrophy* (ACSM, 2012; Haff and Triplett, 2016).

At the beginning of the resistance training program, strength gains occur due to neural factors, such as an increase in neural muscle stimulation, an increase in motor unit synchronization, and an improvement in contractile protein activation (Wilmore and Costill, 2008). After six to eight weeks of progressive resistance training, gains in hypertrophy of the muscle fibers begin to occur due to an increase in the number of filaments of actin and myosin. Other adaptations that lead to improvements in strength include increases in the concentration of muscle phosphocreatine (PCr) and activity of the glycolytic enzymes (ACSM, 2012).

For correct resistance training, we should highlight the following details (ACSM, 2012; Dias, et al. 2017; Haff and Triplett, 2016):

- The execution speed is normally slow to moderate and high speed in some specific cases.
- The number of repetitions is 2RM to 6RM.
- The rest between the sets is two to five minutes.
- The number of sets is two to six.
- The rest between training days may vary from 48 hours to seven days.

To show how to perform resistance training effectively and injury-free, we invited UFC fighters Shawn Jordan, Carmelo Marrero, Thiago "Marreta" Santos, and Santiago Ponzinibbio (also called the "Argentine Dagger") to demonstrate.

Normally after a brief warm-up (5-15 minutes), we begin resistance training with more complex exercises and movements that demand more energy, such as squats, bench presses, and rowing for the back (given that, at the beginning of the training session, athletes have more energy and optimal conditions in the central nervous system). After this, we will work on smaller muscle groups, such as the biceps or triceps, or break the training up (e.g., one day we train all the major muscle groups [legs, chest, and back]; on another day we train the rest of the body [shoulders, biceps, triceps, abdominals, etc.]).

On this occasion, after performing one or two exercises for the lower body, we took a brief rest and moved on to the upper body, working on exercises for the chest or back. After working all the major muscle groups with at least one exercise, including one more exercise for the legs, chest, and back may be recommended, if necessary. At the end of each training session, we also recommend auxiliary exercises for the core and the neck. We recommend training B in table 5.4 to build strength in the shoulders, biceps, triceps, calves, and so on, always alternating between one day of strength work and one day of rest.

Back Squat

The squat has a high degree of difficulty. With the barbell resting on a stand, slide under the bar and place it on the trapezius. Grasp the bar firmly with the hands at a comfortable width and keep the elbows back. Inhale deeply to maintain the intrathoracic pressure, contract the abdominal core, look straight ahead, and remove the barbell from the stand. Step back two steps and stop with both feet parallel to each other and hip-width or shoulder-width apart (see figure 5.31a). Flex forward from the hips and avoid rounding the back to prevent injury. Squat until the angle predetermined by the coach or when the thighs are horizontal to the floor (see figure 5.31b), then extend the knees and lift the torso to return to the initial position. The squat may also be performed on equipment such as the Smith Machine or a back squat machine, or as a free-weight exercise with dumbbells, with these variations to be decided by the coach according to the specific goal and limitations of the athlete. The back squat mainly works the quadriceps, gluteal muscles, adductor group, erector spinae, abdominal muscles, and hamstrings (Delavier, 2010).

Figure 5.31 – Back squat.

Cable Chest Press

The barbell bench press is normally our first choice of exercise for the upper body. The bench press is a basic, multijoint exercise widely used to develop the chest muscles, but we would like to demonstrate a variation here: the cable chest press using the crossover. Sit on the bench with the arms at a 90-degree angle (see figure 5.32a). Head, shoulders, and buttocks stay on the bench, and the feet are flat on the floor. Hold the cables, inhale, and push to full elbow extension (see figure 5.32b). Exhale at the end of the movement. This exercise works similar muscles to the bench press but with a higher degree of complexity due to some instability of the cables requiring extra coordination.

Figure 5.32 – Cable chest press.

Lat Pulldown With a Plate Machine

This articulated machine with weight plates allows the athlete to perform bilateral or unilateral movements. The independent arms ensure a more balanced strength improvement and provide the feel of free weights in a guided environment. Sit and face the machine with the legs under the pads and grip the bar with a wide overhand grip (see figure 5.33a). Inhale and pull the bar down to the sternal notch while pulling the elbows back (see figure 5.33b). Exhale at the end of the movement. This exercise mainly works the upper and central fibers of the latissimus dorsi. The middle and lower portions of the trapezius, the rhomboids, and the biceps brachii (Delavier, 2010) are also engaged.

Figure 5.33 – Lat pulldown with a plate machine.

Plank

This isometric exercise strengthens the abdominal and lumbar regions, which are fundamental during a fight because this is how an athlete maintains posture, fighting stance, and support to be able to execute the widest range of fighting moves. This plank may be performed in a prone position: facedown, on the tips of the toes, feet parallel, legs extended, and the torso supported on the forearms. The isometric contraction and support should be provided by all the muscles in the abdominal, lumbar, and pelvic regions, and it is vitally important to activate and contract the gluteal muscles, thus keeping the back straight along its entire length (see figure 5.34a). This isolation exercise works the entire abdominal wall (Delavier and Gundill, 2013). This same exercise may also be performed laterally. In the side plank (see figure 5.34b), the upper body is supported on the forearm. But unlike the abdominal plank, the body will only be supported on one foot, the outer part of which will be in contact with the floor, with the other foot on top of it. This position should be repeated on both sides. As with the plank, this exercise involves isometric muscle contractions and activates the muscles that stabilize the spine, which, during fights, tend to generate force resulting in punches. It is also responsible for absorbing impacts at waist level.

Figure 5.34 – (a) Plank and (b) side plank.

Table 5.4 presents three programs for maximum strength.

Table 5.4 – Maximum Strength (Total Body) Programs

	Week 1	Week 2	Week 3	Week 4
Training A				
1. Back squat	2 × 8RM	2 × 6RM	3 × 4RM	4 × 2RM
2. Cable chest press	2 × 8RM	2 × 6RM	3 × 4RM	4 × 2RM
3. Lat pulldown with a plate machine	2 × 8RM	2 × 6RM	3 × 4RM	4 × 2RM
4. Plank	2 × 20 sec	3 × 20 sec	3 × 25 sec	3 × 30 sec
5. Side plank	2 × 20 sec each side	3 × 20 sec each side	3 × 25 sec each side	3 × 30 sec each side
Training B				
1. Seated dumbbell press	2 × 8RM	2 × 8RM	3 × 6RM	3 × 6RM
2. Barbell curl	2 × 8RM	2 × 8RM	3 × 6RM	3 × 6RM
3. Triceps pushdown	2 × 8RM	2 × 8RM	3 × 6RM	3 × 6RM
4. Seated machine calf raise	2 × 8RM	2 × 8RM	3 × 6RM	3 × 6RM
5. Crunch	2 × 20 sec	3 × 20 sec	3 × 25 sec	3 × 30 sec
Training C				
1. Deadlift	2 × 8RM	2 × 6RM	3 × 4RM	4 × 2RM
2. Barbell bench press	2 × 8RM	2 × 6RM	3 × 4RM	4 × 2RM
3. Power clean	2 × 6RM	2 × 4RM	3 × 2RM	4 × 1RM
4. Plank	2 × 20 sec	3 × 20 sec	3 × 25 sec	3 × 30 sec
5. Side plank	2 × 20 sec each side	3 × 20 sec each side	3 × 25 sec each side	3 × 30 sec each side

Split Routines (Different Muscle Groups)

Split-routine training isolates different parts of the body on different training days. It is also widely used in hypertrophy programs. First, understand that muscle hypertrophy means the enlargement of the muscle fiber cross-sectional area (CSA) following training. The hypertrophy process involves an increase in the net accretion of the contractile proteins actin and myosin within the myofibril, as well as an increase in the number (hyperplasia) of myofibrils within a muscle fiber (Haff and Triplett, 2016; Dias, et al. 2017). This process arises during the acceleration of protein biosynthesis, reduction in degradation, or both (Haff and Triplett, 2016). Research has revealed four main factors affecting the acceleration of protein biosynthesis in the cell (Dias, et al. 2017):

1. Amino acid reserves in the cell (amino acids accumulate after ingestion of foods rich in proteins)

2. A positive increase in anabolic hormones concentration (naturally) in the blood as a result of psychological stress (effort); the hormones are produced and released according to the increase in the loads and physical stress imposed by training with high intensity or to muscle failure

3. A high concentration of free creatine in the muscle fibers serves as an endogenous stimulus, which increases protein biosynthesis in the muscles (this factor derives from sets in which the contraction time is between 20-50 seconds or between 10-20 repetitions)

4. The increase in hydrogen ion concentration causes membrane labilization (an increase in membrane pore size), facilitating hormone penetration into the muscle cells (for this, a training session with a high volume and a short rest between sets is required, in which fatigue will be felt in the activated muscles)

The second, third, and fourth factors are directly linked to the content of the training exercises, which we will show for the different muscle groups in the sections that follow.

To activate fast-twitch muscle fibers, the exercises must be performed with maximal or submaximal intensity. According to the "size principle" Henneman and colleagues (1965) proposed, slow- and fast-twitch muscle fibers are going to be actively recruited. If muscle contraction is combined with relaxation (such as a brief pause between the repetitions of a set), this will not interrupt blood circulation, and the effects of the exercise will be predominately directed to the fast-twitch muscle fibers.

To achieve the desired objectives, there are various methods and training systems, which gives rise to controversy about the superiority of one method over another. However, because there are few studies on the various methods, claims that one is better than another are generally unfounded. Very often, one person may respond better or worse to a certain system, but that does not mean that the training method is "the best" or "the worst." Rather, it means that this individual responds to it more positively or negatively. Ultimately, when we talk about increasing muscle mass or strength, many variables must be considered, including nutrition and rest, not only the physical training. Other details that should be targeted include the following:

- Exercise execution speed is normally slow or moderate.
- The rest between the sets is one to three minutes and sometimes longer.
- The number of sets per exercise is three to five.
- The rest between training days may vary from 48 hours to seven days.

Leg Training

The legs have a wide variety of muscles. To exercise them all, or at least most of them, many exercises are required using different angles. In this section, we invited former UFC heavyweight Shawn Jordan and UFC and WEC veteran Carmelo Marrero to demonstrate different ways to effectively train the lower body.

Back Squat

The back squat (see figure 5.31 on page 149) may also be performed on equipment such as the Smith Machine or back squat machine, or as a free-weight exercise with dumbbells. The coach should decide variations according to the specific goal and limitations of the athlete.

Single-Leg Squat

This exercise follows similar parameters as the back squat, but with the added difficulty of being performed on one leg. The athlete needs to have coordination and find the point of balance needed to perform the exercise. It may be done with body weight, dumbbells, or a medicine ball. Start by standing on the left foot. Lift the right leg out and hold it out straight and slightly in front of the torso (see figure 5.35a). Another variation is to flex the knee and keep the right leg elevated from the start. Arms are placed along the sides of the body, out in front for balance, or crossed at shoulder level to increase the difficulty of the exercise. Keep the core engaged and torso upright throughout the movement. Inhale and push the hips back as the body lowers into a squat position (see figure 5.35b). The goal is to get low enough so that the hips are parallel to the ground or until the bench is touched. Squeeze the glutes and push into the left foot to stand back up and exhale at the end of the movement. This exercise works the following muscles: glutes, calves, thighs, hamstrings, and, to a lesser degree, core muscles.

Figure 5.35 – Single-leg squat.

Leg Extension

As explained in figure 5.26 on page 144, sit on the machine and extend the legs until completion (if there is any limitation, the coach should control the angle at which the exercise is performed). This exercise works the quadriceps (rectus femoris, vastus lateralis, vastus medialis, and vastus intermedius).

Barbell Deadlift

Like the squat, this exercise also has a high degree of difficulty because the athlete needs to control posture (stabilization of the core). For more information on how to execute the barbell deadlift, see figure 5.20 on page 141. This exercise works many muscles and could be used during leg or back training, depending on the goals.

Single-Leg Romanian Deadlift (RDL)

Stand with the feet shoulder-width apart and knees slightly flexed and raise one leg off the floor. Inhale, flex the knee on the standing or support leg 15 percent to 20 percent to activate the glutes. Without changing the flex in the knee, keep the back naturally arched, flex (hinge) at the hips, and lower the torso until it is almost parallel to the floor. Briefly pause at the bottom, squeeze the glutes, and thrust the hips forward, then raise the torso back to the starting position, exhaling at the end of the movement. Repeat until the prescribed number of repetitions is completed on each leg. To make this exercise harder, hold a dumbbell in the opposite arm (contralateral), like in figure 5.36. This functional exercise strengthens many muscles of the posterior chain, including the hamstrings, gluteal complex, and lumbar erector spinae muscles (Sutton, 2022). This variation is used to develop balance and motor coordination and is used with traditional basic leg exercises.

Figure 5.36 – Single-leg Romanian deadlift (RDL).

Standing Calf Raise With Dumbbells

Stand on a step and slowly dorsiflex the feet (lower the heels) until a light stretch is felt in the calves (see figure 5.37*a*). Then plantarflex (rise on the toes) while keeping the knees extended or slightly flexed (see figure 5.37*b*). This is a specific exercise for the calves in which dumbbells are used to overload the muscles. Variations may be performed with a barbell or on equipment such as a calf machine. This exercise mainly works the triceps surae (made up of the two gastrocnemius and the soleus) as well as the flexor hallucis longus, tibialis posterior, and flexor digitorum longus (Delavier, 2010).

Figure 5.37 – Standing calf raise with dumbbells.

Dumbbell Lunge

Stand with the legs slightly apart and hold a dumbbell in each hand (see figure 5.38*a*). Inhale and take a big step forward, keeping the torso as straight as possible. When the forward thigh reaches horizontal (see figure 5.38*b*), return to the initial position. Exhale at the end of the movement. Perform a complete set on one side and then the other or work the legs alternately doing a walking lunge. This exercise mainly works the gluteus maximus and quadriceps (Delavier, 2010).

Figure 5.38 – Dumbbell lunge.

Dumbbell Lateral Lunge

Following the same idea as in the previous exercise, in the lateral lunge, stand tall with dumbbells in both hands (see figure 5.39a). Arms are at the sides and the palms face in. The feet are hip-width apart. After inhaling, take a big step to the left and land in a wide stance that is approximately double shoulder width. As the left foot lands, hinge at the hips, allowing them to move back and flex. Flex the left knee so the left shin is vertical and in line with the left ankle. Keeping the back straight, continue to hinge at the hips and reach the dumbbells to each side of the left foot (see figure 5.39b). Once at the bottom of the movement, push off the left foot to extend the body and step back to the starting position. Exhale at the end of the movement. Repeat on the other side. This exercise works the hamstrings, adductors, and gluteus.

Figure 5.39 – Dumbbell lateral lunge.

Nordic Hamstring Curl

This is a functional exercise performed with body weight. The Nordic hamstring curl involves kneeling on a pad (for knee comfort) while the ankles are held in place by a partner, a loaded barbell, or any other immovable object (see figure 5.40a). Then extend the hamstring muscles to lean forward from the knees, not from the hips (see figure 5.40b).

The movement should be slow and controlled. Come as forward or low to the floor as possible without using the hands or arms until the leg muscles alone cannot sustain the movements. Then pull back to the starting position. Be aware of possible delayed onset muscle soreness (DOMS) when adding this exercise to training sessions. Start slowly and adhere to a sound progressive overload strategy.

Start with just a few repetitions, do not bring the body lower than can be managed easily, and build to more repetitions and greater range of movement. Nordic hamstring curls can help protect the hamstrings by strengthening them through the lengthened state, eccentric action, and building strength at the end of the range of motion. This work in the lengthened position both strengthens the muscle group and helps prevent injury (Chebbi, et al. 2020).

Figure 5.40 – Nordic hamstring curl.

Dumbbell Step-Up

This exercise is performed with dumbbells and a step, box, or bench. Stand on the floor behind the bench, place the left foot flat on top of the bench (see figure 5.41a), and inhale. Using only the left leg, step onto the bench with the right leg (see figure 5.41b). Using only the left leg, step down to the floor with the right leg. Exhale at the end of the movement. Repeat the stepping action for the desired repetitions and perform on both sides. This exercise works the quadriceps, hamstrings, and gluteal muscles.

Figure 5.41 – Dumbbell step-up.

Table 5.5 presents two programs for training the legs in a split routine. These exercises and programs provide a basis for proper planning for strength and hypertrophy. Should practitioners decide to use both training programs in the same week, we recommend a rest of at least 72 hours between training sessions for the legs.

Table 5.5 – Leg Training Programs

	Week 1	Week 2	Week 3	Week 4
Training A				
1. Back squat	2 × 12RM	2 × 10RM	3 × 8RM	4 × 6RM
2. Dumbbell lunge	2 × 10 each leg	2 × 10 each leg	3 × 10 each leg	3 × 10 each leg
3. Leg extension	2 × 12RM	2 × 12RM	3 × 10RM	3 × 10RM
4. Lying leg curl	2 × 12RM	2 × 12RM	3 × 10RM	3 × 10RM
5. Dumbbell step-up	2 × 10 each leg	2 × 10 each leg	3 × 10 each leg	3 × 10 each leg
6. Single-leg squat	2 × 10 each leg	2 × 10 each leg	3 × 10 each leg	3 × 10 each leg
7. Isoton leg press (see description of Isoton method in chapter 2 or at the end of this chapter)	3 × 30 sec @ 35% 1RM	3 × 30 sec @ 35% 1RM	4 × 30 sec @ 40% 1RM	4 × 30 sec @ 40% 1RM
Training B				
1. Barbell deadlift	2 × 12RM	2 × 10RM	3 × 8RM	4 × 6RM
2. Single-leg RDL	2 × 10 each leg	2 × 10 each leg	3 × 10 each leg	3 × 10 each leg
3. Standing calf raise with dumbbells	3 × 15RM	3 × 15RM	4 × 12RM	4 × 12RM
4. Nordic hamstring curl	1 × 10 BW	2 × 10 BW	3 × 10 BW	4 × 10 BW
5. Dumbbell lateral lunge	2 × 10 each leg	2 × 10 each leg	3 × 10 each leg	3 × 10 each leg
6. Isoton leg press (see description of Isoton method in chapter 2 or at the end of this chapter)	3 × 30 sec @ 35% 1RM	3 × 30 sec @ 35% 1RM	4 × 30 sec @ 40% 1RM	4 × 30 sec @ 40% 1RM

BW: body weight

Chest Training

In this section, we invited the top-level participant in The Ultimate Fighter (TUF): Brazil and a person in the top five in UFC rankings, Thiago "Marreta" Santos, to demonstrate how to increase chest muscle volume. The chest muscles are divided into two parts, the pectoralis major and minor, which perform the following actions: horizontal adduction, medial or internal rotation, horizontal flexion, and depression of the shoulders.

Cable Crossover Fly

Stand with the legs staggered. Lean the torso forward a little, keeping the arms spread and the elbows slightly flexed (see figure 5.42*a*). Inhale and squeeze the arms together until the handles touch (see figure 5.42*b*). Exhale at the end of the movement. Return in a controlled manner to the initial position and repeat. Variations of different angles may be created according to the settings of the equipment used to exercise the pectoralis major and pectoralis minor muscles.

Figure 5.42 – Thiago Santos performing cable crossover fly.

Dumbbell Fly

The dumbbell fly is a single-joint exercise. The body is in supine position (belly up) and the arms are lowered out to the sides, toward the floor. The glenohumeral joint is the main axis of movement. Pay attention to the angles of this movement for best results. This exercise may be used to generate a state of pre-exhaustion before a compound lift. For example, the athlete can pre-exhaust the auxiliary musculature of the chest with the chest fly before performing a bench press. Lie on a narrow bench that will not interfere with shoulder movement and hold a dumbbell in each hand, the arms in a vertical position with the elbows slightly flexed to relieve stress on the elbow joint (see figure 5.43*a*). Inhale and open the arms to a horizontal position (see figure 5.43*b*). Raise the arms to a vertical position while exhaling. This exercise works the pectoralis major and should be performed with moderate loads to avoid injury.

Figure 5.43 – Dumbbell fly.

Incline Bench Press

Sit on an incline bench at 45 to 60 degrees and grasp the barbell with an overhand grip wider than shoulder width (see figure 5.44a). Inhale and lower the barbell to the sternal notch (see figure 5.44b). Extend the arms and exhale at the end of the movement. This exercise works the clavicular head of the pectoralis major, anterior deltoid, triceps brachii, serratus anterior, and pectoralis minor (Delavier, 2010).

Figure 5.44 – Incline bench press.

Incline Dumbbell Fly

This exercise has the same technique as the dumbbell fly. Only the bench angle differs (see figure 5.45).

Figure 5.45 – Incline dumbbell fly.

Push-Up

This exercise is performed with an overload of the person's own body weight and may be executed anywhere with a flat surface. Lie facedown on the ground with the arms extended and hands shoulder-width apart or making a fist to increase exercise difficulty. The feet should be touching or slightly apart (see figure 5.46a). Inhale and flex the elbows to bring the rib cage close to the ground without arching the low back (see figure 5.46b). Push back up to complete the arm extension, exhaling at the end of the movement. The push-up could be used with a narrow hand placement. The advantage over the bench press is that the shoulder blades are not immobilized on a bench. This forces the serratus anterior to stabilize the shoulder blades. The serratus muscles also help project the arm when extending, so these muscles could increase punching power (Delavier and Gundill, 2013). This exercise works the pectoralis major, triceps brachii, and anterior deltoid. Some variations of angle and range of motion may be used with the aid of steps, a medicine ball, and so on.

Figure 5.46 – Push-up.

Dumbbell Bench Press

This exercise is similar to the barbell bench press, but dumbbells allow a greater range of motion with a greater degree of difficulty in terms of execution, balance, and stabilization (Dias, et al. 2017). Lie faceup on a flat bench, feet on the ground for stability and elbows flexed. Hold the dumbbells with an overhand grip at chest level (see figure 5.47a). Inhale and extend the arms vertically until the dumbbells touch each other (see figure 5.47b). Exhale at the end of the movement. This exercise works the pectoralis muscles, triceps brachii, and anterior deltoid.

Figure 5.47 – Dumbbell bench press.

Incline Dumbbell Press

This exercise is similar to the dumbbell press. The main difference is that the athlete uses a bench with no more than a 60-degree angle to avoid overworking the deltoid (see figure 5.48). This exercise works the pectoralis (mainly the clavicular head), the anterior deltoid, the serratus anterior, and the triceps brachii (Delavier, 2010).

Figure 5.48 – Incline dumbbell press.

Punching With Resistance Bands

This exercise was developed in adapted training for MMA, boxing, and Muay Thai. Stand, holding the resistance bands behind the body in fighting stance. Then, grab the handle and strike as fast as possible (see figure 5.49) before returning to the initial position. This exercise works the pectorals, deltoid, triceps brachii, serratus anterior, thighs, calves, and various other muscles to stabilize movement, such as the core muscles (Dias, et al. 2017).

Figure 5.49 – Punching with resistance bands.

Table 5.6 includes two programs for training the chest muscles.

Table 5.6 – Chest Training Programs

	Week 1	Week 2	Week 3	Week 4
Training A				
1. Barbell bench press	2 × 12RM	2 × 10RM	3 × 8RM	4 × 6RM
2. Dumbbell fly	2 × 12RM	2 × 12RM	3 × 10RM	3 × 10RM
3. Incline bench press	2 × 12RM	2 × 10RM	3 × 8RM	3 × 6RM
4. Cable crossover fly	2 × 12RM	2 × 12RM	3 × 10RM	3 × 10RM
5. Isoton push-up (see description of Isoton method in chapter 2 or at the end of this chapter)	3 × 30 sec, BW	3 × 35 sec, BW	4 × 30 sec, BW	4 × 35 sec, BW
Training B				
1. Dumbbell bench press	2 × 12RM	3 × 10RM	4 × 8RM	1 × 12RM + 1 × 10RM + 1 × 8RM + 1 × 6RM
2. Incline dumbbell press	2 × 12RM	2 × 10RM	3 × 8RM	4 × 6RM
3. Cable chest press	2 × 12RM	2 × 12RM	3 × 10RM	3 × 10RM
4. Cable crossover fly	2 × 12RM	2 × 12RM	3 × 10RM	3 × 10RM
5. Punching with resistance bands	2 × 10 each arm	2 × 15 each arm	3 × 15 each arm	3 × 20 each arm
6. Isoton push-up (see description of Isoton method in chapter 2 or at the end of this chapter)	3 × 30 sec, BW	3 × 35 sec, BW	4 × 30 sec, BW	4 × 35 sec, BW

BW: body weight

Back Training

In this section, we visited the Institute of Human Performance (IHP) in Boca Raton, Florida, and invited Santiago Ponzinibbio, who is ranked in the top 10 in the UFC, to demonstrate back muscle training.

Seated Row

This exercise varies according to the machine available to perform the movement. We are using a Technogym machine with dual pulleys, which allows some variations in the execution with the option to perform it bilaterally or unilaterally. Sit, keeping the chest at the height of the machine backrest and the arms aligned (see figure 5.50a). Inhale and pull the elbows back as far as possible (see figure 5.50b). Exhale at the end of the movement and return to the initial position. This exercise works the latissimus dorsi, teres major, posterior deltoid, biceps brachii, brachioradialis, and, at the end of the movement, the trapezius and rhomboids (Delavier, 2010).

Figure 5.50 – Seated row.

Clinch on MV^2 VersaPulley Machine

This machine is a gravity-free resistance system using a rotational inertia mechanism with an infinitely variable cam to store the energy a trainee provides through the concentric contraction. Then it releases the energy right back for the trainee to dissipate during the eccentric action. This exercise works on the clinch with additional load. The clinch is a movement characteristic of Muay Thai and is widely used in MMA competitions. Stand with the legs apart in a staggered position and the arms extended (see figure 5.51a), gripping in a manner similar to the clinch. Then pull the arms to the chest (see figure 5.51b). This exercise may be performed on any cable machine, such as the crossover, pulley, and so on. We usually use the MV^2 VersaPulley machine, because the faster and stronger the athlete pulls the clinch, the greater the resistance. This exercise works the arms, forearms, and back muscles.

Figure 5.51 – Clinch on the MV pulley machine.

Wide-Grip Chin-Up

This exercise uses body weight and may be performed in gyms, parks, or anywhere such equipment is available. The movement may be performed using wide or narrow grips according to the program chosen. In this case, priority is given to the wide grip. To execute this exercise, hang from a fixed bar with an overhand grip. Inhale and pull the chest up to the level of the bar (see figure 5.52). Exhale at the end of the movement and return to the initial position in a controlled manner. This exercise works the latissimus dorsi, teres major, rhomboids, middle and lower portion of the trapezius, biceps brachii, brachialis, and brachioradialis (Delavier and Gundill, 2013).

Figure 5.52 – Wide-grip chin-up.

Cable Lat Pulldown

This exercise varies according to the equipment. The dual pulleys the Technogym offers enable work to be performed at different angles and unilaterally or bilaterally. This exercise may also be performed on a regular pulley with narrow or wide grips or using the articulated machine with weight plates as shown in figure 5.33. Sit facing the machine with the thighs under the pads and with the upper body straight (see figure 5.53a). Inhale and pull the cable down while pulling the elbows back (see figure 5.53b). Exhale at the end of the movement. This exercise works the latissimus dorsi, the middle and lower portions of the trapezius, the rhomboids, the biceps brachii, and the brachialis.

Figure 5.53 – Cable lat pulldown.

Dumbbell Pullover

This exercise may be performed with a dumbbell, barbell, or cable. Lie down with the upper part of the back on a bench, keeping the torso straight and the hips raised. Hold a dumbbell in the palms of both hands in line with the chest with a narrow grip. Inhale and lower the dumbbell behind the head, flexing slightly at the elbows (see figure 5.54). Exhale at the end of the movement and return to the initial position. While we chose to place the pullover exercise within the back training program, it involves both the back and chest muscles. This exercise works the pectoralis major, long head of the triceps brachii, teres major, latissimus dorsi, serratus anterior, rhomboids, and pectoralis minor (Delavier, 2010).

Figure 5.54 – Dumbbell pullover.

Standing Cable Row

This exercise is performed in a parallel stance, rather than seated with the legs resting on the machine. Facing the loading point, stand in a parallel stance with the feet shoulder-width apart and a handle in each hand. Slightly flex the knees and lean back as necessary to counterbalance the load (see figure 5.55a). Inhale and pull the handles back simultaneously until the hands are outside the chest while keeping the core tight (see figure 5.55b). Exhale at the end of the movement and return the hands to the starting position. This variation builds the back muscles by generating a greater degree of difficulty in terms of posture and movement stabilization.

Figure 5.55 – Standing cable row.

One-Arm Dumbbell Row

Put one knee and one arm on a flat bench and the other leg on the ground. Grasp a dumbbell with the palm facing in (see figure 5.56). Inhale and lift the upper arm and elbow as high as possible next to the body with the elbow flexed. Exhale at the end of the movement. Repeat until the prescribed number of repetitions is completed for each arm. This exercise works the latissimus dorsi, teres major, posterior deltoid, trapezius, rhomboids, and forearm flexors.

Figure 5.56 – One-arm dumbbell row.

Row Against the Wall With Rope

This exercise illustrates the possibilities of creating exercises with different equipment. A rope is used to perform various exercises. The horizontal row or pull on the rope involves the athlete placing their feet against the wall with the body suspended off the ground (see figure 5.57a). Thus, the exercise may be performed with body weight and with a neutral grip. Inhale, make a pulling motion, and hold 5 seconds at the top of the movement in isometric contraction (see figure 5.57b). Exhale at the end of the movement and repeat the motion. To perform the exercise correctly, the posture should be aligned using the core muscles to stabilize the movement. This exercise works the back, arms, and forearm muscles and is important for developing grip strength.

Figure 5.57 – Santiago performs the row against the wall with rope exercise.

Seated Row With a Plate Machine

This exercise is very similar to the seated row (see figure 5.50), but the main difference is that this machine provides the feel of free weights in a guided environment. Sit, keeping the chest at the height of the machine backrest and the arms aligned (see figure 5.58a). Inhale and pull the elbows back as far as possible (see figure 5.58b). Exhale at the end of the movement and return to the initial position. This exercise works the latissimus dorsi, teres major, posterior deltoid, biceps brachii, brachioradialis, and, at the end of the movement, the trapezius and rhomboids.

Figure 5.58 – Seated row with a plate machine.

Table 5.7 illustrates two programs for training the back muscles.

Table 5.7 – Back Training Programs

	Week 1	Week 2	Week 3	Week 4
Training A				
1. Barbell deadlift	2 × 12RM	2 × 10RM	3 × 8RM	4 × 6RM
2. Seated row	2 × 12RM	2 × 10RM	3 × 8RM	4 × 6RM
3. Clinch on MV² VersaPulley machine	2 × 30 sec Fast pace	2 × 30 sec Fast pace	3 × 30 sec Fast pace	3 × 30 sec Fast pace
4. Wide-grip chin-up	2 × 10 BW	2 × 12 BW	2 × 15 BW	2 × 20 BW
5. Cable lat pulldown	2 × 12RM	2 × 12RM	3 × 10RM	3 × 10RM
6. Isoton dumbbell pullover (see description of Isoton method in chapter 2 or at the end of this chapter)	3 × 30 sec @ 35% 1RM	3 × 30 sec @ 35% 1RM	4 × 30 sec @ 40% 1RM	4 × 30 sec @ 40% 1RM

	Week 1	**Week 2**	**Week 3**	**Week 4**
		Training B		
1. Barbell deadlift	2 × 12RM	2 × 10RM	3 × 8RM	4 × 6RM
2. Standing cable row	2 × 12RM	3 × 10RM	4 × 8RM	1 × 12RM + 1 × 10RM + 1 × 8RM + 1 × 6RM
3. Seated row with a plate machine	2 × 12RM	2 × 10RM	3 × 8RM	4 × 6RM
4. One-arm dumbbell row	2 × 12RM each arm	2 × 12RM each arm	3 × 10RM each arm	3 × 10RM each arm
5. Row against the wall with rope	4 × 5 with 5 sec isometric contraction	4 × 5 with 5 sec isometric contraction	6 × 5 with 5 sec isometric contraction	6 × 5 with 5 sec isometric contraction
6. Isoton cable lat pulldown (see description of Isoton method in chapter 2 or at the end of this chapter)	3 × 30 sec @ 35% 1RM	3 × 30 sec @ 35% 1RM	4 × 30 sec @ 40% 1RM	4 × 30 sec @ 40% 1RM

BW: body weight

Shoulder Training

We invited former UFC fighter Marcelo Guimarães to demonstrate how to effectively train the shoulder muscles. The shoulder muscles are divided into the anterior deltoid, middle deltoid, and posterior deltoid; the muscles that form the rotator cuff: supraspinatus, infraspinatus, subscapularis, and teres minor; and the trapezius and rhomboid muscles. Being a joint involved in most upper-body exercises, the shoulder and its surrounding area are in constant motion and are important to a fighter's program.

Low-Pulley Lateral Raise

Grasp the handle with the arm next to the body (see figure 5.59a). Inhale and raise the arm to horizontal (see figure 5.59b). Exhale at the end of the movement. Repeat until the prescribed number of repetitions is completed for each arm. In this lateral raise movement, in addition to the main musculature (middle deltoid), we have the muscles that assist in both upper-body stabilization and the exercise itself.

Figure 5.59 – Low-pulley lateral raise.

Lateral Dumbbell Raise

When using dumbbells to perform this shoulder exercise, pay attention to the angles using biomechanical analysis, because the action of force vectors differs from exercises performed using machines or cables. In the lateral dumbbell raise, stand with a straight back, legs slightly apart, and arms hanging next to the body. Hold a dumbbell in each hand (see figure 5.60a). Inhale and raise the arms to horizontal, keeping the elbows slightly flexed (see figure 5.60b). Return to the initial position and exhale at the end of the movement. This exercise works mainly the middle portion of the deltoid and, to a lesser degree, the supraspinatus and upper and middle portion of the trapezius.

Figure 5.60 – Lateral dumbbell raise.

Low-Pulley Front Raise

This arm movement is performed to head height. Use a pronated, supinated, or neutral grip. Stand with the feet slightly apart and the arms next to the body and grasp the handle with each hand (see figure 5.61a). Inhale and raise the arms to horizontal or eye level (see figure 5.61b). Exhale at the end of the movement and return to the initial position. The goal of this exercise is to work the anterior deltoid and a portion of the chest.

Figure 5.61 – Low-pulley front raise.

Seated Low-Pulley Shoulder Press

Sit on a bench, keeping the back straight, and hold the handles at shoulder level with an overhand grip (see figure 5.62a). Inhale and extend the arms vertically (see figure 5.62b). Exhale at the end of the movement and return to the initial position. The shoulder press is considered a multijoint movement, mobilizing the shoulder and elbow joints, so the exercise activates various muscles, including the deltoids, triceps brachii, trapezius, and serratus anterior.

Figure 5.62 — Seated low-pulley shoulder press.

High-Pulley Lateral Extension (Horizontal Abduction)

This exercise is performed with a horizontal abduction movement using a cross-grip, which is gripping the right handle with the left hand and the left handle with the right hand (see figure 5.63a). Stand facing the pulleys and grasp the handles. Inhale and extend the arms to the side and back (see figure 5.63b). Exhale at the end of the movement and return to the initial position. This movement works the shoulder muscles, mainly the posterior deltoid and, to a lesser degree, infraspinatus, teres minor, trapezius, and rhomboids (Delavier, 2010).

Figure 5.63 — High-pulley lateral extension (horizontal abduction).

Seated Dumbbell Press

Like the seated low-pulley shoulder press, the seated dumbbell press may be performed on a bench or while standing. Sit on a bench, keeping the back straight, and hold dumbbells at shoulder level with an overhand grip (see figure 5.64a). Inhale and extend the arms vertically (see figure 5.64b). Exhale at the end of the movement and return to the initial position. This exercise works the middle deltoid, triceps brachii, trapezius, and serratus anterior.

Figure 5.64 – Seated dumbbell press.

Upright Row

When the deltoid (shoulder) muscles and the trapezius need to be built up, the upright row becomes an ally and may be performed with a barbell, dumbbells, or cables. Stand with the legs slightly apart and the back straight. Grasp the barbell with an overhand grip and rest it against the thighs (see figure 5.65a). Inhale and pull the barbell up along the body to the chin (see figure 5.65b). Lower the bar in a controlled manner and exhale at the end of the movement. This exercise works the deltoid, trapezius, biceps, and, to a lesser degree, the forearm muscles.

Figure 5.65 – Upright row.

Front Raise With a Weight Plate

This movement is performed to head height. It uses a neutral grip or has the arms slightly flexed. Stand with the legs slightly apart, back straight, and the core muscles contracted. Grasp a plate with both hands and rest it against the thighs (see figure 5.66a). Inhale and raise the plate to eye level (see figure 5.66b). Exhale at the end of the movement and return to the initial position. The goal of this exercise is to build the anterior shoulder musculature along with a portion of the chest and, to a lesser degree, the short head of the biceps.

Figure 5.66 – Front raise with a weight plate.

Dumbbell Single-Arm Full Swing

The full swing is a complex exercise using the muscles of the lower and upper body. Hold the dumbbell in front of the body. Inhale and hinge the hips with a straight back, flexing the knees (see figure 5.67a). Quickly extend the entire body to propel the dumbbell up in a circular path, so that at the end of the movement, the position is almost upright (see figure 5.67b). Exhale at the end of the movement and repeat on both sides. This exercise works both the lower and upper body but focuses on the shoulders.

Figure 5.67 – Dumbbell single-arm full swing.

Low-Pulley Bent-Over Lateral Raise

This exercise is performed using the pulley. Stand with the feet apart and knees slightly flexed. Lean forward from the waist, keeping the back flat, and grip the handle with the cable crossing in front of the body (see figure 5.68*a*). Inhale and raise the arm to the side until it is horizontal to the floor (see figure 5.68*b*). Exhale at the end of the movement and repeat on both sides. In this movement, we have the action of the shoulder muscles, especially the posterior deltoid, the trapezius, and rhomboids, among others.

Figure 5.68 – Low-pulley bent-over lateral raise.

Table 5.8 presents two programs for training the shoulder muscles.

Table 5.8 – Shoulder Training Programs

	Week 1	Week 2	Week 3	Week 4
Training A				
1. Seated dumbbell press	2 × 12RM	2 × 10RM	3 × 8RM	4 × 6RM
2. Dumbbell single-arm full swing	2 × 10 each arm	2 × 10 each arm	3 × 10 each arm	3 × 10 each arm
3. Low-pulley bent-over lateral raise	2 × 10 each arm	2 × 10 each arm	3 × 10 each arm	3 × 10 each arm
4. Low-pulley front raise	2 × 12RM	2 × 12RM	3 × 10RM	3 × 10RM
5. Upright row	2 × 12RM	2 × 12RM	3 × 10RM	3 × 10RM
6. Isoton low-pulley lateral raise (see description of Isoton method in chapter 2 or at the end of this chapter)	3 × 30 sec @ 35% 1RM	3 × 30 sec @ 35% 1RM	4 × 30 sec @ 40% 1RM	4 × 30 sec @ 40% 1RM
Training B				
1. Seated dumbbell press	2 × 12RM	2 × 10RM	3 × 8RM	4 × 6RM
2. Front raise with a weight plate	2 × 10	2 × 15	3 × 12	3 × 15
3. Lateral dumbbell raise	2 × 12RM	2 × 12RM	3 × 10RM	3 × 10RM
4. Low-pulley front raise	2 × 12RM	2 × 12RM	3 × 10RM	3 × 10RM
5. Isoton high-pulley lateral extension (see description of Isoton method in chapter 2 or at the end of this chapter)	3 × 30 sec @ 30% 1RM	3 × 30 sec @ 30% 1RM	4 × 30 sec @ 35% 1RM	4 × 30 sec @ 35% 1RM
6. Isoton seated low-pulley shoulder press (see description of Isoton method in chapter 2 or at the end of this chapter)	3 × 30 sec @ 35% 1RM	3 × 30 sec @ 35% 1RM	4 × 30 sec @ 40% 1RM	4 × 30 sec @ 40% 1RM

Biceps and Forearm Training

For this section, we invited former middleweight UFC fighter Caio "Monstro" Magalhães to demonstrate exercises that may be used to increase hypertrophy of the anterior arms. We will show some of the best exercises to develop the biceps brachii, brachialis, and brachioradialis, and forearm muscles that help stabilize the wrist joint. We also show how to create alternative exercises to stimulate these muscles.

The forearm consists of various muscles that may be divided into flexor and extensor muscles of the hand and wrist. The flexor muscles are the flexor carpi radialis, palmaris longus, and flexor carpi ulnaris (superficial layer); flexor digitorum superficialis (intermediate layer); and flexor pollicis longus and flexor digitorum profundus (deep layer). The extensor muscles of the hand and wrist are extensor digitorum, extensor digiti minimi, extensor carpi ulnaris, extensor carpi radialis longus, and extensor carpi radialis brevis.

The biceps brachii is divided between the short and long head of the biceps and has the function of flexing the elbow joint, supinating (turning) the forearm, and aiding shoulder flexion. The brachialis muscle helps in elbow flexion. The brachioradialis assists in elbow flexion, pronation from supination to neutral, and supination from pronation to neutral, while the coracobrachialis acts in the flexion, horizontal adduction, and diagonal adduction of the arm (Floyd, 2018).

Barbell Curl (Olympic Bar)

This exercise is commonly performed by athletes who wish to strengthen or increase the muscle volume of the arms. It is a variation of the EzBar biceps curl that was described in figure 5.24 and can be performed in a standing position with the legs parallel or with a staggered stance and the back straight. Grasp the bar with an underhand grip and hands slightly wider than shoulder-width apart (see figure 5.69a). The abdominal and spinal muscles are used to stabilize the exercise. Inhale and raise the bar by flexing the elbows (see figure 5.69b). Exhale at the end of the movement. This movement contracts the biceps brachii, brachialis, and, to a lesser degree, the brachioradialis, pronator teres, and wrist flexor muscles (Floyd, 2018).

Figure 5.69 – Caio Magalhães executes a barbell curl with an Olympic bar.

Seated Dumbbell Hammer Curl

This exercise is performed in a sitting position. Hold a dumbbell in each hand with the palms facing each other (see figure 5.70a). Inhale and raise the forearms alternately (as in figure 5.70b), or both at the same time. Exhale at the end of the movement. This exercise works the biceps brachii and brachialis, and it is one of the best exercises for developing the brachioradialis (Delavier, 2010). It also works the extensor carpi radialis longus and extensor carpi radialis brevis.

Figure 5.70 – Seated dumbbell hammer curl.

Preacher Curl (Adapted)

This exercise is a variation of the traditional preacher curl. Here, we demonstrate how to adapt exercises according to the equipment available. Stand and support the arm on an incline bench, holding a dumbbell with a supinated grip (see figure 5.71a). Inhale and raise the forearm by flexing the elbow (see figure 5.71b). Exhale at the end of the movement. Repeat until the prescribed number of repetitions is completed for each arm. In this exercise, we focus on biceps brachii development with the aid of the brachialis muscle.

Figure 5.71 – Preacher curl (adapted).

High-Pulley Curl

This exercise is important because it can be used to overload the biceps at different angles through the cables and pulleys. Stand with the knees slightly flexed. Hold the arms perpendicular to the torso with the cables at the same height as, or a little above, the shoulders so that the movement is horizontal (see figure 5.72a). Grasp the handles of the high pulleys with an underhand grip. Inhale and flex the elbows to bring the hands toward the body (see figure 5.72b). Exhale at the end of the movement. This exercise allows the biceps brachii to be worked on as well as its short head, which is under tension due to the position of the arms. We do not recommend performing this exercise with heavy loads because of the greater risk of injury. Consider this exercise to be moderately difficult and focus on controlling the posture (stabilization of the core).

Figure 5.72 – Caio Magalhães demonstrates the high-pulley curl.

Reverse Barbell Curl

The reverse curl is considered a basic exercise but has a greater degree of difficulty since it is performed using a reverse grip (in pronation). It has the same procedure as the barbell curl and should be performed in a standing position with the legs parallel or with one leg forward (staggered stance). The torso and shoulder joints should be aligned (with the shoulder blades pulled in toward each other). The athlete can use an Olympic bar or an EzBar to minimize the tension on the wrists. Grasp the bar with an overhand grip (see figure 5.73a). Inhale and raise the forearms by flexing the elbows (see figure 5.73b). Exhale at the end of the movement. This exercise works the brachioradialis, brachialis, and, to a lesser extent, the biceps brachii. Additionally, it also works the extensor muscles of the wrist: the extensor carpi radialis longus, extensor carpi radialis brevis, extensor digitorum, extensor digiti minimi, and extensor carpi ulnaris. These muscles are important for strengthening the wrist joint and minimizing the difference in strength between the flexor muscles of the wrist and the extensors (Delavier and Gundill, 2013). For this reason, it is recommended for MMA fighters, boxers, and weightlifters. The abdominal and spinal muscles are used to stabilize the exercise.

Figure 5.73 – Reverse barbell curl.

Biceps Curl With Chains

This is another variation that we use to develop the fighter's arms. The chains provide additional load, allowing for a linear increase in the applied resistance. This type of training should be used only with experienced intermediate and elite-level athletes—individuals who have stable exercise technique. The resistance the chain provides depends on its structure, density, length, and diameter. To quantify the resistance, the absolute load is determined for the top and the bottom portion of the movement, then the average of these two loads is calculated and used to train the athlete (Haff and Triplett, 2016). Hold the chains at the sides using a neutral grip (see figure 5.74a). Inhale and raise the forearms by flexing the elbows (see figure 5.74b). Exhale at the end of the movement. This exercise works the brachioradialis, brachialis, and the biceps brachii. It is also a good exercise to develop the forearms.

Figure 5.74 – Biceps curl with chains.

Standing Dumbbell Curl

Like the barbell curl, perform this movement with dumbbells and using a supinated grip with the palms facing forward (see figure 5.75a). Inhale and raise the forearms by flexing the elbows (see figure 5.75b). Exhale at the end of the movement. This exercise works the biceps brachii and the brachialis.

Figure 5.75 – Standing dumbbell curl.

Preacher Hammer Curl

This exercise is a variation of the preacher curl demonstrated in figure 5.71. The main difference is the neutral or hammer grip. Inhale and flex the elbow, raising the forearm (see figure 5.76). Exhale at the end of the movement. Repeat until the prescribed number of repetitions is completed for each arm. This exercise works the brachioradialis, biceps brachii, and brachialis and, to a lesser extent, the extensor carpi radialis longus and extensor carpi radialis brevis.

Figure 5.76 – Caio Magalhães performs the preacher hammer curl.

Single-Arm Olympic Barbell Curl

This exercise has a very high degree of difficulty in relation to balance of the barbell. Grasp the middle of the bar with an underhand grip. The core and leg muscles are used to stabilize the exercise. Inhale and raise the bar by flexing the elbow (see figure 5.77). Exhale at the end of the movement. Repeat on both sides. This is an advanced exercise to strengthen the arm, forearm, and wrist muscles. MMA athletes need to develop a good muscular base in this area to withstand the overload of punches and grappling movements used in training and competition.

Figure 5.77 – Single-arm Olympic barbell curl.

Low-Pulley Curl

In cable exercises, pay attention to the angles imposed by the cables themselves and by the joints involved in the movement. Keep the legs parallel and the torso and shoulders aligned (see figure 5.78a). The movement can be done using a small bar in a two-handed curl or a one-arm variation. Inhale and flex the elbows, raising the forearms (see figure 5.78b). Exhale at the end of the movement. This exercise allows the effort to be concentrated on the biceps brachii, which in turn acts on more than one joint: the elbow and shoulder. The biceps brachii can flex the forearm, raise the elbow, put the forearm in a position of supination, and move the arm close to the thorax. This exercise also works the brachialis, which acts on a single joint, the elbow, and is called a pure flexor because it only mobilizes the elbow joint and only flexes the forearm (Delavier, 2010).

Figure 5.78 – Low-pulley curl.

Lying Curl With Resistance Band

This exercise is a good option for the biceps because the athlete is lying down and cannot perform torso flexion or extension movements. Hold the handles with an underhand grip (see figure 5.79a). Inhale and flex the elbows so the handles move toward the head (see figure 5.79b). Exhale at the end. This movement is concentrated in the arms and uses similar muscles to those in the low-pulley curl mentioned previously.

Figure 5.79 – Lying curl with resistance band.

Table 5.9 includes two programs for training the biceps and forearms.

Table 5.9 – Biceps and Forearm Training Programs

	Week 1	Week 2	Week 3	Week 4
Training A				
1. Barbell curl	2 × 12RM	2 × 10RM	3 × 8RM	4 × 6RM
2. Seated dumbbell hammer curl	2 × 10RM each arm	2 × 10RM each arm	3 × 10RM each arm	3 × 10RM each arm
3. Preacher curl	2 × 12RM each arm	2 × 12RM each arm	3 × 10RM each arm	3 × 10RM each arm
4. Lying curl with resistance band	2 × 10 Fast pace	2 × 10 Fast pace	3 × 10 Fast pace	3 × 10 Fast pace
5. Isoton reverse barbell curl (see description of Isoton method in chapter 2 or at the end of this chapter)	3 × 30 sec @ 30% 1RM	3 × 30 sec @ 30% 1RM	4 × 30 sec @ 35% 1RM	4 × 30 sec @ 35% 1RM
Training B				
1. Single-arm Olympic barbell curl	2 × 10 Slow pace	2 × 10 Slow pace	3 × 8 Slow pace	3 × 8 Slow pace
2. Standing dumbbell curl	2 × 10RM	2 × 10RM	3 × 10RM	3 × 10RM
3. Preacher hammer curl	2 × 10RM each arm	2 × 10RM each arm	3 × 10RM each arm	3 × 10RM each arm
4. Biceps curl with chains	2 × 10 Fast pace	2 × 10 Fast pace	3 × 10 Fast pace	3 × 10 Fast pace
5. Isoton high-pulley curl (see description of Isoton method in chapter 2 or at the end of this chapter)	3 × 30 sec @ 35% 1RM	3 × 30 sec @ 35% 1RM	4 × 30 sec @ 40% 1RM	4 × 30 sec @ 40% 1RM

Triceps Training

In this section, we invited former Bellator champion Atilla Végh and Hungarian fighter Robert Sarkozi to demonstrate exercises used to increase the muscle volume or hypertrophy of the triceps muscles. The triceps brachii is a broad, three-headed skeletal muscle. It runs along the posterior surface of the arm, and its main function is arm extension.

The triceps brachii muscle is generally simply called the *triceps*, which in Latin means "three heads" and may be used for any muscle that has three heads. The origins and positions of the three heads are:

- *Medial head*: arises from the posterior surface of the humerus, just inferior to the groove of the radial nerve
- *Lateral head*: arises from the posterior surface of the humerus, superior to the groove of the radial nerve
- *Long head*: arises from the infraglenoid tubercle of the scapula

Triceps Dip

This traditional triceps exercise is normally done between benches. We have added a Swiss ball to generate some difficulty in stabilizing the movement. Place the hands on the edge of one bench and the feet on the edge of the other bench or on top of the Swiss ball (see figure 5.80a). Inhale and "dip" by flexing the elbows (see figure 5.80b) and then rise back up by extending the elbows. Exhale at the end of the movement. This exercise works the triceps, pectorals, anterior deltoid, and, to a lesser degree, the core muscles and legs to stabilize the movement.

Figure 5.80 – Triceps dip.

Diamond Push-Up

The diamond (close-grip) push-up is a variation of the traditional push-up exercise described in figure 5.46. Lie in a prone position, facedown on the ground with the arms extended and the hands together, either forming a diamond with the hands (fingertips and thumbs touching) or with just the thumbs touching (see figure 5.81a). Legs are either touching or slightly apart. Inhale and flex the elbows to bring the rib cage close to the ground without arching the low back (see figure 5.81b). Push back up to complete the arm extension, exhaling at the end of the movement. This exercise focuses on the triceps brachii and the sternal head of the pectoralis major.

Figure 5.81 – Diamond push-up.

One-Arm Triceps Kickback

This exercise could be done standing or using a bench for support. Maintaining a straight back, flex the elbow and hold the upper arm horizontally next to the body (see figure 5.82a). Inhale and extend the elbow (see figure 5.82b). Exhale at the end of the movement. Repeat until the prescribed number of repetitions is completed for each arm. When using free weights, we must take precautions with the angles and range of motion to ensure proper form and technique to avoid injuries. Therefore, this exercise prioritizes a higher number of repetitions and lighter weights. This is a good exercise for the triceps brachii and anconeus.

Figure 5.82 – One-arm triceps kickback.

Lying Triceps Extension

This exercise is a variation of the triceps extension using an EzBar as described in figure 5.25. The movement may be performed with a straight bar, as in figures 5.83*a* and 5.83*b*, or dumbbells, as in figures 5.83*c* and 5.83*d*. The difference will depend on the morphology of the athlete. For example, with the straight bar, the hands may be far apart and the elbows open during the movement. Using dumbbells or an EzBar allows the exercise to be performed without excessive stress on the wrist joint. This is important for a combat athlete who just fought or is recovering from a wrist injury. Lie supine on a horizontal bench, holding the bar with an overhand grip and the arms extended (vertical) (see figure 5.83*a*). Inhale and lower the barbell to the forehead or until it has passed head level (see figure 5.83*b*). Return to the starting position, extending the arms fully and exhale at the end of the movement. This exercise is important for the triceps brachii muscles.

Figure 5.83 – Lying triceps extension with a bar (*a-b*) and dumbbells (*c-d*).

Seated Dumbbell Triceps Extension

Sit on a bench, back straight and both hands holding a dumbbell behind the neck (see figure 5.84a). Inhale and extend the elbows (see figure 5.84b). Exhale at the end of the movement. This movement is very good for developing the long head of the triceps. The core muscles help maintain the correct posture and technique. This exercise may also be performed on a bench with a low backrest for more stability.

Figure 5.84 – Seated dumbbell triceps extension.

Triceps Pushdown With Rope

Stand with the feet parallel or in a staggered stance. Face the machine, lean forward, and align the upper body with the angle of the cable to make the exercise biomechanics most efficient (see figure 5.85a). Holding the rope, inhale and extend the elbows, keeping the elbows tucked into the body (see figure 5.85b). Exhale at the end of the movement. This exercise works the triceps brachii and the anconeus. Performing this exercise with a rope attachment places more intense demands on the lateral head of the triceps brachii (Delavier, 2010).

Figure 5.85 – Triceps pushdown with rope.

Close-Grip Bench Press

Using a horizontal bench, lie down with the buttocks on the bench and the feet on the ground. Grip the barbell with an overhand grip and keep the wrists 5 to 15 inches (12 to 38 cm) apart, according to the size and flexibility of the athlete (see figure 5.86a). Inhale and lower the bar to the chest in a controlled manner (see figure 5.86b). Extend the arms and exhale at the end of the movement. This exercise works the pectorals and triceps muscles and should be used to make punches and hammer fist strikes more powerful. It is also important for pushing an opponent off when on the back but may cause pain in the elbows and places heavy strain on the clavicular part of the deltoid (Delavier and Gundill, 2013). Therefore, we do not recommend using maximum loads.

Figure 5.86 – Close-grip bench press.

Overhead Cable Triceps Extension

Using a crossover or a pulley machine that allows work at different angles, stand with a staggered stance, back toward the machine. Grasp the pulley with an overhand grip, arms slightly above horizontal and elbows flexed (see figure 5.87a). Inhale and extend the elbows (see figure 5.87b). Exhale at the end of the movement and switch the stance between sets. The proper posture and machine adjustment are important when performing this movement. This variation works the triceps brachii, anconeus, serratus anterior, and core muscles, and it is a good exercise to target the long head of the triceps.

Figure 5.87 – Overhead cable triceps extension.

One-Arm Overhead Dumbbell Triceps Extension

This exercise is a one-arm variation (shown in figure 5.88) performed in the same manner as the seated dumbbell triceps extension described previously in figure 5.84. It is important to contract the core muscles to maintain the correct technique and posture during the movement. Repeat until the prescribed number of repetitions is completed for each arm.

Figure 5.88 – One-arm overhead dumbbell triceps extension.

Triceps Pushdown With Kimono Fabric

This is similar to the triceps pushdown described in figure 5.85, but instead of using a handle or rope, we vary the grip by using a piece of kimono fabric (see figure 5.89). This variation may be used for jiu-jitsu fighters or those interested in developing their grip strength and strengthening the wrists.

Figure 5.89 – Triceps pushdown with kimono fabric.

Various methods and training systems, as seen in the previous chapters, can be used to achieve the desired objectives, but the following details should be emphasized:

- Do not do more than four exercises for the triceps in a single training session.
- The execution speed of the exercise is slow to moderate.
- The rest between the sets is one to five minutes.
- The number of sets is two to six.
- The rest between training days may vary from 48 hours to seven days.

These exercises and methods are the basis for proper planning for strength and hypertrophy. If practitioners decide to use two of the three proposed training programs in a single week, we recommend a rest of at least 72 hours between the two, and we do not recommend doing the three variations (training A, B, and C) over a period of less than 10 days. The choice of exercises, their order, and training variations form part of an individual analysis of the needs and goals involved in planning for the athlete. Table 5.10 includes three training programs for developing the triceps from the exercises described previously.

Table 5.10 – Triceps Training Programs

	Week 1	Week 2	Week 3	Week 4
Training A				
1. Triceps dip	2 × 15 BW	2 × 20 BW	3 × 15 BW	3 × 20 BW
2. Diamond push-up	2 × 20 BW	2 × 25 BW	3 × 20 BW	3 × 25 BW
3. One-arm triceps kickback	2 × 12RM each arm	2 × 12RM each arm	3 × 10RM each arm	3 × 10RM each arm
4. Isoton triceps pushdown with kimono fabric (see description of Isoton method in chapter 2 or at the end of this chapter)	3 × 30 sec @ 35% 1RM	3 × 30 sec @ 35% 1RM	4 × 30 sec @ 40% 1RM	4 × 30 sec @ 40% 1RM
Training B				
1. Close-grip bench press	2 × 12RM	3 × 10RM	4 × 8RM	4 × 8RM
2. Seated dumbbell triceps extension	2 × 12RM	2 × 12RM	3 × 10RM	3 × 10RM
3. Lying triceps extension	2 × 10RM	2 × 10RM	3 × 10RM	3 × 10RM
4. Isoton overhead cable triceps extension (see description of Isoton method in chapter 2 or at the end of this chapter)	3 × 30 sec @ 35% 1RM	3 × 30 sec @ 35% 1RM	4 × 30 sec @ 40% 1RM	4 × 30 sec @ 40% 1RM
Training C				
1. Triceps pushdown with rope	2 × 12RM	3 × 10RM	4 × 8RM	4 × 8RM
2. Triceps pushdown with kimono fabric	2 × 15RM	2 × 15RM	3 × 15RM	3 × 15RM
3. One-arm overhead dumbbell triceps extension	2 × 12RM each arm	2 × 12RM each arm	3 × 10RM each arm	3 × 10RM each arm
4. Isoton close-grip bench press (see description of Isoton method in chapter 2 or at the end of this chapter)	3 × 30 sec @ 35% 1RM	3 × 30 sec @ 35% 1RM	4 × 30 sec @ 40% 1RM	4 × 30 sec @ 40% 1RM

BW: body weight

Core Training

The importance of developing the body's core for stabilization and force generation in sports is increasingly recognized. However, there is still a lack of clarity regarding what constitutes the "core," both anatomically and physiologically, among athletes and coaches. The body's musculoskeletal core includes the spinal column, hips, pelvis, proximal lower limbs, and abdominal structures. These muscles are responsible for maintaining spine and pelvis stability and generating and transferring energy from large to small parts of the body during many sports activities (Kibler, et al. 2006).

Studies have shown that core stability development reduces pain in adults with problems in the lumbar region. The need to work on the strength, coordination, and muscular endurance of the core in athletes has also been highlighted (Clark, et al. 2018; Kibler, et al. 2006).

According to NASM (Clark, et al. 2018), core musculature has been divided into the local stabilization system, global stabilization system, and movement system. To maintain core stability, neuromuscular control of the local stabilization, global stabilization, and movement systems is required (Clark, et al. 2018). The core muscles, according to NASM (Clark, et al. 2018), are listed in table 5.11.

Table 5.11 – Core Muscles

Local stabilization system	Global stabilization system	Movement system
▪ Transverse abdominis	▪ Quadratus lumborum	▪ Latissimus dorsi
▪ Internal oblique	▪ Psoas major	▪ Hip flexors
▪ Lumbar multifidus	▪ External oblique	▪ Hamstring complex
▪ Pelvic floor muscles	▪ Portions of internal oblique	▪ Quadriceps
▪ Diaphragm	▪ Rectus abdominis	
	▪ Gluteus medius	
	▪ Adductor complex	
	• Adductor magnus	
	• Adductor longus	
	• Adductor brevis	
	• Gracilis	
	• Pectineus	

One of the major goals of core training is to exercise the abdominal muscles and the lumbar region simultaneously or during the same section of training (Dias, et al. 2016a). According to ACSM (2014), reductions in strength and muscular endurance in the torso are associated with a greater prevalence of pain in the lumbar region. Additionally, athletes should spend as much time training the lower-back muscles as they do abdominal muscles.

Hanging Leg Raise

Hang from a chin-up bar. Inhale and raise the knees with straight legs as high as possible. Do not raise the legs so far that there is any back pain (see figure 5.90). Exhale at the end of the movement. This exercise has a high degree of coordination and difficulty and should be performed only by athletes who are physically prepared to do it. In this exercise, we work the rectus abdominis, iliopsoas, rectus femoris, tensor fasciae latae, and the internal and external oblique muscles. The athlete needs to hold the body balanced in suspension to be able to perform the exercise correctly.

Figure 5.90 – Hanging leg raise.

Plank

Planks are isometric exercises and may be performed on stable surfaces (floor) or unstable surfaces (BOSU ball, Swiss ball, or suspended), with a prone posture or as a side plank as described previously in figure 5.34, working many core muscles at the same time.

Bird Dog

Use a soft surface to kneel on and have enough space to extend both an arm and a leg at the same time. An exercise mat, rubber floor, or turf is a good choice for surface. Kneel with knees hip-width apart and hands firmly on the ground about shoulder-width apart. Brace the abdominals. Inhale and lift one hand and the opposite knee while balancing on the other hand and knee and keeping the weight centered (see figure 5.91a). Move on to the full range of motion, pointing the arm out straight in front and extending the opposite leg to the back (see figure 5.91b). To prevent the low back from sagging, raise the leg only as high as possible while keeping the back straight. Hold for 1 to 4 seconds and then return the hands and knees to the starting position. Exhale at the end of the movement. Switch to the other side.

Keep the abs engaged throughout the entire exercise. Work to minimize any extra motion in the hips during the weight shift. For a more advanced variation, perform the exercise with the knee hovering without touching the ground. Both variations involve a high degree of difficulty in terms of balance. Bird dogs are excellent for strengthening the core safely and effectively. It is up to the trainers and coaches to decide which options are best suited to the athlete. Most frequently, we use sets of 15 to 30 seconds on each side, repeating for 2 to 3 sets.

Figure 5.91 – Bird dog.

V-Up

This movement is also called a jackknife. Lie on the ground, arms outstretched behind the head (see figure 5.92a). Keep the arms and legs raised a little off the ground throughout the movement. Inhale and perform a flexion of the torso, thighs, and hips, holding a medicine ball or a weight plate (to make it harder) as an external load (see figure 5.92b). Exhale at the end of the movement. This exercise is designed to strengthen the rectus abdominis, the transversus abdominis muscle, oblique muscles, iliopsoas, tensor fasciae latae, and rectus femoris.

Figure 5.92 – V-up.

Sit-Up With Rotation

Lie on the back with the knees flexed and legs suspended in an isometric position (keep the feet flat on the ground for an easier variation). Inhale and raise the shoulders off the ground, rotating the torso and moving the medicine ball from one side to the other while maintaining balance with the hips on the floor (see figure 5.93). In this exercise, the medicine ball is an external load to increase the difficulty. We typically perform 15 to 30 repetitions on each side to develop muscular endurance. This exercise works the rectus abdominis, obliques, and hip flexors.

Figure 5.93 – Sit-up with rotation.

Core Rotation With Cable

Core rotations (torso rotations) are excellent exercises that resemble the various fighting movements of attack and defense in MMA. Here, we use a pulley machine. Set the loading point at about chest height. Hold one handle in both hands. Keep the knees slightly flexed and the arms straight out in front. Inhale and turn to the left so the loading point is to the right while the core remains stiff. Exhale at the end of the movement and repeat on both sides of the body. Usually, we perform dynamic sets of 10 to 20 repetitions (see figures 5.94a-b) or we use the Isoton method (described in chapter 2). The movement may be performed with the pulley at different heights, such as from high to low (shown in figures 5.94c-d), or from low to high (shown in figures 5.94e-f). This exercise targets the internal and external obliques as well as the rectus abdominis, core, legs, and other muscles.

Figure 5.94 – Core rotation with cable: (a-b) horizontal, (c-d) high to low, and (e-f) low to high.

Superman

Lie on the floor in a prone (belly down) position, with the legs straight and the arms extended in front. Keep the head in a neutral position and slowly lift the arms and legs around 6 inches (15.3 cm) off the ground or until the lower-back muscles are contracting (see figure 5.95). Aim to lift the belly button slightly off the floor to contract the abs. A good way to picture this is to imagine Superman flying in the air. Hold this position for 2 to 3 seconds. Be sure to breathe the entire time. Lower the arms, legs, and belly back to the floor and repeat the movement. This exercise can be done dynamically or isometrically. We chose isometric contraction, keeping the arms and legs extended without any contact with the ground for 15 to 30 seconds. Take a short rest before repeating the movement again. This is important, given that most of the core muscles have a greater concentration of type I muscle fibers, so the muscles recover quickly (Clark, et al. 2018). This work may also be performed using the Isoton method described in chapter 2 and repeated 2 to 4 times a week, alternating between training session A and B, as shown in the training programs that follow. Muscular endurance core training may be done at the end of a specific combat training session or with other strength work on another muscle group. The Superman exercise targets the erector spinae muscles of the lower back, including the spinalis, longissimus, and iliocostalis, which are key for back extension. This exercise also targets the glutes, hamstrings, upper back, shoulders, and abdominal muscles.

Figure 5.95 – Superman.

Table 5.12 presents two programs for training the core based on the exercises described previously.

Table 5.12 – Core Training Programs

	Week 1	Week 2	Week 3	Week 4
Training A				
1. Hanging leg raise	1 × 10 BW	2 × 10 BW	3 × 10 BW	4 × 10 BW
2. Plank	2 × 15 sec BW	2 × 25 sec BW	3 × 20 sec BW	3 × 30 sec BW
3. Bird dog	2 × 10 BW each side	2 × 10 BW each side	3 × 10 BW each side	3 × 10 BW each side
4. Isoton core rotation with cable (see description of Isoton method in chapter 2 or at the end of this chapter)	3 × 30 sec @ 30% 1RM on each side	3 × 30 sec @ 30% 1RM on each side	4 × 30 sec @ 30% 1RM on each side	4 × 30 sec @ 30% 1RM on each side
Training B				
1. V-up	1 × 15 w/ 5 lb MB	2 × 15 w/ 5 lb MB	3 × 15 w/ 5 lb MB	4 × 15 w/ 5 lb MB
2. Side plank	2 × 15 sec BW on each side	2 × 25 sec BW on each side	3 × 20 sec BW on each side	3 × 30 sec BW on each side
3. Superman or cobra	2 × 15 sec BW	2 × 25 sec BW	3 × 20 sec BW	3 × 30 sec BW
4. Isoton core rotation with cable from high to low or from low to high (see description of Isoton method in chapter 2 or at the end of this chapter)	3 × 30 sec @ 30% 1RM on each side	3 × 30 sec @ 30% 1RM on each side	4 × 30 sec @ 30% 1RM on each side	4 × 30 sec @ 30% 1RM on each side

BW: body weight; MB: medicine ball

Agonist-Antagonist Training

Agonist-antagonist training can be an extremely useful addition to the training for MMA athletes. The agonist-antagonist or pull-push method in the form of a bi-set is characteristic of advanced resistance training work, with the option of working opposing muscle groups. Perform the exercises one after the other without any rest or with minimal rest between the movements. Only after two sets does the athlete have a rest period as established by the coach.

We normally divide training into a preparatory phase and competitive phase. Each phase lasts about six weeks. In the preparatory phase, we use basic training to build strength and prioritize stress and metabolic stimuli, with varied repetitions between 6 to 12 repetitions at a load of 65 percent to 85 percent RM (repetition maximum) and a rest period of one to five minutes between sets. The number of sets varies from three to six, and the coach is always seeking to extract the maximum performance from the athlete. To demonstrate this training method, we invited former UFC fighter and Bare Knuckle Fighting Middleweight Champion Thiago "Pitbull" Alves.

Seated Bench Press With a Plate Machine

The seated bench press is a basic multijoint exercise widely used to build the upper body. This articulated machine with free weights allows the athlete to perform bilateral or unilateral movements. The athlete performs this exercise bilaterally. Sit on the bench, legs properly aligned and back supported. The placement of the grip should result in the arm and forearm being at a 90-degree angle to improve mechanical efficiency (see figure 5.96a). Inhale and press, making a "pushing" movement toward the midline of the chest (see figure 5.96b). Exhale at the end of the movement and return to the initial position. In this movement, the chest muscles perform the main actions, but auxiliary muscles, such as the triceps brachii and deltoids, are also involved.

Figure 5.96 – Seated bench press with a plate machine.

Lat Pulldown With a Plate Machine

This articulated machine with a plate is important to develop the back muscles (see figure 5.97). For more information about this exercise and the proper form of movement, see figure 5.33.

Figure 5.97 – Lat pulldown with a plate machine.

Dumbbell Press

A dumbbell press is a very popular exercise and was previously described in figure 5.47. The dumbbells allow a greater range of motion with a higher degree of difficulty in terms of execution, balance, and stabilization (see figure 5.98).

Figure 5.98 – Dumbbell press.

Chin-Up

This is a basic exercise using the overload of body weight and may be performed in gyms, parks, or anywhere where such equipment is available. Use wide or narrow grips according to the program chosen. In this case, priority is given to the wide grip (see figure 5.99). For more information about this exercise and proper form of movement, see figure 5.52.

Figure 5.99 – Chin-up.

Standing Cable Press

Stand in the middle of the cable machine with the legs slightly apart in a staggered stance. Lean the torso forward a bit, holding the handles with the arms spread and elbows flexed (see figure 5.100a). Inhale and extend the arms together (see figure 5.100b). Exhale at the end of the movement. Return in a controlled manner to the initial position and repeat. In this exercise, various angles can be created by altering the equipment settings. The coach is responsible for deciding which angle will be used for targeting the pectoralis muscles.

Figure 5.100 – Standing cable press.

One-Arm Seated Row With a Plate Machine

The seated row with a plate machine is a horizontal rowing movement. This articulated machine with free weights allows the athlete to perform bilateral or unilateral movements. Perform the exercise unilaterally (see figure 5.101). Repeat until the prescribed number of repetitions is completed for each arm. For more information about this exercise and proper form of movement, see figure 5.58.

Figure 5.101 – One-arm seated row with a plate machine.

Table 5.13 shows an example program for agonist-antagonist training.

Table 5.13 – Agonist-Antagonist (Push-Pull) Training

	Week 1	**Week 2**	**Week 3**	**Week 4**
Bi-set 1				
1. Seated bench press with a plate machine	3 × 12RM	4 × 10RM	4 × 8RM	4 × 6RM
2. Lat pulldown with a plate machine	3 × 12RM	4 × 10RM	4 × 8RM	4 × 6RM
Bi-set 2				
1. Dumbbell press	3 × 12RM	4 × 10RM	4 × 8RM	4 × 6RM
2. Chin-up	3 × 10 BW	4 × 10 BW	4 × 12 BW	4 × 12 BW
Bi-set 3				
1. Standing cable press	3 × 12RM	4 × 10RM	4 × 8RM	4 × 6RM
2. One-arm seated row with a plate machine	3 × 12RM	4 × 10RM	4 × 8RM	4 × 6RM

BW: body weight

Eccentric Training

Eccentric training occurs when the muscle lengthens while under tension due to an external force greater than the force the muscle can generate. Instead of moving the joint in the direction of the contraction, the muscle decelerates the movement in a controlled manner (this work is also called the negative part of the movement). The loads used in this work are around 110 percent to 120 percent of the maximum load the athlete tolerates.

To demonstrate this eccentric training method, we invited UFC athlete Marcos Rogério "Pezão" de Lima, some of his training partners, and coach Stefane Dias to help lift the load in the concentric or positive part of the movement. Assistance was required because the load exceeds the athlete's maximum strength. It should be noted that this is an advanced training and needs to be correctly prescribed by an exercise science professional and be well supervised.

According to the American College of Sports Medicine (2014, 2012), several principles should be followed:

- The warm-up should last from 5 to 10 minutes.
- During submaximal eccentric training, the load should be lifted in one to two seconds and slowly lowered in four to six seconds.
- When training with maximum load or above maximum load, lift the load with the help of spotters and lower it in a controlled manner.
- Delayed onset muscle soreness may last 24 to 72 hours.
- Maximum loads should only be used once a week.
- Begin with few repetitions and sets and gradually increase them as the weeks go by.

Seated Dumbbell Press

This is considered a multijoint movement in which the athlete mobilizes the shoulder and elbow joints so that the exercise demands the action of various muscles as described in figure 5.64. In this exercise, the coach hands the dumbbells to the athlete, monitors the lowering and lengthening movement (eccentric phase), and assists in the return to the initial position of the movement (concentric phase) (see figure 5.102). The sets are performed at a slow pace until muscle failure.

Figure 5.102 – Seated dumbbell press with a spotter.

Back Squat

The back squat is a powerful exercise for the lower body with a high level of difficulty. Perform the exercise following the same instructions provided in figure 5.31, with the assistance of two spotters (see figure 5.103). The exercise is performed so that the athlete squats until the angle predetermined by the coach. The squat may also be performed on equipment such as the Smith Machine or back squat machine, or as a free-weight exercise with dumbbells. The spotters position themselves next to the barbell to monitor the movement during the eccentric phase and assist during the concentric phase of the movement to move the bar back up to the starting position.

Figure 5.103 – Back squat with spotters.

Barbell Bench Press

This multijoint exercise is widely used to build upper-body strength. Perform the exercise following the same instructions provided in figure 5.21 but with the assistance of two spotters (see figure 5.104). The spotters position themselves next to the barbell to monitor the movement during the eccentric phase and assist during the concentric phase of the movement to move the bar back up to the starting position.

Figure 5.104 – Barbell bench press with spotters.

T-Bar Row

Lean forward at the waist with a flat back and the legs slightly flexed. Stabilize the body and grasp the bar with an overhand grip (see figure 5.105a). Inhale and raise the bar to the chest with the assistance of a spotter (see figure 5.105b). Slowly bring the bar back to the initial position and exhale at the end of the movement (see figure 5.105c). This exercise requires great posture and movement stabilization. It targets the latissimus dorsi, teres major, infraspinatus, rhomboids, trapezius, flexors of the forearm, core, and leg muscles.

Figure 5.105 – T-bar row with a spotter.

Dumbbell Bench Press

This exercise is similar to the barbell bench press but uses dumbbells. Perform the exercise following the same instructions provided in figure 5.47. The dumbbells allow a greater range of motion with a higher level of difficulty. In this exercise, two spotters are necessary, each grabbing a heavy dumbbell and giving them to the athlete. After that, the spotters position themselves next to the dumbbells to monitor the movement during the eccentric phase and assist during the concentric phase to move the dumbbell up to the starting position (see figure 5.106).

Figure 5.106 – Dumbbell bench press with spotters.

Chin-Up

The chin-up is a great exercise to develop back muscles and grip strength. Perform the exercise following the same instructions provided in figure 5.52. During the eccentric chin-up, the coach helps the athlete during the concentric phase of the movement, while the athlete returns slowly to the starting position (see figure 5.107). For a lighter athlete (weighing less than 205 lb [93 kg]), we recommend adding a weight vest to make the exercise harder.

Figure 5.107 – Chin-up with a spotter.

EzBar Biceps Curl

Considered a basic exercise in which the action is to flex the elbow, this exercise should be performed in a standing position following the same instructions provided in figure 5.24. During the eccentric EzBar biceps curl, the coach helps the athlete during the concentric phase of the movement, while the athlete returns slowly to the starting position (see figure 5.108).

Figure 5.108 – EzBar biceps curl with a spotter.

EzBar Lying Triceps Extension

Lie down in a supine position, following the same instructions provided in figure 5.25. During the eccentric EzBar lying triceps extension, the coach helps the athlete during the concentric phase of the movement, while the athlete slowly lowers the bar until it has passed head level (eccentric phase) (see figure 5.109).

Figure 5.109 – EzBar lying triceps extension with a spotter.

Supine Leg Raise

Lie down on the floor with the legs straight while holding the legs of a training partner or coach. Inhale and raise the legs, lifting the pelvis as if trying to bring the knees to the head (see figure 5.110). The coach pushes the athlete's feet to the floor while the athlete resists, working to slow down the movement. Exhale at the end of the movement and repeat. This is an excellent exercise to work the iliopsoas, tensor fasciae latae, rectus femoris, and abdominal muscles.

Figure 5.110 – Supine leg raise with a spotter.

Table 5.14 includes two programs for eccentric training. Because it is so intense, this training should not be performed more than twice a week, and the exercises may be divided into two, as in the sample training program. Heavy loads should be used in the sets (90%-120% of the maximum). The athlete should perform relatively few repetitions and use long rest periods ranging from three to five minutes or more.

Table 5.14 – Eccentric Training Programs

	Week 1	**Week 2**	**Week 3**	**Week 4**
Training A				
1. Back squat	3 × 6 @ 100% RM	3 × 6 @ 100% RM	4 × 4 @ 110% RM	4 × 4 @ 110% RM
2. Barbell bench press	2 × 6 @ 100% RM	2 × 6 @ 100% RM	3 × 4 @ 110% RM	3 × 4 @ 110% RM
3. Chin-up	2 × 8 BW Slow pace	2 × 8 BW Slow pace	3 × 10 BW Slow pace	3 × 10 BW Slow pace
4. EzBar biceps curl	2 × 6 @ 100% RM	2 × 6 @ 100% RM	3 × 4 @ 110% RM	3 × 4 @ 110% RM
5. Supine leg raise	2 × 15 BW	2 × 15 BW	3 × 15 BW	3 × 15 BW
Training B				
1. T-bar row	3 × 6 @ 100% RM	3 × 6 @ 100% RM	4 × 4 @ 110% RM	4 × 4 @ 110% RM
2. Dumbbell bench press	2 × 6 @ 100% RM	2 × 6 @ 100% RM	3 × 4 @ 110% RM	3 × 4 @ 110% RM
3. Seated dumb-bell press	2 × 6 @ 100% RM	2 × 6 @ 100% RM	3 × 4 @ 110% RM	3 × 4 @ 110% RM
4. EzBar lying tri-ceps extension	2 × 6 @ 100% RM	2 × 6 @ 100% RM	3 × 4 @ 110% RM	3 × 4 @ 110% RM
5. Supine leg raise	2 × 15 BW	2 × 15 BW	3 × 15 BW	3 × 15 BW

BW: body weight

Functional Training

Success in sports is multifaceted and includes optimal technical and tactical preparation and training of the motor skills involved in the specific demands of each sport. Functional training incorporates various training methods to target strength, speed, power, muscular endurance, and so on to achieve an ideal adaptive response appropriate to the sport or activity for which it is designed and to reduce injury risk from high training volume or inappropriate training loads. However, to design training programs that use these methods, it is necessary to first understand the term *functional training*. Thinking in physical terms, the main function of the human body—its main purpose—is to move on all basic anatomical planes (sagittal, transverse, and frontal) (Cook, et al. 2011).

We may classify human movement patterns into four categories: locomotion, level changes, pulling (horizontally and vertically) or pushing (horizontally and vertically), and rotation (changes of direction) (Boyle, 2016; Santana, 2015; Chek, 2001). These four pillars allow us to design a training program relating the major movements and adapt them to the demands of MMA and other combat sports athletes.

In this section, we invited Russian athletes Alexey Ivanov, combat sambo world champion, and Sergey Belostenny, MMA fighter and Sanda world champion, to perform a functional strength circuit designed for MMA training. We used exercises in all anatomical planes to stimulate muscle power, and they were performed in a circuit to simulate muscle power endurance. Due to the volume in this kind of training, high demand is placed on aerobic metabolism to accelerate the recovery of active muscles, even when the exercises are short, explosive, and high intensity. Mitochondrial synthesis in the type II glycolytic muscle fibers is stimulated.

Medicine Ball Overhead Slam

The medicine ball overhead slam is a multijoint exercise that develops shoulder, core, and throwing power. Using a medicine ball with a low bounce, stand in a parallel stance with feet shoulder-width apart. Hold the medicine ball in front with the arms extended (see figure 5.111a). Inhale, keeping the core tight, and bring the medicine ball overhead by fully extending the body (see figure 5.111b). Slam the ball down about 2 feet (60 cm) in front (to avoid the ball hitting the face when it rebounds) and exhale during the slam (see figure 5.111c). Catch the ball on the bounce and repeat. This exercise requires strong core activation (spine and hip flexors), shoulder extension (mainly the latissimus dorsi), and spine extensors to maintain a flat back during the execution of the rapid and explosive movement.

Figure 5.111 – Medicine ball overhead slam.

Medicine Ball Overhead Lunge

The medicine ball overhead lunge is a multijoint exercise with leg dominance that places high demands on the shoulder girdle to stabilize the shoulders and maintain the ball above the head as the elbows are completely extended. Start with the feet together, standing tall with the ball overhead (see figure 5.112a). Inhale and step forward about 3 feet (0.9 m), keeping the whole core engaged and braced to avoid any unwanted sideways movements. While stepping forward, press the ball toward the ceiling, keeping the elbows locked (see figure 5.112b). Near the bottom position, drop the hips toward the floor until the back knee touches the ground. Exhale at the end of the movement and repeat until the prescribed number of repetitions is completed for each leg. The spine should be kept straight, without excessive curve, during the entire movement. The gluteal muscles and hamstrings are the primary muscles for the movement.

Figure 5.112 – Medicine ball overhead lunge.

Hanging Leg Raise

The hanging leg raise, also called "toes to bar," is a highly efficient movement for developing stability and strength of the midline and core muscles as well as grip strength, given that the individual hangs, supporting their body weight, during the entire movement. For more information on how to properly perform this exercise, see figure 5.90.

Legless Rope Climb

The legless rope climb is an advanced functional exercise that is important for developing grip strength in fighters. Sit on the floor, with the legs in front and hands above the head (see figure 5.113a). Inhale and pull the rope toward the body, keeping the chin above the hands. Once the chin is above the hands, pull the body up by reaching with the lower hand above the upper one. Keep the shoulders engaged (latissimus dorsi should be active) and brace the core as much as possible. Repeat the movement while maintaining breathing until the top of the rope or desired height is reached (see figure 5.113b). This is a powerful exercise to develop the back, arms, and forearm muscles.

Figure 5.113 – Legless rope climb.

Wall Ball

The wall ball is basically a squat in which the load (the ball) is thrown after the full extension of the body. However, what makes this exercise unique is the descending phase, in which the individual develops the capacity to slow the ball, controlling the eccentric phase of the squat, which may be an important characteristic for preventing muscle injuries. Stand tall, holding the ball with both hands underneath the ball and in front of the chest. Stay 2 to 3 feet (0.6-0.9 m) from the wall. Inhale and push the hips back, lowering into a squat position (see figure 5.114a). Quickly extend the hips and legs while throwing the ball upward against the wall (see figure 5.114b). Exhale at the end of the movement. Catch the ball and return to the starting position.

Figure 5.114 – Wall ball.

Box Jump

The box jump is excellent for developing the triple extension, the explosive generation of power produced by the simultaneous extension of the hips, knees, and ankles. Stand in front of the box, feet shoulder-width apart (see figure 5.115a). Inhale and drop down into a quarter squat (see figure 5.115b). Swing the arms back and then up and explode up off the ground. Land on the box as smoothly as possible, in the take-off position on landing (see figure 5.115c). Exhale at the end of the movement. Stand tall on the box (see figure 5.115d), step back down, and repeat the movement. This exercise targets the gluteal muscles, quadriceps, hamstrings, and calf muscles to generate force. The main reason for using jumping exercises is to exploit the stretch-shortening cycle of the lower body and develop elastic energy.

Figure 5.115 – Box jump.

Landmine Core Rotation

Ninety percent of fight movements depend on body rotation. For the body to rotate strongly, rapidly, and explosively, with minimal chance of injury, exercises should work on rotation. The landmine core rotation is designed with this in mind, because the arc made with the bar from one side of the body to the other forces the stabilizing muscles of the core to work efficiently and "teaches" the oblique muscles to efficiently perform the movement of rotating the torso.

To perform this exercise properly, assume a lunge stance, feet shoulder-width apart. Both hands should be under the barbell (see figure 5.116a). Inhale and use the arms in an arc and drive the barbell down to the hip, keeping the arms straight (see figure 5.116b). Exhale at the end of the movement. Bring the barbell up back to the starting position and go to the other side (see figure 5.116c). Then, switch legs and repeat the movement from the other side, always keeping the back straight and the core and hips engaged.

Figure 5.116 – Landmine core rotation.

Table 5.15 presents a training program for a functional strength circuit based on the previous exercises. The circuit was divided into four supersets. Perform all sets of a superset and then actively rest for two minutes (walking, indoor cycling, shadow boxing, etc.). Note that the exercise movements should be performed explosively and with speed. The supersets should be designed with exercises of similar movement patterns. This program may be repeated twice a week: one day at high volume (shock training) and the second day at maintenance volume (50% less than the shock volume), around 48 hours after the shock session (Maksimov, et al. 2011).

Table 5.15 – Functional Training Circuit Program

	Week 1	Week 2	Week 3	Week 4
1. Medicine ball overhead slam	2 × 10 sec work + 10 sec rest; 4 kg ball	3 × 10 sec work + 10 sec rest; 8 kg ball	4 × 15 sec work + 15 sec rest; 8 kg ball	5 × 15 sec work + 10 sec rest; 8 kg ball
2. Medicine ball overhead lunge	2 × 10 sec work + 10 sec rest; 8 kg ball	3 × 10 sec work + 10 sec rest; 10 kg ball	4 × 15 sec work + 15 sec rest; 10 kg ball	5 × 15 sec work + 10 sec rest; 10 kg ball
2 min of active rest				
3. Toes to bar	2 × 10 sec work + 10 sec rest; BW	3 × 10 sec work + 10 sec rest; BW	4 × 15 sec work + 15 sec rest; BW	5 × 15 sec work + 10 rest; BW
4. Legless rope climb	2 × 10 sec work + 10 sec rest; max height	3 × 10 sec work + 10 sec rest; max height	4 × 15 sec work + 15 sec rest; max height	5 × 15 sec work + 10 sec rest; max height
2 min of active rest				
5. Wall ball	2 × 10 sec work + 10 sec rest; 4 kg ball	3 × 10 sec work + 10 sec rest; 8 kg ball	4 × 15 sec work + 15 sec rest; 8 kg ball	5 × 15 sec work + 10 sec rest; 8 kg ball
6. Box jump	2 × 10 sec work + 10 sec rest; 18 in. box	3 × 10 sec work + 10 sec rest; 24 in. box	4 × 15 sec work + 15 sec rest; 24 in. box	5 × 15 sec work + 10 sec rest; 24 in. box
2 min of active rest				
7. Landmine core rotation	2 × 10 sec work + 10 sec rest each leg; 10 kg	3 × 10 sec work + 10 sec rest each leg; 15 kg	4 × 15 sec work + 10 sec rest each leg; 15 kg	5 × 15 sec work + 10 sec rest each leg; 15 kg

BW: body weight

Suspension Training

Another tool that we use to physically prepare athletes is suspension training. Most gyms are equipped with some sort of suspension system like Olympic rings, a system of ropes, and so on. Suspension training offers unique advantages compared to traditional resistance training machines that allow the coaches to modify exercises to meet the needs of virtually any athlete. Most of the exercises use body weight only and are easily manipulated to be either more or less difficult by positioning the body either closer or further from the anchor of the suspension straps. Most exercises are also compound due to the stabilizing component of performing suspension training. This method can be useful for learning and practicing an exercise until good form is solidified before trying it with free weights. For example, if we see an individual struggling to maintain proper form during the walking lunge, static split squat, or alternating rear lunge, holding suspension straps can be a useful tool in that individual's training progression. Suspension training is also used to aid in increasing range of motion, like in a squat movement, by permitting athletes to manipulate the body's position while being provided stability and enabling multiplanar, multijoint exercises in a proprioceptively enriched training environment.

According to Sutton (2022), the physiologic benefits of suspension training include:

- Increased balance
- A potential increase in flexibility and joint mobility
- Increased core muscle activation
- Low compressive loads on the spine
- A potential increase in caloric expenditure

Low Row

Begin with the suspension trainer fully shortened. Face the anchor point. Grasp the handles. The shoulder blades should be externally rotated and depressed (back and down). The elbows are flexed, with the handles positioned at the rib cage. Walk toward the anchor point until the appropriate angle is achieved. Maintain the body in a reverse plank position and lower the trunk until the arms are fully extended (see figure 5.117a). Perform the exercise by pulling the body toward the anchor point where the heels contact the floor by driving the elbows straight back, close to the body (see figure 5.117b). For an advanced variation of the exercise, see figures 5.117c and 5.117d. The primary muscles worked are the latissimus dorsi, rhomboids, trapezius, teres major and minor, brachioradialis, biceps brachii, and brachialis.

Figure 5.117 – Low row: (a-b) beginner and (c-d) advanced.

Chest Press

Start facing away from the anchor point with the straps fully lengthened. Extend the arms in front of the shoulders and choose the appropriate foot stance (see figure 5.118a). The feet closer together or toward the anchor point will increase the difficulty, while feet wider apart or away from the anchor point will make the movement easier. While maintaining a plank position, lower the body by flexing the elbows 90 degrees (see figure 5.118b). Return to the straight-arm starting position by driving through the palms and squeezing the chest. Maintain the plank position. The primary muscles worked are the pectoralis major, anterior deltoid, triceps brachii, and anconeus.

Figure 5.118 – Chest press.

Chest Fly

Begin by facing away from the anchor point with the straps fully lengthened. Holding the straps in a high plank position with the palms facing each other, open the arms, lowering the chest toward the floor (see figure 5.119a). Raise the body by bringing the arms back toward each other and adducting the shoulders (see figure 5.119b). The core is rigid throughout the movement. The primary muscle worked is the pectoralis major.

Figure 5.119 – Chest fly.

Push-Up

Start with the feet in the suspension straps, the hands shoulder-width apart on the floor, and the arms straight (see figure 5.120a). Lower the chest to the floor while gazing forward, keeping the core rigid (see figure 5.120b). Once the downward move is complete, lift the body back up by extending the arms. The primary muscles worked are the pectoralis major, anterior deltoid, triceps brachii, and anconeus.

Figure 5.120 – Push-up.

Knees to Chest

This exercise begins with the feet in the suspension straps and the athlete in a high plank position (see figure 5.121a). Bracing with the abdominal muscles, move the knees toward the chest by flexing the knees and hips (see figure 5.121b). Extend them to return to the initial position. The primary muscles worked are the rectus abdominis, transverse abdominis, internal oblique, pyramidalis, and leg muscles.

Figure 5.121 – Knees to chest.

Squat

Begin by facing the anchor of the suspension straps with the feet hip-width apart. Hold the handles at a distance that creates tension in the straps (see figure 5.122a). Slowly lower down until the buttocks are as close to the heels as possible without causing discomfort to the knees or losing correct exercise form (see figure 5.122b). The primary muscles worked are the quadriceps (vastus lateralis, rectus femoris, vastus intermedius, and vastus medialis), gluteus maximus, and gluteus medius.

Figure 5.122 – Squat.

Pistol Squat

Begin by facing the anchor of the suspension straps, feet hip-width apart. Hold the handles at a distance that creates tension in the straps. Extend one leg (see figure 5.123a) and then perform a squat with the other leg (see figure 5.123b). Slowly lower down by flexing the hips, knees, and ankles until the thighs are parallel to the floor. Return to the starting position by extending through the joints of the lower body. Repeat until the prescribed number of repetitions is completed for each leg. The primary muscles worked are the quadriceps (vastus lateralis, rectus femoris, vastus intermedius, and vastus medialis) and gluteus maximus.

Figure 5.123 – Pistol squat.

Bulgarian Split Squat

Place one foot into the strap of the suspension band, with the back facing the band's anchor point (see figure 5.124a). With the other leg, slowly lower down into a squat by flexing the hips, knees, and ankles (see figure 5.124b). Return to the initial position by extending through the joints of the lower body. Repeat until the prescribed number of repetitions is completed for each leg. The primary muscles worked are the quadriceps (vastus lateralis, rectus femoris, vastus intermedius, and vastus medialis) and gluteus maximus.

Figure 5.124 – Bulgarian split squat.

Pike

Place the tops of the feet into the suspension straps and take a high plank position (see figure 5.125a). Initiating from the abdomen, lift the hips into the air, maintaining straight arms, back, and legs (see figure 5.125b). Slowly lower the body and return to the starting position. The primary muscles worked are the rectus abdominis, transverse abdominis, internal oblique, and biceps femoris.

Figure 5.125 – Pike.

Hamstring Curl

Lying face up, place the heels into the suspension straps. Raise the hips off the floor, as in a straight-legged bridge (see figure 5.126a). From this position, flex the knees and hips, bringing the knees toward the chest (see figure 5.126b). Return to the initial position by extending through the hips and knees, sustaining the hip lift throughout the movement. The primary muscles worked are the gluteus maximus and biceps femoris (short and long head).

Figure 5.126 – Hamstring curl.

Table 5.16 presents two sample suspension training programs.

Table 5.16 – Suspension Training Programs

	Week 1	Week 2	Week 3	Week 4
Training A				
1. Low row	3 × 10	3 × 12	4 × 10	4 × 12
2. Squat	3 × 20	3 × 30	4 × 20	4 × 30
3. Chest press	3 × 10	3 × 12	4 × 10	4 × 12
4. Bulgarian split squat	3 × 10 on each side	3 × 12 on each side	4 × 10 on each side	4 × 12 on each side
5. Pike	3 × 20	3 × 30	4 × 20	4 × 30
6. Hamstring curl	3 × 10	3 × 12	4 × 10	4 × 12
Training B				
1. Low row	3 × 10	3 × 12	4 × 10	4 × 12
2. Squat	3 × 20	3 × 30	4 × 20	4 × 30
3. Chest fly	3 × 10	3 × 12	4 × 10	4 × 12
4. Pistol squat	3 × 10 on each side	3 × 12 on each side	4 × 10 on each side	4 × 12 on each side
5. Push-up	3 × 20	3 × 30	4 × 20	4 × 30
6. Knees to chest	3 × 10	3 × 12	4 × 10	4 × 12

Power Training

Combat athletes and mixed martial artists rely on many physical components, such as stamina, strength, and technique to execute skills during competition. These specific metrics can affect overall performance in a single match as well as the ability to maintain high performance levels consistently during a tournament or training camp taking place over several months.

Relatively high strength levels have long been considered a significant attribute to enhance general sport skills, such as jumping, sprinting, and change-of-direction movements. Research indicates that stronger athletes tend to produce superior performances during sport-specific tasks, specifically those that are anaerobic in nature, such as American football, volleyball, jumping events, and weightlifting (Suchomel, et al. 2016). However, for the mixed martial artist, maximal strength levels may not serve as the most important sports performance characteristic compared to quickness and power (Dias and Oliveira, 2013). Due to the violent nature of combat sports, explosive movements—the ability of the athlete to generate high force levels in a split second—should be considered one of the most important physical abilities to possess. This can be both in peak power measurements taken in a single movement or repetition as well as average power that can be measured through several repetitions performed repeatedly.

Strength is most often associated with lower velocities while power is associated with significantly higher velocities. However, the suggestion that strength is equivalent to being slow or that power equals fast is not entirely accurate (Haff and Triplett, 2016). The most critical attribute is for the combat athlete to be able to exert force at velocities that are similar to the competitive environment they compete in. This may be enhancing the acceleration of the body (i.e., during a shoot for a takedown) or an implement (i.e., a fist or leg during a strike) to maximize the potential damage that can be caused in the shortest time or by repeated strikes.

Power is defined biomechanically as one's ability to produce a significant amount of work over a specific time and is expressed mathematically as:

$$\text{Power} = \text{work} \div \text{time}$$

Power can also be calculated as a product of the force that is placed on an object and the velocity of that object traveling in the direction that matches the force that is exerted on to it, expressed mathematically as:

$$\text{Power} = \text{force} \times \text{velocity}$$

To provide an example of how power can be measured, an athlete can complete a bench press with a specific percentage of weight like 80 percent 1RM, while the speed of the bar is monitored, allowing a mathematical determination of power to be calculated. Then, to determine if power has increased, the athlete can repeat the assessment either using the same or a greater load than the previous one. If the movement is performed faster than previous assessments, or if the bar speed is the same but with a greater load, an increase in power performance has been demonstrated.

Traditionally, to improve an athlete's ability to perform a movement with more power, an athlete simply increased muscle mass due to the established relationship between the cross-sectional area of a muscle and its ability to produce greater force (Funato, et al. 2000; Maughan, et al. 1984). The combat athlete faces a unique challenge with this traditional idea due to their body weight needing to be within an acceptable range for their weight division. If muscle mass increases too much, the athlete may not be able to make weight resulting in failure to compete. The coach or trainer of a combat athlete should implement specialized resistance training methods that focus on neurological muscle recruitment that will enhance power or rate of force production while not interfering with body weight changes that may occur from resistance training.

Training adaptations to increase strength in this manner can take place neurologically in two ways: via spatial or temporal summation. *Temporal summation* results in an increase in how fast neural impulses recruit a greater amount of muscle fibers during multiple reps or time under tension. *Spatial summation* is the synchronization of neural impulses to fire simultaneously to recruit more muscle fibers in a shorter amount of time in a single repetition with much higher loads (McArdle, et al. 2016). In this section, we will review three methods that significantly enhance the rate of force production and power performance in athletes and how to implement each method in the training of a combat athlete.

Compensatory Acceleration Training

Compensatory acceleration training refers to applying maximum force into the barbell during an exercise movement to move it as fast as possible within the designated range of motion. The purpose is to deliberately try to accelerate the bar through the concentric phase of a movement without allowing the load of the bar to dictate the speed at which it can be moved (Siff, 2003). Typically, in resistance training, a heavier load results in slower movements, thus increasing time under tension and inducing various muscular adaptations (Wilk, et al. 2021). The idea of using compensatory acceleration training is providing a physiological overload stimulus without having to use heavier loads. This method has been shown to significantly increase power and strength in advanced athletes in as little as five weeks and increase the recruitment of faster motor units with greater force during a movement (Jones, et al. 1999; Lee, et al. 2013; Jones, 2014).

According to Newton's second law (law of acceleration), the rate of change of an object's velocity is directly proportional to the forces acting on the body in the same direction of the force. Mathematically, the amount of force exhibited during a specific movement is influenced by the mass of the object and its acceleration, which is expressed as:

$$Force = mass \times acceleration$$

According to this equation, to generate greater force, mass (weight) must increase on the bar or the bar has to move faster with the same load, or both when performing the exercise. Simply increasing the mass has been shown to increase muscle recruitment efficiently; however, the ability to perform the movement sufficiently and safely directly correlates to the athlete's experience with the movement itself (Siff, 2003). Typically, combat athletes spend little time mastering traditional exercise movements, such as the bench press, squat, deadlift, and the Olympic lifts, because this would take considerable time away from skills training and require greater rest periods, which could be detrimental physically and psychologically when approaching a fight. For this reason, using compensatory acceleration as a training technique is a reasonable method because it does not require maximal strength levels, can be effective with loads ranging from 30 percent to 90 percent of 1RM, and merely requires a great deal of concentrated effort on the part of the combat athlete to experience the positive benefits of this training method (Zatsiorsky and Kraemer, 2006; Baker, 1995). Table 5.17 shows an example of a compensatory acceleration training program.

Table 5.17 – Compensatory Acceleration Training Program

	Week 1	Week 2	Week 3	Week 4
Day 1				
1. Shoulder press	5 × 5 @ 65% 1RM	5 × 5 @ 70% 1RM	5 × 3 @ 75% 1RM	4 × 3 @ 80% 1RM
2. Back squat	5 × 5 @ 65% 1RM	5 × 5 @ 70% 1RM	6 × 3 @ 75% 1RM	4 × 3 @ 80% 1RM
Day 2				
1. Bench press	5 × 5 @ 65% 1RM	5 × 5 @ 70% 1RM	5 × 3 @ 75% 1RM	4 × 3 @ 80% 1RM
2. Deadlift	5 × 5 @ 65% 1RM	5 × 5 @ 70% 1RM	6 × 3 @ 75% 1RM	4 × 3 @ 80% 1RM

Accommodating Resistance Training

Accommodating resistance training is commonly used with either elastic bands or chains to simulate an increasing intensity (load) as the athlete performs the concentric part of a movement. This demands a greater amount of force to overcome the increased intensity at the top of an exercise but also requires maximum effort throughout the entire range of movement. This is a simple method to implement into training with little experience required to set up and apply (Zatsiorsky and Kraemer, 2006). It can easily be implemented with various exercises but would probably be best and safest to use with ground-based closed-chain exercises such as the bench press, back squat, deadlift, and shoulder press as well as various body weight movements. Although either chains or elastic bands can be used, elastic bands may be preferred for the combat athlete due to the core rigidity needed to support the tension, which is helpful for the unstable nature of the sport when competing.

Accommodating resistance training is extremely useful for a gym that does not specialize in resistance training due to the lack of equipment, funds, or available space. Elastic bands can be implemented in various settings with or without equipment (see examples in figures 5.127 and 5.128). Table 5.18 presents an example of an accommodating resistance training program.

Figure 5.127 – Push-up with resistance band.

Figure 5.128 – Back squat with resistance band.

Table 5.18 – Accommodating Resistance Training Program

	Week 1	Week 2	Week 3	Week 4
Day 1				
1. Back squat with bands	12 × 2-3 @ 60%-70% 1RM with light resistance bands	10 × 2-3 @ 70%-80% 1RM with light resistance bands	8 × 2-3 @ 60%-70% 1RM with medium resistance bands	6 × 2-3 @ 70%-80% 1RM with medium resistance bands
2. Leg curl and leg extension with bands	3 × 12 @ 60% 1RM with light resistance bands	3 × 10 @ 65% 1RM with light resistance bands	3 × 8 @ 70% 1RM with medium resistance bands	3 × 8 @ 70% 1RM with medium resistance bands
3. Step-up with bands	3 × 12 @ 60% 1RM with light resistance bands per side	3 × 10 @ 65% 1RM with light resistance bands per side	3 × 8 @ 70% 1RM with medium resistance bands per side	3 × 8 @ 70% 1RM with medium resistance bands per side
Day 2				
1. Bench press with bands	12 × 2-3 @ 60%-70% 1RM with light resistance bands	10 × 2-3 @ 70%-80% 1RM with light resistance bands	8 × 2-3 @ 60%-70% 1RM with medium resistance bands	6 × 2-3 @ 70%-80% 1RM with medium resistance bands
2. Triceps extension with bands	3 × 12 with light resistance bands	3 × 12 with light resistance bands	3 × 8 with medium resistance bands	3 × 8 with medium resistance bands
3. Shoulder press with bands	3 × 12 @ 60% 1RM with light resistance bands	3 × 10 @ 65% 1RM with light resistance bands	3 × 8 @ 70% 1RM with medium resistance bands	3 × 8 @ 70% 1RM with medium resistance bands
Day 3				
1. Barbell deadlift with bands	12 × 2-3 @ 60%-70% 1RM with light resistance bands	10 × 2-3 @ 70%-80% 1RM with light resistance bands	8 × 2-3 @ 60%-70% 1RM with medium resistance bands	6 × 2-3 @ 70%-80% 1RM with medium resistance bands
2. Kettlebell swing with bands	3 × 12 with light resistance bands	3 × 12 with light resistance bands	3 × 8 with medium resistance bands	3 × 8 with medium resistance bands
3. RDL with bands	3 × 12 with light resistance bands	3 × 12 with light resistance bands	3 × 8 with medium resistance bands	3 × 8 with medium resistance bands

Contrast Training Method

Contrast training is an effective and time-efficient training method to improve strength and power. It alternates heavy resistance exercise followed by an unloaded or lightly loaded power exercise performed in an explosive manner. This method provides an opportunity to train both sides of the force-velocity curve equation in one session (Sutton, 2022). An example of contrast training would be performing 1 set × 10 repetitions of back squats followed by 1 set × 10 box jumps. The athlete would repeat this format until all the sets have been completed.

This method has resulted in significant improvements in power performance and is supported in various studies (Gago, et al. 2020; Lowery, et al. 2012; Johnson, et al. 2019). Due to the nature of the sport, combat athletes may want to incorporate the contrast method to take advantage of *post-activation potentiation* (PAP), the primary method on which contrast training is based. PAP refers to the condition by which acute muscle-force generation is increased as a result of the inner contractions of the muscle. This causes nervous system stimulation, which is created by the heavy loads lifted (Sutton, 2022).

One can set up a contrast training session easily with hardly more than a standard barbell or kettlebell set to perform typical exercise movements such as the back squat, bench press, deadlift, and shoulder press. In figures 5.129 and 5.130, we invited UFC veteran Ben Saunders and Professor Brian Binkley to show sample exercises that can be used after heavy sets of back squat or deadlift exercises using the contrast method. Table 5.19 presents an example of a contrast training program.

Figure 5.129 – Ben Saunders doing a suspension pendulum squat jump.

Figure 5.130 – Suspension pendulum ski jump.

Table 5.19 – Contrast Training Method Program

	Week 1	Week 2	Week 3	Week 4
Day 1				
1A. Back squat	8 × 3 @ 75% 1RM	8 × 3 @ 75% 1RM	8 × 2 @ 80% 1RM	8 × 2 @ 80% 1RM
1B. Tuck jump	8 × 2 BW	8 × 3 BW	8 × 2 BW	8 × 3 BW
2A. Front squat	3 × 12 @ 60% 1RM	3 × 12 @ 60% 1RM	3 × 10 @ 65% 1RM	3 × 8 @ 70% 1RM
2B. Suspension pendulum squat jump	3 × 5 BW	3 × 5 BW	3 × 5 BW	3 × 5 BW
3A. Dumbbell lateral lunge	3 × 12 per side	3 × 12 per side	3 × 10 per side, explosive	3 × 10 per side, explosive
3B. Suspension pendulum ski jump	3 × 5 BW	3 × 5 BW	3 × 8 BW	3 × 8 BW
Day 2				
1A. Bench press	8 × 3 @ 75% 1RM	8 × 3 @ 75% 1RM	8 × 2 @ 80% 1RM	8 × 2 @ 80% 1RM
1B. Plyo push-up	8 × 3 BW	8 × 3 BW	8 × 5 BW	8 × 5 BW
2A. Shoulder press	3 × 12 @ 60% 1RM	3 × 12 @ 60% 1RM	3 × 10 @ 65% 1RM	3 × 8 @ 70% 1RM
2B. Medicine ball overhead throw	3 × 5	3 × 5	3 × 5	3 × 5
3A. T-bar row	3 × 12 @ 60% 1RM	3 × 12 @ 60% 1RM	3 × 10 @ 65% 1RM	3 × 8 @ 70% 1RM
3B. Medicine ball overhead slam	3 × 5	3 × 5	3 × 5	3 × 5
Day 3				
1A. Barbell deadlift	8 × 3 @ 75% 1RM	8 × 3 @ 75% 1RM	8 × 2 @ 80% 1RM	8 × 2 @ 80% 1RM
1B. Long jump	8 × 3 BW	8 × 3 BW	8 × 5 BW	8 × 5 BW
2A. Dumbbell lunge	3 × 12 per side	3 × 12 per side	3 × 10 per side, explosive	3 × 10 per side, explosive
2B. Split squat jump	3 × 6 BW	3 × 6 BW	3 × 8 BW	3 × 8 BW
3A. Dumbbell thruster	3 × 12 @ 60% 1RM	3 × 12 @ 60% 1RM	3 × 10 @ 65% 1RM	3 × 8 @ 70% 1RM
3B. Medicine ball overhead throw	3 × 5	3 × 5	3 × 5	3 × 5

BW: body weight

Power Training Circuit

Power training may be performed in different ways, as demonstrated earlier in this chapter, so for this section, we invited veteran former UFC fighter George Sotiropoulos to demonstrate how to combine strength and velocity training to develop power in the form of a circuit. The circuits consist of a mix of exercises with weights (dumbbells) and a medicine ball in which the athlete develops strength and velocity (power) of movements similar to the ones used in combat.

In the resistance training exercises, moderate or high loads are used with repetitions that range from 4RM to 10RM, but to appropriately develop velocity, workloads of between 10 percent and 40 percent of the maximum should be used. The exercises should be performed at maximum speed but be of short duration, varying between 5 and 15 seconds. The rest intervals must allow the fighter to fully recover between exercise sets (rests that vary between 1-5 minutes). The number of sets in each circuit varies from two to five, and the frequency of the training may not be less than one session or greater than three sessions per week. The strength and velocity training must be incorporated within the annual program and, in general, is performed four to eight weeks before the fight (Dias, et al. 2017).

First Circuit

Start with the dumbbell fly, in which the strength of the chest and deltoid muscles is developed, along with providing isometric work for the biceps (see figure 5.131). The range of motion is limited so that there is a greater emphasis on the target muscles. Then move on to a medicine ball, without a rest, throwing it at maximum velocity, and repeating this five times (see figure 5.132).

Figure 5.131 – Sotiropoulos performing dumbbell fly.

Figure 5.132 – Throwing a medicine ball at maximum velocity.

Second Circuit

This exercise sequence is for the lower body. It begins with a dumbbell lunge, which develops leg strength (see figure 5.133). After the lunge, the athlete moves on, without any rest, to a horizontal jump (the athlete is required to jump with maximum force and velocity five times) (see figure 5.134).

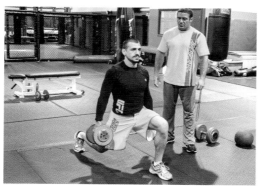

Figure 5.133 – Dumbbell lunge.

Figure 5.134 – Horizontal jump.

Third Circuit

This works the upper body and lower back. Begin with the one-arm dumbbell row (see figure 5.135). It is important to emphasize control of posture and breathing during this movement. After the row, move on to the medicine ball overhead slam onto the floor, working the total body. Repeat it five times with maximum velocity (see figure 5.136).

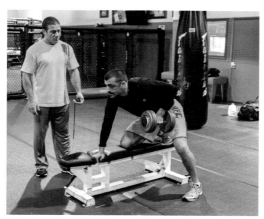

Figure 5.135 – One-arm dumbbell row.

Figure 5.136 – Medicine ball overhead slam.

At the end of the training, some abdominal exercises (see figure 5.137) are performed with the medicine ball in sets of 50 repetitions until fatigue.

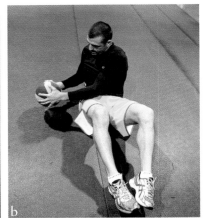

Figure 5.137 – Abdominal exercises with medicine ball.

Table 5.20 presents a sample program for the power circuit.

Table 5.20 – Power Circuit Program

	Week 1	Week 2	Week 3	Week 4
First circuit				
1. Dumbbell fly	2 × 10	2 × 10	3 × 8	4 × 6
2. Medicine ball throw	2 × 5	2 × 5	3 × 5	4 × 5
Second circuit				
1. Dumbbell lunge	2 × 10 per side	2 × 10 per side	3 × 8 per side	4 × 6 per side
2. Horizontal jump	2 × 5 BW	2 × 5 BW	3 × 5 BW	4 × 5 BW
Third circuit				
1. One-arm dumbbell row	2 × 10 per side	2 × 10 per side	3 × 8 per side	4 × 6 per side
2. Medicine ball overhead slam	2 × 5	2 × 5	3 × 5	4 × 5

BW: body weight

Specific Power Training

Determining which exercises are important in each period of the training is an indispensable factor for the success of the training process. According to Verkhoshansky and Siff (2009), strength is highly dependent on the context, the pattern of movement, and technique in which it is used.

Resistance training exercises may be classified into three major groups: general, special, or specific, depending on their biomechanical structures and the effect on the neuromuscular system.

- *Specific exercises* repeat the movements of the competitive activity (e.g., straight punch) in training and may also be used with external load
- *Special exercises* train the same muscle group, muscular activities, and physiological systems as the specific exercises but do not imitate them (e.g., medicine ball chest pass)
- *General exercises* do not imitate competitive activity and do not train the physiological systems specific to the sport (e.g., bench press)

To explain the hierarchical pyramid of the resistance training exercises, we have adapted the exercise classification Bondarchuk (2007) proposed to prepare MMA athletes (see figure 5.138).

The more specific exercises at the top are exactly what the fighter will perform in the competition: punches, kicks, takedowns, and so on. Any other exercise variation will be moved to lower levels of the pyramid. Toward the base are general exercises.

Verkhoshansky and Siff (2009) determined five laws of dynamic correspondence (a criterion proposed to determine the positive effect of a training program on an athlete's performance). These laws are as follows:

1. Amplitude and direction of movement
2. Accentuated region of force production
3. Dynamics of the effort
4. Rate and time of maximal force production
5. Regimen of muscular work

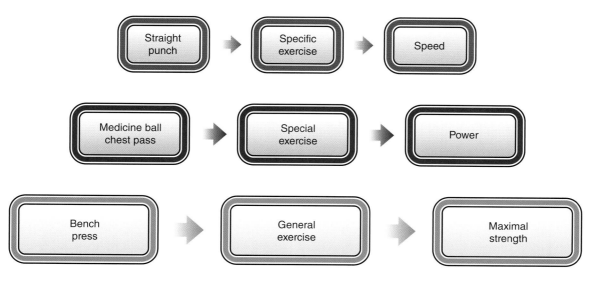

Figure 5.138 – Example of exercises and their classification for MMA athletes.

Adapted by permission from A. Bondarchuk, *Transfer of Training Sports*, vol. 1 (Muskegon, MI: Ultimate Athlete Concepts, 2007).

A resistance training method quite widely used to improve muscle power in fighters is called *contrast training* and was described previously in this chapter. Under this training method, two exercises with the same movement pattern are used in one superset. The first exercise should be high resistance, and the subsequent exercise is lighter but is performed at a faster speed. According to Baker (2003), because the lighter exercise is performed with less resistance than the first heavier exercise, the power subsequently applied is increased in the lighter exercise.

In this section, we invited former UFC athlete Leandro "Buscape" Silva and the striking coach of American Top Team (ATT), Luciano "Macarrão" Dos Santos, to perform an example of contrast training (see figure 5.139*a*) using the general exercise of horizontal pushing on the PowerMax 360 paired with the specific exercise of punching the pads with Coach Macarrão (see figure 5.139*b*).

Another example of contrast training is attaching a resistance band to a fixed point or pulley and completing the movement with accommodating resistance (resistance band), generating a greater peak power at the end of the movement, followed by the same movement without load at the fastest execution speed possible. Should the chosen exercise be a movement specific to the sport, consider that using a very high resistance on the resistance band means there is a greater chance of the athlete's technique worsening, so it is important to find a load that the athlete can move through the range of movement without compromising technique. In the examples shown in figures 5.140 through 5.142, we used three specific exercises (jab, cross, and front kick) as the conditioning activity (with a load), followed by the same exercise without resistance and at full speed.

Figure 5.139 – Horizontal pushing a high load using the PowerMax 360 (*a*); punching the pad without resistance and at full speed (*b*).

Figure 5.140 – A jab with a resistance band (a moderate load) (*a-b*); punching the pad without resistance and at full speed (*c-d*).

Figure 5.141 – A cross with a resistance band (a moderate load) (*a-b*); punching the pad without resistance and at full speed (*c-d*).

Figure 5.142 – A front kick with a resistance band (a moderate load) (*a-b*); kicking the pad without resistance and at full speed (*c-d*).

A variation on complex training is *French contrast training*, where we use more than two exercises in a single set. The key difference between these two training methods is that in French contrast training, more methods are used to develop the athlete's power. As an example, to improve power in a front kick, in figure 5.143, we first use the general exercise of hip and knee flexion and extension on a high-resistance pneumatic machine for the lower body called The Real Runner.

Figure 5.143 – Hip and knee flexion and extension using The Real Runner.

This is followed by a special hip flexion movement using low resistance (light super-band) (see figures 5.144a-b); and finally, the specific exercise of kneeing the pad with the coach, with no resistance but performing at maximum speed (see figures 5.144c-d).

Figure 5.144 – A special hip flexion movement with a resistance band (a light load) (a-b); kneeing the pad without resistance and at full speed (c-d).

Today, it is possible to find machines that use these training methods such as the KINEO (Kineo Intelligent Load) system where the individual can vary the resistance of the cable according to the focus of the training (see figure 5.145).

Figure 5.145 – Horizontal pushing a high load using the KINEO system (a); punching the pad with a light load and at full speed (b).

This advanced training method benefits individuals with a greater level of muscle strength the most, because they have already mastered the specific movements and have a track record of training with greater strength compared to amateur and less well-trained athletes.

Table 5.21 presents two programs for specific power training that incorporates contrast training.

Table 5.21 – Specific Power Training Programs

	Week 1	Week 2	Week 3	Week 4
Program 1: Contrast training superset*				
1a. Pushing on the PowerMax 360	3 × 6 reps per side	4 × 6 reps per side	5 × 6 reps per side	6 × 6 reps per side
1b. Hitting the pads with coach (cross) or punching bag	3 × 10 sec per side	4 × 10 sec per side	5 × 10 sec per side	6 × 10 sec per side
2a. Jab exercise with resistance band	3 × 6 reps per side	4 × 6 reps per side	5 × 6 reps per side	6 × 6 reps per side
2b. Hitting the pads with coach (jab) or punching bag	3 × 10 sec per side	4 × 10 sec per side	5 × 10 sec per side	6 × 10 sec per side
3a. Front kick exercise with resistance band	3 × 6 reps per side	4 × 6 reps per side	5 × 6 reps per side	6 × 6 reps per side
3b. Hitting the pads with coach (front kick) or punching bag	3 × 10 sec per side	4 × 10 sec per side	5 × 10 sec per side	6 × 10 sec per side
Program 2: French contrast training triset**				
1. Hip and knee flexion/extension on The Real Runner machine	2 × 10 sec	4 × 10 sec	6 × 10 sec	8 × 10 sec
2. Hip flexion with superband on the ankle	2 × 10 sec per side	4 × 10 sec per side	6 × 10 sec per side	8 × 10 sec per side
3. Hitting the pads with coach (kneeing) or punching bag	2 × 10 sec per side	4 × 10 sec per side	6 × 10 sec per side	8 × 10 sec per side

Note: All the exercises should be done as fast as possible.

*Rest for 60 seconds to 90 seconds between each set. No rest between each superset exercise.

** Rest for 60 seconds to 90 seconds between each set. Rest for 10 seconds between each triset exercise.

Power Endurance Training

The words *power* and *endurance* are not commonly seen together because they refer to different things. Power refers to the ability to generate force very quickly over a short time, and endurance typically is associated with lower forces generated over a longer time. For this book, *power endurance* is defined as the ability to perform movements at a higher percentage of maximal force repetitively. This is important for mixed martial arts and other combat sports that require repeated bouts of high-intensity effort (Zatsiorsky and Kraemer, 2006). Intensities used to improve this training characteristic typically range from 60 percent to 80 percent of 1RM or only allowing 8 to 10 repetitions until failure.

However, the particular session design is critical to consider. The session should allow for optimal recovery before repeating the exercise at the specific intensity prescribed to ensure that correct technique and optimal speed are achieved. This training can also help protect the athlete from injury due to decreased motor control brought on by an onset of fatigue during the session (Haff and Triplett, 2016; Zatsiorsky and Kraemer, 2006). Because the exercise is already at a high intensity, it is in the athlete's best interests to increase the session density by reducing the rest intervals between each exercise performed from three to five minutes to as low as 30 to 60 seconds so that muscular endurance capacity within the prescribed intensity is developed. However, rest intervals should only be reduced when the athlete will still achieve optimal recovery.

Power Endurance Training (Program 1)

Repeat five to eight times over several weeks, progressing intensity by decreasing rest time between each exercise and group of exercises (this is also called a *circuit* or *cluster*).

Circuit A
Bench press @ 75% 1RM × 8-10 reps → Back squat @ 75% 1RM × 8 reps → Shoulder press @ 75% 1RM × 8-10 reps → Sled or tire sprint 20-30 yd as fast as possible. Rest for 2-3 min.

Circuit B
Suspension pendulum squat jump with weight vest × 8 reps → Band-resisted push-up × 8 reps → Ground to overhead movement (using kettlebell, dumbbell, or medicine ball) × 8 reps → Dummy takedown to ground and pound (punch/elbow/alternating) as many and as fast as possible in 30-60 sec. Rest for 2-3 min.

Circuit C
Kettlebell or dumbbell thruster 10RM × 8 reps → Plyo/clapping push-up with weight vest × 5-8 reps → Knee strikes with ankle weights to dummy bag × 20 (alternating/same side) → Dummy carry 20-30 yd × 8-10 reps. Rest for 2-3 min.

Power Endurance Training (Program 2)

In this section, we are going to demonstrate a circuit with weights used in the preparation of several UFC fighters, such as veteran UFC and Bellator Italian athlete, Alessio "Legionarius" Sakara. This work is normally performed twice a week for six weeks so that the last heavy training session ends 10 days before the contest (Dias, et al. 2017).

We have devised the training in stations, mixing complex exercises with basic exercises in resistance training, like bench press and row, in which the goal is to develop power endurance.

First Combination or Triplex

This station consists of a weightlifting-type exercise, abdominal core work, and the bench press. The first exercise is the clean pull (a highly difficult exercise in which the athlete develops strength and coordination and strengthens the arm and leg muscles; see figure 5.146, but note that not all three pulls are shown). Start in deadlift position and keep the feet hip-width apart. Grip the bar with both hands slightly wider than shoulder width. Lower the hips until the shins touch the bar; the hips should be slightly lower than the traditional deadlift setup. Pinch the shoulder blades and look forward (not down as in a standard deadlift). The exercise can be broken down into three pulls:

1. *First pull:* The first pull is moving the bar from the floor to just above the knee. This is the most controlled pull in the clean pull. Keep the back tight and try to turn the armpits forward to engage the lats. Inhale and pull the bar off the floor, shifting weight back to the heels. Lead with the chest rising and try to maintain the angle of the hips and shoulders. The bar should shift back toward the torso. It is critical to keep the bar close and not let it shift forward. Keep the shoulders in front of the bar as long as possible.

2. *Second pull:* The second pull is moving the bar from just above the knee to the upper thigh, a "power position" that will permit acceleration. Now focus on aggressively extending at the hips and knees (essentially standing up) by shifting the hips forward. Pull the bar back toward the torso, keeping it in close contact with the quads. The torso angle should become more vertical as this occurs. Do not let the bar lose contact with the quads. Keeping the lats engaged, continue pulling the bar back toward the hips.

3. *Third pull:* In the third and final pull, max acceleration is achieved. Hips, knees, and ankles all fully extend. As this triple extension occurs, the shoulders shrug, and the weight shifts onto the toes (as if jumping) as the acceleration of the bar forces the heels off the floor. Think of this as a jump and shrug that gets the bar moving vertically, but do not over-involve the arms. The arms should remain straight (except during the shoulder shrug), elbows pointed out. The momentum of the final pull will propel the bar upward to finish above the hips. Exhale at the end of the movement.

Figure 5.146 – Alessio Sakara performs the clean pull.

The second exercise should be executed to strengthen the abdominal core muscles as described in table 5.12. Choose any logical exercise to target the core.

Finally, the third exercise is a traditional bench press and promotes strengthening the pushing muscles (using a spotter) as shown in figure 5.147.

Figure 5.147 – Bench press with a spotter.

Second Combination or Triplex

This station includes a clean and press, abdominal core work, and a one-arm standing row on the machine. The first exercise (see figure 5.148) has a high degree of difficulty, allowing the athlete to develop strength and movement coordination. It strengthens the muscles of the lower and upper body. Squat down with a straight back and grab the barbell with an overhand grip. Inhale, and in one swift movement, lift the barbell to shoulder height and sink back down into a squat. Push up through the heels and extend the arms to press the barbell above the head. Lower safely to the shoulders and drop back to the floor while maintaining a straight back. Exhale at the end of the movement.

Figure 5.148 – Clean and press.

Next, select a different exercise targeting the abdominal core muscles as described in table 5.12 and perform it for 30 seconds.

To finish the second combination, we use the one-arm standing row to strengthen the back muscles. This version has a moderate degree of difficulty, because the athlete adopts a semi-squatting position and executes it unilaterally (see figure 5.149).

Figure 5.149 – One-arm standing machine row.

Third Combination or Triplex

This station consists of a low cable squat, medicine ball crunch, and medicine ball overhead slam followed by a sprawl. The first exercise uses a low-pulley machine with adapted tubes instead of handles to simulate an open wrist grip in grappling. Begin the low cable squat by standing in front of the cable machine, with the feet about shoulder-width apart and facing forward. The cables (and attachments) should be low, at the feet. Engage the core and keep the shoulders retracted. Grab the tubes and slowly lower the body as if sitting in a chair by flexing at the knees and hips in a squatting motion (see figure 5.150a). Inhale and squeeze the glute muscles, rising to the starting position until the knees are back into full extension (see figure 5.150b). Exhale at the end of the movement and repeat this motion for as many desired repetitions within the set.

Figure 5.150 – Low cable squat.

For the medicine ball crunch, start on the ground, with the knees flexed and the medicine ball held against the chest. Extend the arms up in a straight line. Keep them straight and perform a sit-up, then reach back on the way down so the medicine ball touches the chest. Repeat the movement for as many desired repetitions within the set (see figure 5.151).

Figure 5.151 – Medicine ball crunch.

To finish the third combination, perform the medicine ball overhead slam (see figure 5.111) but finish with a sprawl movement (see figure 5.152), with the hands remaining on top of the ball. This is a dynamic exercise that seeks to adapt real fight movements to condition the athlete for defending takedowns with less fatigue.

Figure 5.152 – The sprawl (performed after the medicine ball overhead slam).

At the end of the work described previously, aerobic work (average duration 10-20 min) is performed on the elliptical trainer to help maintain body weight (see figure 5.153).

Figure 5.153 – Aerobic work on the elliptical trainer.

The exercises are performed as a trio, with minimal rest between them, and only at the end of the three exercises does the athlete take a transition break of 30 to 45 seconds. The exercises are performed as a circuit, totaling five to six minutes in each combination. The number of repetitions varies between 2RM and 6RM in the first exercise of the group, the second is normally executed for 30 seconds, and the last varies between 10RM and 15RM repetitions. The number of sets is between two and four in each combination.

The basic localized exercises should be mixed with more complex exercises in which the whole body is mobilized, like we see with the clean pull, clean and press, or medicine ball overhead slam with sprawl.

This power endurance circuit is performed in only one of the final preparation phases of the athlete and is normally executed twice a week. Table 5.22 shows how to use this circuit over the course of four weeks.

Table 5.22 – Power Endurance Training Circuit Program

	Week 1	Week 2	Week 3	Week 4
First triplex				
1a. Clean pull	2 × 6RM	2 × 6RM	3 × 4RM	3 × 4RM
1b. Abdominal work	2 × 30 sec	2 × 30 sec	3 × 30 sec	3 × 30 sec
1c. Bench press with a spotter	2 × 15RM	2 × 15RM	3 × 15RM	3 × 15RM
Second triplex				
2a. Clean and press	2 × 4RM	2 × 4RM	3 × 2RM	3 × 2RM
2b. Abdominal work	2 × 30 sec	2 × 30 sec	3 × 30 sec	3 × 30 sec
2c. One-arm standing machine row	2 × 12RM on each side	2 × 12RM on each side	3 × 10RM on each side	3 × 10RM on each side
Third triplex				
3a. Low cable squat	2 × 6RM	2 × 6RM	3 × 4RM	3 × 4RM
3b. Medicine ball crunch	2 × 30 sec	2 × 30 sec	3 × 30 sec	3 × 30 sec
3c. Medicine ball overhead slam followed by a sprawl	2 × 10	2 × 10	3 × 10	3 × 10
Aerobic training				
Elliptical machine	1 × 10 min Slow pace	1 × 10 min Slow pace	1 × 15 min Slow pace	1 × 20 min Slow pace

Speed Training

The term *speed*, according to leading researcher Vladimir Zatsiorsky (1995), is defined as "the ability to perform motor actions as quickly as possible under certain conditions." Speed is a component of the essential explosive strength and power required during striking, while success during grappling depends on isometric and concentric strength (Barley, et al. 2019). Additionally, technical actions must be performed correctly, using the most efficient movements, at a very high rate (Bompa, 1999). Statistics such as amateur boxers averaging 1.4 actions per second during competition (Loturco, et al. 2016) represent how important speed is to programming sport-specific training for combat sport athletes.

While we can develop an athlete's speed through strength and conditioning, speed is a physical ability that depends greatly on the athlete's genetics. Athletes born with a higher ratio of fast-twitch to slow-twitch muscle fibers will always be faster than athletes with normal concentrations (normally about 50/50) of fast- and slow-twitch muscle fibers. As coaches we can ensure our programming is increasing the athlete's speed by testing the athlete at regular intervals and comparing the results to previous scores. We can also compare them to athletes of other sports using normative data to determine where they place in the bigger picture of professional athletic abilities (Zatsiorsky apud Dias, et al. 2016b).

For example, a high-level athlete weighing around 80 kilograms (176 lb) should be able to do a long jump with a standing start of 2.38 meters (7.97 ft) or more, whereas an average athlete jumps 2.28 meters (7.48 ft) or less. The vertical jump is over 58 centimeters (22.83 in.) for high-level athletes and about 51 centimeters (20 in.) for mid-level athletes.

The running speed of 30 meters (33 yd) with a standing start is around 3.94 seconds and 100 meters (109 yd) is 13 seconds for high-level athletes. In beginner athletes, it is 4.08 seconds for a 30-meter race and 14.11 seconds in a 100-meter race (Dias, et al. 2016b).

Based on data collected using various methods described in chapter 3, we can ascertain the current speed of our athletes and create a baseline for comparison. Performing these evaluations allows us to develop speed more accurately in sport-specific movements.

There are factors specific to upper-body striking that should be considered in speed training. While the legs are at zero velocity, the athlete initiates force against the ground and accelerates the body after overcoming inertia, and the final arm extension happens at a very high speed. Therefore, the kinematic (properties of motion in an object) and kinetic (resulting from motion) characteristics of striking must be considered in training (Chaabène, et al. 2015).

Another factor we need to consider in speed training for MMA athletes is that punching and other upper-body strikes occur both standing and on the ground, yet another physical demand unique to the sport. The athlete must be able to produce high forces at a high velocity and must move quickly to avoid being struck, nimbly moving around in and out of the strike zone while on their feet, against the cage, and the ground.

For the best results through the most effective training, follow these recommendations:

- Exercises should be done at the maximum speed but be short in duration. Work time should range from 5 to 15 seconds.
- Rest intervals should enable the fighter to fully recover between exercise sets. Intervals should range from one to five minutes.
- Training frequency may not be less than one workout per week.
- To properly develop speed, we must maintain workloads from 0 to 40 percent of the athlete's maximum effort.
- Speed training should be within the annual periodization program, usually a few weeks before fights or competitions.

Coaches and athletes need to be concerned with optimal load. There is often a motivation to work "hard" by lifting heavy loads to develop strength over a long time, which limits athletes' speed capabilities. Exercises must cause the desired neural adaptation without significantly altering fat free mass (FFM) (Kostikiadis, et al. 2018). This is why functional training for combat sport athletes is popular. The athlete becomes stronger without gaining size or weight. Neuromuscular adaptation occurs through the whole body being engaged in movements that mimic the sport (Santana, 2015).

In the following section, former UFC fighter and No-Gi world champion Roan "Jucão" Carneiro demonstrates selected exercises that professionals use to develop the speed of different muscle groups in mixed martial arts athletes.

Bicycle
Begin training with a general and specific warm-up lasting 5 to 10 minutes to raise body temperature and increase blood flow to the muscles, preparing the body to work and reducing the chance of injury. In this instance, we chose to work on the spin bicycle, which works the lower body, calves, hamstrings, and quadriceps. To a degree, depending on the resistance used, the spin bicycle will work the core and gluteal muscles as well.

Keiser Air300 Runner
In this first circuit, the athlete performs an exercise targeting the lower body on a pneumatic machine (see figure 5.154). These machines use air resistance through an adapted compressor, allowing movements with an overload of up to 490 pounds (222 kg). This exercise specifically trains acceleration, speed, and power endurance in the legs. The sets performed for this exercise were 5 to 15 seconds long with an active recovery interval of 60 to 90 seconds, sometimes longer, repeated 4 to 6 times, with a load of 20 percent to 40 percent of the athlete's 1RM in the back squat.

Figure 5.154 – Roan "Jucão" Carneiro on the Air300 Runner.

Arm Ergometer
After performing high-intensity lower body work, we switch the segment to the upper body using an arm cycle ergometer to develop speed endurance (see figure 5.155). Speed endurance is the capacity of an athlete to withstand high-intensity movement for a longer period. With the aid of the cycle ergometer, we can develop these capabilities in the arms and increase maximal oxygen uptake and anaerobic threshold. In this exercise, we performed 4 to 6 series for a 15-second duration in each direction (forward and backward), with an active recovery range of 60 to 120 seconds.

Figure 5.155 – Roan "Jucão" Carneiro using an arm ergometer.

VersaClimber

The VersaClimber simulates climbing with dynamic and cyclic arm and leg movements. It is used to train speed or speed endurance (see figure 5.156). In this exercise, we perform 4 to 6 sets of 5 to 15 seconds for speed or 20 to 30 seconds in duration for speed endurance, using a 60- to 90-second active interval.

Figure 5.156 – Roan "Jucão" Carneiro on the VersaClimber.

Battle Rope

Battle ropes can be used for increasing speed and speed endurance (see figure 5.157). It is very well suited for combat sport athletes due to the degree of difficulty and variability of executing movements that enhance speed, coordination, balance, and core stabilization. The proposed series for this phase of training was 10 to 15 seconds of rope work with 60 to 90 seconds of either passive or active rest (shadow boxing) interval, depending on the athlete's conditioning, until 5 minutes total time is reached.

Figure 5.157 – Roan "Jucão" Carneiro using battle ropes.

NordicTrack Incline Trainer

For this exercise, run on a 30 percent to 50 percent incline at a speed of 6 to 8 miles per hour (9.5-12 km/h), for 5 to 15 seconds with a 45-second active rest interval, totaling 5 minutes of work (see figure 5.158).

Figure 5.158 – Roan "Jucão" Carneiro on the incline trainer.

Running Sprint on the Tread Sled

Another exercise used to develop speed, especially for the legs, is the tread sled (see figure 5.159a). This exercise can be used in place of the incline trainer exercise or as an additional exercise. Work on the tread sled not only increases speed but also enhances movements specific to fighters, both defensively, when pushing the opponent away, and offensively, when holding the opponent against the cage. Sprint at maximum speed for 5 to 15 seconds with a 45-second active rest interval, totaling 5 minutes of work. In figure 5.159b, the data panel includes the acceleration graph, the power in watts, and other data that help control the load and effectively train speed.

Figure 5.159 – Roan "Jucão" Carneiro on the tread sled (*a*) with a close-up of the data panel (*b*).

Table 5.23 shows two examples of speed training programs.

Table 5.23 – Speed Training Programs

	Week 1	Week 2	Week 3	Week 4
Training A				
1. Bicycle warm-up	1 × 5 min	1 × 6 min	1 × 8 min	1 × 10 min
2. Keiser Air300 Runner	4 × 5 sec @ 20% of 1RM	4 × 10 sec @ 20% of 1RM	5 × 10 sec @ 20% of 1RM	6 × 10 sec @ 20% of 1RM
3. Arm ergometer	4 × 15 sec forward and 15 sec backward	4 × 15 sec forward and 15 sec backward	5 × 15 sec forward and 15 sec backward	6 × 15 sec forward and 15 sec backward
4. Tread sled sprint	3 × 10 sec BW	4 × 10 sec BW	5 × 10 sec BW	6 × 10 sec BW
Training B				
1. Bicycle warm-up	1 × 5 min	1 × 6 min	1 × 8 min	1 × 10 min
2. VersaClimber	4 × 15 sec	4 × 15 sec	5 × 15 sec	6 × 15 sec
3. Battle rope	3 × 15 sec	4 × 15 sec	5 × 15 sec	6 × 15 sec
4. Incline trainer	4 × 10 sec 6 mph @ 35% incline	4 × 10 sec 6 mph @ 40% incline	5 × 10 sec 6 mph @ 45% incline	6 × 10 sec 6 mph @ 50% incline

BW: body weight

Agility Training

The time spent on strength and conditioning is very small compared to the time an athlete will spend cultivating the skills of their sport. Yet, we know that through strength and conditioning, indicators of sport success such as highly developed anaerobic conditioning, power, agility, and coordination are enhanced (Andrade, et al. 2019). Therefore, rapid change of direction, agility, strategically responding to tactical situations, and carrying out preplanned changes in direction are key factors in success for competitive MMA and other combat sports. Athletes should be agile enough to change direction quickly and skillfully while engaged in competition and still maintain their perceptual and cognitive abilities.

The aspects of agility we train are change of direction and speed, maneuverability, and perceptual and cognitive ability. These physical abilities depend on neurophysiological requirements being met. Agility demands acceleration, deceleration, reacceleration, and braking, which depend on high-velocity forces and high-force eccentric actions. The neuromuscular adaptations to eccentric and concentric loading are not the same, with adaptations to eccentric loading being directly related to the velocity of the load (Haff and Triplett, 2016).

Important factors that influence agility are ground contact time and ground reaction force. The force in most movements is generated from ground forces. We must have ground interaction to generate high force. In other words, the reaction force is the result of ground contact (Santana, 2015). When an athlete performs a shallow-angle movement, less ground contact time is needed (<250 ms), but when the angle is steep, the ground contact time increases (>250 ms) to compensate for the greater deceleration or braking intensity. To develop better change-of-direction capacity, the athlete needs to train dynamic, isometric, and specifically eccentric strength (Haff and Triplett, 2016).

When selecting exercises to develop agility, remember that we are improving the athlete's:

- Change of direction and speed: accelerate, decelerate, reaccelerate
- Maneuverability: multiple changes in direction
- Perceptual and cognitive demands: reaction time, decision making, anticipating, searching, determining if the situation requires offensive or defensive tactics (Haff and Triplett, 2016)

In this section, UFC veteran Adriano Martins demonstrates the described agility-enhancing exercises, followed by two training programs. Note that training B is designed for sports that have a striking element, like MMA or Muay Thai.

Warm-Up

Begin training by warming up the whole body with a dynamic warm-up. For this series we recommend running in place or doing mountain climbers (see figure 5.160). To execute mountain climbers, begin in a high plank position and alternate bringing each knee to the chest, maintaining good form and then increasing in speed. The warm-up should last between 3 and 10 minutes to properly get the athlete's body ready for work.

Figure 5.160 – Dynamic warm-up: (*a*) running in place and (*b*) mountain climber.

Agility Ladder

The agility ladder may be the most popular piece of agility training equipment. It is important to focus on the movement pattern first, then on increasing the movement speed. Switch steps proceeding down the ladder were used for this training program, and the athlete held his hands in a guard position to make the exercise more specialized to MMA. One of the reasons we ask athletes to hold dumbbells is because fighters usually drop their hands during a fight, especially if they get tired. This makes them an easier target for the opponent. Maintaining the hands up, like in a close guard position, increases the exercise intensity. However, hand placement or adding weight as shown in figure 5.161 is optional.

Figure 5.161 – Agility ladder.

Push-Up Sprint

Begin in a wide push-up position and at the starting cue lower the trunk and push up (see figure 5.162*a*), exploding to standing and directly into the sprint (see figure 5.162*b*). The sprint should be performed for a distance of 10 to 30 meters (11-33 yd), 4 to 10 times, focusing on maximum reaction time and velocity.

Figure 5.162 – Push-up sprint.

Jump Followed by a Sprawl (and a High Kick)

Place 4 to 10 hurdles that are 8 to 18 inches (20-45 cm) tall on the ground approximately 20 inches (about 50 cm) apart. Begin by jumping simultaneously with both feet over the hurdles (see figure 5.163*a*), directly sprawl after landing (see figure 5.163*b*), and then spring up into fight stance and execute a high kick (see figure 5.163*c*). If the sport does not require striking, perform only the jump and sprawl portion of the exercise. Ten sets of this exercise are performed at maximal speed.

Figure 5.163 – Jump, sprawl, and kick.

5-10-5 Shuttle Run

This exercise focuses on reaction time and maneuverability. Two cones are placed 10 meters (11 yd) apart. Take a starting position at a cone placed in the center (see figure 5.164a). At the verbal signal of "start" (a whistle can also be used if preferred), run until reaching the cone to the left (see figure 5.164b), then quickly change directions and run past the center to the right cone (see figure 5.164c). Change directions one more time and run past the center at which point the exercise is complete (see figure 5.164d). This combination should be repeated 5 to 10 times at maximum velocity.

Figure 5.164 – The 5-10-5 shuttle run.

Table 5.24 includes two agility training programs.

Table 5.24 – Agility Training Programs

	Week 1	Week 2	Week 3	Week 4
Training A				
1. Warm-up	1 × 2 min mountain climbers	2 × 2 min mountain climbers	3 × 2 min mountain climbers	4 × 2 min mountain climbers
2. Agility ladder	Switch steps: 1 × 3 min	Switch steps: 2 × 3 min	Switch steps: 3 × 3 min	Switch steps: 4 × 3 min
3. Push-up sprints	20 meters × 4 repetitions	20 meters × 6 repetitions	20 meters × 8 repetitions	20 meters × 10 repetitions
4. Jump, sprawl, and kick	6 × 8 sec low hurdles; 4 sets	6 × 8 sec low hurdles; 6 sets	6 × 8 sec low hurdles; 8 sets	6 × 8 sec low hurdles; 10 sets
5. 5-10-5 shuttle run	6 repetitions	6 repetitions	8 repetitions	8 repetitions
Training B				
1. Warm-up	1 × 2 min running in place	2 × 2 min running in place	3 × 2 min running in place	4 × 2 min running in place
2. Push-up sprints	30 meters × 6 repetitions	30 meters × 6 repetitions	30 meters × 8 repetitions	30 meters × 8 repetitions
3. Jump, sprawl, and high kick	6 × 12 sec low hurdles; 4 sets	6 × 12 sec low hurdles; 4 sets	6 × 12 sec low hurdles; 6 sets	6 × 12 sec low hurdles; 6 sets
4. 5-10-5 shuttle run	5 repetitions	6 repetitions	8 repetitions	10 repetitions
5. Agility ladder	Switch steps: 1 × 1 min max speed	Switch steps: 2 × 1 min max speed	Switch steps: 3 × 1 min max speed	Switch steps: 4 × 1 min max speed

Precompetition Training

The use of preparation circuits for MMA and grappling is becoming increasingly developed and well organized, but some training options offer better results for certain athletes. For this reason, we invited Melvin Guillard (veteran UFC and World Series of Fighting [WSOF]) and Mike Bruno (wrestler, grappler, and MMA fighter) to demonstrate how to perform a precompetition circuit effectively.

This circuit is a model for developing power and muscular endurance and lasts approximately five minutes to simulate rounds of a fight. The number of repetitions varies according to the number of rounds that the athlete is going to fight. For example, for athletes who compete in up to three rounds, we have one general warm-up round, one specific warm-up round, and three rounds of the circuit. Normally, the general warm-up has aerobic exercises, such as running or cycling, and stretching.

Figure 5.165 – Melvin Guillard and Mike Bruno warm up on stationary bicycles.

First Round (5-10 min): Use stationary or spinning bicycles (see figure 5.165), an elliptical trainer, or a treadmill to do a general warm-up.

Figure 5.166 – Mike Bruno performs rotations on a Technogym machine. In the background, Melvin Guillard is engaged in active recovery on the elliptical trainer. The men repeat (and alternate) the movements until the end of the round.

Second Round (5-6 min): Here, the idea is to imitate the movements of wrestling pummeling by using a specialized machine that regulates the resistance of rotation (see figure 5.166). Normally, the rotation is in a forward direction for 30 seconds and then the direction of rotation is reversed, and the athlete performs backward rotations for another 30 seconds followed by an active recovery on the elliptical trainer.

Third Round (5-6 min): This round consists of three exercises:

1. *Medicine ball throw:* Hold the ball at chest height with the arms aligned and throw the medicine ball against the wall (see figure 5.167). In this movement, the idea is to work the muscles responsible for pushing or punching movements (here, the chest, deltoid, and triceps brachii muscles, as well as the core muscles, which stabilize the movement). The ball is thrown 10 times as fast as possible.

Figure 5.167 – Medicine ball throw.

Figure 5.168 – Guillotine choke executed against the cage.

2. *Guillotine choke*: This is an attack that seeks strangulation and an end to the contest. This exercise was developed to improve the athlete's force of submission attack, with the fighter adopting a horizontal position, holding the entire body in an isometric position (see figure 5.168). The muscles required in this exercise are the back muscles, the arms, forearm muscles, and the core, to stabilize the position. The exercise duration may vary between 15 and 30 seconds.

3. *Run with sprawl*: For this exercise, we use a mattress. Run in place with high knees, and at the coach's command of "sprawl," execute a traditional takedown defensive movement, called the sprawl (see figure 5.169). Greater action is required of the lower-body muscles, and 10 sprawls should be performed at maximum speed. We normally use only a few seconds between each sprawl, but change the pattern after every repetition to stimulate attention and reaction time.

Figure 5.169 – Run with sprawl on mattress.

Figure 5.170 – Ground and pound performed on a cable machine.

Fourth Round (5-6 min): This round consists of three exercises:

1. *Ground and pound*: Use a cable machine to simulate the movements of vertical punches (ground and pound) (see figure 5.170). In this exercise, perform the movement with one hand, extending the arm while rotating the torso and generating high power. Sometimes, we place a dummy below the athlete to get hit and make the movement even more specific. In that case, we suggest using MMA gloves to avoid hurting the hand and wrist. The muscles used to execute the exercise are the chest, deltoid, and triceps brachii muscles, as well as the core. We normally perform between 10 and 15 punches with each arm.

Figure 5.171 – Core rotation with medicine ball throw.

2. *Core rotation with medicine ball throw*: This is a dynamic exercise in which the athlete rotates the torso and throws the medicine ball against the wall (see figure 5.171). It is specifically designed to develop the core endurance. We recommend performing 15 repetitions on each side.

3. *Single-leg press*: This is a variation of the traditional 45-degree leg press. Position the back properly against the backrest on the machine and one leg on the machine (see figure 5.172a). Inhale and release the safety bars, then flex the knee so that the thigh nearly touches the torso (see figure 5.172b). Return to the initial position and exhale at the end of the movement. This exercise develops the legs, especially the quadriceps (rectus femoris, vastus lateralis, vastus medialis, and vastus intermedius), and acts on the other muscles of the thigh as a whole. We suggest sets of 8 to 12 repetitions on each leg.

Figure 5.172 – Single-leg press.

Fifth Round (5-6 min): This round consists of three exercises:

1. *Jump on the Shuttle MVP machine*: Position the back properly against the backrest on the machine, with the feet on the platform (see figure 5.173a). Hold the handles, inhale, and jump as explosively as possible (see figure 5.173b). Exhale at the end of the movement, return to the initial position, and repeat. The benefit of using this machine is that we can regulate the intensity of the jump by adding elastic bands with extra resistance. The muscles used in this exercise are mainly those of the lower body. We recommend 10 to 15 jumps.

Figure 5.173 – Plyometric jump on a Shuttle MVP machine.

2. *Rope climb*: This powerful exercise develops the back, arms, and forearm muscles as previously described in figure 5.113. In this round of exercises, the athletes climb up and down the rope two to three times as fast as possible (see figure 5.174).

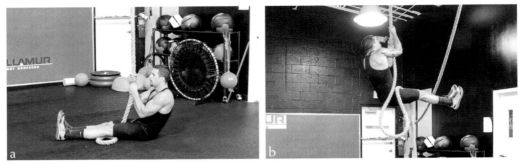

Figure 5.174 – Rope climb.

3. *Technogym press*: This exercise was previously described in the agonist-antagonist method section (see figure 5.101 on page 193). On this equipment, it is possible to work on one-arm pushing to simulate punching movements with overload (see figure 5.175). The muscles involved are the chest, triceps brachii, and deltoid muscles. We recommend 10 to 15 pushes with each arm.

Figure 5.175 – One-arm pushing movements with overload.

Table 5.25 presents a program for a precompetition circuit. This circuit is generally performed during the final phase of preparation, with an average duration of four weeks. Note that the station order always alternates between exercises for the upper and lower body to avoid acidity buildup in the muscles. The rounds should last for five minutes, or slightly longer. It is better to have more five- to six-minute rounds than longer rounds of six to eight minutes, for example. We always end the circuit with a round of shadow boxing and stretching to help cool down the body.

Table 5.25 – Precompetition Circuit Training Program

	Week 1	Week 2	Week 3	Week 4
	First round			
Warm-up	1 × 5 min	1 × 6 min	1 × 8 min	1 × 10 min
	Second round			
Pummeling on machine + active recovery using elliptical trainer	15 sec forward rotations and 15 sec backward + 45 sec of active recovery and repeat until the end of the round	20 sec forward rotations and 20 sec backward + 45 sec of active recovery and repeat until the end of the round	25 sec forward rotations and 25 sec backward + 45 sec of active recovery and repeat until the end of the round	30 sec forward rotations and 30 sec backward + 45 sec of active recovery and repeat until the end of the round
	Third round			
1. Medicine ball throw	8 throws	8 throws	10 throws	10 throws
2. Guillotine choke	15 sec BW	20 sec BW	25 sec BW	30 sec BW
3. Run with sprawl	8 sprawls	8 sprawls	10 sprawls	10 sprawls
	Fourth round			
1. Ground and pound	10 punches each arm	10 punches each arm	15 punches each arm	15 punches each arm
2. Core rotations with medicine ball	10 × per side	10 × per side	15 × per side	15 × per side
3. Single-leg press	8 × per side	8 × per side	10 × per side	10 × per side
	Fifth round			
1. Jump on MVP machine	10 jumps	10 jumps	12 jumps	12 jumps
2. Rope climbing	2 BW	2 BW	3 BW	3 BW
3. Technogym press	10 punches each arm	10 punches each arm	15 punches each arm	15 punches each arm

BW: body weight

MMA-Specific Cross Training

In this part of the chapter, we are going to talk about important aspects and physical capacities that should be developed in young athletes. It talks about specific programs that were designed to accommodate the limitations of our athletes and their needs while preparing for a world jiu-jitsu competition, grappling, or MMA. We also address the important changes in training that must be made to accommodate the athlete's transition from amateur to professional, then becoming part of an organization such as the UFC, PFL, or Bellator.

Sensitive Periods in the Physical Development of Children

There is thought to be an ideal period in a child's physical development for developing speed and motor skills that will contribute to the athlete's long-term success. The athletic components of speed, sports skills, stamina, strength, and flexibility can all be cultivated in the child athlete in the hopes of increasing their physical capacity and long-term athletic success (Van Hooren and De Ste Croix, 2020).

Sensitive periods can be understood as being the time during which an individual is most susceptible to a certain external influence (physical training) and are not to be confused with *critical periods* (Malina and Bouchard, 2002). Critical periods should not be seen only as a time in which certain events have a decisive influence on a physiological function or organ but also as the time in which an individual is more susceptible to the influence of training (Filin, et al. 1996). As we will see in table 5.26, physical capacities develop in a heterochronic way; that is, in different periods, they present growth acceleration in some moments and deceleration in others. Therefore, when it comes to the long-term training of young fighters, the theory of sensitive periods is part of correct planning of physical preparation for young athletes. Additionally, males and females have different growth and development rates, with girls tending to complete the biological maturation process before boys (Filin and Volkov, 1998).

Speed ability shows accelerated growth rates around 7 to 11 years of age, both in boys and girls, after which, only boys show slight changes. To develop this ability, we use short sprints ranging from 15 to 60 meters (16-66 yd) or a maximum time of 5 to 10 seconds with maximum speed (see figure 5.176).

Figure 5.176 – Jorjão developing speed capacity.

The speed-strength capacity shows the highest growth rates at ages 9 to 11 years for girls and ages 13 to 15 for boys. To enhance this capacity, we can use different jumps on the ground or mat or with the help of hurdles, sled push, and medicine balls (see figure 5.177).

Figure 5.177 – Jorjão developing speed-strength capacity.

Strength shows an accelerated growth rate at 10 to 11 years for girls and, after this period, only changes slightly. In males, this occurs after 13 years of age, with the greatest changes only occurring after 16 years of age. We typically use body weight exercises like push-ups and pull-ups and rubber bands for pull, push, squat, rotation, and other working movements (see figure 5.178).

Figure 5.178 – Jorjão developing strength capacity.

Coordination shows an accelerated growth at ages 7 to 10 and 13 to 14 in girls, and at 10 to 12 in boys. In MMA, athletes can only compete professionally when they are 18 years old. The International Mixed Martial Arts Federation (IMMAF, 2021) rules outline what makes an athlete eligible to compete in Amateur MMA and Youth World Championships:

- The contestant shall be of legal age according to the laws of the country where the competition is held.
- The contestant shall be in good physical and mental condition.
- The contestant will be examined during the medical check.
- The contestant shall be prepared to compete in MMA.
- The contestant shall have experience from competing in full-contact martial arts.
- When entering a competition, the contestant is responsible for ensuring that all relevant martial arts experience is reported.
- The contestant must have a passport valid for a minimum of two years.

Because athletes cannot compete professionally until 18 years old, we recommend young athletes start practicing other important modalities for MMA, such as jiu-jitsu, judo, wrestling, Muay Thai, and boxing, among others. In the specific case of Jorge "Jorjão" Fernandes, he began to develop his coordination and technique very early on, around age five when he started training jiu-jitsu and judo at age eight. At age 12, the young talent representing American Top Team in Fort Lauderdale has already won numerous competitions, including two Pan American Kids jiu-jitsu championships, four Florida championships, United States Judo Federation US Open Judo championships, and more (see figure 5.179).

Figure 5.179 – Jorjão competing in *(a)* judo and *(b)* jiu-jitsu.

Flexibility has the greatest growth at ages 7 to 10 and 14 to 17 years of age in girls. In boys it occurs at ages 9 to 10 and 15 to 16 years of age. To develop flexibility, we use movements that involve the largest muscle group and recommend isometric contractions for two to three sets of 30 seconds performed at the end of training or as a separate training session (see figure 5.180). For more information on how to properly develop a flexibility program, please read chapter 6 of this book.

Figure 5.180 – Jorjão developing flexibility.

Endurance shows the greatest growth at ages 10 to 12 in girls, whereas in boys, it occurs at ages 14 to 16. To develop muscular endurance, we recommend using low-impact aerobic exercises such as cycling, elliptical training, swimming, or treadmill running at medium intensity for 15 to 45 minutes (see figure 5.181).

Figure 5.181 – Jorjão developing muscular endurance.

Table 5.26 presents how physical capacities range in males and females from ages 7 to 8 to 16 to 17. Emphasis should be placed on capabilities that are represented with XX or XXX.

Table 5.26 – Changes in Physical Capacities (Sensitive Periods) From Ages 7 to 17

Physical capacities	7-8 M	7-8 F	8-9 M	8-9 F	9-10 M	9-10 F	10-11 M	10-11 F	11-12 M	11-12 F	12-13 M	12-13 F	13-14 M	13-14 F	14-15 M	14-15 F	15-16 M	15-16 F	16-17 M	16-17 F
Speed	XXX	XXX	XX	XXX	X	XX	XX	XX			X				X		X			
Speed-strength		X	X	X		XXX	X	XXX		X			XX		XX					
Strength			X	X		X	X	XXX		X			XX		X		X		XXX	X
Coordination or skills	X	XXX	X	XXX	X	XXX	XX		XX		X		XX							
Flexibility	X	XX	X	X	XX	XXX				X	X	X	X	X		XX	XX			XX
Endurance						X		XX	X	XX	X				XX		XXX		X	

Empty = Changes in indices *below* the average annual increase over 10 years.

X = Changes in indices *equaling* the average annual increase over 10 years.

XX = Changes in indices that *exceed 1.5 times* the average annual increase over 10 years.

XXX = Changes in indices that *exceed 2 times* the average annual increase over 10 years.

Adapted from Van Hooren and De Ste Croix (2020) and Filin, Gomes, and da Silva (1996).

Changes in Training to Transition From Amateur to Professional

After developing all the necessary physical capacities and skills during the initial career of the young combat athlete, the amateur athlete is ready for the increased intensity of MMA training. After learning the basic skills in jiu-jitsu, wrestling, boxing, Muay Thai, and so on, the task is to combine the fighter's skill set into effective MMA, which is developed through sparring sessions. We recommend no more than two sessions a week with full protective gear (chin guard, helmet, gloves, mouthpiece) for a few rounds (1-3).

The number of rounds and sparring intensity should gradually increase over three to six months, until the young athlete and their coach feel that they are ready for the first amateur fight. Every fight is very serious during this time because building as close to a perfect career record as possible until transitioning into a professional is advantageous to the fighter. It is recommended that 3 to 10 amateur fights (all victories) are needed to gain adequate experience before the athlete is ready for the professional level. After becoming a professional athlete, it is even more important to remain undefeated to be able to earn more and compete against better opponents.

The training of amateur athletes differs from that of veteran athletes. This is because younger athletes, in general, exhibit a greater hormonal response, which enables faster recovery and allows a greater training volume than veteran athletes over age 35 (Dias, et al. 2017). Based on these principles, we show an explosive power circuit that was developed within the ATT for Mirsad Bektic at the beginning of his professional career until signing with the UFC. Note that we use different training methods to develop power and strength, like functional training, agility, and speed exercises. One specificity of this training was the modification of the exercise group. Here, exercises are performed in groups of three, two of them general and one specific.

Each training session begins with a dynamic warm-up lasting between 5 and 10 minutes. Then the following exercises are performed.

Part 1

Part 1 consists of three exercises:

1. *Dumbbell bench press*: In this exercise, perform eccentric action in its initial phase and concentric contraction in its end or return phase (see figure 5.182). The sets are repeated 2 to 4 times for 6 to 10 repetitions each.

Figure 5.182 – Dumbbell bench press.

2. *Plyometric push-up on BOSU ball*: This exercise was designed to develop explosive power in the arms and promote the use of the legs and core muscles. Place the hands flat on the platform, equidistant from the center, or grab the side handles of the BOSU. Extend the legs to come to the top of a push-up or plank. Flex the elbows until the chest hovers over the platform. Then, explode up, pushing the ball into the floor and bouncing back into the air (see figure 5.183). The sets are repeated 2 to 4 times and may vary from 20 to 30 seconds executed at maximum speed.

Figure 5.183 – Plyometric push-up on BOSU ball.

3. *Pad work for straight and cross punches:* This is a specific exercise used in the technical preparation of Muay Thai and boxing, in which the fighter executes a technical sequence to generate a contrast within the preparative training (see figure 5.184). It may also be used as an active rest. The duration will vary from 1 to 2 minutes, depending on the goal.

Figure 5.184 – Pad work for straight and cross punches.

Part 2
Part 2 consists of three exercises:

1. *Barbell deadlift:* This exercise is important and special attention should be given to the proper form of young athletes. See figure 5.20 for more information. The sets are repeated 2 to 4 times and vary from 2 to 6 repetitions according to the training phase.
2. *Plyometric jump with hurdles:* The hurdles should be organized so several jumps may be performed in sequence, with the specific aim of adding power to the lower body (see figure 5.185). The sets are repeated 2 to 4 times and vary from 20 to 30 seconds.

Figure 5.185 – Plyometric jump with hurdles.

3. *Pad work for kicks and knees:* This is specific work for technical development and agility within the planning adapted to the special needs of the athlete (see figure 5.186). The duration varies from 1 to 2 minutes, depending on the training goal.

Figure 5.186 – Pad work for kicks and knees.

Part 3

Part 3 consists of three exercises:

1. *Front raise with a weight plate:* Stand up straight, holding a weight plate in front of the hips with both hands (see figure 5.187a). Keeping the back straight and the elbows slightly flexed, exhale and raise the plate out in front of the body in an arcing motion until the arms are parallel with the floor or, if desired, above the head (see figure 5.187b). Hold for a second or two. Inhale and lower the plate in a controlled manner to the starting position and repeat. This exercise develops strength and muscular endurance in the arms and shoulders. The muscles of the upper body are used throughout every fight, whether standing or on the floor. The sets are repeated 2 to 4 times and vary from 10 to 12 repetitions.

Figure 5.187 – Front raise with a weight plate.

2. *Double-arm wave battle rope*: Start with the feet hip-width apart, toes pointing forward and knees slightly flexed. Grip the ropes with the palms facing the floor and move both arms at the same time up, then down, using full range of motion (see figure 5.188). The sets are repeated 2 to 4 times and vary from 20 to 30 seconds.

Figure 5.188 – Double-arm wave battle rope.

3. *Pad work for uppercuts*: After the weightlifting and rope exercises, we perform technical pad work using uppercuts that are specific to fight training (see figure 5.189). The duration may vary from 1 to 2 minutes, depending on the goal.

Figure 5.189 – Pad work for uppercuts.

Part 4

Part 4 consists of two exercises:

1. *Medicine ball throw*: This exercise is used to develop the muscles responsible for pushing and punching (see figure 5.167 for more information). The difference when applied to young athletes as opposed to a professional is the weight of the ball. We usually recommend lighter balls, no more than 5 to 10 pounds (2-5 kg) (see figure 5.190). This movement develops the ability to generate explosive power. The sets are repeated 2 to 4 times, 10 repetitions per side.

Figure 5.190 – Medicine ball throw with lighter ball.

2. *Tire flip*: Flipping a tractor tire involves a high degree of difficulty and coordination, combined with work on strength and explosive power. To flip a tire properly, squat down and keep the hips lower than the shoulders. Take a wide grip and dig the fingers under the tire so the forearms touch the tire (see figure 5.191a). If able, get the chest against the tire as well. Inhale, lean in, and drive, pushing through the legs and lifting the tire up at a 45-degree angle (see figure 5.191b). Stand up quickly and get a knee into the tire to help continue pushing the tire up. Flip the hands over and push the tire over. The movement must be fully committed to once it is begun, driving all the way through the tire or it will stall and come back against the athlete. This is a quick and powerful movement with no stopping point. Keep the momentum moving up and forward. Exhale at the end of the movement. For young athletes, the weight of the tire is lighter than for a veteran athlete; no more than 200 pounds (91 kg) is recommended. The sets are repeated 2 to 4 times with 6 flips per set.

Figure 5.191 – Tire flip.

Younger athletes can withstand a greater training volume, which is advantageous when high-volume, specific fighting exercises in the physical preparation of young UFC athletes need to be implemented. Table 5.27 shows a sample training program for young amateur athletes that can be performed two to three times a week.

Table 5.27 – Training Program for Young Athletes

	Week 1	Week 2	Week 3	Week 4
Part 1				
1. Dumbbell bench press	1 × 8RM	2 × 8RM	3 × 6RM	4 × 6RM
2. Plyometric push-up on BOSU ball	1 × 20 BW	2 × 20 BW	3 × 20 BW	4 × 20 BW
3. Pad work for straight and cross punches	1 × 1 min	2 × 1 min	3 × 2 min	4 × 2 min
Part 2				
1. Barbell deadlift	1 × 8RM	2 × 8RM	3 × 6RM	4 × 6RM
2. Plyometric jump with hurdles	1 × 20 BW	2 × 20 BW	3 × 20 BW	4 × 20 BW
3. Pad work for kicks and knees	1 × 1 min	2 × 1 min	3 × 2 min	4 × 2 min
Part 3				
1. Front raise with a weight plate	1 × 12 @ 45 lb	2 × 12 @ 45 lb	3 × 12 @ 45 lb	4 × 12 @ 45 lb
2. Double-arm wave battle rope	1 × 20 sec	2 × 20 sec	3 × 20 sec	4 × 20 sec
3. Pad work for uppercuts	1 × 1 min	2 × 1 min	3 × 1 min	4 × 1 min
Part 4				
1. Medicine ball throw	1 × 10 per side	2 × 10 per side	3 × 10 per side	4 × 10 per side
2. Tire flip	1 × 6	2 × 6	3 × 6	4 × 6

Training for Adaptive MMA Athletes

When working with combat sport athletes, traditional training methods using machines or free weights are used, but sometimes we encounter fighters with certain functional limitations. Therefore, adapting exercises to accommodate the individual needs of an athlete to achieve optimum performance may be necessary.

Exceeding limits and overcoming in a quest to achieve goals: This is how we define North American athlete Nick "Notorious" Newell. He was born without half of his left arm due to a congenital amputation, but this did not stop him from fighting MMA against high-level opponents and becoming an Xtreme Fighting Championships (XFC) champion. Nick also fought for the WSOF and currently has a contract with Bellator.

In this section, we will show how training can be adapted with the aid of resistance bands, medicine balls, and "out of the box" creativity to offer quality, individualized training.

Pull-Up Bar

This exercise is performed with body weight and an adapted grip. In the starting position, this athlete begins with the grip of the left arm fully extended and with the right arm flexed, due to the physical limitation (see figure 5.192a). In the ending position, Nick performs a full pull-up until the angle to which he is limited (i.e., his movement is not considered complete in terms of the traditional angles) (see figure 5.192b). However, it may be said that it is a full exercise for his needs. The goal of the pull-up is strengthening the back muscles with the aid of the biceps brachii and the core region to stabilize the movement. Normally, 2 to 4 sets of 10 to 15 repetitions are performed.

Figure 5.192 – Adapted pull-up.

Pulley Lat Pulldown

This exercise has a goal similar to the pull-up bar for the back muscles. However, on this equipment, it is possible to regulate the loads and adapt the different training methodologies. In Nick's case, he performs 4 sets with increasing loads but reduces repetitions (12, 10, 8, and 6 repetitions) (see figure 5.193).

Figure 5.193 – Adapted pulley lat pulldown.

One-Arm Cable or Resistance Band Angled Row

This exercise was adapted with a Velcro armband to improve the clinch movement (see figure 5.194). The sets are performed to failure, following the Isoton method in a superset format as described in chapter 2 or later in this chapter. This exercise is performed to develop the back, posterior deltoid, and core muscles.

Figure 5.194 – Adapted one-arm cable angled row.

Clinch Walk

This exercise was created to strengthen the muscles that help the athlete to maintain their guard high in the fight, even when fatigued. For this, the execution was adapted with the use of a dumbbell and a medicine ball. In the starting position, Nick raises his arms and holds a dumbbell with his right arm and balances a medicine ball with his left (see figure 5.195a). After lifting the loads, the athlete walks with his arms and shoulders performing isometric exercise and abdominal stabilization (see figure 5.195b). This exercise works the arms and shoulders. Normally, 4 sets of 30 seconds each are performed.

Figure 5.195 – Adapted clinch walk.

Cable Punches

This exercise may be performed to specifically strengthen the muscles involved in punching movements (jab, straight, cross, etc.). In the starting position, adapt a tensioner to the left arm, so that the complete movement of the chosen punches can be performed. Keep the knees slightly flexed and the torso in rotation. In the finishing position, Nick performs the punch extending the arm with a rotation of the torso. This exercise works the deltoids, chest, triceps brachii, and core, among other muscles. We recommend 3 to 4 sets of 20 punches on each arm to develop muscular endurance (see figure 5.196).

Figure 5.196 – Adapted cable punches.

Push-Up

This exercise uses body weight to generate an overload to develop the "pushing" muscles that are so important in striking and grappling. In this exercise, a medicine ball is adapted to enable the execution of the movement. In the starting position, Nick extends his arms and stands on tiptoe, his hips in line with the floor. In the finishing position, he performs a flexion toward the floor, getting as close as possible to the ground (see figure 5.197). This exercise works the chest muscles, triceps brachii, and anterior deltoid. The sets are performed until failure and repeated 5 times, with active rest consisting of shadow boxing for 1 minute.

Figure 5.197 – Adapted push-up with medicine ball.

Zercher Squat

This is an exercise with a high degree of difficulty to develop strength in the posterior muscles. Assume a squat position. An adaptation is made in the barbell grip, in which the left arm is in position to support the load (see figure 5.198a). After gripping the barbell correctly, extend the legs and torso completely (see figure 5.198b), in addition to using the legs, back, and core muscles, performing an isometric exercise with the arms to support the barbell.

Figure 5.198 – Adapted Zercher squat.

Knee With Cables

Using the VertiMax platform, cables are affixed to tensioners on one of the legs and kneeing movements are made against the pad (see figure 5.199), varying between 20 and 30 repetitions for 3 sets.

Figure 5.199 – Adapted knee with cables.

Table 5.28 presents an adapted training program. All adapted work takes into account the unique needs and specific goal of each athlete. Using physical assessments, coaches should direct the training in accordance with the phase that the athlete has reached within their annual program.

Table 5.28 – Adapted Training Program

	Week 1	Week 2	Week 3	Week 4
1. Adapted pull-up	3 × 15 BW	3 × 15 BW	4 × 15 BW	4 × 15 BW
2. Adapted pulley lat pulldown	2 × 12RM 2 × 10RM	2 × 12RM 2 × 10RM	2 × 8RM 2 × 6RM	2 × 8RM 2 × 6RM
3. Adapted one-arm angled row with cable—Isoton	3 × 30 sec @ 30% 1RM per side	3 × 30 sec @ 30% 1RM per side	4 × 30 sec @ 30% 1RM per side	4 × 30 sec @ 30% 1RM per side
4. Adapted clinch walk	1 × 30 sec	2 × 30 sec	3 × 30 sec	4 × 30 sec
5. Adapted punch with cables	2 × 20 per side	2 × 20 per side	3 × 20 per side	3 × 20 per side
6. Adapted push-up	3 × Max # of reps with BW	3 × Max # of reps with BW	4 × Max # of reps with BW	4 × Max # of reps with BW
7. Adapted Zercher squat	3 × 8RM	3 × 8RM	4 × 6RM	4 × 6RM
8. Adapted knee with cables	2 × 20 per side	2 × 20 per side	3 × 20 per side	3 × 20 per side

BW: body weight

Training to Improve MMA Takedowns

One important aspect of an MMA fight is using takedowns to put an opponent on their back on the ground. This leads to the athlete being awarded points by the ringside judges, allows the use of jiu-jitsu with finishing moves, or even allows for a knockout using ground and pound. Veteran UFC fighter Gleison Tibau is well known for his takedown performance, and for this reason we will demonstrate with his help how to improve takedown attacks for MMA based on his training.

Normally, the general warm-up encompasses aerobic exercises, such as jumping rope (see figure 5.1a), shadow boxing in front of a mirror (see figure 5.1b), and dynamic stretching. We also use specific combat movements as well as body weight exercises.

Tire Flip

This is a very good exercise for takedowns or to pressure an opponent against the cage and was previously explained in figure 5.191. The tire used may weigh up to 500 pounds (227 kg) (see figure 5.200) and the sets vary from 6 to 10 flips, with the option to perform jumps into the rests.

Figure 5.200 – Tire flip.

Takedown With Resistance Band

Begin with the resistance band under tension (the coach determines the tension of the resistance band) and perform a takedown movement with a training partner, who, in this case, is a UFC fighter and former world champion in the 170-pound division, Tyron Woodley (see figure 5.201). The takedown is also determined according to the technical ability of the athlete and may be a double-leg or single-leg takedown. After lifting the training partner (see figures 5.201a-b), Tibau walks with the athlete on his shoulders and the overload of the resistance band, generating an opposing force that forces him to maintain his technical posture (see figure 5.201c). The core, upper-body, and lower-body muscles are called upon to perform the movement. We repeat this movement for 5 to 10 takedowns on each side.

Figure 5.201 – Takedown training with resistance band.

Striking Tire With Sledgehammer

Start the movement in a fighting stance, with the left leg forward and the right leg back. Grip with the right hand forward and the left hand back, alternating in the same order when the stance changes. The exercise is characterized by the raising and circumduction (circular movement of the arm around the shoulder joint) of the arms, in which the fighter strikes the tire with the sledgehammer using the arms and torso to give power to the movement (see figure 5.202). This is a great exercise for improving the ground and pound power. Normally, 16- to 30-pound (7-14 kg) sledgehammers are used 20 times, with each arm striking the tire 10 times.

Figure 5.202 – Striking tire with sledgehammer.

Ground and Pound With Resistance Band

This exercise has a movement adapted from a real fight situation. The fighter must remain with the resistance band under tension and adopt a real fighting stance. They may use a dummy or a bag to assist the training. Thus, they perform the planned set of punches and adopt the specific grappling positions (see figure 5.203). The aim of the work is to take the specific situation of a fight to the training room with the overload necessary to develop strength, power, and muscular endurance. The muscles recruited in these movements are generally the arms and legs, either in direct or indirect action. During this work, the sets are timed, with between 15 to 30 seconds of action and 1 to 3 minutes of active recovery such as jumping in place, footwork, or shadow boxing.

Figure 5.203 – Ground and pound with resistance band.

Strengthening of Neck Muscles

For a fighter, an important region for absorbing blows and finishing moves during the course of training and fights is the neck, and the coach should pay attention to specific strengthening exercises for the neck and trapezius muscles. To make this region strong and resistant, special equipment is used for anteroposterior and lateral movements (see figure 5.204). This equipment allows fight training methods to be adapted. The sets are executed until local failure, normally using the Isoton method described in chapter 2 or later in this chapter.

Figure 5.204 – Strengthening the neck muscles.

Single-Leg Proprioception on Gel X-PAD

This exercise develops balance, strength, and stability (described in figure 5.2). Balance training can reduce the injury risk in competitive athletes. When designing preseason and in-season injury-prevention programs, balance training should be incorporated to improve performance and injury resistance (Sutton, 2022). This work should be done in 3 sets of 10 repetitions on each side.

Core Rotation With Medicine Ball

During preparatory training for a fight, we always seek to analyze the aspects necessary to optimize the athlete's performance and the exercises that may boost their training. In this exercise, the aim is to strengthen the core muscles with the upper-body and lower-body muscles, which assist wrestling takedown techniques (see figure 5.205). The recommendation is 3 sets, 10 times on each side.

Figure 5.205 – Core rotation with medicine ball.

Cable or Resistance Band Guillotine Choke

The cable or resistance band guillotine choke exercise is an excellent option for developing strength for this submission technique. Remain in a squatting position with the arms in an isometric position, thus extending the torso and strengthening the back, arms, and forearms (see figure 5.206). Perform 2 to 4 sets of 15 to 30 seconds in duration on each side.

Figure 5.206 – Cable or resistance band guillotine choke.

Punching Dummy With Takedown

To finish, we chose a specific fighting exercise in which the athlete performs striking and grappling or wrestling movements (see figure 5.207). There is a combination of punching techniques, and, after, a takedown technique and ground and pound work may also be performed. This work is repeated several times in 30-second sets, with active recovery ranging from 1 to 5 minutes.

Figure 5.207 – Punching dummy with takedown.

Table 5.29 presents a training program to improve MMA takedowns. Note that the exercises chosen for the training of Gleison Tibau are advanced, and some movements may be removed or added according to the individual requirements of the athlete or coach. It is recommended that this work be repeated twice a week and executed for four to six weeks before the fight.

Table 5.29 – MMA Takedown Training Program

	Week 1	Week 2	Week 3	Week 4
1. Warm-up with shadow boxing and jumping rope	2 × 1 min jump rope and 1 min shadow boxing	2 × 1 min jump rope and 1 min shadow boxing	3 × 1 min jump rope and 1 min shadow boxing	3 × 1 min jump rope and 1 min shadow boxing
2. Tire flip	2 × 10	2 × 10	3 × 10	3 × 10
3. Takedown with partner	2 × 5 per side	2 × 5 per side	3 × 5 per side	3 × 5 per side
4. Sledgehammer on the tire	2 × 10 per side	2 × 10 per side	3 × 10 per side	3 × 10 per side
5. Ground and pound	3 × 30 sec	3 × 30 sec	4 × 30 sec	4 × 30 sec
6. Neck—Isoton	3 × 30 sec @ 30% 1RM per side	3 × 30 sec @ 30% 1RM per side	4 × 30 sec @ 30% 1RM per side	4 × 30 sec @ 30% 1RM per side
7. Proprioception on gel X-PAD	2 × 10 BW per side	2 × 10 BW per side	3 × 10 BW per side	3 × 10 BW per side
8. Core rotation with medicine ball	2 × 10 per side	2 × 10 per side	3 × 10 per side	3 × 10 per side
9. Guillotine choke (isometric exercise)	3 × 30 sec per side	3 × 30 sec per side	4 × 30 sec per side	4 × 30 sec per side
10. Punches and ground and pound	3 × 30 sec	4 × 30 sec	5 × 30 sec	6 × 30 sec

BW: body weight

MMA, Muay Thai, and Jiu-Jitsu Preparation Training for Women

Combat sports for women have grown significantly in popularity over recent years. This growth has been influenced by the media, especially television, initially with shows such as Strikeforce and Bellator, leading to an event exclusively for women, Invicta, and the inclusion of female weight classes in the biggest MMA promotion in the world, UFC (Dias and Oliveira, 2013).

There is an increase in the demand for female fights, and many athletes earn a living exclusively from these fights, something that was practically impossible a few years ago. Due to this growth in the sport and the participation of women, we invited the UFC athletes Tecia Torres from Invicta, Ediane "Índia" Gomes, Thaís "Nega" Souza, Jessica Branco, and five-time jiu-jitsu world champion Gezary "Ge" Matuda to demonstrate a training circuit developed for female fighters who wish to improve their physical capabilities (strength, power, agility, balance, and muscular endurance) for their competitive events (see figure 5.208). Following are examples of exercises that may be performed in female fight training.

Figure 5.208 – From left to right: Tecia Torres, Ediane "Índia" Gomes, Thaís "Nega" Souza, Gezary "Ge" Matuda, and Jessica Branco.

Exercise 1

This exercise is specifically to improve the submission movement called the guillotine choke, which may be used by MMA, jiu-jitsu, and grappling athletes. In this exercise, we seek to develop the strength of the arms and the core with dynamic work and isometric exercise. In the initial phase, the MMA athlete starts in a squatting position, with the torso leaning to align with the movement (see figure 5.209a). In the final phase, the exercise is performed with an extension of the torso and lifting the arms up and pulling back (squeezing), in which an overload is created in the muscles of the back, arms, shoulders, trapezius, and legs (see figure 5.209b). The exercise is repeated 5 to 10 times and ends in isometric contraction at the end of the movement for 10 to 20 seconds.

Figure 5.209 – Ediane Gomes performs an exercise for the guillotine choke submission.

Exercise 2

The VertiMax platform is used to improve muscular endurance in Muay Thai athletes. In the initial phase, Muay Thai techniques are used to train footwork (see figure 5.210a). Next, punches are performed (jabs, straights, crosses, among others, with bands) (see figure 5.210b), in which we work the total body, with the sets being performed by time or repetition.

Figure 5.210 – Thaís Souza performs footwork and punches on the VertiMax platform.

Next, muscular endurance is developed using the knee technique, which recruits muscles in the lower body and the core area (see figure 5.211*a*). To end the set, training is performed using various kicks (see figure 5.211*b*). The time allowed for each set is between 3 and 5 minutes to simulate the duration of rounds of Muay Thai or MMA.

Figure 5.211 – Lower-body training on the VertiMax platform.

Exercise 3

This is specifically designed for jiu-jitsu athletes and uses the VertiMax platform as an accessory to improve performance in fighting movements. Begin in a squatting position (characteristic of standing guard passes), using a grip variation specific to Brazilian jiu-jitsu (BJJ) fighters (see figure 5.212*a*). In this exercise, total body work is performed (both upper- and lower-body muscles). Then, perform a lateral guard pass technique (see figure 5.212*b*). These movements are repeated 20 to 50 times per side at top speed.

Figure 5.212 – Gezary Matuda performing a lateral guard pass exercise geared toward jiu-jitsu.

Exercise 4

This variation of the bent-over row is important to increase strength for the standing guard pass. The overload generates difficulty in performing the exercise, which causes an increase in the strength of the leg, torso, arm, and back muscles. In the initial phase, a squat is performed (remembering the importance of correct posture in the execution of the exercise and isometric working of the stabilizer muscles) (see figure 5.213a). In the intermediate phase of the exercise, perform an extension of the legs and the trunk (see figure 5.213b). In the final phase, maintain the posture and perform a flexion of the arms, bringing the apparatus toward the chest and holding this position for a few seconds (see figure 5.213c). With a single exercise, we manage to work muscles in the back, legs, arms, and abdominals. The sets consist of 4 to 8 repetitions with heavy loads and isometric contractions of 1 to 2 seconds in each phase of the movement.

Figure 5.213 – Strength work for standing guard pass.

Exercise 5

Here we present the machine squat with kimono grip. A deep squat is performed on a machine that facilitates the movement in a safe manner. The exercise is performed in this way to gain strength and strengthen the grip. In the initial phase, adopt a posture with the feet aligned with the hips, the arms outstretched, and the shoulders back, thus requiring an isometric contraction of the muscles of the shoulder girdle (see figure 5.214a). Next, the athlete performs a deep squat, always thrusting the hips backward and maintaining the alignment of the knees and the spine (see figure 5.214b). In this exercise, the main goal is to develop leg, hip, and forearm strength. Normally, each set is performed to muscle failure in an interval of 45 seconds to 1 minute 30 seconds for muscular endurance.

Figure 5.214 – Jessica Branco performs a machine squat with kimono grip.

Exercise 6

Geared toward MMA athletes, in this exercise, the athlete will perform takedowns with the aid of a high-resistance band attached to a vest, making the performance more difficult and creating a high overload in the movement. In the initial phase, adopt a fighting stance with the band slightly stretched (see figure 5.215a). Next, one athlete starts walking toward their partner, performing a double-leg takedown (see figure 5.215b). At this point, the full technique is performed with the overload of the band, which stretches, and the body weight of the training partner (see figure 5.215c). In this exercise, it is possible to develop the muscles of the upper and lower body and improve technique. Each set consists of 5 takedowns to the left and 5 takedowns to the right.

Figure 5.215 – Ediane Gomes and Tecia Torres train takedowns with a high-resistance band attached to a vest.

Exercise 7

In this exercise, a piece of equipment called the VersaClimber is used, which simulates a climbing movement to work on the arms and legs (see figure 5.216). Generally, this equipment is used to develop aerobic capacities, speed, and power. The sets are arranged by time and vary in length between 15 seconds and 1 minute.

Figure 5.216 – Jessica Branco simulates climb on the VersaClimber.

Exercise 8

Another piece of equipment that is very useful for developing muscular endurance, speed, and explosive power is the Hydra-Gym Powermax 360 on which exercises are performed that simulate punches and circular movements such as pummeling because this machine can work up to 360 degrees. The work is normally arranged into sets of 15 to 45 seconds (see figure 5.217).

Figure 5.217 – Tecia Torres performs movements on the Hydra-Gym Powermax 360.

Table 5.30 presents a training program for women.

Table 5.30 – Training Program for Female MMA Athletes

	Week 1	**Week 2**	**Week 3**	**Week 4**
1. Guillotine choke	2 × 5 + 10 sec isometric contraction	2 × 5 + 10 sec isometric contraction	3 × 5 + 15 sec isometric contraction	3 × 5 + 15 sec isometric contraction
2. VertiMax for striking	2 × 3 min	3 × 3 min	4 × 3 min	5 × 3 min
3. VertiMax for BJJ standing guard passes	2 × 30 per side	2 × 30 per side	2 × 40 per side	2 × 40 per side
4. Strength work for standing guard pass	2 × 8RM with 2 sec isometric contractions in each phase	2 × 8RM with 2 sec isometric contractions in each phase	3 × 6RM with 2 sec isometric contractions in each phase	3 × 6RM with 2 sec isometric contractions in each phase
5. Squat with kimono grip	2 × 45 sec	2 × 45 sec	3 × 45 sec	3 × 45 sec
6. Takedowns with a high-resistance band	2 × 5 per side	2 × 5 per side	3 × 5 per side	3 × 5 per side
7. VersaClimber	2 × 15 sec fast + 1 min slow	3 × 15 sec fast + 1 min slow	4 × 15 sec fast + 1 min slow	5 × 15 sec fast + 1 min slow
8. Hydra-Gym Powermax 360	2 × 15 sec fast + 1 min shadow boxing	3 × 15 sec fast + 1 min shadow boxing	4 × 15 sec fast + 1 min shadow boxing	5 × 15 sec fast + 1 min shadow boxing

Training for Wrestlers and Grapplers

Wrestlers and grapplers have been dominating the fight scene in recent years, with athletes such as Jon Jones, Kamaru Usman, Colby Covington, Tyron Woodley, Daniel Cormier, Khabib Nurmagomedov, and Henry Cejudo being just a few of them. These athletes exhibit important characteristics in the world of MMA, including:

- They demonstrate muscular strength, which is the maximum strength that can be generated by a muscle or by a muscle group.

- They demonstrate localized muscular endurance, which is the capacity to perform muscular work without losing effectiveness for a prolonged time, including dynamic and isometric work.

- They have high maximum aerobic capacity ($\dot{V}O_2$max), a reproducible measure of the capacity of the cardiovascular system to release blood to a muscle involved in dynamic work. Normally, the training programs for this physical capacity involve major muscle groups in dynamic exercises, such as running, the elliptical trainer, swimming, the VersaClimber, and so on for 15 to 60 minutes per session, three to five times a week, at an intensity of 70 percent to 85 percent of $\dot{V}O_2$max.

In this section, we invited veteran Bellator wrestler and American FILA grappling champion Kelly "Crossface" Anundson to demonstrate some details of training for grapplers or wrestlers.

Warm-Up
Begin training with aerobic exercises on the elliptical trainer (see figure 5.218), moving for 5 minutes to warm up the body. Gradually increase the intensity and speed of rotation each minute until 70 percent to 85 percent of the maximum is reached. Maintain this pace for 5 to 15 minutes.

Figure 5.218 – Warming up on an elliptical trainer.

Dumbbell Snatch
The dumbbell snatch is very similar to the kettlebell snatch exercise that was described in figure 5.14. One of the reasons that coaches often use dumbbells instead of kettlebells is because they are easier to find in local gyms and have various weight options ranging from 5 to 120 pounds (2-54 kg) or more (see figure 5.219). Perform 3 to 4 sets with rests of 1 to 2 minutes and moderate loads for 8 to 12 repetitions on each arm.

Figure 5.219 – Dumbbell snatch.

Lateral Bench Hop

This exercise strengthens the core musculature, prioritizing stabilization and support while the hops are performed. The body is supported with the elbows half flexed in an isometric contraction, thus allowing the performance of the planned movements (see figure 5.220). The sets are performed with rests of 30 seconds to 1 minute for 20 to 30 hops and are repeated for 3 to 4 sets.

Figure 5.220 – Lateral bench hop.

Barbell Deadlift

The deadlift is important for wrestlers to improve power during takedowns. For more information about this exercise and proper form, see figure 5.20. These sets are performed with long rests and heavy loads, 80 percent to 90 percent of the maximum, for 4 to 6 repetitions and repeated for 3 to 4 sets. When we notice signs of fatigue due to an increase in acidity in the muscles, we perform low-intensity aerobic exercises like shadow boxing or light wrestling movements for 45 seconds to 2 minutes to accelerate recovery.

Seated Low Row

The seated low row is important for grapplers. This exercise helps develop strength for specific fighting techniques and is used to develop strength in the back muscles and arms. Sit facing the machine, feet resting on the foot pads and the torso flexed forward (see figure 5.221a). Inhale and bring the handle to the base of the sternum by pulling the elbows back (see figure 5.221b). Exhale at the end of the movement and return to the initial position. The sets (3-4) are performed with moderate rests and loads of 60 percent to 80 percent of the maximum for 8 to 15 repetitions.

Figure 5.221 – Seated low row.

Takedown With Resistance Band

This exercise was previously described in figure 5.201, and it is very helpful for improving takedowns and the athlete's ability to sustain this exhausting movement during a fight. We repeat 3 to 4 sets of this movement for 5 to 10 takedowns on each side.

Plank

This isometric exercise strengthens the abdominal and lumbar regions, which are important for developing the base and supporting and assisting specific fighting movements (see figure 5.34a). The sets are performed for 20 to 30 seconds in each isometric position with short rests of 30 seconds to 1 minute. Repeat for 3 sets.

Sprints on the Bike or 30-Meter (33-yd) Sprints

We generally perform this part of training separately or end the training session with 10- to 15-second sprints with maximum intensity to develop speed (see figure 5.222). The athlete is pushed to their maximum followed by an active recovery of low-intensity exercise. Repeat 5 to 10 times.

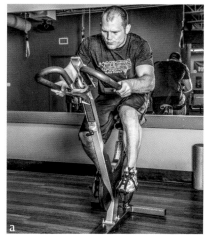

Figure 5.222 – Sprints on the stationary bike (a) or maximum intensity sprints (b) to end the session.

Table 5.31 presents a training program for wrestlers and grapplers.

Table 5.31 – Training Program for Wrestlers and Grapplers

	Week 1	**Week 2**	**Week 3**	**Week 4**
1. Warm-up	1 × 5 min	1 × 5 min	2 × 5 min	3 × 5 min
2. Dumbbell snatch	2 × 10RM per side	2 × 10RM per side	3 × 8RM per side	4 × 8RM per side
3. Lateral bench hop	3 × 20 per side	3 × 20 per side	3 × 25 per side	4 × 25 per side
4. Barbell deadlift + shadow boxing	2 × 4RM + 2 min shadow boxing	2 × 4RM + 2 min shadow boxing	3 × 4RM + 2 min shadow boxing	4 × 4RM + 2 min shadow boxing
5. Seated low row	2 × 15RM	2 × 15RM	3 × 15RM	3 × 15RM
6. Takedown with resistance band	2 × 5 per side	2 × 5 per side	3 × 5 per side	4 × 5 per side
7. Plank	2 × 30 sec per side	2 × 30 sec per side	3 × 30 sec per side	4 × 30 sec per side
8. Sprints + active recovery	5 × 10 sec sprints + 1 min active recovery	5 × 10 sec sprints + 1 min active recovery	8 × 10 sec sprints + 1 min active recovery	8 × 10 sec sprints + 1 min active recovery

Training for Jiu-Jitsu

The current success of MMA has led to many martial arts enthusiasts learning the techniques of jiu-jitsu, and because of this, "the gentle art" has spread around the world. With this increase in the number of jiu-jitsu practitioners, the sports calendar has grown, and the intensity of training and competitions has increased significantly. In the quest for victories and medals, physical preparation takes fundamental importance in improving the performance of jiu-jitsu athletes.

Coaches and athletes should consider the availability of time and physical space to perform any training. For this reason, we have tried to create physical preparation exercises for athletes and practitioners of jiu-jitsu that can be performed on the mat without needing a resistance training gym.

Jiu-Jitsu Training Program 1

For this training program, we visited the American Top Team in East Orlando and invited black belts Jayson Patino and Tarsis da Gama e Paula Neto to demonstrate. This work may be performed 2 or 3 times a week, and serves to improve muscular endurance, speed of takedown, agility of movement, strength for gripping the cloth of a kimono, and so on.

The exercises demonstrated here are only a few examples of an enormous range of possibilities within training geared toward the martial arts, especially jiu-jitsu. This training may be performed in different ways, with the exercises being done individually with 2 to 4 sets per exercise for 15 to 30 seconds and a 1-minute rest or in the form of a long circuit where the athlete does a set at each station and changes exercises until the end of the round stipulated by the coach. Rounds may vary from 5 to 10 minutes. This training may be performed soon after jiu-jitsu training or on a separate day from sports practice.

Grip Strengthening for Standing Guard Pass

In this work, Tarsis develops grip strength with overload offered by his training partner's (Jayson's) body (see figure 5.223). Start in a deep squat position. Hold the partner's lapels, inhale, and lift their body to a half-squat position. Hold this position for a few seconds. Exhale at the end of the movement and repeat. This type of resistance uses back, arm, forearm, core, and lower-body muscles to stabilize the movement correctly. Perform the technique using a training methodology that develops isometric strength and muscular endurance for jiu-jitsu in a movement similar to a standing guard pass.

Figure 5.223 – Grip strengthening for standing guard pass.

Adapted Leg Press

The adapted leg press is a variation of the traditional 45-degree leg press. We opted to work with the overload of the partner and develop the leg musculature, especially the quadriceps (rectus femoris, vastus lateralis, vastus medialis, and vastus intermedius). The difference here is that at the end of the movement, the athlete pushes their partner, who is standing, and then ends in an attacking half-kneeling position (see figure 5.224).

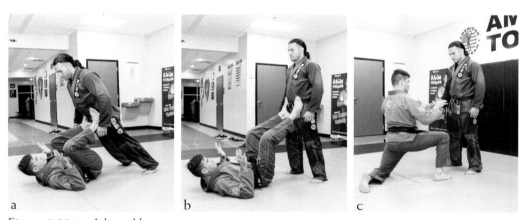

a   b   c

Figure 5.224 – Adapted leg press.

Squat With Partner

Begin the squat by standing, legs aligned. Carry the partner in a fireman's carry, which requires stabilization of the core (see figure 5.225). The main objective is to develop the strength and muscular endurance of lower-body muscles.

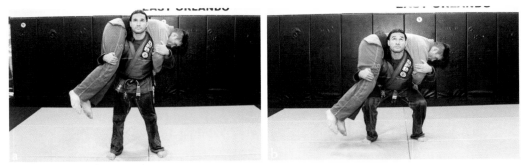

Figure 5.225 – Squat with partner.

Jump Over Punchbags

We use the bags as an alternative, but we can use benches or hurdles to perform plyometric exercises. We organize it so that the athlete performs various jumps in sequence with the specific aim of adding power to the lower body (see figure 5.226).

Figure 5.226 – Jump over punchbags.

Medicine Ball Throw With Partner

Hold the ball at chest height with the arms aligned, and throw the medicine ball to the partner, who throws it back (see figure 5.227). In this movement, we seek to work the muscles responsible for pushing movements—in this case, the chest, deltoid, triceps brachii, and core muscles that stabilize the movement.

Figure 5.227 – Medicine ball throw with partner.

Agility Ladder

Agility exercises develop speed, agility, and footwork and will aid with movement in fights (see figure 5.228).

Figure 5.228 – Agility ladder exercise.

Battle Rope

With the nautical rope, we may work on movements with maximum execution speed at various angles. This exercise targets the arms and shoulders and strengthens the shoulder-stabilizing muscles (see figure 5.229).

Figure 5.229 – Battle rope.

Lateral Jump With Sprawl

We use a bag as an alternative, but we can use hurdles for plyometric exercises. Start in a fighting stance (see figure 5.230a). Jump from one side of the bag to the other (see figure 5.230b), then execute a sprawl technique and repeat (see figure 5.230c). We organize it so that the athlete performs various jumps in sequence to add power, or power endurance, to the lower body.

Figure 5.230 – Lateral jump with sprawl.

Isometric Hold on the Pull-Up Bar With Kimono Grip

This exercise was developed to improve grip strength. Adopt a horizontal position, holding the entire body in an isometric position (see figure 5.231). Various muscles are required in this exercise, and it is very challenging.

Figure 5.231 – Isometric hold on the pull-up bar with kimono grip.

The training program presented in table 5.32 provides two training options for jiu-jitsu.

Table 5.32 – Jiu-Jitsu Training Program 1

	Week 1	Week 2	Week 3	Week 4
Training A				
1. Grip strengthening for standing guard pass	2 × 5 with partner holding 5 sec each rep	2 × 5 with partner holding 5 sec each rep	3 × 5 with partner holding 5 sec each rep	3 × 5 with partner holding 5 sec each rep
2. Medicine ball throw	2 × 10	2 × 10	3 × 10	3 × 10
3. Lateral jump with sprawl	2 × 10 per side	2 × 10 per side	3 × 10 per side	3 × 10 per side
4. Battle rope	1 × 30 sec	2 × 30 sec	3 × 30 sec	4 × 30 sec
5. Squat with partner	3 × 10	3 × 10	4 × 10	4 × 10
Training B				
1. Agility ladder	2 × 30 sec	3 × 30 sec	4 × 30 sec	5 × 30 sec
2. Adapted leg press	3 × 10	3 × 10	4 × 10	4 × 10
3. Battle rope	3 × 15 sec Max speed	3 × 15 sec Max speed	4 × 15 sec Max speed	4 × 15 sec Max speed
4. Jump over punchbags	2 × 20	2 × 20	3 × 20	3 × 20
5. Isometric hold on the pull-up bar with kimono grip	1 × 30 sec	2 × 30 sec	3 × 30 sec	4 × 30 sec

Jiu-Jitsu Training Program 2

In this section, we concentrate on developing specific preparation exercises for jiu-jitsu. We invited five-time world champion Gezary "Ge" Matuda, former American champion Bruno "Brunim" Bastos, and former Brazilian champion Jonatas "Tagarela" Gurgel to demonstrate (see figure 5.232).

Figure 5.232 – From left to right: Bruno "Brunim" Bastos, Jonatas "Tagarela" Gurgel, and Gezary "Ge" Matuda.

This work is normally performed once a week outside of competition and two or three times a week during the training camp for a tournament. It serves to improve muscular endurance, takedown speed and guard passes, agility, and grip strength, with or without a kimono.

The exercises demonstrated here are only a few examples of an enormous range of possibilities within training geared toward martial arts, especially jiu-jitsu. This training may be performed in different ways, in which the sets may be composed of time intervals (e.g., lateral jump for 30 sec) or number of repetitions (as with climbing up and down a rope 3 times).

Perform a warm-up that varies between 5 and 10 minutes made up of exercises that are chosen according to the daily plan.

Guard Pass With a Knee on the Belly

In this work, the idea is to develop guard pass techniques with an overload from an elastic band around the waist (see figure 5.233). This type of resistance forces the core muscles and legs to activate to stabilize the movement correctly. Perform the technique within a training methodology applied to develop muscular endurance within jiu-jitsu.

Figure 5.233 – Guard pass with a knee on the belly with overload from elastic band tied around the waist.

Long Jump and Lateral Plyometric Jump Over Hurdles

In the first exercise (see figures 5.234a-b), perform various jumps over the high hurdles in sequence. In the second exercise, start in a fighting stance. Jump from one side to the other of the low hurdle and repeat (see figures 5.234c-d). Both exercises are good choices to add power and power endurance to the lower body.

Figure 5.234 – Jonatas Gurgel performs long jump (a-b) while Gezary Matuda performs lateral plyometric jump over hurdles (c-d).

Overhead Medicine Ball Throw and Sprawl

This exercise was developed so that the athlete perfects their capacity for explosive muscle power in the anterior region of the torso. The medicine ball accomplishes this due to the ease of a single throw. With the medicine ball close to the chest and the legs aligned in the traditional squatting position (see figure 5.235a), throw the ball overhead, keeping the elbows flexed and close to the torso but extending them when throwing the medicine ball (see figure 5.235b), and then immediately perform a sprawl (takedown defense technique) (see figure 5.235c).

Figure 5.235 – Overhead medicine ball throw and sprawl.

Ippon Seoi Nage Drills

With physical preparation training, technical exercises may be included with the clear goal of specific conditioning but without forgetting perfecting the technique chosen at the time. We use ippon seoi nage drills to improve muscular endurance for the takedown technique (see figure 5.236).

Figure 5.236 – Ippon seoi nage drills.

Double-Leg Takedown With Resistance Bands

This exercise was created to develop strength and muscular endurance adapted for one of the takedown techniques most widely used by jiu-jitsu athletes: the double-leg takedown (see figure 5.237).

Figure 5.237 – Double-leg takedown with resistance bands.

Bent-Over Row With Partner

This exercise was created specifically for this training, in which the partner's body weight is used to create the overload necessary to develop strength in posterior muscles and strengthen the traditional jiu-jitsu grip. Adopt a position with the knees flexed and with the torso leaning forward and make a horizontal pulling motion (see figure 5.238).

Figure 5.238 – Bent-over row with partner.

Rope Climb

The goal of this exercise is to develop strength and muscular endurance in the musculature of the arms, back, core, and lower body, if they are used in the execution (see figure 5.239). This kind of work also strengthens grip.

Figure 5.239 – Rope climb.

Table 5.33 presents a training program for jiu-jitsu.

Table 5.33 – Jiu-Jitsu Training Program 2

	Week 1	Week 2	Week 3	Week 4
1. Guard pass exercise with knee on the belly	2 × 10 per side	2 × 10 per side	3 × 10 per side	3 × 10 per side
2. Long jump and lateral plyometric jump over hurdles	2 × 10 long jumps; rest for 1 min and 2 × 30 sec lateral jumps	2 × 10 long jumps; rest for 1 min and 2 × 30 sec lateral jumps	3 × 10 long jumps; rest for 1 min and 3 × 30 sec lateral jumps	3 × 10 long jumps; rest for 1 min and 3 × 30 sec lateral jumps
3. Overhead medicine ball throw and sprawl	2 × 15	2 × 15	2 × 20	2 × 20
4. Ippon seoi nage drills	2 × 10	2 × 10	3 × 10	3 × 10
5. Double-leg takedown with resistance bands	1 × 20	2 × 20	3 × 20	4 × 20
6. Bent-over row with partner	1 × 8 with partner	2 × 8 with partner	3 × 8 with partner	4 × 8 with partner
7. Rope climb	1 × 2 BW	2 × 2 BW	3 × 2 BW	4 × 2 BW

BW: body weight

Outdoor Training for MMA

The use of training circuits for MMA is becoming increasingly developed and well organized, but some training nuances may be improved, or exploited to a greater extent, such as the structuring of outdoor training (Dias, et al. 2017). In this section, we will demonstrate an outdoor circuit with Brett Rogers and Thiago "Big Monster" Santos.

The circuit in table 5.34 develops power endurance according to the MMA circuit model (Dias, et al. 2017). Lasting approximately five minutes to simulate the rounds of a fight, the repetitions vary according to the number of rounds that the athlete is going to fight. For example, for athletes who compete in up to three rounds, we have a general warm-up round, a specific warm-up round, and three rounds of the circuit. Normally, the general warm-up encompasses aerobic exercises, such as running or cycling, and stretching. In the specific warm-up round, half of one round has at least one repetition performed at each station of the circuit to improve the athlete's transition and memorization, and in the other half, there is pad work with the assistance of ATT striking coach Luciano "Macarrão" Dos Santos.

Note that the station order in this circuit training always alternates between exercises for the upper and lower body to avoid a buildup of lactic acid, hydrogen ions, and excessive fatigue. The rounds should last for five minutes, or slightly longer. Between the stations, the rest is minimal, and at the end of each round, we have a one-minute rest to simulate the recovery time during a fight. It is better to have more five- to six-minute rounds than rounds longer than six minutes (Dias, et al. 2017).

Battle Rope Alternating Waves

This exercise is performed for 30 seconds, making waves, to work the upper body (see figure 5.240).

Figure 5.240 – Thiago Santos demonstrates battle rope alternating waves.

Car Push

This exercise is performed for 30 to 50 meters (33-54 yd), with intense exercise for the lower body and isometric exercise for the torso and arms (see figure 5.241).

Figure 5.241 – Brett Rogers pushes an SUV.

Striking a Tire With Sledgehammer

This exercise is performed 20 times, 10 times with each arm. To make the exercise more challenging, there is resistance to traction provided by the special resistance band affixed to the torso (see figure 5.242). The sledgehammer may weigh 18 to 33 pounds (8-15 kg).

Figure 5.242 – Striking a tire with sledgehammer with a resistance band affixed to the torso.

Tire Flip With Jump

The tire flip was previously demonstrated in figure 5.191 and is performed 10 times. The difference here is that the athlete is required to jump into and out of the tire to change sides (see figure 5.243). The tire may weigh between 300 and 500 pounds (136-227 kg).

Figure 5.243 – Brett Rogers executes the tire flip and jump.

Car Pull With Rope

This is an intense workout for the back, arms, and forearms and is an isometric exercise for the lumbar spine (see figure 5.244). It is performed over 15 meters (16 yd).

Figure 5.244 – Thiago Santos pulls an SUV with a rope.

Hitting Pads With Coach

This last training station exercise consists of hitting pads at high speed until the end of the round (approximately 1 min) (see figure 5.245).

Figure 5.245 – Brett Rogers hitting pads with Coach Luciano.

At the end of the circuit, we perform an extra round of pad work with the striking coach to correct any technical details and as a cool-down. For athletes in lighter weight divisions, we recommend a lighter sledgehammer, using a car rather than a van or SUV, and using a smaller tire than those heavyweights use.

Table 5.34 includes an outdoor training circuit adapted for MMA.

Table 5.34 – Outdoor Training Circuit for MMA

	Week 1	Week 2	Week 3	Week 4
1. Battle rope alternating waves	2 × 30 sec	2 × 30 sec	3 × 30 sec	3 × 30 sec
2. Car push	2 × 30 m	2 × 40 m	3 × 35 m	3 × 40 m
3. Sledgehammer on the tire	2 × 10 per side	2 × 10 per side	3 × 10 per side	3 × 10 per side
4. Tire flip with jump	2 × 10	2 × 10	3 × 10	3 × 10
5. Car pull with rope	2 × 15 m	2 × 15 m	3 × 15 m	3 × 15 m
6. Hitting pads with coach (plus extra round, if desired)	2 × 1 min hard (1 × 5 min light)	2 × 1 min hard (1 × 5 min light)	3 × 1 min hard (1 × 5 min light)	3 × 1 min hard (1 × 5 min light)

High-Intensity Interval Training for MMA

Endurance may be defined as the ability to continue to endure a stress, hardship, or discomfort level. In sport, *muscular endurance* is the ability to sustain a specific activity for a prolonged time. Muscular endurance depends on energy potential, the adaptation level to the demands of an event, technical and tactical efficiency, and the athlete's psychological stamina. This capacity helps the athlete to demonstrate a high level of muscular activity during training sessions and competitions and delay or cancel out the process of fatigue (Platonov, 2004).

For MMA, muscular endurance is indispensable for high-level combat, especially with the increase in the number of five-round fights (Dias, et al. 2017). For this reason, we invited John Lineker, UFC veteran and ONE-FC athlete, to demonstrate an HIIT circuit that may be used during the training camp four to six weeks before a fight.

The circuit is a model to develop muscular endurance, lasts approximately five to six minutes to simulate the rounds of a fight, and the number of repetitions varies according to the number of rounds that the athlete is going to fight.

Normally, the general warm-up has aerobic exercise, such as running or cycling, and dynamic stretching. In the specific warm-up round, a little of each station to be used in the circuit is completed as a warm-up in which the loads and speeds of movement are reduced by half.

First Round (5-6 min): This round uses an arm ergometer with movements that simulate pummeling and that may be performed in a forward and backward direction (see figure 5.246). In general, the movements are performed for 10 to 30 seconds in a forward direction and 10 to 30 seconds in a backward direction. After that, we have 1 to 2 minutes of active recovery. Repeat these movements until the end of the round.

Figure 5.246 – Use of an arm ergometer to simulate the movements of pummeling.

Second Round (5-6 min): This round uses the Hydra-Gym Powermax 360 (which offers concentric resistance, with independent unilateral movement for body exercises). This platform uses OmniKinetics resistance, which allows movements at all angles and at all speeds, provides the opportunity to work the arms at different angles and in movements that recruit agonist and antagonist muscles (e.g., chest and back muscles), and prepares for a sequence of ground and pound exercises after the Hydra (see figure 5.247). Normally, 15- to 30-second sets are performed on the Hydra, followed by a sequence that involves strike simulations for 15 to 30 seconds, after which we have 1 to 2 minutes of active recovery. These movements are repeated until the end of the round.

Figure 5.247 – Movement on the Hydra-Gym Powermax 360 platform, followed by ground and pound.

Third Round (5-6 min): This round includes a sequence of sprints performed on the Air300 Runner (see figure 5.248), in an interval of 10 to 30 seconds, alternating with 1 to 2 minutes of active recovery. These movements are repeated until the end of the round.

Figure 5.248 – Sprints on the Air300 Runner.

Fourth Round (5-6 min): Here, we look to work on the anterior and posterior muscles of the torso using resistance bands while simulating punches and clinches. In this circuit, we work either with time intervals or repetitions. In the specific case of John Lineker, we use 10- to 30-second intervals with maximum execution speed using the resistance band (see figures 5.249a-b) and 45 or more seconds of slow work, without the resistance band, performing shadow boxing movements to accelerate recovery. Then, another 10 to 30 seconds on the VersaPulley at maximum speed to simulate the clinch movement (see figures 5.249c-d). Repeat these movements until the end of the round.

Figure 5.249 – Using resistance bands to simulate punches (*a-b*), followed by work on the VersaPulley to simulate the clinch movement (*c-d*).

Fifth Round (5-6 min): The VersaClimber simulates a climb with resistance, and the athlete works on the upper and lower body at the same time (see figure 5.250). The athlete accelerates for 10 to 20 seconds and takes 45 or more seconds of active rest (at low speed), developing aerobic endurance through interval training. This may be performed for up to 5 to 6 minutes.

Figure 5.250 – VersaClimber climb.

Sixth Round (5-10 min): In figure 5.251, we use an elliptical trainer that simulates skiing as continuous aerobic exercise at a moderate to slow pace (with a heart rate of around 130-150 bpm) or as a cool-down. We recommend switching between an elliptical trainer, treadmill, bicycle, and skiing machine to help deter overuse injury and excessive use of certain musculature or joints. Variety also prevents mental fatigue. This work may be done for 5 to 10 minutes, depending on the athlete's goal and training status.

Figure 5.251 – Simulation of skiing on elliptical trainer.

Table 5.35 presents a sample program for HIIT training.

Table 5.35 – Sample HIIT Training Program

	Week 1	Week 2	Week 3	Week 4
First round				
Arm ergometer	15 sec forward 15 sec back; 2 min active recovery and repeat 2 times	15 sec forward 15 sec back; 2 min active recovery and repeat 2 times	15 sec forward 15 sec back; 1 min active recovery and repeat 3 times	15 sec forward 15 sec back; 1 min active recovery and repeat 3 times
Second round				
Hydra-Gym Powermax 360 + ground and pound	15 sec of Hydra + 30 sec of ground and pound; 2 min active recovery and repeat 2 times	15 sec of Hydra + 30 sec of ground and pound; 2 min active recovery and repeat 2 times	15 sec of Hydra + 30 sec of ground and pound; 1 min active recovery and repeat 3 times	15 sec of Hydra + 30 sec of ground and pound; 1 min active recovery and repeat 3 times
Third round				
Sprint on Air300 Runner	30 sec sprint; 2 min active recovery and repeat 2 times	30 sec sprint; 2 min active recovery and repeat 2 times	30 sec sprint; 1 min 30 sec active recovery and repeat 3 times	30 sec sprint; 1 min 30 sec active recovery and repeat 3 times
Fourth round				
Punches with resistance bands + VersaPulley clinch	30 sec of punches; 1 min 30 sec active recovery + 30 sec clinch and repeat 2 times	30 sec of punches; 1 min 30 sec active recovery + 30 sec clinch and repeat 2 times	30 sec of punches; 1 min active recovery + 30 sec clinch and repeat 3 times	30 sec of punches; 1 min active recovery + 30 sec clinch and repeat 3 times
Fifth round				
VersaClimber	20 sec fast; 1 min 30 sec slow and repeat until the end of the round	20 sec fast; 1 min 30 sec slow and repeat until the end of the round	20 sec fast; 1 min slow and repeat until the end of the round	20 sec fast; 1 min slow and repeat until the end of the round
Sixth round				
Elliptical trainer	1 × 5 min @ 130-150 bpm	1 × 5 min @ 130-150 bpm	2 × 5 min @ 130-150 bpm	2 × 5 min @ 130-150 bpm

Circuits for Five-Round Matches

In this chapter, we have seen various training programs involving physical preparation for grappling or striking. Now we will demonstrate a few of the five-round fight preparation circuits that were developed based on specific fights for championship belts or main events with five rounds. When the MMA athlete gets to this point, they must be in top shape to achieve peak performance to win a belt, maintain a belt, or both in the case of Amanda Nunes from American Top Team. By training a variation of the programs and with the help of strength and conditioning coach Everton Bittar, she was able to become undisputed champion in two UFC divisions.

Circuit Program 1

In this example, we are going to show a circuit that was developed for António "Big Foot" Silva, based on different training methods including strength, functional training, agility, and speed exercises.

The training not only involves work in the resistance training room with machines and free weights but may also be applied using several accessories, such as resistance bands, as well as the body weight itself, which, depending on the exercise, makes the exercise more difficult than with free weights (Dias and Oliveira, 2013). In this section, we are going to show how it is possible to do this kind of training.

First Round: The first round includes a warm-up, which ranges from 5 to 10 minutes.

Second Round: This round consists of three exercises:

1. *Barbell bench press:* This exercise was previously described in figure 5.21. During this round, there are 2 to 5 sets, each with 4 to 10 repetitions (see figure 5.252).

Figure 5.252 – Barbell bench press.

2. *Hydra-Gym Powermax 360:* This device has been used in different ways because it enables work at various angles, offering pneumatic resistance with air cylinders. In this round, the Hydra-Gym Powermax 360 is used for push-pull (chest and back) training (see figure 5.253). Sets may vary from 2 to 5, ranging from 20 to 30 seconds of execution at maximum speed.

Figure 5.253 – Push-pull exercise performed on the Hydra-Gym Powermax 360 platform.

3. *Russian kettlebell swing:* The kettlebell has proved to be a powerful ally in combat training (see figure 5.13). Here, it is used to develop muscular endurance (see figure 5.254). Sets may be repeated 2 to 5 times with 20 to 30 seconds of execution.

Figure 5.254 – Russian kettlebell swing.

Third Round: This round consists of three exercises:

1. *Front raise with resistance bands:* This functional exercise is adapted for MMA to simulate wrestling pummeling movements or defense against takedowns. Perform the movement with the legs parallel or in a fighting stance and with the arms in bilateral elevation (see figure 5.255). It may also be performed alternately. The resistance band tension facilitates muscular endurance or speed work, which varies according to the length and intensity of the resistance bands. We recommend 2 to 5 sets from 20 to 30 seconds of execution at maximum speed.

Figure 5.255 – Front raise with resistance bands.

2. *Medicine ball throw*: This exercise targets punching or pushing movements and was described in figure 5.167. We recommend 2 to 5 sets with the throw repeated 4 or 5 times at maximum speed (see figure 5.256).

Figure 5.256 – Medicine ball throw.

3. *Medicine ball overhead slam*: This exercise is similar to attacks used by MMA fighters during ground and pound. For more information on how to properly perform this exercise, see figure 5.111. We recommend 2 to 5 sets of 10 to 20 repetitions or 20 to 30 seconds per set (see figure 5.257).

Figure 5.257 – Medicine ball overhead slam.

Fourth Round: This round consists of two exercises:

1. *Barbell deadlift:* This exercise plays an important role in the strength and explosive power of combat athletes (see figure 5.258). For more information on how to properly perform this exercise, see figure 5.20. In this round we use 2 to 5 sets with 3 to 6 repetitions.

Figure 5.258 – Barbell deadlift.

2. *Sprints with resistance band:* In the sprint exercises, a resistance band is used around the torso to produce overload and increase the intensity of the exercise (see figure 5.259). In this work, a variation could be to perform a deep penetration step (wrestling movement) at the end of the sprint, improving takedown technique. We recommend 2 to 5 sets, which may vary from 6 to 10 sprints executed at maximum speed.

Figure 5.259 – Sprints with resistance band.

Fifth Round: This round includes agility exercises (speed and agility ladders) that are used to develop speed, agility, and footwork and will aid movement in fight training (see figure 5.260).

Figure 5.260 – Agility work with ladder.

Table 5.36 demonstrates how to use this circuit over four weeks.

Table 5.36 – Five-Round Circuit Training Program

	Week 1	Week 2	Week 3	Week 4
First round				
Warm-up	1 × 5-10 min	1 × 5-10 min	1 × 5-10 min	1 × 5-10 min
Second round				
1. Barbell bench press	2 × 10RM	3 × 8RM	4 × 6RM	5 × 4RM
2. Hydra-Gym Powermax 360	2 × 20 sec	3 × 20 sec	4 × 20 sec	5 × 20 sec
3. Russian kettlebell swing	2 × 20 sec	3 × 20 sec	4 × 20 sec	5 × 20 sec
Third round				
1. Front raise with resistance bands	2 × 20 sec	3 × 20 sec	4 × 20 sec	5 × 20 sec
2. Medicine ball throw	2 × 5	3 × 5	4 × 5	5 × 5
3. Medicine ball overhead slam	2 × 20 sec	3 × 20 sec	4 × 20 sec	5 × 20 sec
Fourth round				
1. Barbell deadlift	2 × 8RM	3 × 8RM	4 × 6RM	5 × 4RM
2. Sprints with resistance band	2 × 6	3 × 6	4 × 6	5 × 6
Fifth round				
Agility	2 × 1 min work +1 min rest	3 × 1 min work +1 min rest	4 × 1 min work +1 min rest	5 × 1 min work +1 min rest

Circuit Program 2

In this program, we invited Jessica Aguilar to detail a variation of a circuit of five rounds that was used in some of her fights for a championship belt. The main focus of this training was to develop muscular strength and endurance exercises to maintain performance during a long five-round fight.

First Round: Initially, during the first round, perform a warm-up including some mobility movements, ranging from 5 to 10 minutes. Then perform the exercises listed for the subsequent rounds. Note that some exercises could be used more than one time in different rounds. To make it easy to understand, table 5.37 demonstrates how to use this circuit over 4 weeks of training.

Second Round: This round consists of three exercises:

1. *Dumbbell bench press:* The bench press is a powerful exercise for the upper body and was previously described in this chapter. For more information on how to properly perform this exercise, see figure 5.47. In this specific training, Jessica had some back pain due to wrestling practice, so we decided to keep the feet on the bench to reduce the tension in the lower back (see figure 5.261). We normally do 4 to 6 sets of 8 repetitions with 60 percent to 80 percent of maximum.

Figure 5.261 – Dumbbell bench press.

2. *Cable core rotation with arm extension:* This functional exercise was developed specifically for fighters (see figure 5.262). The choice of this exercise was the result of a technical analysis of her fight training with the goal of adding power to her punching. The sets are performed with a moderate load (50% of maximum) and taken to failure with an average time of 30 seconds on each side.

Figure 5.262 – Cable core rotation with arm extension.

3. *Isoton front raise with resistance bands:* In the fight world, the front raise may be adapted to add power to specific movements such as defense against takedowns or punches, as described in figure 5.255. In this exercise, keep the legs parallel (see figure 5.263) and use the Isoton method in a superset format with 30 seconds of contraction followed by 30 seconds of rest, repeated 3 times (one superset). Take active rest consisting of shadow boxing for 30 to 45 seconds and repeat the work for 2 to 3 sets to develop muscular endurance.

Figure 5.263 – Front raise with resistance bands.

Third Round: This round consists of three exercises:

1. *Medicine ball overhead throw:* The medicine ball overhead throw is a functional exercise adapted for fighting. Using the medicine ball, keep the arms extended and the core tight. Perform a half squat and hinge at the hips to bring the ball between the legs (see figure 5.264a). Inhale, explode up, and throw the ball vertically overhead into the air (see figures 5.264b-c). We repeat this movement for 10 to 20 throws broken down into 2 to 3 sets.

Figure 5.264 – Medicine ball overhead throw.

2. *Standing hammer curl:* This traditional exercise is widely used at gyms. Stand gripping a dumbbell in each hand with the palms facing each other. Inhale and raise the forearms together or alternately. Exhale at the end of the movement. We recommend 4 sets of this exercise with loads of between 60 percent and 75 percent of maximum (see figure 5.265).

Figure 5.265 – Standing hammer curl.

3. *Ropes alternating up and down:* Nautical rope has become an accessory in functional fight training. Here, it was used to continue our work on our athlete's arms and shoulders. Sets could be alternated or using bilateral movements to develop muscular endurance, recruiting the arm, shoulder, and core muscles (see figure 5.266). For this exercise, we use 2 to 4 sets performed until failure with an average time of 30 seconds.

Figure 5.266 – Ropes alternating up and down.

Fourth Round: This round consists of two exercises:

1. *Back squat:* One of the most well-known exercises for the lower body, the back squat was already described in depth in this chapter (see figure 5.31). We recommend 2 to 4 sets with 75 percent of maximum performed to failure.

2. *Chin-up with neutral grip:* This movement was described in figure 5.52, but the grips are different. In Jessica's case, the exercise intent was to develop dynamic and isometric strength using a neutral grip (see figure 5.267). We normally use 3 to 4 sets of 10 repetitions with 5 seconds of isometric contraction at the end of each set.

Figure 5.267 – Chin-up with neutral grip.

Fifth Round: This round consists of two exercises:

1. *Rope pushdown with BOSU ball:* This is an adaptation of the traditional rope pushdown on the pulley, only on top of an inverted BOSU ball, thus causing difficulty in maintaining balance (see figure 5.268). In Jessica's case, this exercise was chosen to work the triceps brachii muscle and create instability for the lower body rendering the exercise more difficult. Long sets of 20 repetitions with moderate loads (55% of maximum) were used.

Figure 5.268 – Rope pushdown with BOSU ball.

2. *Bent-over row:* This is another great exercise for the back muscles. Straddle the bar with the legs slightly bent and lean forward at the waist to about 45 degrees, keeping the back flat. Grasp the bar with an overhand grip. Contract the core, inhale, and raise the bar to the chest. Exhale at the end of the movement. The bent-over row is very useful for MMA due to its similarity to grappling movements (see figure 5.269). In this exercise, we use 3 sets of heavy loads (80%-85% of maximum) repeated until failure.

Figure 5.269 – Bent-over row.

Table 5.37 demonstrates how to use this circuit over four weeks.

Table 5.37 – Five-Round Circuit Training Program

	Week 1	Week 2	Week 3	Week 4
First round				
Warm-up, mobility	1 × 5-10 min	1 × 5-10 min	1 × 5-10 min	1 × 5-10 min
Second round				
1. Dumbbell bench press	2 × 8 @ 70% 1RM	2 × 8 @ 70% 1RM	3 × 8 @ 70% 1RM	3 × 8 @ 70% 1RM
2. Cable core rotation with arm extension	2 × 25 sec per side	2 × 25 sec per side	3 × 25 sec per side	3 × 25 sec per side
3. Isoton front raise with resistance bands (see description of Isoton method in chapter 2 or at the end of this chapter)	3 × 30 sec with 30 sec rest with light resistance bands	3 × 30 sec with 30 sec rest with light resistance bands	4 × 30 sec with 30 sec rest with medium resistance bands	4 × 30 sec with 30 sec rest with medium resistance bands
Third round				
1. Medicine ball overhead throw	2 × 15	2 × 20	3 × 15	3 × 20
2. Standing hammer curl	2 × 15RM	2 × 15RM	3 × 12RM	3 × 12RM
3. Ropes alternating up and down	2 × 25 sec	2 × 30 sec	3 × 25 sec	3 × 30 sec
Fourth round				
1. Back squat	2 @ 75% 1RM to failure	2 @ 75% 1RM to failure	3 @ 75% 1RM to failure	3 @ 75% 1RM to failure
2. Chin-up with neutral grip	2 × 10 BW	2 × 10 BW	3 × 10 BW	3 × 10 BW
Fifth round				
1. Rope pushdown with BOSU ball	2 × 20RM	2 × 20RM	3 × 20RM	3 × 20RM
2. Bent-over row	2 × 8RM	2 × 8RM	3 × 6RM	3 × 6RM

BW: body weight

Circuit Program 3

For this circuit program, we invited the UFC fighter Tecia Torres, strawweight fighter (115 lb [52 kg]) and participant in TUF. In this section, we will show another variation of a five-round circuit, which may be used by any athlete.

First Round: We begin the training with dynamic movements to move the joints for a general and specific warm-up. Next, we start footwork and agility work using a speed or agility ladder for 5 to 10 minutes of movement (see figure 5.270).

Figure 5.270 – Footwork training with agility ladder.

Second Round: This round consists of three exercises: EzBar hang clean and press, hanging leg raise, and cable core rotation (see figures 5.271-5.273). In this round, we prioritize work with overload to develop strength endurance, performing the exercises at moderate execution speed to the limit. The sets designed in this work vary between 2 and 4 with 10 to 20 repetitions.

Figure 5.271 – EzBar hang clean and press.

Figure 5.272 – Hanging leg raise.

Figure 5.273 – Cable core rotation.

Third Round: This round consists of two exercises: alternating cable pulldown and medicine ball lift with sprawl. In this round, we prioritize the muscles of the posterior region and functional exercise with a medicine ball in the form of a circuit. The alternating cable pulldown (see figure 5.274) allows us to adapt dynamic movements with constant speed, and the medicine ball lift with sprawl (see figure 5.275) develops strength and muscular endurance within a specific fighting movement. In this round we used sets based on time rather than repetitions. The duration is between 20 and 30 seconds of execution in each exercise, with a 30- to 40-second rest. The intensity is measured at 8 or 9 using the rating of perceived exertion (RPE) scale, with 1 being very light and 10 maximal effort. Then we repeat 4 or 5 times until the round has been completed.

Figure 5.274 – Alternating cable pulldown.

Figure 5.275 – Medicine ball lift with sprawl.

Fourth Round: This round consists of three exercises: low cable front raise, medicine ball throw, and running in place with high knees. In this round, we direct the work toward the anterior region and legs. We use the same idea of contrasting stimuli as in the previous round, with one exercise on a cable machine and one using a medicine ball. On the cable machine, perform a simultaneous front raise movement (see figure 5.276). This exercise is similar to takedown defense movements like the under hook. This may be adapted to attack movements, such as punches followed by medicine ball throws on a mini trampoline (see figure 5.277). During the active rest interval, run in place with high knees on the mini trampoline (see figure 5.278). These exercises work the chest, deltoid, triceps brachii, and leg muscles.

Figure 5.276 – Low cable front raise.

Figure 5.277 – Medicine ball throw on mini trampoline.

Figure 5.278 – Running in place with high knees on the mini trampoline.

Fifth Round: This round consists of two specific plyometric exercises: a jump and push-up with a BOSU ball (used for balance exercises). For the jump, start on top of a 39-inch (99 cm) bench for the first jump, and reduce the height of the bench one after another, from 32 inches (81 cm) to 16 inches (41 cm) (see figure 5.279). Shortly after, perform push-ups with the BOSU ball as described in figure 5.183. These plyo push-ups are used to work on the upper body (see figure 5.280). This work is performed based on time or repetitions with transition breaks between one full set, which consists of performing the jump and push-up. The exercises are performed with maximum execution speed and power in each repetition.

Figure 5.279 – Plyometric jump.

Figure 5.280 – Plyo push-up with BOSU ball.

Table 5.38 demonstrates how to use this particular circuit over four weeks.

Table 5.38 – Five-Round Circuit Training Program

	Week 1	Week 2	Week 3	Week 4
First round				
Warm-up, agility	1 × 5-10 min	1 × 5-10 min	1 × 5-10 min	1 × 5-10 min
Second round				
1. EzBar hang clean and press	2 × 12RM	2 × 12RM	3 × 10RM	3 × 10RM
2. Hanging leg raise	2 × 20 BW	2 × 20 BW	3 × 20 BW	3 × 20 BW
3. Cable core rotation	2 × 25 sec per side	2 × 25 sec per side	3 × 25 sec per side	3 × 25 sec per side
Third round				
1. Alternating cable pulldown	2 × 20 sec @ 8 RPE	2 × 20 sec @ 8 RPE	3 × 20 sec @ 8 RPE	3 × 20 sec @ 8 RPE
2. Medicine ball lift with sprawl	2 × 20 sec @ 8 RPE	2 × 20 sec @ 8 RPE	3 × 20 sec @ 8 RPE	3 × 20 sec @ 8 RPE
Fourth round				
1. Low cable front raise	2 × 15RM	2 × 15RM	3 × 15RM	3 × 15RM
2. Medicine ball throw	2 × 10	2 × 10	3 × 10	3 × 10
3. Running in place with high knees	2 × 30 sec	2 × 30 sec	3 × 30 sec	3 × 30 sec
Fifth round				
1. Plyo jump	2 × 8 BW	2 × 10 BW	3 × 8 BW	3 × 10 BW
2. Plyo push-up with BOSU ball	2 × 8 BW	2 × 10 BW	3 × 8 BW	3 × 10 BW

BW: body weight

Resistance Band Training

In this chapter, we demonstrated many exercises using pulleys, also called *cables*. They usually offer constant mass and are preferred to train heavy and moderate to slow movements. In contrast, bands offer variable resistance and allow explosive movements typically found in MMA.

Resistance bands are an extremely useful training tool because they can be applied toward achieving a wide variety of outcomes. Nowadays, we see them used in physiotherapy situations, for specific sport training, and other strength and conditioning focuses. Many benefits have been demonstrated by training with resistance bands including improving functional capacity and increasing muscle activation, strength, and muscular endurance. For some individuals, training with resistance bands carries less chance of injury than traditional resistance training modes like barbells and dumbbells. (Lopes, et al. 2019). Research has shown resistance bands to be beneficial for increasing overall strength during specific sport movements or movements that simulate activities of daily living (ADLs) (Iverson, et al. 2017). Additionally, bands are very practical and easy to use in most environments. During the COVID-19 lockdowns, the versatile nature of resistance bands for training was most important as untraditional training environments became essential. Bands are portable, low cost, and able to be anchored to any secure post or rail.

Training With Resistance Bands for Striking

In this section, we demonstrate training with resistance bands that was developed with striking coaches Katel Kubis and Luciano "Macarrão" Dos Santos.

This work is normally performed once a week outside competition periods and twice a week during the training camp. It improves the power and speed of punches, kicks, and knees (Dias, et al. 2017). Training usually consists of five to seven rounds lasting five minutes each in sets of 30 seconds of exercise with the resistance band at moderate speed, followed by one minute without the resistance band at maximum speed, hitting the pads with the coach. This sequence of 30 seconds with the resistance band and one minute without the resistance band is repeated until a five-minute round has been completed.

In general, the following sequence of rounds is used (see figures 5.281-5.285).

Figure 5.281 — First round: five-minute warm-up of jumping rope.

Figure 5.282 – Second round: punches, jabs, and cross.

Figure 5.283 – Third round: specific exercises to improve knees.

Figure 5.284 – Fourth round: exercises to increase the power of kicks.

Figure 5.285 – Fifth round: exercises with resistance bands working all the previous movements.

In the final round, the resistance bands are removed and only pad work with the coach is done, seeking maximum power and speed.

The exercises are performed in sets. At the end of each one, the movements are repeated without the resistance bands to increase speed, coordination, and balance. The training with resistance bands strengthens specific muscle groups used in each punching, kicking, and kneeing movement and stabilizes the movement throughout the core. In beginning athletes, after a preassessment, the work starts with between two and five rounds for up to four weeks, with a frequency of once or twice a week. Table 5.39 presents a training program with resistance bands for striking.

Table 5.39 – Training Program With Resistance Bands for Striking

	Week 1	Week 2	Week 3	Week 4
First round				
Warm-up	1 × 5 min	1 × 5 min	2 × 5 min	2 × 5 min
Second round				
Punches, jabs, and cross	30 sec with resistance bands, rest 30 sec + 30 sec without bands and repeat until the end of the round	30 sec with resistance bands, rest 30 sec + 30 sec without bands and repeat until the end of the round	30 sec with heavy resistance bands, rest 30 sec + 1 min without bands and repeat until the end of the round	30 sec with heavy resistance bands, rest 30 sec + 1 min without bands and repeat until the end of the round
Third round				
Specific exercises to improve knees	30 sec with resistance bands + 30 sec without bands and repeat until the end of the round, alternating sides	30 sec with resistance bands + 30 sec without bands and repeat until the end of the round, alternating sides	30 sec with resistance bands + 45 sec without bands and repeat until the end of the round, alternating sides	30 sec with resistance bands + 45 sec without bands and repeat until the end of the round, alternating sides
Fourth round				
Exercises to increase the power of kicks	5 kicks with resistance bands + 5 without bands and repeat until the end of the round, alternating sides	5 kicks with resistance bands + 5 without bands and repeat until the end of the round, alternating sides	5 kicks with resistance bands + 10 without bands and repeat until the end of the round, alternating sides	5 kicks with resistance bands + 10 without bands and repeat until the end of the round, alternating sides
Fifth round				
Exercises with resistance bands	30 sec with bands for the upper body, rest 30 sec + 30 sec with bands for the lower body and repeat until the end of the round	30 sec with bands for the upper body, rest 30 sec + 30 sec with bands for the lower body and repeat until the end of the round	30 sec with bands for the upper body + 30 sec with bands for the lower body and repeat until the end of the round	30 sec with bands for the upper body + 30 sec with bands for the lower body and repeat until the end of the round
Final round				
Hitting pads with coach	1 × 5 min medium speed	1 × 5 min medium speed	1 × 5 min fast speed	1 × 5 min fast speed

Training With Resistance Bands for Power Takedowns

In this section, we demonstrate the training with resistance bands for power takedowns that was developed with Russian coach and owner of Fitsambo, Pavel Vladimirovich Pashkin. This work and its variations have been used for more than 20 years by Russian and European athletes who achieved great results at different competition levels.

Exercise for Throwing the Opponent From the Back

Begin with the feet shoulder-width apart and hold the resistance band with an overhand grip (see figure 5.286*a*). Imitate pulling the opponent off-balance by stepping behind while thrusting one hand upward toward the face and drawing the band toward the chest with the other hand (see figures 5.286*b-c*). Turn as if to throw the opponent from the back (see figure 5.286*d*). Keep one hand at the chest and the other hand in line with the shoulder. Turn the head to increase the amplitude of motion. The twisting motion is performed in the direction of the opposite shin to shoulder that is imitating the throw.

Figure 5.286 – Exercise for throwing an opponent from the back (with resistance bands).

Exercise for Takedowns With Two Hands on the Opponent

Begin with the feet shoulder-width apart and hold the resistance band with an overhand grip (see figure 5.287a). Imitate pulling the opponent off-balance by stepping behind with a cross-step. Thrust one hand upward toward the face and with the other hand draw the band toward the chest (see figure 5.287b). Step to turn, imitating the takedown by pulling the band, as if bringing the opponent close and off-balance. Tighten the resistance band at the chest with one hand (see figure 5.287c). With the other hand, press the resistance band forward. Continue moving forward with a twisting action (see figure 5.287d). Continually tighten the resistance band along the chest with one hand. With the other hand, stop the motion moving forward and away and move toward the opposite lower leg, pivoting on the foot that is on the same side as the resistance band. Turn the head in the direction of movement to increase the amplitude and efficiency of the motion.

Figure 5.287 – Exercise for takedowns with two hands on the opponent.

Exercise for Takedowns With a Grip on One of the Opponent's Hands, or on the Arm, and Grasping the Torso

Begin with the feet shoulder-width apart and hold the resistance band with the left hand close to the body. Use the right hand to simulate holding the opponent's kimono (see figure 5.288a). Turn with a back step to imitate the takedown, bringing the opponent off-balance toward you. The right hand pulls the resistance band up and forward; the left hand presses it forward only (see figures 5.288b-c). Perform a partial rotation, holding the resistance band and turning away from the wall. The right arm stays forward, and the left arm pulls the resistance band around the body in the direction of the movement (see figures 5.288d-e). Turn the head in the direction of motion (see figure 5.288f). The rotation is performed toward the opposite lower leg from the side of the start of the movement.

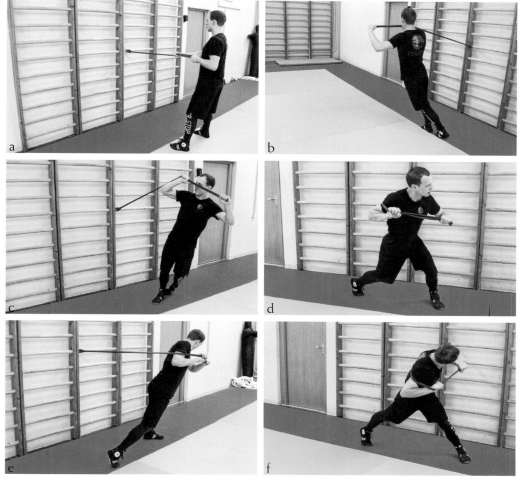

Figure 5.288 – Exercise for takedowns with a grip on one of the opponent's hands and grasping the torso.

Exercise to Simulate a Lift to Shoulder Carry

Stand with the feet shoulder-width apart. Grip the resistance band with one hand (see figure 5.289*a*). Thrust the resistance band up and over the head. Dive underneath and perform a half squat while the resistance band lies on the trapezius (see figure 5.289*b*). Extend the legs and hips, simulating lifting the opponent onto the shoulders (see figures 5.289*c-d*).

Figure 5.289 – Exercise to simulate a lift to shoulder carry.

Exercise to Simulate a Lift to Shoulder Carry From the Knees

Stand with the feet shoulder-width apart. Grip the resistance band with one hand (see figure 5.290a). Drop into a preparation position, contracting the core, and prepare as if for a takedown (see figures 5.290b-c). Thrust the resistance band above the head and toward the body, diving underneath it (see figure 5.290d). Move to two knees, pulling the resistance band behind the head, over the shoulders, and forward (see figure 5.290e). Pull on the resistance band while it lies on the trapezius (see figure 5.290f). Tighten the resistance band against the abdomen. Tilt the body in the direction of the pull. With the free hand, simulate grasping the opponent's leg (see figure 5.290g).

Figure 5.290 – Exercise to simulate a lift to shoulder carry from the knees.

Exercise for Throwing the Opponent From the Chest (Suplex Takedown)

Place the resistance band behind the back and under the arms as pictured and stand at a distance that puts tension on the band (see figures 5.291*a-c*). Drop into a shallow squat to prepare to pull the resistance band back and imitate a throw (see figure 5.291*d*). Take a step forward with one foot (right) from the preparation position and begin to pull the resistance band upward (see figure 5.291*e*). Perform a short step with the second foot (left), maintaining the semi-squat, and continue to pull the resistance band upward (see figure 5.291*f*). To simulate the throw from the chest (suplex takedown), extend the legs. Continue to pull the resistance band upward and over, hyperextending the back (see figure 5.291*g*).

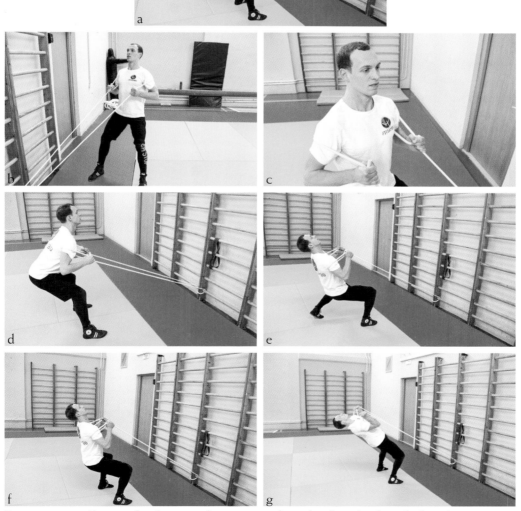

Figure 5.291 – Exercise for throwing the opponent from the chest (suplex takedown).

Exercise Variation to Prepare for Takedowns

Hold the resistance band and push it away, using one hand. With the other hand, pull the resistance band toward the chest (see figures 5.292*a-b*). Step forward diagonally, keeping the knee in line with the toe of the forward foot (see figures 5.292*c-d*). Bring the right leg forward, flexing at the knee to raise the leg up (see figures 5.292*e-g*). Put the foot back on the mat and simulate the throw. Flexing the front knee, continually put pressure on the resistance band and push it away (see figures 5.292*h-i*).

Figure 5.292 – Exercise variation to prepare for takedowns.

Exercise for Trip Takedowns From the Outside Leg

Attach the resistance band around the ankle and place the hands in combat position (see figure 5.293a). Step to the side and simulate a side trip takedown (see figures 5.293b-c).

Figure 5.293 – Exercise for trip takedowns from the outside leg.

Exercise for Trip Takedowns From the Inside Leg

Place the resistance band around the ankle and increase the tension slightly (see figure 5.294a). Perform the exercise by flexing the knee and pulling the resistance band back with the thigh (see figure 5.294b). Move the thigh back and perform a circular movement with the hip, moving from the inside out (as if tripping from the inside) (see figure 5.294c). Keep the leg flexed at the knee and increase the tension in the resistance band.

Figure 5.294 – Exercise for trip takedowns from the inside leg.

These exercises can be used by either young or experienced athletes for general or specific sport preparation. The exercises we recommend in the training program serve as a baseline. Normally an athlete will need to work on only a couple techniques at a time until mastery is achieved before progressing on to the next techniques. Once the athlete is proficient in all the techniques shown, they can select as many as they need during their training program.

The program is individualized in every case and exercise selection depends on the training level. The trainer or coach selects the number of exercises, reps, training days, and pace. The resistance band tension will need to increase from light to heavy according to each athlete's ability and training objective. Table 5.40 presents an example of a resistance band training program (technical exercises) to develop the power of takedowns using two exercises previously described. Coaches and trainers should change or incorporate the rest of the exercises in the program every four to six weeks.

Table 5.40 – Training Program With Resistance Bands for Power Takedowns

	Week 1	Week 2	Week 3	Week 4
Exercise for throwing the opponent from the back (with resistance bands)	3 × 30 times × 3 days; focus on performing the skills with proper form	5 × 30 times × 3 days; focus on performing the skills with proper form	3-5 × 30 sec × 3 days; focus on high-speed throwing skills	5 × 10 sec × 3 days; focus on performing the skills at maximum speed
Exercise for takedowns with two hands on the opponent (with resistance bands)	3 × 30 times × 3 days; focus on performing the skills with proper form	5 × 30 times × 3 days; focus on performing the skills with proper form	3-5 × 30 sec × 3 days; focus on high-speed throwing skills	5 × 10 sec × 3 days; focus on performing the skills at maximum speed

Training With Resistance Bands for Strength and Muscular Endurance

Resistance bands improve movement efficiency, resulting in a lowered risk of noncontact injury during training and competition. The resistance varies throughout the range of motion along the same natural lines as nonresisted training, enforcing correct joint action along the line of motion. This is important when quickly throwing the limbs in striking actions. Bands have proven to increase strength and muscular endurance at a low cost and could be used as an alternative training method so athletes and coaches don't need to rely only on machines or free weights.

In this section, we will demonstrate how to work with the Fitsambo jacket, a kimono top with loops used to facilitate functional training. The jacket is a dense sambo kimono jacket with cutouts for the belt and loops sewn into the jacket. The loops are where the opponent grips the jacket. The bands are attached to the loops of the jacket by a carabiner.

Standing Row With Two Hands

Stand with the feet shoulder-width apart, grip the resistance band, and pull until there is slight tension (see figure 5.295a). Flex the arms and pull the shoulders back, drawing the shoulder blades together (see figure 5.295b).

a   b

Figure 5.295 – Standing row with resistance band.

Chest Press

Hold the resistance band in two hands and place the feet in a stable split stance, making sure there is tension in the resistance band (see figures 5.296a-b). Extend the arms at chest height (see figures 5.296c-d).

a   b

c   d

Figure 5.296 – Chest press with resistance band.

Standing One-Arm Row

Stand in a shallow split squat position, emphasizing knee placement of the leg opposite the working arm. Grip the resistance band with one hand and place the free hand on the knee of the standing leg for support (see figure 5.297a). Make sure there is always tension in the band. Pull the resistance band toward the body, moving the shoulder blade toward the midline (see figure 5.297b).

Figure 5.297 – Standing one-arm row with resistance band.

Front Raise

Grip the resistance band with the shoulders slightly retracted (see figure 5.298a). The band should have some tension. Pull the band forward and slightly upward (see figure 5.298b). There should be no, or very minimal, movement in the elbow joint during this exercise.

Figure 5.298 – Front raise with resistance band.

Straight-Arm Pull

Face the band's anchor, with the arms extended near the sides, and grip the resistance band (see figure 5.299a). With straight arms, pull the resistance band back and the shoulder blades toward the midline (see figure 5.299b).

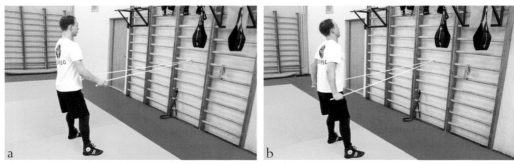

Figure 5.299 – Straight-arm pull with resistance band.

Alternating Arm Swings

With the back to the band's anchor, grip the resistance bands at the sides (see figure 5.300*a*). Perform locomotion with the arms, alternating swinging them from the shoulder joint and extending and flexing the elbows (see figures 5.300*b-e*).

Figure 5.300 – Alternating arm swings with resistance band.

Lying Back Extension

This exercise strengthens the muscles of the back, arms, and glutes. Lying on the stomach, extend the arms and legs away from the trunk. Keep the arms shoulder-width apart and the feet hip-width apart. Pull the band, maintaining constant tension (see figure 5.301*a*). Perform extension in the lower back, raising the legs and arms off the mat (see figure 5.301*b*). Stretch the resistance even further, creating more resistance. At the same time, spread the legs so the feet are at the same width as the hands and hold this position (see figure 5.301*c*).

Figure 5.301 – Lying back extension with resistance band.

Exercises using the Fitsambo jacket can be dynamic, static, or static and dynamic, depending on how the exercises are performed. We explain a few examples of resistance training exercises using the Fitsambo jacket.

Exercise 1

Starting with feet shoulder-width apart, facing where the band is anchored, select a distance to create slight tension in the band (see figure 5.302a). Inhale, and on the exhalation, bring the shoulder blades together toward the spine while flexing the elbows until the band stretches in line with the body (see figure 5.302b). Inhale again and return to the original starting position.

Figure 5.302 – Exercise 1 demonstration using the Fitsambo jacket.

Exercise 2

With the feet shoulder-width apart and the back toward the band's anchor, which is attached to the jacket sleeves, select a distance that creates some tension in the band (see figure 5.303a). Inhale, and on the exhalation, extend the elbow joints until the hands are in front (see figure 5.303b). The height of the extension (upward, downward, or straight out from the chest) depends on the muscle group being focused on.

Figure 5.303 – Exercise 2 demonstration using the Fitsambo jacket.

Exercise 3

Begin as if in the low point of a squat, legs shoulder-width apart, flexed at the knees, and arms outstretched (see figure 5.304a). The band is attached to the loops on the sleeves. Face the anchor. Start at a distance that creates some tension in the band and keep the back straight. Inhale, and then on the exhale, bring the shoulder blades toward each other while flexing the elbows (see figure 5.304b). The band will stretch to where it is fixed on the jacket along the pull line of the elbow. Inhale and return the band to its initial position.

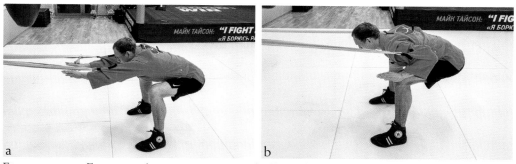

Figure 5.304 – Exercise 3 demonstration using the Fitsambo jacket.

Exercise 4

Face the band's anchor with the feet shoulder-width apart (see figure 5.305a). The band is attached to the loops in the jacket's chest area. Select a distance to create slight tension in the band. Inhale, and then on exhalation, rotate the body to the right, upward, and diagonally. Lean back in the direction of the rotation (see figures 5.305b-c). While inhaling, return to the original starting position. The exercise is performed in both directions.

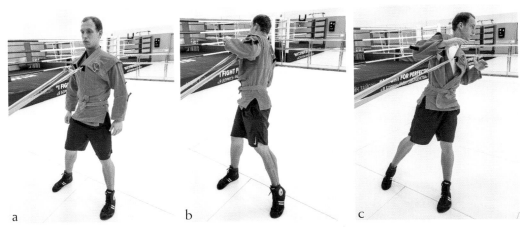

Figure 5.305 – Exercise 4 demonstration using the Fitsambo jacket.

Exercise 5

Assume a position as in the low part of a squat, with the knees flexed and legs shoulder-width apart (see figure 5.306a). The band is attached to the loops on the jacket lapel around the neck. Face the band's anchor. Select a distance to create slight tension in the band. Extend the back and knees to pull the band into higher tension (see figure 5.306b). Return to the starting position and repeat.

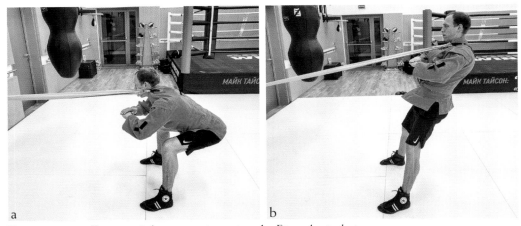

Figure 5.306 – Exercise 5 demonstration using the Fitsambo jacket.

Exercise 6

Start with the feet shoulder-width apart, with the back to where the band is anchored (see figure 5.307a). The band is attached to the loops on the back of the jacket in the area of the shoulder blades and the center of the back. Start at a distance that creates slight tension in the band. Swing the arms back at the same time as performing a squat (see figure 5.307b). Throw the arms forward and long jump (see figure 5.307c). Return to the starting position and repeat.

Figure 5.307 – Exercise 6 demonstration using the Fitsambo jacket.

Exercise 7

Stand with the feet shoulder-width apart and with the back to the band's anchor (see figure 5.308a). The band is attached to the loops on the back of the jacket in the area of the shoulder blades and the center of the back. Select a distance to create slight tension in the band. Perform a forward lunge with the right foot (see figure 5.308b). Return to the starting position and repeat with the left foot.

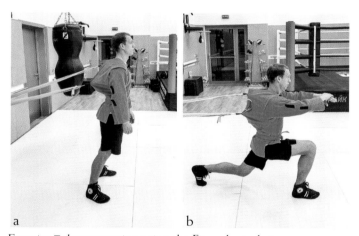

Figure 5.308 – Exercise 7 demonstration using the Fitsambo jacket.

The principal benefit of training in the Fitsambo jacket is creating a constraining tension that simulates a feeling of being gripped by an opponent. Some examples of wrestling- and grappling-specific exercises using the Fitsambo jacket follow.

Exercise 8

Start with the feet shoulder-width apart and face the band's anchor (see figure 5.309a). The band is attached to the loops on the jacket lapel at the chest and the sleeve area. Select a distance that creates slight tension in the band. Hold the band and perform a crossover turn. Continue the movement to imitate a throw over the back (see figures 5.309b-d). Return to the starting position and repeat on the opposite side of the body.

Figure 5.309 – Exercise 8 demonstration using the Fitsambo jacket.

Exercise 9

Start standing with the feet shoulder-width apart, facing the band anchors attached to the loops on the jacket lapel at the chest area (see figure 5.310a). Select a distance that creates slight band tension. Holding the band in each hand, use the left hand to perform a circular motion inward underneath and around the band. Hold the elbow against the band, making sure there is tension (see figures 5.310b-c). Lunge with the left leg to the side and carry out an unwinding motion (see figure 5.310d).

Figure 5.310 – Exercise 9 demonstration using the Fitsambo jacket.

Punching and kicking techniques can also be trained in the Fitsambo jacket, which can benefit an MMA or combat sambo athlete because of the combination of strikes, grappling, and throws. Some examples of exercises that target striking techniques follow.

Exercise 10

Direct strike with the left hand (jab) (see figure 5.311).

Figure 5.311 – Exercise 10 demonstration by Coach Pavel Pashkin of direct strike with the left hand (jab) using the Fitsambo jacket.

Exercise 11

Direct strike with the right hand (cross) (see figure 5.312).

Figure 5.312 – Exercise 11 demonstration of direct strike with the right hand (cross) using the Fitsambo jacket.

Exercise 12

Strikes from below with the right and left hand (uppercut) (see figure 5.313).

Figure 5.313 – Exercise 12 demonstration of strikes from below with the right and left hand (uppercut) using the Fitsambo jacket.

Exercise 13

Side strike with the right and left hand (hook) (see figure 5.314).

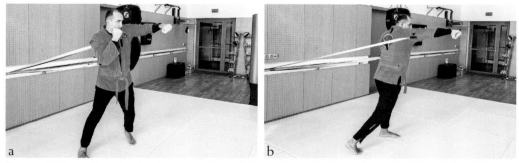

Figure 5.314 – Exercise 13 demonstration of side strike with the right and left hand (hook) using the Fitsambo jacket.

Exercise 14
Elbow strikes with the right and left arm (see figure 5.315).

Figure 5.315 – Exercise 14 demonstration of elbow strikes using the Fitsambo jacket.

Table 5.41 presents four programs for developing strength and muscular endurance with resistance bands.

Table 5.41 – Training Programs With Resistance Bands and Fitsambo Jacket for Strength and Muscular Endurance

	Week 1	Week 2	Week 3	Week 4
Training A				
1. Standing row with resistance band	3 × 8	3 × 10	3 × 12	4 × 12*
2. Chest press with resistance band	3 × 8	3 × 10	3 × 12	4 × 12*
3. Lying back extension with resistance band	15 sec hold, 30 sec rest × 3 sets	20 sec hold, 30 sec rest × 3 sets	30 sec hold, 30 sec rest × 3 sets	30 sec hold, 30 sec rest × 4 sets
4. Front raise with resistance band	3 × 8	3 × 10	3 × 12	4 × 12*
Training B				
1. Standing one-arm row with resistance band	3 × 8	3 × 10	3 × 12	4 × 12*
2. Front raise with resistance band	3 × 8	3 × 10	3 × 12	4 × 12*
3. Alternating arm swings with resistance band	3 × 8	3 × 10	3 × 12	4 × 12*
4. Straight-arm pull with resistance band	3 × 8	3 × 10	3 × 12	4 × 12*
Training C				
Exercise 1 with Fitsambo jacket	2 × 15	2 × 15	3 × 15	4 × 15*
Exercise 2 with Fitsambo jacket	2 × 15	2 × 15	3 × 15	4 × 15*
Exercise 3 with Fitsambo jacket	2 × 15	2 × 15	3 × 15	4 × 15*

	Week 1	**Week 2**	**Week 3**	**Week 4**
Training C				
Exercise 4 with Fitsambo jacket	2 × 10 per side	2 × 10 per side	3 × 10 per side	3 × 10 per side*
Exercise 5 with Fitsambo jacket	2 × 15	2 × 15	3 × 15	3 × 15*
Exercise 6 with Fitsambo jacket	2 × 8	2 × 8	3 × 6 explosive	3 × 6 explosive*
Exercise 7 with Fitsambo jacket	2 × 10 per side	2 × 10 per side	3 × 10 per side	3 × 10 per side*
Training D				
Exercise 10 with Fitsambo jacket	2 × 10 per side	2 × 10 per side	3 × 10 per side	3 × 10 per side Max speed
Exercise 11 with Fitsambo jacket	2 × 10 per side	2 × 10 per side	3 × 10 per side	3 × 10 per side Max speed
Exercise 12 with Fitsambo jacket	2 × 10 per side	2 × 10 per side	3 × 10 per side	3 × 10 per side Max speed
Exercise 13 with Fitsambo jacket	2 × 10 per side	2 × 10 per side	3 × 10 per side	3 × 10 per side Max speed
Exercise 14 with Fitsambo jacket	2 × 10 per side	2 × 10 per side	3 × 10 per side	3 × 10 per side Max speed

*May also need to increase the band's resistance.

Training With Resistance Bands for Flexibility and Joint Mobility

Flexibility is important so that the full range of motion of each joint can be performed without inhibiting correct form. Without full range of motion, the athlete will not be able to fully contract or extend the muscle. Actions such as punches and kicks could be limited. Being "stacked," in the case of grappling, for example, could end the match if the athlete does not have the flexibility to tolerate the position even though it is not a submission.

Shoulder Mobility and Chest and Arm Stretches

Start by holding the band in front of the body and move it above the head. Grasp both ends and pull until some tension is created (see figures 5.316a-b). Bring the arms down to shoulder level (see figure 5.316c), then pull the band behind the head and down (see figures 5.316d-e). Hold this final position a few seconds to stretch the pectoralis and anterior deltoid and then return to the starting position. Keep the head in line with the shoulders and not forward or down as the band is pulled behind the head. Adjust the grip according to flexibility level.

Figure 5.316 – Shoulder mobility and chest and arm stretches with resistance band.

Side Stretches

Side stretches work the calves, glutes, hamstrings, oblique muscles of the abdomen, latissimus dorsi, and popliteal ligaments. There are three variations:

1. *Variation 1*: Begin by sitting on the mat in a half-straddle position. Place the resistance band around one foot and pull the band with the hand on the same side as the outstretched leg, flexing the foot (see figure 5.317*a*).

2. *Variation 2*: Begin this variation the same way as in variation 1, but continue flexing the upper body toward the outstretched leg. Reach over the head and toward the band with the opposite arm (see figure 5.317*b*).

3. *Variation 3*: Begin by sitting on the mat in a half-straddle position. Place the resistance band around one foot. Reach over the head and grip the resistance band with the hand opposite the outstretched leg. Reach the arm on the same side as the outstretched leg forward for stability (see figure 5.317*c*).

Figure 5.317 – Side stretches with resistance band.

Rocking Stretch

The rocking stretch unloads back and spine muscles, develops abdominal muscle stabilizers, and enhances balance. Begin in a "boat pose," placing the band under the feet and holding it securely (see figure 5.318a). Round the back and roll backward until the hips come off the mat (see figure 5.318b). Immediately return to the starting position and maintain balance momentarily before repeating the movement (see figure 5.318c).

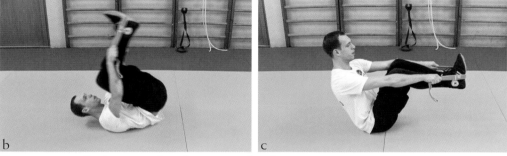

Figure 5.318 – Rocking stretch with resistance band.

Standing Back Stretch

In a wide stance with the knees slightly flexed, hold the resistance band and move away from the band's anchor. Keeping the back straight, extend the arms forward and allow the resistance band to pull while resisting in order to stretch the back muscles (see figure 5.319).

Figure 5.319 – Back stretch with resistance band.

Triceps and Shoulder Stretch

Position the body so the side is to the resistance band's anchor. With the hand on the opposite side of the body, reach across to grasp the band. Move away from the band's anchor until the triceps and posterior deltoid (see figure 5.320) stretch. Increase the stretch by increasing the tension in the band or by using a band with a heavier resistance weight.

Figure 5.320 – Triceps and shoulder stretch with resistance band.

Biceps Stretch

Turn so the side is to the resistance band's anchor. With the hand on the same side as the anchor, reach to grasp the band. Move away from the band's anchor until the biceps (see figure 5.321) stretch. Increase the stretch by increasing the tension in the band or by using a band with a heavier resistance weight.

Figure 5.321 – Biceps stretch with resistance band.

Abdominal and Chest Stretch

Kneel, sitting on the heels. With the back to the band's anchor, grasp the resistance band with extended arms above the head (see figure 5.322a). Move the body until the hips are extended (see figure 5.322b).

Figure 5.322 – Abdominal and chest stretch with resistance band.

Seated Hamstring Stretch

Sitting on the ground, feet toward the anchor, tuck the chin and begin to roll back, letting the resistance band stretch forward while the spine is lengthened. Try to keep the legs straight throughout the entire exercise. Figures 5.323*a-b* show an easier version with the band anchored high. Figures 5.323*c-d* show a more difficult version with the resistance band anchored low.

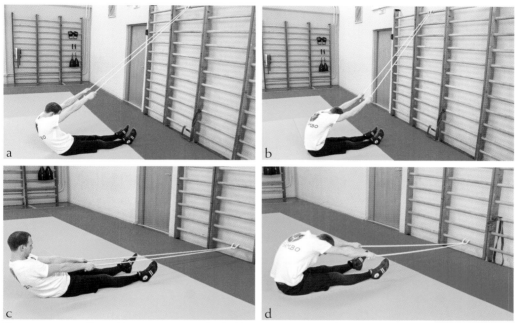

Figure 5.323 – Seated hamstring stretch: (*a-b*) easier version with band anchored high; (*c-d*) harder version with band anchored low.

We have shown examples of exercises and stretches that can be done with resistance bands. Some of these can be done as part of a dynamic stretch as part of the warm-up before training or at the end of the training session as a passive static stretch. For more details on stretching, refer to chapter 6. Table 5.42 includes two training programs for developing flexibility and joint mobility.

Table 5.42 – Training Programs With Resistance Bands for Flexibility and Joint Mobility

	Week 1	Week 2	Week 3	Week 4
Training A				
1. Shoulder mobility and chest and arm stretches with resistance band	2 × 15 sec	2 × 20 sec	3 × 20 sec	3 × 30 sec
2. Side stretch with resistance band	2 × 15 sec each side	2 × 20 sec each side	3 × 20 sec each side	3 × 30 sec each side
3. Triceps and shoulder stretch with resistance band	2 × 15 sec each side	2 × 20 sec each side	3 × 20 sec each side	3 × 30 sec each side
4. Biceps stretch with resistance band	2 × 15 sec each side	2 × 20 sec each side	3 × 20 sec each side	3 × 30 sec each side
5. Standing back stretch with resistance band	2 × 15 sec	2 × 20 sec	3 × 20 sec	3 × 30 sec

(continued)

Table 5.42 – Training Programs With Resistance Bans for Flexibility and Joint Mobility (*continued*)

	Week 1	Week 2	Week 3	Week 4
Training B				
1. Rocking stretch with resistance band	2 × 15 sec	2 × 20 sec	3 × 20 sec	3 × 30 sec
2. Abdominal and chest stretch with resistance band	2 × 15 sec	2 × 20 sec	3 × 20 sec	3 × 30 sec
3. Standing back stretch with resistance band	2 × 15 sec	2 × 20 sec	3 × 20 sec	3 × 30 sec
4. Shoulder mobility and chest and arm stretches with resistance band	2 × 15 sec	2 × 20 sec	3 × 20 sec	3 × 30 sec
5. Seated hamstring stretch with resistance band	2 × 15 sec	2 × 20 sec	3 × 20 sec	3 × 30 sec

Training Using the Isoton Method

This section was designed with ProSportLab, one of the largest and most distinguished labs tasked with training Olympic and other national athletes, including world champion wrestlers and judo, sambo, combat sambo, MMA, and other combat sport athletes. The founder and scientific director of the laboratory was Professor Victor Nikolaevich Seluyanov (1946–2017).

Isoton, first introduced by Russian scientist Victor Nikolaevich Seluyanov, is static-dynamic in nature (that is, exercises are performed under constant muscular tension through the most difficult range of motion of the exercise, never allowing total relaxation of the working muscle). Isoton exercises force type I muscle fibers to work anaerobically. Due to the range of motion being very limited and the constant tension in the muscle, blood flow is obstructed, and a hypoxic state is induced while the muscle is under tension (Seluianov, 2001; Dias, et al. 2017). For more detailed information on how Isoton training effects the systems of the body, refer to chapter 2.

The exercise intensity should guarantee slow-twitch fiber recruitment only, usually between 30 percent to 60 percent of 1RM. The exercise duration should not exceed 60 seconds; otherwise, the accumulation of hydrogen ions (H^+) may become excessive and lead to muscle damage (Dias, et al. 2017).

Practice of partial range of motion exercises is increasing as the benefits continue to be proven. The short range of motion and low intensity make Isoton suitable for rehabilitative environments as well as for individuals who want more localized, specific muscular hypertrophy (Newmire and Willoughby, 2018).

Practice the exercises in successive series (superset). After finishing the superset, an extended rest of 5 to 10 minutes is needed, or the athlete may perform an exercise that concentrates on another muscle group or engage in active rest, such as walking or jogging (Dias, et al. 2017).

To realize the maximum benefits of this method, the following conditions must be observed:

- All exercises should use a partial range of motion under constant muscular tension, through the most difficult range of motion (greatest effort) of the exercise, never allowing the working muscles to totally relax.

- The exercises need to be conducted in a superset: 30 seconds of work followed by 30 seconds of rest, repeated in the same muscle three to six times.
- Intensity of the load must be 30 percent to 60 percent 1RM.
- The exercise should last between 30 and 45 seconds, until there is necessary stress (caused by exercise) for hormone stimulation, often felt as a burning sensation in the muscle.
- The interval between each superset is also between 30 to 60 seconds.
- The interval of active recovery between each superset is 5 to 10 minutes.
- Rest must be active. It is possible to use another muscle group (distant from the muscle worked) as an interval between the supersets.
- The number of sets per muscle group ranges from 4 to 10 for muscular development and 1 to 3 for muscular toning.
- The number of daily workouts can be one, two, or more.
- Per week, the exercise is repeated within two to five days for the same muscle group.
- If performed to maximum volume of supersets, only do one time per week per muscle group.

Standing Dumbbell Press

This exercise is similar to the seated dumbbell press that was described in figure 5.64. Here, we use it while standing, using a partial range of motion under constant muscular tension, through the most difficult range of motion (greatest effort) of the exercise, never allowing total relaxation of the working muscles (see figure 5.324). It targets all three heads of the triceps brachii, along with the middle, anterior, and posterior deltoid and, to a lesser degree, the trapezius and serratus anterior.

Figure 5.324 – Standing dumbbell press.

Dumbbell Split Squat

From a standing position, take a long step forward as if performing a lunge (see figure 5.325a). The heel of the back foot should be raised. Keeping the torso straight, lower slowly until the back knee almost touches the floor (see figure 5.325b), then push back up using partial range of motion under constant muscular tension through the most difficult range of motion (greatest effort) of the exercise. Complete all repetitions on one leg, then switch to the other. Keep the knees in line with the toes, especially on the front leg. This is a great exercise for strengthening the gluteus maximus and entire quadriceps muscle (rectus femoris and the vastus lateralis, medialis, and intermedius). This exercise can be performed with a narrower stance, which will target the quadriceps more intensely, or with a wider stance to focus on working the gluteus maximus.

Figure 5.325 – Dumbbell split squat.

Dumbbell Bench Press

This exercise was described in figure 5.47. Here, it uses a partial range of motion and never allows the working muscles to relax. This exercise works the pectoralis major, anterior deltoid, triceps brachii, and anconeus, which is important for stabilizing the elbow. The main exercise variations are pressing with a forearm rotation so that the palms face each other or without any rotation as shown here (see figure 5.326) (Delavier, 2010).

Figure 5.326 – Dumbbell bench press.

Standing Dumbbell Curl

This exercise was described in figure 5.75. Here, it uses a partial range of motion under constant muscular tension (see figure 5.327). This exercise works the biceps brachii, brachialis, and brachioradialis (another important elbow stabilizer).

Figure 5.327 – Standing dumbbell curl.

Triceps Pushdown With Rope

This exercise was described in figure 5.85. Here, it uses a partial range of motion under constant muscular tension. This is an excellent exercise for working all three heads of the triceps and anconeus (important for elbow flexion, extension, and stabilization) in a very isolated manner. Using the rope concentrates more of the work into the lateral head of the triceps than when using the straight bar (see figure 5.328). To focus the exercise on the medial head, an underhand grip can be used (Delavier, 2010).

Figure 5.328 – Triceps pushdown with rope.

Cable Crunch

Also called a high-pulley crunch, this exercise works the rectus abdominis, external oblique, and pyramidalis (abdominal muscle superior to the pubis). This exercise adapts very well to the Isoton method because the exercise does not need to be performed with heavy weights and the focus is on abdominal contraction. Perform this exercise slowly, lowering the sternum toward the knees and rolling gently through the spine under constant muscular tension (see figure 5.329).

Figure 5.329 – Cable crunch.

Straight-Arm Lat Pulldown

Grab the bar with an overhand grip slightly wider than the shoulders and take a couple steps away from the cable machine to move the weight off the cable stack (see figure 5.330a). Stand tall with a neutral head and neck position and the shoulders slightly ahead of the hips. The arms should be long in front of the body. The chin should remain tucked throughout the movement. While maintaining long arms, initiate the downward movement by squeezing the lats and pulling the bar toward the hips (see figure 5.330b). Allow the shoulder blades to move naturally. Squeeze the lats at the bottom position. While maintaining alignment, allow the arms to slowly return to the starting position using a partial range of motion under constant muscular tension and repeat. This exercise concentrates on the latissimus dorsi as well as the teres major and the long head of the triceps brachii (Delavier, 2010).

Figure 5.330 – Straight-arm lat pulldown.

Dumbbell Front Raise

This exercise was previously described in figure 5.28 using alternating arms. Here, it uses both arms simultaneously and a partial range of motion under constant muscular tension. This exercise works the anterior deltoid and the clavicular head of the pectoralis major to a much lesser extent. Shown in figure 5.331 with dumbbells, this exercise is easily adapted to a cable or barbell.

Figure 5.331 – Dumbbell front raise.

Chest-Supported Dumbbell Rear Delt Fly

This exercise was previously described in figure 5.68 using the pulley. If the traditional dumbbell rear delt fly causes strain on the lower back, try using an incline bench. Instead of relying on the core to stabilize the body, rest the weight on the bench, which will help to better isolate the rear (posterior) deltoid. Keep a partial range of motion, never allowing the working muscles to totally relax. This exercise targets the posterior deltoid but also works the middle and anterior deltoid along with the infraspinatus and teres minor, which are important shoulder stabilizers. The trapezius, rhomboids, and upper portion of the latissimus dorsi are also engaged during this exercise (Delavier, 2010). It can be done either against a bench as pictured in figure 5.332, with the feet on the floor, or to increase the difficulty and recruit more core stabilizers, place the knees on the seat of the bench. This exercise can also be performed bent over, standing in hip flexion, with the torso facing the ground, with a straight back, and with flexed knees.

Figure 5.332 – Chest-supported dumbbell rear delt fly.

Table 5.43 presents two sample training programs of Isoton exercises.

Table 5.43 – Isoton Method Training Programs

	Week 1	Week 2	Week 3	Week 4
Training A (to be done as a superset)				
1. Dumbbell bench press	3 × 30 sec of work with a 30 sec rest @ 35% 1RM	4 × 30 sec of work with a 30 sec rest @ 35% 1RM	5 × 30 sec of work with a 30 sec rest @ 40% 1RM	6 × 30 sec of work with a 30 sec rest @ 40% 1RM
2. Standing dumbbell curl	3 × 30 sec of work with a 30 sec rest @ 30% 1RM	4 × 30 sec of work with a 30 sec rest @ 30% 1RM	5 × 30 sec of work with a 30 sec rest @ 35% 1RM	6 × 30 sec of work with a 30 sec rest @ 35% 1RM
3. Dumbbell split squat	3 × 30 sec of work with a 30 sec rest @ 30% 1RM per side	4 × 30 sec of work with a 30 sec rest @ 30% 1RM per side	5 × 30 sec of work with a 30 sec rest @ 35% 1RM per side	6 × 30 sec of work with a 30 sec rest @ 35% 1RM per side
4. Straight-arm lat pulldown	3 × 30 sec of work with a 30 sec rest @ 35% 1RM	4 × 30 sec of work with a 30 sec rest @ 35% 1RM	5 × 30 sec of work with a 30 sec rest @ 40% 1RM	6 × 30 sec of work with a 30 sec rest @ 40% 1RM
5. Cable crunch (until failure)	3 × 30 sec of work with a 30 sec rest	4 × 30 sec of work with a 30 sec rest	5 × 30 sec of work with a 30 sec rest	6 × 30 sec of work with a 30 sec rest

(continued)

Table 5.43 – Isoton Method Training Programs *(continued)*

	Week 1	Week 2	Week 3	Week 4
Training B (to be done as a superset)				
1. Standing dumbbell press	3 × 30 sec of work with a 30 sec rest @ 35% 1RM	4 × 30 sec of work with a 30 sec rest @ 35% 1RM	5 × 30 sec of work with a 30 sec rest @ 40% 1RM	6 × 30 sec of work with a 30 sec rest @ 40% 1RM
2. Dumbbell split squat	3 × 30 sec of work with a 30 sec rest @ 30% 1RM per side	4 × 30 sec of work with a 30 sec rest @ 30% 1RM per side	5 × 30 sec of work with a 30 sec rest @ 35% 1RM per side	6 × 30 sec of work with a 30 sec rest @ 35% 1RM per side
3. Dumbbell front raise	3 × 30 sec of work with a 30 sec rest @ 30% 1RM	4 × 30 sec of work with a 30 sec rest @ 30% 1RM	5 × 30 sec of work with a 30 sec rest @ 35% 1RM	6 × 30 sec of work with a 30 sec rest @ 35% 1RM
4. Chest-supported dumbbell rear delt fly (until failure)	3 × 30 sec of work with a 30 sec rest	4 × 30 sec of work with a 30 sec rest	5 × 30 sec of work with a 30 sec rest	6 × 30 sec of work with a 30 sec rest
5. Triceps pushdown with rope	3 × 30 sec of work with a 30 sec rest @ 30% 1RM	4 × 30 sec of work with a 30 sec rest @ 30% 1RM	5 × 30 sec of work with a 30 sec rest @ 35% 1RM	6 × 30 sec of work with a 30 sec rest @ 35% 1RM
6. Cable crunch (until failure)	3 × 30 sec of work with a 30 sec rest	4 × 30 sec of work with a 30 sec rest	5 × 30 sec of work with a 30 sec rest	6 × 30 sec of work with a 30 sec rest

Training to Increase Muscular Endurance and Number of Mitochondria in Type II Muscle Fibers

The following are examples of exercises used in interval training to increase the number of mitochondria in fast-twitch muscle fibers and glycolytic muscle fibers. This will increase power output at the anaerobic threshold for the muscles involved in these exercises, increase the duration the athlete is able to work at a higher anaerobic threshold, and increase local muscular endurance. Details on how to use these exercises in a training program and what is meant by the "type of training" (i.e., interval training type I, the 10 × 10 method) is explained starting on page 343.

Power Clean (see figure 5.333):

- *Type of training*: interval training type I
- *Type of exercise*: multijoint
- *Joints involved*: ankle, knee, hip, elbow, shoulder
- *Main muscle groups affected*: gluteal muscles, quadriceps, hamstrings, anterior tibialis, soleus, gastrocnemius, back muscles, deltoids, and arm muscles

Figure 5.333 – Grigor Chilingaryan demonstrating the power clean.

Barbell Deadlift (see figure 5.334):

- *Type of training*: interval training type I
- *Type of exercise*: multijoint
- *Joints involved*: ankle, knee, hip
- *Main muscle groups affected*: gluteal muscles and muscles of the thigh, back, and forearm

Figure 5.334 – Barbell deadlift.

Low Box Jump (see figure 5.335):

- *Type of training*: interval training type I and the 10 × 10 method
- *Type of exercise*: multijoint
- *Joints involved*: ankle, knee, hip
- *Main muscle groups affected*: gluteal muscles, quadriceps, hamstrings, and muscles of the lower leg

Figure 5.335 – Low box jump (20 inches [50 cm]).

Chest-Supported Barbell Bench Pull (see figure 5.336):

- *Type of training*: interval training type I and the 10 × 10 method
- *Type of exercise*: multijoint
- *Working joints*: ulnar, shoulder
- *Main muscle groups affected*: latissimus dorsi, posterior deltoid, infraspinatus, teres major and teres minor, rhomboids, erector spinae, trapezius, biceps, and forearm muscles

Figure 5.336 – Vitaly Rybakov demonstrating the chest-supported barbell bench pull.

Barbell Bench Press (see figure 5.337):

- *Type of training*: interval training type I and the 10 × 10 method
- *Type of exercise*: multijoint
- *Working joints*: elbow, shoulder
- *Main muscle groups affected*: pectoral major and minor muscles, anterior deltoid, and triceps

Figure 5.337 – Barbell bench press (with a small pause when the bar touches the chest).

Tire Push With Partner (see figure 5.338):

- *Type of training*: 10 × 10 method
- *Type of exercise*: multijoint
- *Working joints*: elbow, shoulder
- *Main muscle groups affected*: pectoral major and minor muscles, deltoids, biceps, triceps, and forearm muscles

Figure 5.338 – Tire push with partner.

Striking Tire With Sledgehammer (see figure 5.339):

- *Type of training*: interval training type I and the 10 × 10 method
- *Type of exercise*: multijoint
- *Working joints*: elbow, shoulder
- *Main muscle groups affected*: pectoral muscles, deltoids, arm muscles, back muscles, and core muscles

Figure 5.339 – Striking tire with sledgehammer.

Body Weight Row (see figure 5.340):

- *Type of training*: interval training type I and the 10 × 10 method
- *Type of exercise*: multijoint
- *Working joints*: elbow, shoulder
- *Main muscle groups affected*: latissimus dorsi, posterior deltoid, infraspinatus, subscapularis, brachialis, long head of the triceps, teres major and minor, and rhomboids

Figure 5.340 – Body weight row.

Pull-Up (see figure 5.341):

- *Type of training*: interval training type I and the 10 × 10 method
- *Type of exercise*: multijoint
- *Working joints*: elbow, shoulder
- *Main muscle groups affected*: latissimus dorsi, posterior deltoid, infraspinatus, subscapularis, brachialis, long head of the triceps, rhomboids, and teres major

Figure 5.341 – Pull-up.

Bent-Over Row With Resistance Bands or Cables (see figure 5.342):

- *Type of training*: interval training type I and the 10 × 10 method
- *Type of exercise*: multijoint
- *Working joints*: elbow, shoulder
- *Main muscle groups affected*: latissimus dorsi, posterior deltoid, infraspinatus, rhomboids, trapezius, and biceps

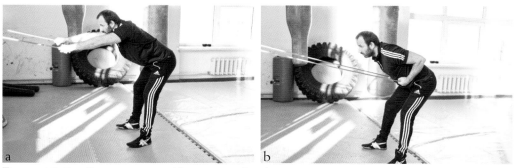

Figure 5.342 – Bent-over row with resistance bands.

Chest Press in Split Stance With Resistance Bands or Cables (see figure 5.343):

- *Type of training*: interval training type I and the 10 × 10 method
- *Type of exercise*: multijoint
- *Working joints*: elbow, shoulder
- *Main muscle groups affected*: pectoral major and minor muscles, deltoids, and triceps

Figure 5.343 – Chest press in split stance with resistance bands.

Plyo Push-Up (see figure 5.344):

- *Type of training*: interval training type I and the 10 × 10 method
- *Type of exercise*: multijoint
- *Working joints*: elbows, shoulder
- *Main muscle groups affected*: pectoral muscles, deltoids, triceps, serratus anterior, and anconeus

Figure 5.344 – Plyo push-up (with a small pause when the chest touches the floor).

Rope Climb (see figure 5.345):

- *Type of training*: interval training type I and the 10 × 10 method
- *Type of exercise*: multijoint
- *Working joints*: elbows, shoulder
- *Main muscle groups affected*: latissimus dorsi, posterior deltoid, infraspinatus, subscapularis, brachialis, long head of the triceps, and biceps

Figure 5.345 – Rope climb.

Sprawl and Simulated Takedowns (see figure 5.346):

- *Type of training*: interval training type I and the 10 × 10 method
- *Type of exercise*: multijoint
- *Joints involved*: ankle, knee, hip
- *Main muscle groups affected*: gluteus maximus, gluteus medius, quadriceps, hamstrings, latissimus dorsi, rhomboids, and abdominal muscles

Figure 5.346 – Sprawl and simulated takedowns.

Interval Training Type I

This type of training increases the power of fast-twitch and glycolytic muscle fibers, increases the number of mitochondria in fast-twitch and glycolytic muscle fibers, increases the aerobic capacity of muscles, and increases power at the anaerobic threshold. It also increases resistance to fatigue by increasing the anaerobic threshold. For this method, it is important to rest one or two seconds between every repetition in a set until local fatigue. This method could be used with technical and MMA-specific exercises such as hitting the heavy bag, pad work, or traditional strength and conditioning exercises such as those described previously.

Training Method Parameters

- *Intensity of muscle contraction:* 60 percent to 80 percent of 1RM
- *Form of exercise:* Perform one repetition, wait for one to two seconds (pause), and repeat until the end of the set
- *Duration of work (time):* 30 seconds to 120 seconds; until local fatigue
- *Rest interval between sets:* 2 to 5 minutes (depending on the time spent under tension)
- *Number of sets:* tonus (maintaining) 5 to 10; developing (to increase capacity) 10 to 20
- This training method can be repeated 1 to 3 times a week

Interval Training 10 × 10 Method

This type of training increases the number of mitochondria in fast-twitch and glycolytic muscle fibers and increases the aerobic capacity of muscles and muscular endurance. The main difference between this method and the type I method is the lighter loads used in the 10 × 10, the faster tempo, and switching the exercises after the first signs of local muscular fatigue. This method is normally used with agonist-antagonist exercises or in a circuit format. For example, the athlete performs one set of 10 push-ups with a little pause between every repetition, rests for one minute, and executes one set of 10 body weight rows. Rest for one minute and repeat until 10 sets of both exercises are completed. Another example would be doing 1 × 10 plyo push-ups, 1 × 10 pull-ups, 1 × 10 low box jumps, and repeat this circuit until completing 10 sets.

Training Method Parameters

- *Intensity of muscle contraction*: 40 percent to 60 percent of 1RM
- *Form of exercise*: Move quickly, with a pause between repetitions and at the end of each set. Avoid severe local muscle fatigue and work only until the first signs of fatigue are felt. The exercises and their combination should be made to target all major muscle groups (chest, back, shoulders, and legs).
- *Number of repetitions in a set*: 10
- *Number of exercises in a circuit*: 2 to 3
- *Number of sets*: 5 to 10 (10 being optimal for high-level athletes)
- *Rest interval between sets (if necessary)*: ≤1 minute
- *Number of different circuits*: 1 to 3
- *Rest interval between circuits*: 5 to 15 minutes (stretching, work with low intensity)
- This training method can be repeated 1 to 3 times a week

Interval Training Type II

This type of training increases the power of fast-twitch and glycolytic muscle fibers, increases the number of mitochondria in fast-twitch and glycolytic muscle fibers, and increases power at the anaerobic threshold. It also increases resistance to fatigue by increasing the anaerobic threshold. The main difference between this method and interval training type I is the use of heavy and near maximal weights for a shorter duration. This is an advanced method and should be performed only with a spotter or coach's assistance. This method improves biomechanics and strength of sports movements and stimulates modeling of competitive activity. This type of training can be used for MMA-specific fighting exercises, such as those demonstrated in figures 5.282-5.285.

Training Method Parameters

- *Intensity of muscle contraction*: 80 percent to 100 percent of 1RM
- *Tempo*: fast and explosive
- *Number of repetitions in a set*: 1 to 5
- *Duration of work (time)*: 20 to 30 seconds; until local fatigue
- *Rest interval between sets*: 2 to 5 minutes (depending on the duration of work)
- *Number of sets*: tonus (maintaining) 5 to 10; developing (to increase capacity) 10 to 20
- This training method can be repeated only once a week with maximum volume or two times a week if volume is lower

Training to Increase Strength and Power in Type II Muscle Fibers

The following are examples of exercises used in developmental training of high-threshold motor units (fast-twitch muscle fibers) to increase absolute strength and high-speed power capabilities. Details for using these exercises in a training program and what is meant by the "type of training" (i.e., activation of fast-twitch muscle fibers) is explained on page 347.

Barbell Bench Press (see figure 5.347):

- *Type of training*: activation of fast-twitch muscle fibers
- *Type of exercise*: multijoint
- *Joints involved*: elbow, shoulder
- *Main muscle groups affected*: pectoral major and minor muscles, deltoids, serratus anterior, and triceps

Figure 5.347 – Barbell bench press with a heavy weight and a spotter.

Power Clean (see figure 5.348):

- *Type of training*: activation of fast-twitch muscle fibers
- *Type of exercise*: multijoint
- *Joints involved*: ankle, knee, hip, elbow, shoulder
- *Main muscle groups affected*: gluteal muscles, quadriceps, hamstrings, lower leg muscles, back muscles, and deltoids

Figure 5.348 – Salim Kharkovsky demonstrating the power clean on an Olympic platform.

Weighted Pull-Up (see figure 5.349):

- *Type of training*: activation of fast-twitch muscle fibers
- *Type of exercise*: multijoint
- *Joints involved*: ulnar, shoulder
- *Main muscle groups affected*: latissimus dorsi, posterior deltoid, infraspinatus, subscapularis, brachialis, long head of the triceps, rhomboids, and biceps

Figure 5.349 – Weighted pull-up.

Back Squat (see figure 5.350):

- *Type of training*: activation of fast-twitch muscle fibers
- *Type of exercise*: multijoint
- *Joints involved*: hip, knee
- *Main muscle groups affected*: gluteal muscles and thigh muscles

Figure 5.350 – Back squat.

High Box Jump (see figure 5.351):

- *Type of training*: activation of fast-twitch muscle fibers
- *Type of exercise*: multijoint
- *Joints involved*: ankle, knee, hip
- *Main muscle groups affected*: gluteal muscles, thigh muscles, and lower leg muscles

Figure 5.351 – High box jump.

Leg Press (see figure 5.352):

- *Type of training*: activation of fast-twitch muscle fibers
- *Type of exercise*: multijoint
- *Joints involved*: hip, knee
- *Main muscle groups affected*: gluteal muscles, quadriceps, and hamstrings

Figure 5.352 – Leg press.

Activation of Fast-Twitch Muscle Fibers

This type of training increases absolute strength and increases the strength capacity of high-threshold motor units.

Training Method Parameters

- *Intensity of muscle contraction*: 90 percent to 100 percent of 1RM
- *Number of repetitions in a set*: 1 to 3; to failure
- *Rest interval between sets*: 2 to 5 minutes
- *Number of sets*: tonus (maintaining) 1 to 5; developing (to increase capacity) 10 to 12

Training to Increase Speed

The following exercises are used in high-speed interval training to increase the number of mitochondria in glycolytic muscle fibers, which can lead to the athlete being able to work for a longer time at a higher intensity by raising the anaerobic threshold. These exercises are meant to increase local muscular endurance and speed-power capabilities. Details on how to use these exercises in a training program and what is meant by the "type of training" (i.e., high-speed interval training) is explained starting on page 349.

Medicine Ball Slam (see figure 5.353):
- *Type of training*: high-speed interval training
- *Type of exercise*: multijoint
- *Joints involved*: ankle, knee, hip, shoulder, elbow
- *Main muscle groups affected*: gluteal muscles, quadriceps, hamstrings, rhomboids, trapezius, deltoids, and rectus abdominis

Figure 5.353 – Medicine ball slam.

One-Arm Medicine Ball Throw (see figure 5.354):
- *Type of training*: high-speed interval training
- *Type of exercise*: multijoint
- *Working joints*: elbow, shoulder
- *Main muscle groups affected*: pectoral muscles, deltoids, arm muscles, rectus abdominis, and external oblique

Figure 5.354 – One-arm medicine ball throw.

Rope Climb (see figure 5.355):

- *Type of training*: high-speed interval training
- *Type of exercise*: multijoint
- *Working joints*: elbow, shoulder
- *Main muscle groups affected*: latissimus dorsi, posterior deltoid, infraspinatus, subscapularis, brachialis, long head of the triceps, rhomboids, rectus abdominis, transversus abdominis, and iliopsoas

Figure 5.355 – Rope climb.

Medicine Ball Overhead Throw (see figure 5.356):

- *Type of training*: high-speed interval training
- *Type of exercise*: multijoint
- *Joints involved*: ankle, knee, hip, shoulder, elbow
- *Main muscle groups affected*: gluteal muscles, quadriceps, hamstrings, back muscles, chest, and abdominals

Figure 5.356 – Medicine ball overhead throw.

High-Speed Interval Training

This type of training increases speed and power capabilities and increases resistance to fatigue by increasing the anaerobic threshold.

Training Method Parameters

- *Intensity of effort*: 80 percent to 100 percent of maximum
- *Pace*: fast or maximum speed, depending on the exercise

- *Duration of work (time)*: 5 seconds (95%-100% of maximum effort); 10 to 15 seconds (80%-90% of maximum effort)
- *Rest interval between sets*: 2 to 3 minutes (depending on the duration of work)
- *Number of sets*: tonus (maintaining) 5 to 10; developing (to increase capacity) 10 to 20

MMA-Oriented Training

This type of training increases the number of mitochondria in fast-twitch and glycolytic muscle fibers, increases the power at the anaerobic threshold, and minimizes acidity in the muscles. This training improves biomechanics and sports movement skills, aiding the determination of optimal tactics for competitive fights (sparring).

Training Method Parameters
- *Intensity of muscle contraction*: competitive
- *Pace*: competitive
- *Duration of work (time)*: 30 seconds to 120 seconds; until local fatigue
- *Rest interval between sets*: 5 to 10 minutes (depending on the duration of the work)
- *Number of sets*: tonus (maintaining) 1 to 5; developing (to increase capacity) 5 to 10

Tables 5.44 through 5.49 show how the training covered in previous sections can be used to create a microcycle or combined into a mesocycle.

Table 5.44 – Microcycle Training Program to Increase the Number of Mitochondria

Monday	Tuesday	Wednesday	Thursday	Friday	Saturday	Sunday
High-speed interval training (development)	Interval training 10 × 10 (tonus)	Interval training type I (development)	Interval training 10 × 10 (tonus)	High-speed interval training (development)	Interval training type I (tonus)	Rest day

Table 5.45 – Microcycle Training Program to Increase Speed-Strength Capacity

Monday	Tuesday	Wednesday	Thursday	Friday	Saturday	Sunday
High-speed interval training (development)	Interval training type I (tonus)	Resistance training* (development)	Interval training 10 × 10 (tonus)	High-speed interval training (tonus)	Isoton training (development)	Rest day

*See the section on training for the hypertrophy of the glycolytic muscle fibers through hyperplasia in chapter 2.

Table 5.46 – Mesocycle Variation A

	Monday	Tuesday	Wednesday	Thursday	Friday	Saturday	Sunday
Week 1	Interval training type II (tonus)	Interval training 10 × 10 (tonus)	Interval training type I (tonus)	Interval training 10 × 10 (tonus)	MMA-oriented training (tonus)	Resistance training* (development)	Rest day
Week 2	Interval training type II (tonus)	Interval training 10 × 10 (tonus)	Interval training type I (tonus)	Interval training 10 × 10 (tonus)	MMA-oriented training (tonus)	Isoton training (development)	Rest day
Week 3	Interval training type II (development)	Interval training 10 × 10 (tonus)	Interval training type I (development)	Interval training 10 × 10 (tonus)	MMA-oriented training (development)	Interval training type I (tonus)	Rest day

*See the section on training for the hypertrophy of the glycolytic muscle fibers through hyperplasia in chapter 2.

Table 5.47 – Mesocycle Variation B

	Monday	Tuesday	Wednesday	Thursday	Friday	Saturday	Sunday
Week 1	High-speed interval training (tonus)	Interval training type I (tonus)	Interval training type I (tonus)	Interval training 10 × 10 (tonus)	MMA-oriented training (tonus)	Resistance training* (development)	Rest day
Week 2	Interval training type I (tonus)	High-speed interval training (tonus)	Interval training type I (tonus)	Interval training 10 × 10 (tonus)	MMA-oriented training (tonus)	Isoton training (development)	Rest day
Week 3	Interval training type II (development)	Interval training type I (tonus)	Interval training type II (tonus)	Interval training type I (tonus)	MMA-oriented training (development)	Interval training type I (tonus)	Rest day

*See the section on training for the hypertrophy of the glycolytic muscle fibers through hyperplasia in chapter 2.

Table 5.48 – Mesocycle Variation C

	Monday	Tuesday	Wednesday	Thursday	Friday	Saturday	Sunday
Week 1	Interval training type I (tonus)	Interval training type I (tonus)	Resistance training (for upper body)* (development)	Interval training 10 × 10 (tonus)	Interval training type II (tonus)	Resistance training (for lower body)* (development)	Rest day
Week 2	Interval training 10 × 10 (tonus)	Interval training type I (tonus)	Isoton training (lower body) (development)	Interval training 10 × 10 (tonus)	MMA-oriented training (tonus)	Isoton training (upper body) (development)	Rest day
Week 3	Interval training type II (development)	Interval training type I (tonus)	Interval training type II (tonus)	Interval training type I (tonus)	MMA-oriented training (development)	Interval training type I (tonus)	Rest day

*See the section on training for the hypertrophy of the glycolytic muscle fibers through hyperplasia in chapter 2.

Table 5.49 – Mesocycle Variation D

	Monday	Tuesday	Wednesday	Thursday	Friday	Saturday	Sunday
Week 1	High-speed interval training (tonus)	Interval training type I (tonus)	Isoton training (upper body) (development)	Interval training 10 × 10 (tonus)	Interval training type II (tonus)	Isoton training (lower body) (development)	Rest day
Week 2	Fast-twitch muscle fiber (development)	Fast-twitch muscle fiber (development)	Fast-twitch muscle fiber (development)	Rest day	Fast-twitch muscle fiber (development)	Interval training type I (tonus)	Rest day

When working with children and youth, sensitive periods in their physical development should be considered within the frame of their strength and conditioning program to maximize their performance potential in the long term and increase their chances of achieving professional, elite-level athleticism. When the athlete is at an amateur level, all the periodization principles should be applied. For the best outcome, athletes must follow a process of planned periodization, starting with anatomical adaptation and then a hypertrophy phase, transitioning to maximum strength, and then power, power endurance, and circuit MMA before a longer transition period (i.e., a vacation).

Another consideration in the athlete's long-term career is to treat the fights during the amateur period as important. It is critical that the athlete be undefeated within the first five amateur fights before their professional debut. Afterward, the first of their professional fights needs to be won to fortify their professional status. The result is better-promoted fights with higher-ranked opponents and the chance to advance their own ranking as well as the potential to earn higher pay.

Once they are professionals with a place in the UFC, Bellator, PFL, and so on, the training can become more tailored to their preferences, fighting style, and experience gained from each fight but will still be designed according to a process of planned periodization like the programs we have outlined in this chapter. As an athlete becomes more elite and ranks higher, certain phases may be eliminated and the focus of the training sessions may shift to mainly strength, power endurance, and circuit MMA. The training needs to be carefully planned, as we showed in this chapter.

Another important detail to minimize training plateaus or overtraining is to avoid more than two sequential heavy days of training with a development focus. One day should be development and the next day a lighter day (tonus), for example, and alternate the load. There will be two to three peak days of load within a week. If there are more than four training peak load days in a single week, the chance of overtraining is high. To deter overtraining, plan a deload week every two to six weeks for the athlete. This deload week uses approximately 30 percent less volume, so the intensity of the work remains, and performance is maintained in this period.

The Isoton method we presented is a way to increase the aerobic threshold and muscular endurance, especially in type I muscle fibers. The 10 × 10 method and the type I method both increase aerobic capacity in intermediate and fast-twitch muscle fibers. These methods are not as demanding on the body in terms of neurological load, so they can be incorporated into training up to three times per week. Split routines are incorporated only in cases where the athlete has a specific deficiency that we are trying to correct or during the off-season and are not normally used within a training camp. Training with elastic resistance bands can be an important tool to develop power and power endurance, and they are also highly adaptable to any environment. In cases like the COVID-19 lockdown, the portability and versatility of resistance bands was taken advantage of to maintain training performance intensity using nontraditional environments and outdoor settings.

Coaches should understand all the principles we have explained in the previous chapters to apply the best training program to their athlete. In the next chapter we talk in depth about injury prevention and flexibility exercises, both of which are necessary tools to better prepare our athletes physically for optimal performance and positive competition outcomes.

6

PREVENTION OF MMA–RELATED INJURIES

Charla-Yvonne Girtman, DHSc(c), MBA

Howard Gelb, MD

Tone Ricardo Benevides Panassollo, PT, MS

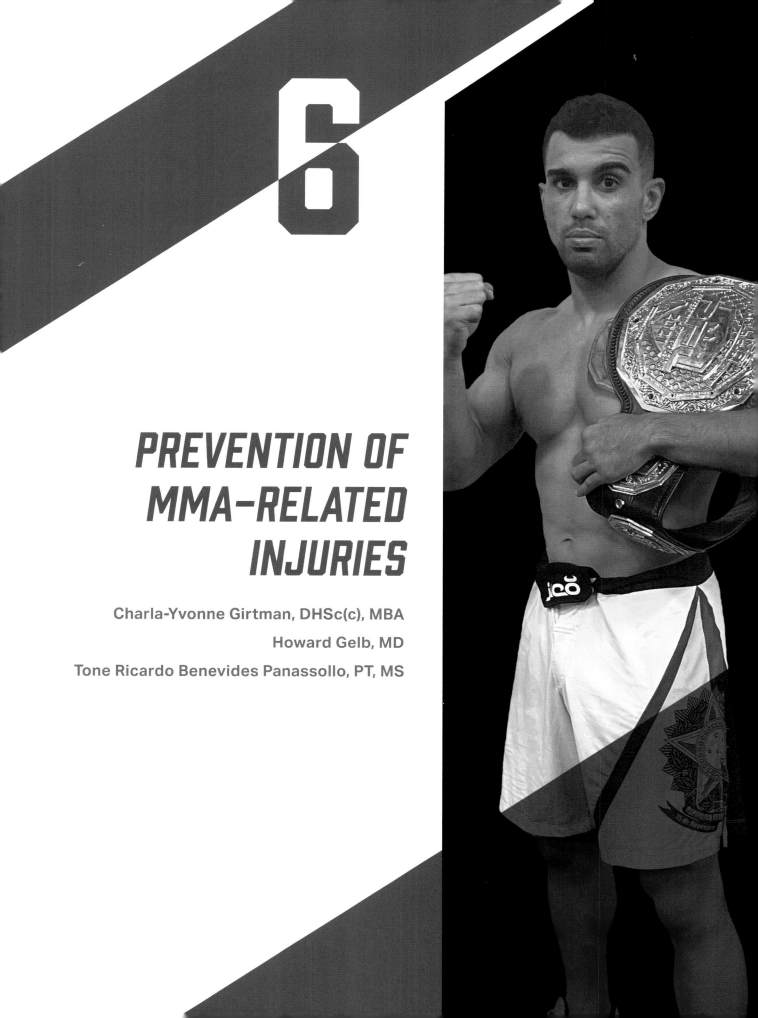

While the goal of sport is to participate at the highest level possible for as long as possible, injuries may derail achievement of this goal. Injuries are somewhat commonplace in sport participation, especially in contact sports. Contact sports by nature have a higher potential for injury because of the increased chance for unintended or uncontrolled contact. Other injuries occur due to over- or improper training. Not all injuries are career- or season-ending, but an injury could delay participation or change the outcome of a season. It is important to prevent injuries whenever possible. This chapter will highlight a system of testing an athlete's current status and strategies to increase prevention of and facilitate recovery from the most common injuries in MMA.

Injury Prevention in MMA Fighters

MMA is a high-intensity activity that can lead to physical and mental exhaustion (Dias and Oliveira, 2013). Moreover, it is a contact sport that includes striking actions (punches, kicks, elbows, etc.) and accompanying falls and other tactical maneuvers. This can lead to numerous contact injuries such as bone fractures, joint dislocation, concussion, and bruising, as well as noncontact and overuse injuries, such as tendonitis, muscle strains, and ligament injuries.

The number of injuries during training and competition has been a point of concern. Jensen and colleagues (2017) noted that injuries occurred at a rate of 22.9 to 28.6 per 100 fighters. The UFC (2021) reported that between 2017 and 2020, 80.7 percent of injuries were fight-related and only 19.3 percent occurred during training.

In contrast, Rainey (2009) reported 77.9 percent of injuries occurred during training and only 22.1 percent occurred during competitions. Since more time is spent during training compared with fighting, it may increase the probability of injuries during training, especially noncontact injuries. Training injuries may even be undercounted because athletes do not always report them. The contention that the percentage of training-related injuries is high (and could be higher due to underreporting) highlights the importance of a balanced training program.

Muscle strength and muscular endurance are critical for injury prevention due to muscles' role in joint stabilization and force production. The ability of a muscle to generate more force is associated with a lower risk of injury in athletes (Barber-Westin and Noyes, 2017; McLean and Samorezov, 2009). Thus, training periodization (chapters 1 and 5) plays an important role in preventing sports injuries (Monsma, et al. 2009; Mujika, et al. 2018; UFC, 2021). It is important, during training periodization, to avoid developing a muscle imbalance in any joint or region, because an imbalance can lead to serious injuries. For example, an imbalance in the knee (posterior and anterior muscles) can result in anterior cruciate ligament injury (da Silva Junior, et al. 2018; Stuber, et al. 2014).

Additionally, including supplementary injury-prevention exercises in training is critical in decreasing the chance of injury in athletes. For example, in soccer, there is an activity program, FIFA 11+, which is based on core stabilization exercises, eccentric thigh muscle training, proprioceptive training, dynamic stabilization, and plyometric exercises. It has had excellent results in injury prevention. For instance, studies have shown injury reductions ranging from 30 percent to 70 percent in athletes on teams that had implemented the FIFA 11+ program (Barengo, et al. 2014). The UFC recommends exercises to improve mobility and to activate muscles from the hips and shoulders, with the objective of reducing injuries (UFC, 2021). However, there is a lack of studies reporting the effectiveness of these exercises in reducing injury in MMA athletes. Our recommendation for injury prevention is to prioritize mobility and muscle activation. This chapter also discusses mobility and flexibility.

Another important factor in injury prevention in MMA is changes in sport rules, such as the mandatory use of gloves, prohibition of kneeing the face while the opponent is grounded, and banning strikes to the spine. These changes have played an important role in maintaining the athlete's physical safety and preventing injury (Gregory, et al. 2006). Each MMA fighter also uses a combination of different fighting styles, which influences the type and severity of their injuries (Noh, et al. 2015).

In this chapter, we will cite some of the most common injuries fighters experience to different parts of the body and focus on resistance training exercises to prevent injuries. Some of these exercises can also be used in injury rehabilitation settings.

Head and Face Injuries

Injuries to the head and face are the most common in MMA, which is not surprising given that fights for all categories generally end with punches (Jensen, et al. 2017; UFC, 2021; Bueno, et al. 2022). Head injuries accounted for 32.5 percent of total fight injuries but only 3.8 percent of injuries that occurred during training (UFC, 2021). Cuts (lacerations) on the upper eyelid and eyebrow region and hematomas are "part of the job," and it is almost impossible not to have them, especially during fights (Fernandes, et al. 2018; Bueno, et al. 2022). Concussion is also common in combat sports that include striking (Ji, 2016) and can occur from direct or indirect blows that cause an acceleration and deceleration in the head or neck called *whiplash*. This results in visual disturbances and impairment in memory, concentration, and attention (Hynes and Dickey, 2006; Koh, et al. 2003; Ryan and Warden, 2003). After a more severe concussion, such as from a knockout, the athlete may also undergo a second trauma by hitting their head on the ground when they fall (Hutchison, et al. 2014).

Prevention of Head and Face Injuries

One way to prevent head injury is to wear gloves with more padding and helmets. This can reduce the number of injuries sustained during training since during professional (regulated) fights, a helmet is not allowed and glove size is standardized. Studies using larger gloves and a protective helmet show fewer injuries such as cuts and lacerations to the head and face, although their effect on concussion prevention is not significant (Hutchison, et al. 2014; Karpman, et al. 2016). Normally, contact causes head and face injuries, which are difficult to prevent in MMA. The head acceleration and deceleration caused by strikes and falls can be reduced by strengthening the neck muscles (as previously described in figure 5.204 in chapter 5), which can also hopefully reduce the number and frequency of concussion (Eckner, et al. 2014).

Spinal Injuries

The number of spinal injuries that occur during competitive fights is relatively small in MMA athletes. Gregory and colleagues (2006) conducted a study that spanned from September 2001 to December 2004 and found that the incidence of spinal injuries was only 0.58 per 100 competitors. However, athletes may experience spinal pain during an intense training period. For example, 6.9 percent of 1,344 injuries from 2017 to 2020 were associated with lumbar spine pain during MMA training. This number is reduced to only 0.8 percent during competition (UFC, 2021). Lumbar spine pain is common in both high-level athletes and the general population. Decreased muscle strength and neuromuscular control of the spine may be related to pain in the lumbar region (Moreno, et al. 2018).

Prevention of Spinal Injuries

A sound knowledge of takedown defense and falling techniques can help to prevent spinal and neck injuries. Core-strengthening exercises have also been recommended to prevent lumbar spine pain; however, more studies need to be performed to prove their effectiveness (Stuber, et al. 2014). Muscles involved in core stability are the abdominal, diaphragm, paraspinal, and gluteal muscles. In addition to protection, the core muscles transfer energy from the trunk to the extremities during physical activity. Core training (as described in figures 5.90-5.95 and figures 6.1-6.3) is important not only for injury prevention but also for performance enhancement (McGill, 2010; Wheeler, 2015).

Single-Leg Elevated Bridge
In addition to being an excellent exercise for strengthening the glutes, this exercise also works the lumbar spine muscles (see figure 6.1). It can be done for 3 sets of 15 to 20 repetitions on each side. However, the athlete's fitness level must be considered in the application of the exercise.

Figure 6.1 – Single-leg elevated bridge.

Swiss Ball Abdominal Crunch
Working on the Swiss ball is a good option for training the abdominal muscles (see figure 6.2). This exercise can be done in sets to failure or for 3 sets × 30 repetitions.

Figure 6.2 – Swiss ball abdominal crunch.

Swiss Ball Plank

During the plank exercise on the Swiss ball, the coach can move the ball in different directions while the athlete maintains a neutral position of the plank (see figure 6.3). The exercise can be performed in a range of 2 to 3 sets, for 45 to 60 seconds or until muscle failure.

Figure 6.3 – Swiss ball plank.

Elbow, Wrist, and Hand Injuries

Hand and wrist injuries are the second most common injuries in MMA. In an evaluation of 455 fighters, Ji (2016) reported that 8.5 percent and 7.8 percent of the total number of injuries occurred in hands and wrists, respectively. However, the study does not specify the type and severity of the injuries. The number of injuries in this part of the body is higher during competitions (15.2%), compared with 10.7 percent during training activities (UFC, 2021).

The mixed combat nature of MMA includes a multiplicity of fighting styles and techniques from judo, jiu-jitsu, wrestling, and so on. As such, athletes are susceptible to arm, hand, or wrist locks, which can lead to ligament injuries and compromise other structures of the hand and elbow joint. For example, armbar (armlock) is one of the most common causes of submission in UFC fights and can lead to severe injury in the elbow joint (UFC, 2021).

Prevention of Elbow, Wrist, and Hand Injuries

In addition to strengthening and stretching exercises, especially for the arm muscles, improved technique and the use of hand wraps can decrease the incidence of injuries in this region (Drury, et al. 2017). Figures 6.4 and 6.5 show exercises that can improve muscle strength around the wrists and provide joint stability.

Upside Down Kettlebell Exercise

This exercise can be used for strengthening the wrist. Keep the wrist steady to stabilize the weight (see figure 6.4) or perform small flexion and extension movements of the wrist. This exercise is also useful for increasing shoulder stabilization and is performed on each side for 3 sets of 45 to 60 seconds, or until muscle fatigue.

Figure 6.4 – Tone Panassollo demonstrating the upside down kettlebell exercise.

EzBar (or Dumbbell) Wrist Extension and Flexion Exercises

These exercises can strengthen the wrist, working for 3 sets of 15 to 20 repetitions (see figure 6.5). Either can be done using an EzBar or dumbbells.

Figure 6.5 – Wrist extension exercise using an EzBar (*a-b*) and wrist flexion exercise using dumbbells (*c-d*).

Shoulder Injuries

In MMA, grappling attacks of the shoulder joint are common, representing 7.9 percent of injuries during fights and 16.5 percent during training as reported by the UFC (2021). Examples of techniques that target the shoulder joint are Americana and Kimura, both leading to injury of the ligamentous structures and cartilage of this joint. Shoulder cartilage injuries and those associated with shoulder instability can be treated initially without surgery and with the help of physical therapy and strengthening of the rotator cuff, which is the dynamic stabilizer of the shoulder. The muscles around the shoulder blade, including the trapezius, latissimus dorsi, triceps, and rhomboids, should also be strengthened, helping athletes with shoulder instability.

In chronic rotator cuff injuries, for example, cortisone injections can be used in addition to physical therapy and resistance training to avoid surgery procedures (see figure 6.6). If there is a large amount of ligament stretching or laxity after an injury, and the shoulder recurrently dislocates, a surgical procedure is likely necessary. This will usually be performed via arthroscopy, making small holes in the shoulder to repair the ligaments and cartilage. In successful surgeries, the athlete can return to training after three to four months and compete again after six months.

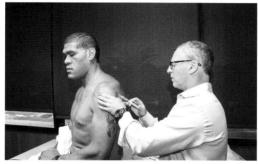

Figure 6.6 – Dr. Howard Gelb doing a cortisone injection on António "Big Foot" Silva.

Prevention of Shoulder Injuries

In this section, we invited sports injury practitioner Dr. Howard Gelb and physical therapist Jay Itzkowitz to demonstrate some of the strengthening exercises of the muscles around the shoulder blade (see figures 6.7-6.12) that were done with António "Big Foot" Silva during the recovery from his shoulder injury. These exercises can be included in a well-rounded injury-prevention program for combat athletes.

Figure 6.7 – Single-arm adducted external rotation with resistance band.

Figure 6.8 – Single-arm adducted internal rotation with resistance band.

Figure 6.9 – Abducted external rotation with resistance band.

Figure 6.10 – Crossbody lateral raises with resistance band.

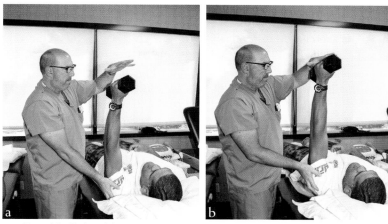

Figure 6.11 – Dumbbell shoulder protraction.

Figure 6.12 – Straight-arm lat pulldown with resistance bands (*a-b*) and seated high cable row (*c-d*).

Recovery From Shoulder Injuries

There are important exercise considerations to follow after injury. Stretches for the shoulder after injury should be static, last 30 seconds to one minute, and be repeated at least three times with each movement. Band and machine exercises should be performed in a progression in which the athlete is stimulated in various ways with dynamic and isometric contractions, and the number of sets changes with the athlete's progress according to the physiotherapist, athletic trainer, and strength coach's planning. As an example, use two to four sets lasting 30 seconds in band exercises and three sets of 15 to 25 repetitions on machine exercises.

Hip and Thigh Injuries

Hip and thigh injuries are more frequent during training (4.6%) than during competition (1.7%). Hamstring strains are a relatively common injury in MMA, being 2.2 percent of the total injuries from 2017 to 2020 (UFC, 2021). Hamstring strains are common in sports composed of movements that require high speed or excessive knee extension (Chan, et al. 2012; Sherry, et al. 2011; Bueno, et al. 2022). MMA fighters use various kicking techniques performed at high speed, which may cause hamstring injuries. As an example, the speed of a karate and taekwondo fighter's kick can range from 5.20 to 14.14 meters per second (Wąsik, 2011). High training volume can also lead to injuries in the hip joint and hamstring muscles. For example, the adductor muscles and hip flexion (iliopsoas) can be overloaded during a high volume of kicks. A technical or skills training session can also create overexertion. Therefore, a well-planned training session is important to avoid overtraining injuries.

Prevention of Hip and Thigh Injuries

The Nordic hamstring curl, sometimes called the Russian hamstring curl, is a great eccentric exercise for preventing hamstring injuries (see figure 6.13). This exercise is associated with a lower risk of muscle strain and used by soccer, football, and rugby teams (Al Attar, et al. 2017; van der Horst, et al. 2015). In the Nordic hamstring curl, the athlete controls the lowering of their body to the limits of their hamstring strength using a wall anchor (see figures 6.13*a-c*) or a coach (see figures 6.13*d-f*). The descent should be slow, with three sets of six to eight repetitions.

Another excellent exercise for eccentric hamstring strengthening is the hamstring curl on a Swiss ball, which can be performed bilaterally or unilaterally (see figure 6.14). Maintain spinal alignment by elevating the hip and flexing the knee. We recommend three sets of 12 to 15 repetitions, depending on the athlete's physical preparedness.

Figure 6.13 – Nordic hamstring curl using a wall anchor (*a-c*) or a coach (*d-f*).

Figure 6.14 – Hamstring curl on a Swiss ball.

Knee Injuries

Knee injury is one of the most common injuries in any sport. In a study that tracked injuries in different sports over 10 years, Majewski and colleagues (2006) reported that 39.8 percent of injuries were to the knee, with 49.48 percent being an anterior cruciate ligament (ACL) injury. In UFC fights, knee injuries represented 13.2 percent of all injuries (UFC, 2021). The same study reported the knee as the most common nonfight injury in MMA athletes. Knee injuries can occur either directly, as in the case of Thiago "Pitbull" Alves, or indirectly, through knee sprain or joint overload.

Pitbull received a kick in the lower leg, and the force of that kick destroyed the ACL and posterior cruciate ligament (PCL) of his left knee. The two ligaments, along with other knee structures such as the meniscus, lateral collateral ligament (LCL), and the medial collateral ligament (MCL), play an important role in stabilizing the knee joint. An ACL injury combined with a PCL injury can end an athlete's career, especially if their recovery is incomplete and does not include medical care, physical therapy, and a good strength and conditioning program.

Fortunately, Pitbull had excellent support from a range of professionals during his rehabilitation, and the athlete continued his career in search of more wins. He underwent successful surgery and subsequently demonstrated excellent knee stability. Pitbull's knee injury occurred by direct contact to the knee, and it would have been difficult to prevent it. However, exercises to improve muscle strength and joint stability can prevent noncontact injuries to the knee. The exercises used during Pitbull's treatment are included in this section, because these exercises can be used during rehabilitation and to prevent injury.

Prevention of Knee Injuries

Strong hamstrings and quadriceps muscles minimize the risk of ACL and other injuries in the knee joint. In case of rehabilitation, amplitude of movement and range of motion will progressively increase according to the rehabilitation phase. We recommend the use of closed-kinetic chain exercises to improve muscle strength in this area such as: squats, lunges, Romanian deadlifts, side lunges (see figure 6.15), and unilateral leg presses (see figure 6.16) with a reduced range of motion. Open-kinetic chain exercises (i.e., leg curls and leg extensions) are important to include in the ACL and knee injury prevention program. During ACL rehabilitation, some open-kinetic chain exercises need to be avoided, but this is beyond the scope of this book. Resistance training exercises can be done until failure (muscle fatigue) or based on sets and repetitions, according to the objective of the rehabilitation phase.

Figure 6.15 – Thiago "Pitbull" Alves demonstrating the side lunge used for rehab.

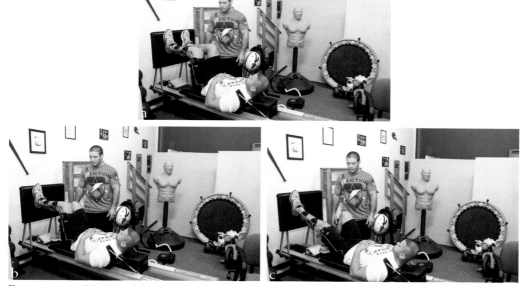

Figure 6.16 – Unilateral leg press with reduced range of motion used for rehab.

Proprioception exercises are an essential part of a rehabilitation program, but they are also important for injury prevention. Proprioception refers to the conscious perception of limb and body position and motion in space (Aman, et al. 2015). The purpose of proprioception is to stress the joint providing instability, forcing the muscles to activate and keep the joint stable (see figure 5.2 in chapter 5). There is no need to add loads during these activities, but closing the eyes, using a different surface (BOSU or foam), or adding specific movements during the exercise can make them more complex. These exercises are usually based on time (for example, 30 seconds) or repetitions (10 × pistol squats on a BOSU ball); see figure 6.17.

Figure 6.17 – Adriano Martins demonstrating the pistol squat on BOSU ball.

Ankle and Foot Injuries

MMA athletes do not use foot protection, either in training or in official (regulated) fights, and they suffer various foot and ankle injuries, such as fractures and other injuries to the ligaments (Jensen, et al. 2017; Ji, 2016; Karpman, et al. 2016). Injuries can be caused by blocking kicks or from foot and ankle locks. Ankle and foot injuries represented 12.3 percent of fight injuries and 10.7 percent of nonfight injuries (UFC, 2021).

Prevention of Ankle and Foot Injuries

Strengthening and proprioception exercises (see figures 6.18-6.19) should be used to prevent ligament injuries. These exercises are also effective during injury rehabilitation. Foot inversion, eversion, and dorsiflexion strengthening movements can prevent injuries in the foot and ankle and can be performed in three sets until fatigue or for 20 to 30 repetitions. Proprioception exercises are also important for maintaining good ankle and foot stabilization and therefore prevent injury. In addition, specific athletic and physio tapes may help maintain ankle joint integrity, especially in MMA activities (Evans and Clough, 2012; Han, et al. 2015; Kadakia and Haddad, 2003; Kaminski, et al. 2019; Strøm, et al. 2016).

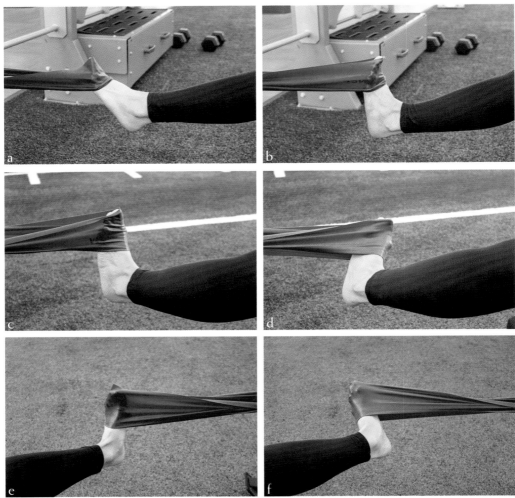

Figure 6.18 – Ankle-strengthening exercises with elastic band: *(a-b)* ankle dorsiflexion, *(c-d)* ankle inversion, and *(e-f)* ankle eversion.

In figure 6.19, we use a proprioceptive disc (a BOSU ball or a proprioceptive pad can also be used). We recommend three sets of 45 to 60 seconds each set in this exercise. This exercise can also be used for developing knee stability.

Figure 6.19 – Proprioception ankle exercise on a BOSU ball.

The Science of Stretching and Flexibility

As an athlete increases the volume and intensity of their training program, the risk of injury increases. Therefore, improving the athlete's strength, muscular endurance, power, cardiorespiratory capacity, and flexibility can decrease the likelihood of injury (Parsons, 2017). Most programs effectively address the former components; however, it is also necessary to specifically address flexibility. The ability to move the joints through a full range of motion is important in sport, and the loss of flexibility can lead to reduced movement economy and possibly injuries (Ruan, et al. 2018).

For this reason, regular stretching exercises are recommended to increase flexibility to optimize movement and to prevent injury. Although flexibility has not been fully scientifically proven to prevent injury specifically for MMA (Dias, et al. 2017), the National Strength and Conditioning Association (NSCA) upholds flexibility as an important component of the strength and conditioning program for all athletes, especially for elite performance and athletic competition preparation (Haff and Triplett, 2016). An increase in flexibility can also positively affect an athlete's performance through improved balance and reaction time (Prentice, 2020).

Flexibility is defined as the ability of a joint or series of joints to move through a full range of motion (ROM). Flexibility is characteristic to each joint and depends not only on the structure of the joint but also on the surrounding tissue, namely ligaments, muscles, and tendons. The range of motion of a given joint depends on several factors, including genetics, muscle properties, physical activity and exercise, anatomical structure, age, and sex.

There are two types of ROM in flexibility: active and passive. Active ROM is the total movement available at the joint through muscular contractions without external assistance. Passive ROM is the total movement available at a joint through inactive muscular movement, generally meaning that a second person or object is assisting to accomplish the total movement. To determine which type of flexibility is most important to the athlete, the sport movement and timing within the training program where flexibility training is incorporated become important to consider. While passive ROM speaks to the total ability of the joint to move, is greater than active ROM, and accounts for looseness or stiffness at the joint, it may not deal with movement efficiency that is seen with active ROM.

According to the American College of Sports Medicine (ACSM, 2009, 2012), there are four modes of training for flexibility: static, ballistic, proprioceptive neuromuscular facilitation (PNF), and dynamic. American Top Team athletes use dynamic flexibility, and it is becoming increasingly popular in the sport, especially in warm-up routines. In this section, we invited veteran Bellator fighter Cristiano "Soldado" Souza to demonstrate how we can develop flexibility.

Types of Stretching

One of the key factors in reducing injury is how an athlete prepares for performance through warm-up, training, and recovery. Training methods are discussed in chapter 5. In this section, we will discuss various forms of stretching that can be part of warm-up and recovery sessions to increase flexibility and improve balance and coordination.

Static Stretching

This is the most commonly used stretching method and consists of slow, steady movement until a final position is maintained, generally at a point of slight discomfort, for 15 to 30 seconds (see figure 6.20). Normally, each stretch is repeated a maximum of four times, because gains are minimal with more sets. Static stretching, as indicated in current research, may be beneficial for short-duration, high-intensity activities and can help reduce injuries when incorporated into a comprehensive warm-up (Chaabene, et al. 2019).

Figure 6.20 – A static stretch option for the abdominal muscles.

However, there must be much more caution when incorporating static stretches in the warm-up routine for high-performance athletes, especially when considering longer-duration practice and participation times in high-intensity activities. e Lima and colleagues (2019) noted that when participating in longer sessions of explosive or maximal force and power, the potential for decreased maximal voluntary contraction (MVC) exceeds the benefits generally garnered in a single session of static stretching. This form of stretching would be more appropriate in active recovery and cool-down programs instead (Bogdanis, et al. 2019).

Ballistic Stretching

This method is a bouncing, or jerking, movement with repetitive agonist muscular contractions that quickly stretch the antagonist (Prentice, 2020). These rapid movements extend a joint to a full range of motion. Those participating in ballistic stretching may have a greater tendency to include uncontrolled, quick movements, which may increase the likelihood for increased muscle soreness and subsequent altered movement (Prentice, 2020). While this method has proven to be effective at increasing available ROM, there is concern that injury may occur due to the forceful nature of the technique. Some athletes and coaches still use this method to increase blood flow and assist in precompetition warm-up or before training sessions. When the sport movement mimics this method, similar to a floor routine in gymnastics, this may warrant incorporation within a longer, more inclusive warm-up protocol.

Proprioceptive Neuromuscular Facilitation

Proprioceptive neuromuscular facilitation (PNF) is a set of techniques that combine passive stretching with isometric and concentric muscle actions. The physiological basis of PNF is that muscle relaxation is followed by an isometric contraction that stimulates the Golgi tendon organ, which inhibits contraction during a subsequent stretching exercise (Sozbir, et al. 2016). Due to the physiological response of this method, there are three PNF techniques: (1) hold-relax, (2) contract-relax, and (3) hold-relax with agonist contraction, each requiring varying amounts of active ROM, passive ROM, and isometric contraction. Our athletes use the contract-relax form of stretching, and it often requires two people (see figure 6.21). The partner moves the joint through its range of motion, and after reaching the end point of the movement, the target muscle is contracted isometrically for 10 seconds (against the partner). There is a 10-second relaxation phase next, where the worked muscle is stretched again by the partner into an even greater range of motion (Prentice, 2020; Haff and Triplett, 2016).

Figure 6.21 – Examples of stretching using the proprioceptive neuromuscular facilitation (PNF) method in the posterior chain for the lumbar spine, gluteal, leg, hamstring, and calf muscles.

Dynamic Stretching

This stretching method refers to the increased ROM an athlete achieves through functional and sport-specific movements in warm-up (Haff and Triplett, 2016). Dynamic flexibility requires the athlete to maintain balance and proprioception while trying to increase sport-specific ROM (see figure 6.22). It becomes important to not only monitor the amount of ROM an athlete has at a joint but also the type of movement they use to obtain it. Similar to previously described techniques, dynamic flexibility uses slow, controlled, sport-specific movements designed to increase core body temperature and improve activity-related flexibility and balance. However, dynamic flexibility requires both stretching and active movement from the athlete with minimal if any assistance. Some studies have shown that when comparing a warm-up composed of static stretching and another with dynamic flexibility, the second was superior in improving sports performance, proving the efficiency of dynamic flexibility before training and competition (Opplert and Babault, 2019). American Top Team athletes use dynamic stretching as a warm-up, performing these moves before sparring sessions and competitions for about 5 to 10 minutes (Dias, et al. 2017).

Figure 6.22 – Stretching of the inner and posterior thigh (adductor and hamstring) (*a-d*), used for dynamic flexibility.

Recommendations for Stretching Techniques

Table 6.1 compares various stretching techniques (Gibson, et al. 2019). While each method increases flexibility and may have a place in the overall program of the fighter, there are occasions where one method is more beneficial than others. Consideration for energy consumption, resistance to stretch, and timing or time limits within the exercise session affect the method chosen.

Table 6.1 – Comparison of Stretching Techniques

	Ballistic	**Static**	**Dynamic**	**PNF**
Risk of injury	High	Low	Medium	Medium
Degree of pain	Medium	Low	Medium	High
Resistance to stretch	High	Low	Medium	Medium
Practicality (time and assistance needed)	Good	Excellent	Excellent	Poor
Efficiency (energy consumption)	Poor	Excellent	Good	Poor
Effective for increasing ROM	Good	Good	Good	Excellent

PNF = proprioceptive neuromuscular facilitation; ROM = range of motion.

Reprinted by permission from A.L. Gibson, D.R. Wagner, and V.H. Heyward, *Advanced Fitness Assessment and Exercise Prescription*, 8th ed. (Champaign, IL: Human Kinetics, 2019), 332.

When performing stretching exercises, we recommend the following general precautions and principles (Dias, et al. 2017).

- Warm up before beginning the flexibility program. Regardless of the method used, preparing the muscle for increasing the available ROM reduces the risk of injury during the stretch.
- Avoid sudden movements, because they increase the tone of muscle flexibility and make stretching more difficult. Do not use ballistic stretching for a fighter without proper warm-up and a qualified professional's supervision.
- Stretch before and after the main part of physical activity.
- Use dynamic stretching during preactivity to increase flexibility.
- Use PNF or static stretching for the cool down or active recovery sessions for long-term improvements in ROM.
- Stretch to the point of mild resistance or tightness. It should not cause pain.
- Pain is an indication of concern.
- Do not continue stretching at a joint in pain. Evaluate these joints for injury.
- Avoid asymmetrical stretching (e.g., excessive stretching of one arm and little of the other). This activity leads to altered movement patterns and decreased performance.
- Maintain normal breathing patterns. The Valsalva maneuver, holding the breath and increasing abdominal pressure, may lead to other health complications.
- Stretches should last 15 to 30 seconds and can be repeated between two to four times at each joint.
- Have flexibility evaluated by a trained professional.
- While it is appropriate to stretch muscles with decreased ROM or that are tight, not every tight muscle needs to be stretched. It may be an indication of being overworked due to movement deficiencies.

Figures 6.23 and 6.24 include some examples of stretching exercises that MMA athletes perform.

Figure 6.23 – Stretching exercises for: anterior deltoid and pectorals (*a*), anterior upper arm (biceps brachii) and forearm (*b*), and posterior deltoid (*c*).

Figure 6.24 – Advanced examples of positions that can be achieved by developing flexibility over years of training.

Assessment of Flexibility

The analysis of the movement and flexibility of athletes remains a highly researched topic today. Scientific advancements and recent research have shown a relationship between ROM and movement deficiencies, decreased performance, and an increased prevalence of injury. The relationship between motor pattern dysfunction at the hip and a high risk of knee injuries is one such example (Svoboda, et al. 2016). Therefore, it is of great importance to incorporate movement analysis in performance and fitness assessments (McKeown, et al. 2014).

There is agreement that screening is needed, especially for high-performance athletes, but there are many flexibility and movement assessments available to practitioners. New assessments and technologies are being researched daily, and there is no consensus concerning the choice of assessment (Haff and Triplett, 2016). Therefore, we suggest the assessment chosen must connect closely to the joint flexibility and movement patterns of the athlete within the sport.

To assess such deficiencies in an MMA population, use the Thomas Test and overhead squat test. Each test uses the concept of the kinetic chain and the connection of each joint to another's movement ability. Using the Thomas Test serves to quantify the flexibility of the hip flexor and quadriceps muscles. With the overhead squat test, we can measure dynamic flexibility, core strength, balance, and overall neuromuscular control. For this part, we invited UFC veteran athlete Ben Saunders to demonstrate how to perform the Thomas Test and overhead squat test.

Thomas Test

The Thomas Test can indicate contracture or lack of mobility of the hip flexors (iliopsoas, rectus femoris, pectineus, gracilis, sartorius, and tensor fasciae latae). Have this test performed by a highly qualified practitioner (athletic trainer, physical therapist, chiropractor, or strength and conditioning professional) for the most reliable and in-depth assessment. Traditionally, the Thomas Test has been performed with the extended thigh flat on the table (Prentice, 2020). However, the modified version of the test has the client with a flat back and the thigh extended slightly beyond the table to better assess rectus femoris and iliopsoas flexibility (Peeler and Anderson, 2008; Vigotsky, et al. 2016; Gabbe, et al. 2004).

For this exam, the test begins with the athlete lying supine (face up) on the treatment table with the gluteal muscles at the edge of the testing surface. The athlete holds both legs with the knees brought to the chest (see figure 6.25a). At the practitioner's command, and ensuring the low back is flat, the athlete will then release the testing leg, allowing it to relax to the final position and rest with the thigh as close to parallel to the floor as possible. Relax the knee to a flexed position at an approximate angle of 80 to 90 degrees at the knee (see figure 6.25b). The practitioner is checking to see whether the thigh or knee is raised from the table and by how much. A raised thigh will indicate potential contracture in the hip. Next, the practitioner will note the lower leg and knee position. If the knee is extended, there is additional indication the rectus femoris has a greater involvement in hip tightness.

Figure 6.25 – Professor Girtman conducting the Thomas Test.

In figure 6.26, we notice that the thigh is parallel to the floor but not flexed at 80 to 90 degrees at the knee. This indicates shortening of the rectus femoris. If this happens, we recommend doing a rectus femoris (quadriceps) stretch for 15 to 30 seconds, repeating the movement on each leg for 2 to 4 sets (see figure 6.27).

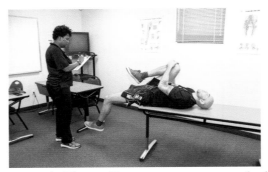

Figure 6.26 – When examining the Thomas Test, it is imperative to use both the side and front view to fully assess the athlete's results.

Figure 6.27 – Due to the athlete's tight rectus femoris muscle, we recommended a quadriceps stretch while maintaining an engaged core to reduce back arch.

If the leg is flexed at 80 to 90 degrees in the knee but is not parallel to the floor, this is often from iliopsoas shortening at the hip flexors (see figure 6.28). To correct this deficiency, we must use the hip flexor stretches shown in figure 6.29 for 15 to 30 seconds, repeating the movement on each leg for 2 to 4 sets.

Figure 6.28 – An example of a tight iliopsoas muscle but a normal rectus femoris muscle. The thigh is not on the table, but the knee is within 80 to 90 degrees.

Figure 6.29 – The kneeling lunge stretch is another stretch for the rectus femoris and the iliopsoas. The addition of trunk rotation incorporates the lower back.

In figure 6.30, notice that the thigh is not parallel to the floor or flexed at 80 to 90 degrees at the knee, indicating shortened iliopsoas, hip flexors, and rectus femoris. In figure 6.31, the leg moved away from the body's center line to the side, indicating a shortening of the iliotibial band. If so, we can suggest the same stretches shown in figures 6.27 and 6.29 for 15 to 30 seconds by repeating the movements on each leg for 2 to 4 sets.

Figure 6.30 – An example of a tight iliopsoas muscle and a tight rectus femoris muscle.

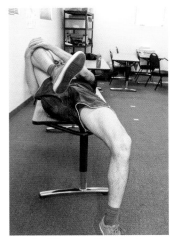

Figure 6.31 – An anterior view of the Thomas Test. In this view, the leg may fall outside of shoulder width when rested; this could be an indication of a tight iliotibial band or hip rotators.

Overhead Squat Test

Athletic performance depends on far more than the ability of a joint to move in isolation. It becomes important to not only monitor the amount of ROM an athlete has at a joint but also the movement they use to obtain it. Joint ROM is directly connected to its shape, size, and location within the body. Different joints are explained in table 6.2. Multiaxial joints, the hip and shoulder, especially, have a greater range of motion than other joints and are more affected by the lack of stability of joints above and below them.

Table 6.2 – Joint Classification by Structure and Function

Type of joint	Axes of rotation	Movements	Examples
Gliding	Nonaxial	Gliding, sliding, twisting	Intercarpal, intertarsal, tarsometatarsal
Hinge	Uniaxial	Flexion, extension	Knee, elbow, ankle, interphalangeal
Pivot	Uniaxial	Medial and lateral rotation	Proximal radioulnar, atlantoaxial
Condyloid and saddle	Biaxial	Flexion, extension, abduction, adduction, circumduction	Wrist, atlantooccipital, metacarpophalangeal, first carpometacarpal
Ball and socket	Triaxial	Flexion, extension, abduction, adduction, circumduction, rotation	Hip, shoulder

We use the overhead squat test to measure dynamic flexibility, core strength, balance, and overall neuromuscular control. The clinician can monitor active range of motion in connection with multijoint movements, noting that dysfunction at one joint may affect another along the kinetic chain. This is the concept that the upper and lower body are interconnected by muscle fascia and connective tissues. Therefore, if movement is hindered at one joint or segment of the chain, there will be some effect on another segment of the chain (Prentice, 2020; McKeown, et al. 2014). The overhead squat test begins with the athlete standing with hands extended above the head, shoulder-width apart and lined up as close to the ears as possible. Be barefoot for a more precise assessment. Keep the feet approximately shoulder-width apart and the toes pointed straight (see figure 6.32 for a frontal view).

Figure 6.32 – In the starting position of the overhead squat test, the athlete stands with the hands overhead, shoulder-width apart. When using the National Strength and Conditioning Association (NSCA) version of the assessment, include the bar; when using the National Academy of Sports Medicine (NASM) version, exclude the bar.

At the coach's command, the athlete does a full squat. Point the knees forward. If they start to move outward as in figure 6.33, it means that the tensor fasciae latae, piriformis, biceps femoris, and gluteus minimus and medius muscles are overactive or shortened.

Figure 6.33 – This is the lowered position of the overhead squat test in the anterior view. The athlete in this image has underactive adductors.

We recommend performing the basic strengthening exercise shown in figure 6.34 or a more advanced variation with a medicine ball shown in figure 6.35 for 2 to 5 sets until light fatigue for 2 to 3 days per week, and stretching the tensor fasciae latae, piriformis, biceps femoris, and gluteus minimus and medius muscles if they are overactive or shortened.

Figure 6.34 – The body weight squat with foam roller hold increases adductor strength and activation. This exercise is traditionally done against the wall but can be done without it for a more advanced exercise.

Figure 6.35 – The body weight squat with medicine ball hold increases adductor strength and activation. This exercise is traditionally done against the wall but can be done without it for a more advanced exercise.

In the anterior (see figure 6.36a) or posterior view (see figure 6.36b), if the knees go inward, we should strengthen the gluteus maximus, medius, and minimus muscles and the posterior portion of the thigh (hamstrings) and incorporate stretches of the adductor, posterior thigh, and calf muscles (gastrocnemius). Another effective exercise to reduce activation of the gastrocnemius or soleus is myofascial release, as shown in figure 6.37. Start rolling the body forward so that the foam roller goes toward the knee. Do this in a controlled manner, and when a pain or discomfort point is felt that is between 6 and 9 on an RPE scale of 1 to 10, hold it for 20 to 30 seconds. Then look for one or two new pain points before switching to the other leg.

Figure 6.36 – This is the lowered position of the overhead squat test in the anterior view (*a*) and posterior view (*b*). The athlete in this image has overactive adductors and tight calves.

Figure 6.37 – Self-myofascial rolling can be used to reduce tightness in the medial calf.

In a lateral view, we can see the optimal squat in figure 6.38*a* and incorrect movement in figure 6.38*b*, with an excessive forward tilt of the torso and arms. To prevent excessive forward tilt, perform the squat exercise with a stability ball at the back (see figure 6.39), concentrating on correct posture and core stabilization until light muscle fatigue in a series of 2 to 4 repetitions and a 1-minute interval between sets. (Note: A practitioner should do the assessment to identify incorrect movement patterns and deficiencies and customize the exercises according to individual needs.)

Figure 6.38 — The side view of the overhead squat profile (*a*) and an excessive forward lean (*b*).

Figure 6.39 — The Swiss ball wall squat teaches activation of the quadriceps, glutes, and abdominals.

MMA athletes are susceptible to a high number of contact and noncontact injuries during their sports careers. Muscle strength, stretching exercises, sports gear, and technique help minimize and prevent both contact and noncontact injuries. A well-planned training periodization schedule needs to incorporate preventive exercises and activities to improve athletes' performance by improving skills related to the sport (i.e., speed, agility, balance, coordination, and reaction time). A well-rounded program includes attention to flexibility, mobility, and recovery. This combination leads the athlete to achieve peak performance and successfully participate in high-level competitions.

The region of the body most often affected by contact injury is the head, a consequence of the objective of this sport. Joints are also commonly affected by techniques that seek opponents' submission. Injuries during training are reported less frequently but account for a high percentage of MMA injuries and are likely to be noncontact injuries. Incorporating assessments of an athlete's potential deficits that may lead to injury and taking appropriate actions (e.g., improve strength, flexibility, and mobility) present an opportunity to improve performance, and therefore, season outcomes.

REFERENCES

Chapter 1

Bompa, T.O. Treinando Atletas de Desporto Coletivo. São Paulo: Phorte, 2003.

Brauer, A., Drigo, A., Kirchner, B., Pimenta, T.F.D.F. and Scorsato, Y. Produção acadêmica em lutas, artes marciais e esportes de combate. Cadernos da Escola de Educação e Humanidades, Curitiba, v. 1, n. 7, 2012.

Brauer Junior, André G.; Souza, Ricardo M.; Andrade Sérgio L.F.; Dias, Stéfane B.C.D.; Pimenta, Thiago F.F. Esportes de Combate: a ciência no treinamento de atletas de MMA. Curitiba: Editora Juruá, 2019.

Dantas, E.H.M. A prática da preparação física. 5. ed. Rio de Janeiro: *Shape*, 2003.

Dantas, E.H.M. Adequabilidade dos principais modelos de periodização do treinamento esportivo. Rev. Bras. Ciênc. *Esporte, Florianópolis*, v. 33, n. 2, p. 483-494, Abr./Jun. 2011.

Dias, S.B.C.D. and Oliveira, E.B.; Júnior, A.G. *Teoria e Prática do treinamento para o MMA*. São Paulo, SP : Phorte Editora, 2017.

Dias, S.B.C.D. and Oliveira, E.B. A ciência do alongamento. Tatame: a revista do lutador, v. 214, p. 80-3, 2013.

Foster, C., Daines, E., Hector, L., Snyder, A.C. and Welsh, R. Athletic performance in relation to training load. *Wisconsin Medical Journal*, Madison, v. 95, no. 6, p. 370-374, 1996.

Foster, C. Monitoring training in athletes with reference to overtraining syndrome. *Medicine and Science in Sports and Exercise*, Hagerstown, v. 30, no. 7, p. 1164-1168, 1998.

Gomes, A.C. Treinamento Desportivo estruturação e periodização. Porto alegre: Artmed, 2009.

Issurin, V.B. Block periodization versus traditional training theory: A review. *J Sports Med Phys Fitness.* 2008;48(1):65-75.6.

Issurin, V.B. New Horizons for the Methodology and Physiology of Training Periodization. Sports Med 2010; 40 (3): 189-206.

Kelly, V.G.; Coutts, A.J. Planning and monitoring training loads during the competition phase in team sports. *Strength and Conditioning Journal*, v. 29, no. 4, p. 32-37, 2007.

Matveev, L.P. Teoriya i metodika fizicheskoi kulturi. Moscou: Fizkultura i Sport – Sportacadem Press, 2008.

Matveev, L.P. Teoriya i metodika fizicheskoi kulturi. Moscou: Nauka, 1991.

Matveev, L.P. Teoría general del entrenamiento deportivo. Barcelona: Paidotribo; 2001.

Maughan, R.; Gleeson, M.; Greenhaff, P.L. *Biochemistry of Exercise and Training.* Oxford: Oxford University, 1997.

McGuigan, M.R., Al Dayel, A., Tod, D., Foster, C., Newton, R.U. and Pettigrew, S. Use of session rating of perceived exertion for monitoring resistance exercise in children who are overweight or obese. *Pediatric Exercise Science*, v. 20, no.3, p. 333-341, 2008.

Moreira, A. Testes de campo para monitorar desempenho, fadiga e recuperação em basquetebolistas de alto rendimento. *Revista da Educação Física, Maringá*, v. 19, n. 2, p. 241-250, Apr./Jun. 2008.

Moreira, A. La periodización del entrenamiento y las cuestiones emergentes: el caso de los deportes de equipo. *Rev Andal Med Deporte.* 2010;3(4):170-178.

Mujika, I.; Halson, S.; Burke M.; Balagué, G.; Farrow, D. An integrated, multifactorial approach to periodization for optimal performance in individual and team sports. *International Journal of Sports Physiology and Performance*, 2018, 13, 538-561.

Nakamura, F.Y.; Moreira A.; Aoki M.S. Monitoramento da carga de treinamento: a percepção subjetiva do esforço da sessão é um método confiável? Revista da Educação Física, Maringá, v. 21, n. 1, p. 1-11, Jan./Mar. 2010.

Platonov, V.N. Tratado geral de treinamento desportivo. São Paulo: Phorte, 2008.

Platonov, V.N. Obshaia teoriya podgotovki sportmenov v olimpiskom sporte. Kiev: Olimpiskaia Literatura, 2007.

Platonov, V.N. Teoria geral do treinamento desportivo olímpico. Porto Alegre: Artmed, 2004.

Santana, J.C. *The essence of program design: The ultimate guide for trainers and coaches.* Florida: [s.n.], 2007.

Seluianov, V.N., Dias, B.C.D., and Andrade, S.L.F. *Musculação*: nova concepção russa de treinamento. Curitiba: Juruá, 2008.

Suslov, F.P. Teoria i metódica Sporta: utchebnoe posobie dlia utchilich olimpiskovo reserva. Moskva, 1997.

Tubino. M.J.G. Moreira, S.B. Metodologia científica do treinamento desportivo. 13. ed. Rio de Janeiro: Shape, 2003.

Verkhoshansky, Y., Lazarev V.V. Principles of planning speed and strength/speed endurance training in sports. *Strength and Conditioning Journal.* 1989;11(2):58-61.17.

Verkhoshansky, Y. Entrenamiento deportivo: planificación y programación. Barcelona: Martínez Roca; 1990.

Volkov, V.I. Bioenergetica napriajonei muichnoi deatelnosti cheloveka i sposobi povichenia rabotasposobnosti sportsmenov. Moskva: Nauka, 1990.

Volkov, V.I. Biojimiia. Moskva: Fizkultura i Sport, 1986, p 462.

Wallace, L.K., Slattery, K.M., and Coutts, A.J. The ecological validity and application of the session-RPE method for quantifying training loads in swimming. *Journal of Strength and Conditioning Research*, v. 23, no. 1, p. 33-38, 2009.

Chapter 2

Ahtiainen, J.P., Pakarinen, A., Alen, M., Kraemer, W., Hakkinen, K. Short vs. long rest period between the sets in hypertrophic resistance training: influence on muscle strength, size, and hormonal adaptations in trained men. *J Strength Cond Res*, v. 19, n. 3, p. 572-82, Aug 2005.

Ahtiainen, J.P., Pakarinen, A., Alen, M., et al., Muscle hypertrophy, hormonal adaptations and strength development during strength training in strength-trained and untrained men. *Eur. J. Appl. Physiol.*, v. 89, n. 6, p. 555, 2003.

Alekseev, G.A. Vliyaniye nazhruskirasz napravlennosti v sprinterskisredini distancie. Moskva: RGFK, p. 22, 1981.

American College of Sports Medicine (ACSM) position stand. Progression models in resistance training for healthy adults. *Medicine & Science in Sports & Exercise*, Madison, v.41, n.3, p.687-708, 2009.

Andrews R. All About High Intensity Interval Training (HIIT), Precisionnutrition.com.

Arruda, Antonio et al. Reliability of meta-analyses to evaluate resistance training programmes. *Journal of Sports Sciences*, v. 35, n. 20, p. 1982-1984, 2017.

Astorino T.A., Allen R.P.; Roberson D.W.; Jurancich M. Effect of High-Intensity Interval Training on Cardiovascular Function, $\dot{V}O_2$max, and Muscular Force. *Journal of Strength and Conditioning Research.* January 2012: 26(1) p. 138-145.

Aulik, I.V. Opredileierabotasposobnosti v clinike i sporte. Mosvka: Medicina, 1990. p. 234.

Barcelos, L.C., Nunes, P.R.P., Ferreira de Souza, L.R.M., Alves de Oliveira, A., Furlanetto, R., Marocolo, M., Orsatti, F.L. Low-load resistance training promotes muscular adaptation regardless of vascular occlusion, load, or volume. Eur J Appl Physiol, Mar 3, 2015.

Bickel, C.S., Cross J.M., Bamman M.M. Exercise dosing to retain resistance training adaptations in young and older adults. *Med Sci Sports Exerc.* 2011 Jul;43(7):1177-87.

Billat V.L., Slawinksi J., Bocquet V., Chassaing P., Demarle A., Koralsztein J.P. Very short (15s-15s) interval-training around the critical velocity allows middle-aged runners to maintain $\dot{V}O_2$max for 14 minutes. *Int J Sports Med.* 2001 Apr;22(3):201-8.

Billat, V.L., Hill, D.W., Pinoteau, J., Petit, B. and Koralsztein, J.P. Effect of protocol on determination of velocity at $\dot{V}O_2$max and on its time to exhaustion. *Archives of Physiology and Biochemistry*, 104(3), 313-321, 1996.

Bloomquist, K., et al. Effect of range of motion in heavy load squatting on muscle and tendon adaptations. *European Journal of Applied Physiology*, v. 113, n. 8, p. 2133-2142, 2013.

Booth, F.W. Effects of endurance exercise on cytochrome C turnover in skeletal muscle. *Annals of the New York Academy of Sciences*, v. 301, p. 431-9, 1977.

Brandon Richey, January 23, 2018, 3 Top HIIT Workouts For MMA Fitness, BrandonRicheyfitness.com.

Buchheit, M., and Laursen, P.B. (2013). High-intensity interval training, solutions to the programming puzzle. Sports medicine, 43(5), 313-338.

Carpenter, S., and Karpati, G. Pathology of skeletal muscle. New York: Churchill-Livingstone, 1984. p. 149-309.

Carroll, T.J.; Riek, S.; Carson, R.G. Neural adaptations to resistance training. *Sports Medicine*, v. 31, n. 12, p. 829-840, 2001.

Cheetham, M.E., Boobis, L.H., Brooks, S., Williams, C. Human muscle metabolism during sprint running. *Journal of Applied Physiology* (1985), v. 61, n. 1, p. 54-60, 1986.

Cintineo, H., Freidenreich, D., Blaine, C., Cardaci, T., Pelligrino, J., Arent, S. (2018). Acute physiological responses to an intensity and time under tension equated single vs. multiple set resistance training bout in trained men. *Journal of Strength and Conditioning Research*, 00(00)/1–9.

Cox, M.; Bennett III, J.B.; Dudley, G. Exercise training-induced alterations of cardiac morphology. *Journal of Applied Physiology*, v. 61, n. 3, p. 926-31, 1986.

Cox, V.M., Williams, P.E., Wright, H., James, R.S., Gillott, K.L., Young, I.S., Goldspink, D.F. Growth induced by incremental static stretch in adult rabbit latissimus dorsi muscle. *Exp Physiol*, v. 85, n. 2, p. 193-202, Mar 2000.

Dankel, S.J., Counts, B.R., Barnett, B.E., Buckner, S.L., Abe, T., Loenneke, J.P. Muscle adaptations following 21 consecutive days of strength test familiarization compared with traditional training. *Muscle and Nerve*, v. 56, n. 2, p. 307-314, 2017.

De Salles, B.F., Simão, R., Miranda, H., Bottaro, M., Fontana, F., Willardson, J.M. Strength increases in upper and lower body are larger with longer inter-set rest intervals in trained men. *J Sci Med Sport*, v. 13, n. 4, p. 429-33, Jul 2010.

de Souza, T.P. Jr, Fleck, S.J., Simão, R., Dubas, J.P., Pereira, B., de Brito Pacheco, E.M., da Silva, A.C., de Oliveira, P.R. Comparison between constant and decreasing rest intervals: influence on maximal strength and hypertrophy. *J Strength Cond Res.* 2010 Jul;24(7):1843-50.

Delavier, F. (2011) Guia dos: Movimentos de musculacao (5th ed.) Barueri,SP: Editora Manola.

Dias, S.B.C.D.; Oliveira, E.B.; Júnior, A.G.B. (2017) Teoria e Prática do treinamento para o MMA /São Paulo, SP: Phorte Editora.

Dias, S.B.C.D.; Seluianov, V.N.; Lopes, L.A.S. Isoton: uma nova teoria e metodologia para o fitness. Curitiba: Editora Jurua, 2017.

Dixson, M. (2017) Fast-track triathlete: balancing a big life with big performance in long-course. Triathlon Paperback: October 18, 2017.

Dudley, G.A.; Abraham, W.M.; Terjung, R.L. Influence of exercise intensity and duration on biochemical adaptations in skeletal muscle. *Journal of Applied Physiology: Respiratory, Environmental and Exercise Physiology*, v. 53, n. 4, p. 844-50, 1982.

Dupont, G., Akakpo, K., Berthoin, S. The Effect of In-Season, High-Intensity Interval Training in Soccer Players. *Journal of Strength and Conditioning Research*: August 2004 vol. 18, issue 3, p 584–589.

Flann, K.L., LaStayo, P.C., McClain, D.A., Hazel, M., Lindstedt, S.L. Muscle damage and muscle remodeling: no pain, no gain? *J Exp Biol.* 2011 Feb 15;214(Pt 4):674-9.

Fridén, J.; Seger, J.; Ekblom, B. Sublethal muscle fibre injuries after high-tension anaerobic exercise. *European Journal of Applied Physiology and Occupational Physiology*, v. 57, n. 3, p. 360-8, 1988.

Friel, J., and Byrn, G. (2003). Going Long: Training for Ironman-Distance Triathlons. VeloPress.

Fry, A.C. The role of resistance exercise intensity on muscle fiber adaptations. *Sports Med.* 2004;34(10):663-79. Review.

Gayeski, T.; Honlg, C.R. O2 gradients from sarcolemma to cell interior in red muscle at maximal $\dot{V}O_2$. *American Journal of Physiology*, v. 251, n. 4, part 2, p. H789-99, 1986.

Gibala, M.J., Little, J.P., MacDonald, M.J., and Hawley, J.A. (2012). Physiological adaptations to low-volume, high-intensity interval training in health and disease. *The Journal of Physiology*, 590: 1077-1084. doi:10.1113/jphysiol.2011.224725

Glaister, M., Stone, M.H., Stewart, A.M., Hughes, M., Moir, G.L. The influence of recovery duration on multiple sprint cycling performance. *J Strength Cond Res.* 2005 Nov;19(4):831-7.

Gollnick, P.D. Metabolic regulation in skeletal muscle: influence of endurance training as exerted by mitochondrial protein concentration. *Acta Physiologica Scandinavica*, v. 128, n. 556, p. 53-66, 1986. Supplement.

Goodman, C.A. The role of mTORC1 in regulating protein synthesis and skeletal muscle mass in response to various mechanical stimuli. *Rev Physiol Biochem Pharmacol*, v. 166, p. 43-95, 2014.

Gundersen, K. Muscle memory and a new cellular model for muscle atrophy and hypertrophy. *Journal of Experimental Biology*, v. 219, n. 2, p. 235-242, 2016.

Guyton, A.C.; Hall, J.E. Tratado de fisiologia médica. 9. ed. Rio de Janeiro: Guanabara Koogan, 1997.

Hackney, K.J., Engels, H.J., Gretebeck, R.J. Resting energy expenditure and delayed-onset muscle soreness after full-body resistance training with an eccentric concentration. *The Journal of Strength and Conditioning Research*, v. 22, n. 5, p. 1602-1609, 2008.

Häkkinen, K., Alen, M., Kraemer, W.J., et al., Neuro-muscular adaptations during concurrent strength and endurance training versus strength training. *Eur. J. Appl. Physiol.*, 2003, vol. 89, no. 1, p. 42.

Harris, R.C., Edwards, R.H.T., Hultman, E., Nordesjö, L.O., Nylind, B., Sahlin, K. The time course of phosphorylcreatine resynthesis during recovery of the quadriceps muscle in man. *Pflügers Archiv*, v. 367, n. 2, p. 137-142, 1976.

Hartmann, J., Tünnemann, H. Modernes krafttraining. Berlin: Sportverlag, 1989. p. 335.

Henneman, E., Somjen, G., and Carpenter, D.O., Functional significance of cell size in spinal motoneurons. *J. Neurophysiol.*, 1965, vol. 28, p. 560.

Hoeger, W.K., and Hoeger, S.A. *Principles and Labs for Fitness and Wellness*, 13th ed, 2014. Cengage Learning.

Holloszy, J. Adaptation of skeletal muscle to endurance exercise. *Med. and Sci. in Sports*, 7, 3, 1975, p. 155-164.

Holloszy, J.O. Biochemical adaptations in muscle: effects of exercise on mitochondrial oxygen uptake and respiratory enzyme activity in skeletal muscle. *Journal of Biology Chemistry*, v. 242, n. 9, p. 2278-82, 1967.

Holmyard, D.J., Cheetham, M.E., Lakomy, H.K.A., and Williams, C. (1988). Effect of recovery duration on performance during multiple treadmill sprints. Science and football, 134-142.

Hoppeler, G. Effektivnyy nutriskelt nimishitsi pod vliyanie fiziceskie nagruski. TSOONTI, v. 6, p. 3-48, 1987.

Howe, L.P., Read, P., Waldron, M. (2017). Muscle hypertrophy: A narrative review on training principles for increasing muscle mass. *Strength and Conditioning Journal*, v. 39 no. 5 (October 2017), 72-81.

Hubal, M.J., Heather G.D., Thompson P.D., Thomas P.B., Hoffman E.P., Angelopoulos T., Gordon, P., Pescatello L., Richard L., Priscilla M. Variability in muscle size and strength gain after unilateral resistance training. *Medicine and Science in Sports and Exercise*, v. 37, n. 6, p. 964-972, 2005.

Hug, F., Marqueste, T., Le Fur, Y., Cozzone, P.J., Grélot, L. and Bendahan, D., Selective training-induced thigh muscles hypertrophy in professional road cyclists. *European Journal of Applied Physiology*, 97(5), 591-597, 2006.

Hutchinson, A. (2018). How Heat Therapy Could Boost Your Performance.

Hutchinson, A., and Gladwell, M. (2018). Endure: Mind, body, and the curiously elastic limits of human performance. HarperCollins.

Jacobs, I., Tesch, P.A., Bar-Or, O., Karlsson, J., Dotan, R. Lactate in human skeletal muscle after 10 and 30 s of supramaximal exercises. *Journal of Applied Physiology: Respiratory, Environmental and Exercise Physiology*, v. 55, n. 2, p. 365-7, 1983.

Jäger R., Kerksick, C., Campbell, B., Cribb, P., Wells, S., Skwiat, T., Purpura, M., Ziegenfuss, T., Ferrando, A., Arent, S. et al. (2017) International society of sports nutrition position stand: protein and exercise. *Journal of the International Society of Sports Nutrition*, 14(20). doi 10.1186/s12970-017-0177-8.

James, R. S., Cox, V. M., Young, I. S., Altringham, J. D., and Goldspink, D. F. (1997). Mechanical properties of rabbit latissimus dorsi muscle after stretch and/or electrical stimulation. Journal of Applied Physiology, 83(2), 398-406.

James, R.S., Altringham, J.D., Goldspink, D.F. The mechanical properties of fast and slow skeletal muscles of the mouse in relation to their locomotory function. *J Exp Biol*, v. 198, n. Pt 2, p. 491-502, Feb 1995.

Joel J. Never Gas Out- MMA Interval Training, https://www.8weeksout.com/2011/09/28/never-gas-out-mma-interval-training/.

Karlsson, J.; Piehl, K.; Knuttgen, H. Performance and muscle metabolite changes in exercise with repeated maximal dynamic contractions. *International Journal of Sports Medicine*, v. 2, n. 2, p. 110-3, 1981.

Karpman, V.L.; Belosorkovck, Z.B.; Gudkov, I.A. Investigatsi i rabotosposobnosti sportmenov. Moskva: Fizkultura i Sport, 1974. 96 p.

Karpman, V.L., Kruchov, S.V., Borlcova, I.A. Tserdsa i rabotosposobnosti sportmenov. Moskva: Fizkultura i Sport, 1978. 120 p.

Kellogg, E., Cantacessi, C., McNamer, O., Holmes, H., von Bargen, R., Ramirez, R., Gallagher, D., Vargas, S., Santia, B., Rodriguez, K. and Astorino, T.A. Comparison of psychological and physiological responses to imposed vs. self-selected high-intensity interval training. *The Journal of Strength and Conditioning Research*, 33(11), 2945-2952, 2019.

King, I. *How to Write Strength Training Programs*. Toowong (AUS): Kings Sport Publishing. 123, 1998.

Kotsa, A.M. Fiziologiya myshechnyye deyatelnost. Moskva: Fizkultura i Sport, 1982. p. 444.

Kotsa, A.M. Sportivnie fiziologii. Moskva: Fizkultura i Sport, 1986. p. 240.

Kraemer, W.J., Patton, J.F., Gordon, S.E., et al., Compatibility of high-intensity strength and endurance Training on hormonal and skeletal muscle adaptations, *J. Appl. Physiol.*, 1995, vol. 78, no. 3, p. 976.

Kubo, K., Ohgo, K., Takeishi, R., Yoshinaga, K., Tsunoda, N., Kanehisa, H. and Fukunaga, T. Effects of isometric training at different knee angles on the muscle–tendon complex in vivo. *Scandinavian Journal of Medicine and Science in Sports*, 16(3), 159-167, 2006.

Lasevicius, T., Ugrinowitsch, C., Schoenfeld, B.J., Roschel, H., Tavares, L.D., Oliveira De Souza, E., Laurentino, G., and Tricoli, V. (2018) Effects of different intensities of resistance training with equated volume load on muscle strength and hypertrophy, European Journal of Sport Science, 18:6, 772-780, DOI: 10.1080/17461391.2018.1450898

Lauersen, J,B, Bertelsen, D.M., Andersen, L.B. The effectiveness of exercise interventions to prevent sports injuries: a systematic review and meta-analysis of randomised controlled trials. *Br J Sports Med*, v. 48, n. 11, p. 871-877, 2014.

Laursen, P. B., and Jenkins, D. G. (2002). The scientific basis for high-intensity interval training. Sports medicine, 32(1), 53-73.

Lorenzo, S., Halliwill, J.R., Sawka, M.N., and Minson, C.T. Heat acclimation improves exercise performance. *Journal of Applied Physiology*, 109(4), pp.1140-1147, 2010.

Lusikov, V.N. Regulirovaniye formirovaniya mitokhondrii: molekulyarnyy aspekt. Moskva: Nauka, 1980.

Maksimov, D.V., Seluianov, V.N., and Tabakov, S.E. Fizicheskaia Podgotovka Edinobortsiev. Moskva: TVT Division, 2011.

Martineau, L.C. and Gardiner, P.F. Insight into skeletal muscle mechanotransduction: MAPK activation is quantitatively related to tension. *Journal of Applied Physiology*, v. 91, n. 2, p. 693-702, 2001.

Mattocks, K.T., Buckner, S.L., Jessee, M.B., Dankel, S.J., Mouser, J.G., and Loenneke, J.P. (2017). Practicing the test produces strength equivalent to higher volume training. *Medicine and science in sports and exercise*, 49(9), 1945-1954.

Maughan, R., Gleeson, M., and Greenhaff, P.L. *Biochemistry of exercise and training*. Oxford: Oxford University, 1997.

McArdle, W.D., Katch, F.I., and Katch, V.L. *Essentials of exercise physiology*, fifth edition. Lippincott Williams & Wilkins. 2016.

McCall, G., Grindeland, R., Roy, R., and Edgerton, V. Muscle afferent activity modulates bioassayable growth hormone in human plasma. *J. Appl. Physiol.*, 2000, vol. 89, p. 1137.

Meaghen, B. (2016). The Surprising Benefits of training in the Heat. https://www.outsideonline.com/health/surprising-benefits-training-heat/.

Meerson, F.Z. Adaptatsii serdtsa c nagruskoi. Moskva: Nauka, 1975. 263 p.

Meerson, F.Z. Adaptatsii stress i profiliatsii. Moskva: Nauka, 1981. 278 p.

Meerson, F.Z. Miokard pri giperfunktsii, gipertrofii i nedostatochnosti serdtsa. Moskva: Meditsina, 1965. 119.

Mitchell, C. J., Churchward-Venne, T. A., West, D. W., Burd, N. A., Breen, L., Baker, S. K., and Phillips, S. M. (2012). Resistance exercise load does not determine training-mediated hypertrophic gains in young men. Journal of applied physiology, 113(1), 71-77.

Mujika, I. (2013). Endurance training. Science and Practice. Ann Jones.

Mujika, I. (2009). Tapering and peaking for optimal performance. Champaign, IL: Human Kinetics.

Nikityuk, B.A. and Talko, V.I. Adaptatsii sistem serdechno sosudistoy c dolgonitelnoy uprazhneniye. Teoriya i Praktika Fizicheskoy Kultury, v. 1, 1991. p. 23-5.

Nosaka, K., and Clarkson, P.M. Muscle damage following repeated bouts of high force eccentric exercise. *Med Sci Sports Exerc*, v. 27, n. 9, p. 1263-9, Sep 1995.

Ogasawara, R., Loenneke, J. P., Thiebaud, R. S., and Abe, T. (2013). Low-load bench press training to fatigue results in muscle hypertrophy similar to high-load bench press training. International Journal of Clinical Medicine, 4(02), 114.

Ostrowski, K.J., Wilson, G.J., Weatherby, R., Murphy, P.W., and Lyttle, A.D. (1997). The effect of weight training volume on hormonal output and muscular size and function. Journal of strength and Conditioning Research, 11, 148-154.

Paoli, A., Moro, T., and Bianco, A. Lift weights to fight overweight. *Clin Physiol Funct Imaging*, v. 35, n. 1, p. 1-6, Jan 2015.

Platonov, V.N. *Adaptatsia v sporte*. Kiev: Sdorovia, 1988.

Platonov, V.N. Obshaia teoriya podgotovki sportmenov v olimpiskom sporte. Kiev: Olimpiskaia Literatura, 1997.

Platonov, V.N. Podgotovka kvalitsitsirovannyj sportmenov. Moskva: Fizkultura i Sport, 1986.

Platonov, V.N. Teoria geral do treinamento desportivo olímpico. Porto Alegre: Artmed, 2004.

Popov, D.V., Tsvirkun, D.V., Netreba, A.I., et al., Hormonal adaptation determines the increase in muscle mass and strength during low-intensity strength training without relaxation, *Human Physiol.*, 2006, vol. 32, no. 5, p. 609.

Salminen, A., Hongisto, K., and Vihko, V. Lysosomal changes related to exercise injuries and training-induced protection in mouse skeletal muscle. *Acta Physiol. Scand.*, 1984, 72, 3, p. 249-253.

Sapega, A., Sokolow, D., Graham, T., and Chance, B. Phosphorus nuclear magnetic resonance: a non-invasive technique for the study of muscle bioenergetics during exercise. *Med. And Sci. Sports Exerc.* 19, 1987, 4, p. 410-420.

Sarsania, S.K., Seluianov V.N. Analiza dinamike trenirovoch noy gruskev sokokvalifikatsi i sportsmenov v godichinie sicle podgotovki: metodicheskaia recomendatsii. Moskva: RGUFK, 1982. p. 32.

Sayers, S.P., Clarkson, P.M. Force recovery after eccentric exercise in males and females. *European Journal of Applied Physiology*, v. 84, n. 1-2, p. 122-126, 2001.

Schantz, P.G. Plasticity of human skeletal muscle. *Acta Physiol. Scand.* 128, 1986, p. 7-62.

Schmeling, M.D. Structuramichtsii i gipoksii na visate. Moskva: Nauka, 1985. p. 95.

Schoenfeld B.J. *Science and Development of Muscle Hypertrophy.* Champaign, IL: Human Kinetics, 2016. pp. 51–56.

Schoenfeld, B.J., Contreras, B., Krieger, J., Grgic, J., Delcastillo, K., Belliard, R., and Alto, A. (2019). Resistance training volume enhances muscle hypertrophy but not strength in trained men. *Medicine and Science in Sports and Exercise*, 51(1), 94.

Schoenfeld, B.J., Ogborn, D., and Krieger, J.W. Dose-response relationship between weekly resistance training volume and increases in muscle mass: A systematic review and meta-analysis. *J Sports Sci* 19: 1-10, 2016.

Schoenfeld, B.J., Ogborn, D., and Krieger, J.W. Dose-response relationship between weekly resistance training volume and increases in muscle mass: A systematic review and meta-analysis. *Journal of Sports Sciences*, v. 35, n. 11, p. 1073-1082, 2017.

Schoenfeld, B.J., Peterson, M.D., Ogborn, D., Contreras, B., and Sonmez, G.T. (2015). Effects of low-vs. high-load resistance training on muscle strength and hypertrophy in well-trained men. *The Journal of Strength & Conditioning Research*, 29(10), 2954-2963.

Seluianov, V.N., and Sarsania, S.K. Fiziologicheskiemcanism i metodiopredleniaaerobinie i anaerobnieparogi. Teoriya i Praktika Fizicheskoy Kultury, v. 10, p. 10-18, 1991.

Seluianov, V.N. Isoton: texnologi izdorovitelnom fizijesko i culturii. Teoriya i Praktika Fiziches koy Kultury, v. 8, p. C49-54, 2001.

Seluianov, V.N. Sarsania, S.K. Caminhos para o aumento da capacidade de trabalho esportivo. Recomendação metodológica. GTSOLIFK, 1987.

Seluianov, V.N. Teoria e prática da didática da educação de desenvolvimento na formação de especialistas em educação física. Laboratório de pesquisa da Rússia – Supervisor V.N. Seluyanov. - M: Cultura Física, Educação e Ciência, 1996.

Seluianov, V.N., Sarsania, S.K. et al. Classificação das cargas físicas na teoria da preparação física. Teoria e prática da cultura física, 1990, 12, p. 2-8.

Seluianov, V.N., Dias, B.C.D., and Andrade, S.L.F. *Musculação*: nova concepção russa de treinamento. Curitiba: Juruá, 2008.

Seluianov, V.N., Dias, S.B.C.D., Andrade, S.L.F. Musculação: nova concepção russa de treinamento. Curitiba: Editora Juruá, Segunda Edição, 2012.

Seluianov, V.N., Sarsania, S.K., Sarsania, K.S. Futebol: aspectos fisiológicos e metodológicos: tradução de Stefane Dias; Manuel Garrido; André Brauer; Tone Panassollo - Curitiba: Editora Juruá, 5th ED. 2011.

Spriet, L.L., Lindinger, M.I., McKelvie, R.S., Heigenhauser, G.J., and Jones, N.L. (1989). Muscle glycogenolysis and H+ concentration during maximal intermittent cycling. Journal of applied physiology, 66(1), 8-13.

Staron, R.S., Leonardi, M.J., Karapondo, D.L., Malicky, E.S., Falkel, J.E., Hagerman, F.C. and Hikida, R.S. Strength and skeletal muscle adaptations in heavy-resistance-trained women after detraining and retraining. *Journal of Applied Physiology*, 70(2), 631-640, 1991.

Stroeve, P. Myoglobin-facilitated oxygen transport in heterogeneous red muscle tissue. *Annals of Biomedical Engineering*, v. 10, n. 2, p. 49-70, 1982.

Sundberg, C.J. Exercise and Training during Graded Leg Ischemia in Healthy Men with Special Reference to Effects on Skeletal Muscle. *Acta Physiol. Scand. Suppl.*, 1994, vol. 615, p. 1.

Suslov, F.P. Teoriya i metodica sporta: uchebnoe pocobie dlia utchilich olimpiskovo reserva. Moskva: GKRFFKT, 1997.

Takarada, Y., Nakamura, Y., Aruga, S., et al., Rapid increase in plasma growth hormone after low-intensity resistance exercise with vascular occlusion, *J. Appl. Physiol.*, 2000, vol. 88, no. 1, p. 61.

Terjung, R.L. The turnover of cytochrome c in different skeletal-muscle fibre types of the rat. *Biochemistry Journal*, v. 178, n. 3, p. 569-74, 1979.

Thorstensson, A., Sjödln, B., and Karlsson, J. Enzyme activities and muscle strength after "sprint training" in man. *Acta Physiologica Scandinavica*, v. 94, n. 3, p. 313-8, 1975.

Tidball, J.G. Mechanical signal transduction in skeletal muscle growth and adaptation. *J Appl Physiol* (1985), v. 98, n. 5, p. 1900-8, May 2005.

Vigil., J. (1995). Road To The Top. Morning Star Communications; 1st edition (November 1, 1995).

Vinogradova, O.L., Popov, D.V., Netreba, A.I., et al. Optimization of training: new developments in safe strength training. *Hum Physiol* 2013;39(5):511–23.

Viru, M. Mecanismos hormonais de adaptação ao treinamento. L.: Ciência, 1981.

Viru, M., Jansson, E., Viru, A., and Sundberg, C.J., Effect of Restricted Blood Flow on Exercise-Induced Hormone Changes in Healthy Men, Eur. J. Appl. Phys- iol. *Occup. Physiol.*, 1998, vol. 77, no. 6, p. 517.

Volkov, N.I.; Sarsania, S.K., Seluianov V.N. Ingestão de preparados, creatina e aminoácido para o aumento da capacidade de trabalho e efetividade do treinamento no esporte. Recomendação metodológica. M.: RIO GTSOLIFK., 1983.

Volkov, V.I. Bioenergetica napriajonei muichnoi deatelnosti cheloveka i sposobi povichenia rabotasposobnosti sportsmenov. Moskva: Nauka, 1990.

Vorobiov, A.H. Tiajoeliatleticheskii sport: osherki po sportivnoi trenirovki. Moskva: Fizkultura i Sport, 1977.

Walker, J.B. Creatine: biosynthesis, regulation, and function. *Adv. Enzymol. Relat. Areas Mol. Med.*, 1979, 50, p. 177-242.

West, D.W., and Phillips, S.M. Anabolic processes in human skeletal muscle: restoring the identities of growth hormone and testosterone. *The Physician and Sports Medicine*, v. 38, n. 3, p. 97-104, 2010.

Westerblad, H., Allen, D.G., and Lannergren, J. Muscle fatigue: lactic acid or inorganic phosphate the major cause? *News Physiol Sci*, v. 17, p. 17-21, Feb 2002.

Weston, A.R., Myburgh, K.H., Lindsay, F.H., Dennis, S.C., Noakes, T.D., and Hawley, J.A. (1997). Skeletal muscle buffering capacity and endurance performance after high-intensity interval training by well-trained cyclists. Eur J Appl Physiol, 75, 7-13.

Zatsiorsky, V.M. Fisicheskie kachestva sportsmena. Moskva: Fizkultura i Sport, 1970.

Zourdos, M.C., Dolan, C., Quiles, J.M., Klemp, A., Jo, E., Loenneke, J.P., Blanco, R., Whitehurst, M. Eficacia del entrenamiento diario de una repetición de máximo peso en levantadores de pesas bien entrenados: una serie de casos. *Nutr Hosp.* 2016 Mar 25;33(2):129.

Chapter 3

Ahtiainen, J.P., Pakarinen, A., Kraemer, W.J., Häkkinen, K. Acute hormonal and neuromuscular responses and recovery to forced vs maximum repetitions multiple resistance exercises. *International Journal of Sports Medicine*, v. 24, n. 6, p. 410-8, 2003.

Alekseev, G.A. *Vliyaniyenazhruskirasznapravlennosti v sprinterskisredinidistancie.* Moskva: RGFK, 1981. p. 22.

Alm, P., Yu, J. Physiological characters in mixed martial arts. *American Journal of Sports Science*, v. 1, n. 2, p. 12-17, 2013.

American Alliance for Health, Physical Education, Recreation, and Dance. *Youth Fitness Test Manual*, Washington, DC: AAHPERD Publications, 1958.

American College of Sports Medicine. *ACSM's Resources Manual For Guidelines For Exercise Testing and Prescription.* 6th ed. Philadelphia, PA: Lippincott Williams and Wilkins, 2009.

American College of Sports Medicine (ACSM). *ACSM's Resources For The Group Exercise Instructor.* Philadelphia, PA: Lippincott Williams and Wilkins, 2012.

American College of Sports Medicine (ACSM). *ACSM's Guidelines For Exercise Testing And Prescription.* Philadelphia, PA: Lippincott Williams and Wilkins, 2014.

Araújo, C.G.S. Flexiteste: uma nova versão dos mapas de avaliação. *Kinesis*, v. 2, p. 251-67, 1986.

Arruga, S., Tetsuya, O., Kei, A., Yasuhiro, Y., Hidetoshi, N., Hidekaru, S., Ken, Ukubata. Measurement of barbell lifting capacity and making strength standards in Judo Team. *Tokai Journal of Sports Medical Science Research Institute of Sports Medical Science*, Tokai, v. 15, n. 1, p. 7-17, 2003.

Aulik, I.V. *Opredileierabotasposobnosti v clinike i sporte.* Mosvka: Medicina, 1990. p. 234.

Baechle, T. and Earle, R. (2020) *Weight Training: Steps to Success* (5th edition). Champaign, IL: Human Kinetics.

Baker, D. Essential Guide to VBT par 1, 2, 3. 2018.

Bandler, R., Grinder, J. *Estrutura da magia.* 2. ed. Rio de Janeiro: LTC, 1982.

Barley, O.R., Chapman, D.W., Guppy, S.N., and Abbiss, C.R. (2019). Considerations when assessing endurance in combat sport athletes. Frontiers in physiology, 10, 205. https://doi.org/10.3389/fphys.2019.00205

Billat, V. and Koralsztein, J.P. (1996). Significance of the velocity at $\dot{V}O_2$ max and time to exhaustion at this velocity. *Sports medicine* (Auckland, N.Z.). 22. 90-108.

Billat, V.L., Hill, D.W., Pinoteau, J., Petit, B., and Koralsztein, J.P. Effect of protocol on determination of velocity at O2 max and on its time to exhaustion. *Archives of Physiology and Biochemistry*, 104(3), 313-321, 1996.

Billat, V.L. Interval training for performance: a scientific and empirical practice. Special recommendations for middle- and long-distance running. Part 1: aerobic interval training. *Sports Medicine*, v. 31, n. 1, p. 13-31, 2001.

Bjorntorp, P. Importance of fat as a support nutrient for energy: Metabolism of athletes. *Journal of Sport Sciences*, v. 9, n. special, p. 71-6, 1991.

Booth, F.W. Effects of endurance exercise on cytochrome C turnover in skeletal muscle. *Annals of the New York Academy of Sciences*, v. 301, p. 431-9, 1977.

Brown, L.E., Weir, J.P. ASEP procedures recommendation I: accurate assessment of muscular strength and power. *Journal of Exercise Physiology Online*, v. 4, n. 3, 2001.

Brzycki, M. Strength testing: predicting a one-rep max from repetitions to fatigue. *Journal of Physical Education, Recreation and Dance*, v. 64, p. 88-90, 1993.

Bueno, J.C.A., Faro, H., Lenetsky, S., Gonçalves, A.F., Dias, S.B.C.D., Ribeiro, A.L.B., da Silva, B.V.C., Filho, C.A.C., de Vasconcelos, B.M., Serrão, J.C., Andrade, A., Souza-Junior, T.P., & Claudino, J.G. (2022). Exploratory systematic review of mixed martial arts: an overview of performance of importance factors with over 20,000 athletes. *Sports*, 10(6), 80.

Carpenter, S., Karpa ti, G. *Pathology of Skeletal Muscle.* New York: Churchill-Livingstone, 1984. p. 149-309.

Cheetham, M.E., Boobis L.H., Brooks, S., Williams, C. Human muscle metabolism during sprint running. *Journal of Applied Physiology (1985)*, v. 61, n. 1, p. 54-60, 1986.

Christienssen, E. Zubervollarbeit und zubervolltraining. *International Zeitschrift fur Angewandte Physiology Einschliesslich Arbeitsphysiologie*, v. 18, p. 345-96, 1960.

Clarkson, P.M. Minerals: exercise performance and supplementation in athletes. *Journal of Sports Sciences*, v. 9, p. 91-116, 1991.

Cox, M., Bennett III, J.B., Dudley, G. Exercise training-induced alterations of cardiac morphology. *Journal of Applied Physiology*, v. 61, n. 3, p. 926-31, 1986.

da Silva Santos, J.F. and Franchini, E., 2016. Is frequency speed of kick test responsive to training? A study with taekwondo athletes. *Sport Sciences for Health*, 12(3), pp. 377-382.

da Silva Santos, J.F., Valenzuela, T. and Franchini, E. (2015). Can different conditioning activities and rest intervals affect the acute performance of taekwondo turning kick? *Journal of Strength & Conditioning Research*, 29, 1640-1647.

Dantas, E.H.M. *Flexibilidade: Alongamento e Flexionamento.* 5. ed. Rio de Janeiro: Shape, 2005.

De Vries, H.A., and Housh, T.J. *Physiology of Exercise.* 5th ed. Madison, WI: WCB Brown and Benchmark, 1994.

Del Coso, J., Hamouti, N., Aguado-Jimenez, R., and Mora-Rodriguez, R. (2009). Respiratory compensation and blood pH regulation during variable intensity exercise in trained versus untrained subjects. *Eur. J. Appl. Physiol.* 107, 83-93.

Dias, S.B.C.D., Oliveira, E.B. A ciência do alongamento. *Tatame: a revista do lutador*, v. 214, p. 80-3, 2013a.

_____. Circuito de força e velocidade. *Tatame: a revista do lutador*, v. 205, p. 88-91, 2013b.

_____. Circuito de MMA outdoor. *Tatame: a revista do lutador*, v. 200, p. 122-4, 2012a.

_____. Circuito exclusivo para mulheres. *Tatame: a revista do lutador*, v. 208, p. 74-7, 2013c.

_____. Circuito para força de resistência. *Tatame: a revista do lutador*, v. 203, p. 90-3, 2013d.

_____. Força e resistência. *Tatame: a revista do lutador*, v. 213, p. 92-8, 2013e.

_____. Treinamento de MMA adaptado. *Tatame: a revista do lutador*, v. 209, p. 68-72, 2013f.

_____. Treinamento de trocação com elásticos. *Tatame: a revista do lutador*, v. 202, p. 94-5, 2012b.

_____. Treinamento em grupo para lutadores. *Tatame: a revista do lutador*, v. 211, p. 92-5, 2013g.

_____. Treino físico na praia. *Tatame: a revista do lutador*, v. 207, p. 74-7, 2013h.

_____. Tratamento preventivo. *Tatame: a revista do lutador*, v. 206, p. 77-7, 2013i.

Din, P. *Processi raspada v kletke*. Perevod S Angl. Moskva: Mir, 1981.

Dudley, G.A., Abraham, W.M., and Terjung, R.L. Influence of exercise intensity and duration on biochemical adaptations in skeletal muscle. *Journal of Applied Physiology: Respiratory, Environmental and Exercise Physiology*, v. 53, n. 4, p. 844-50, 1982.

Farzad, B., Gharakhanlou, R., Agha-Alinejad, H., Curby, D.G., Bayati, M., Bahraminejad, M., Mäestu, Jarek. Physiological and performance changes from the addition of a sprint interval program to wrestling training. *Journal of Strength and Conditioning Research*, v. 25, n. 9, p. 2392-9, 2011.

Franchini, E., Del Vecchio, F., Sterkowicz, S. (2009). A special judo fitness test classificatory table. *Archives of Budo*. 5. 127-129.

Franchini, E., Del Vecchio, F.B., Matsushigue, K.A., Artioli, G.G. Physiological profiles of elite judo athletes. *Sports Medicine*, v. 41, n. 2, p. 147-66, 2011.

_____. Physical fitness and anthropometrical profile of the Brazilian male judo team. *Journal of Physiological Anthropology*, v. 26, n. 2, p. 59-67, 2007.

Fridén, J. Muscle soreness after exercise: implication of morphological changes. *International Journal of Sports Medicine*, v. 5, p. 57-66, 1984.

Fridén, J., Seger, J., and Ekblom, B. Sublethal muscle fibre injuries after high-tension anaerobic exercise. *European Journal of Applied Physiology and Occupational Physiology*, v. 57, n. 3, p. 360-8, 1988.

Fujise, T., et al. The comparison of strength performance and aerobic capacity between two styles of karatedo athletes. *Bulletin of Niigata University of International Information and Culture, Niigata*, v. 1, n. 2, p. 203-215, 1998.

Fukuda, D.H. (2019). *Assessments for Sport and Athletic Performance*. Champaign, IL: Human Kinetics.

Gayeski, T., and Honig, C.R. O2 gradients from sarcolemma to cell interior in red muscle at maximal $\dot{V}O_2$. *American Journal of Physiology*, v. 251, n. 4, part 2, p. H789-99, 1986.

Ghosh A.K. (2004). Anaerobic threshold: Its concept and role in endurance sport. *The Malaysian journal of medical sciences*, 11(1), 24-36.

Giannichi, R.S., and Marins, J.B. *Avaliação e prescrição de atividade física*: guia prático. 2. ed. Rio de Janeiro: Shape, 1998. p. 96.

Gibson, A.L., Wagner, D.R., and Heyward, V.H. *Advanced fitness assessment and exercise prescription*, 8th ed. (Champaign, IL: Human Kinetics, 2019), 249.

Gochioco, M.K., Brown, L.E., Coburn, J.W., Beam, W., Schick, E., Dabbs, N., Khamoui, A., Tran, T. and Munoz, C. (2011). A comparison of the physiological profiles of mixed martial artists and football, basketball, and baseball players. *Journal of Strength & Conditioning Research*, 25, S55-S56.

Golding, L (ed.). *YMCA fitness testing and assessment manual*, 4th ed. (Champaign, IL: Human Kinetics, 2000).

Gollnick, P.D. Metabolic regulation in skeletal muscle: influence of endurance training as exerted by mitochondrial protein concentration. *Acta Physiologica Scandinavica*, v. 128, n. 556, p. 53-66, 1986. Supplement.

Gollnick, P.D., Piehl, K., and Saltin, B. Selective glycogen depletion pattern in human muscle fibers after exercise of varying intensity and at various pedaling rates. *Journal of Physiology*, v. 241, n. 1, p. 45-57, 1974.

Greenhaff, P.L. Creatine: its role in physical performance and fatigue and its application as a sports food supplement. *Insider*, v. 3, n. 1, p. 1-4, 1995.

Guyton, A.C., and Hall, J.E. *Tratado de fisiologia médica*. 9. ed. Rio de Janeiro: Guanabara Koogan, 1997.

Hartmann, J., Tünnemann, H. *Moderneskrafttraining*. Berlin: Sportverlag, 1989. p. 335.

Henneman, E., Somjen, G., and Carpenter, D.O. Functional significance of cell size in spinal motoneurons. *Journal of Neurophysiology*, v. 28, p. 560-80, 1965.

Hermansen, L. Effect of metabolic changes on force generation in skeletal muscle during maximal exercise. *Ciba Foundation Symposium*, v. 82, p. 75-88, 1981.

Hoeger, W.K., and Hoeger, S.A. *Principles and Labs for Fitness and Wellness.* 13th ed. Boise, ID: Boise State University, 2014.

Holloszy, J.O. Biochemical adaptations in muscle: effects of exercise on mitochondrial oxygen uptake and respiratory enzyme activity in skeletal muscle. *Journal of Biology Chemistry*, v. 242, n. 9, p. 2278-82, 1967.

_____. Muscle metabolism during exercise. *Archives of Physical Medicine and Rehabilitation*, v. 63, n. 5, p. 231, 1982.

Holmyard, D.J., Cheetham, M.E., Lakomy H.K.A., and Williams, C. Effect of recovery duration on performance during multiple treadmill sprints. In: Reilly, T., Lees, A., Davids, K., Murphy, W.J. (Ed.). *Science and Football.* London, New York: E. & F. N. Spon, 1987. p. 134-42.

Hoppeler, G. Effektivnyynutriskeltnimishitsi pod vliyaniefiziceskienagruski. *TSOONTI*, v. 6, p. 3-48, 1987.

Howley, T. *Complete Conditioning for Lacrosse.* Human Kinetics, 2015.

Ivy, J., Katz, A.L., Cutler, C.L., Sherman, W.M. and Coyle, E.F. Muscle glycogen synthesis after exercise: effect of time of carbohydrate ingestion. *Journal of Applied Physiology (1985)*, v. 64, n. 4, p. 1480-5, 1988.

Jacobs, I., Tesh, P.A., Bar-Or, O., Karlsson, J., and Dotan, R. Lactate in human skeletal muscle after 10 and 30 s of supramaximal exercises. *Journal of Applied Physiology: Respiratory, Environmental and Exercise Physiology*, v. 55, n. 2, p. 365-7, 1983.

James, L.P., Beckman, E.M., Kelly, V.G., and Haff, G.G. (2017). The neuromuscular qualities of higher- and lower-level mixed-martial-arts competitors. *International Journal of Sports Physiology and Performance*, 12(5), 612-620.

James, L.P., Haff, G.G., Kelly, V.G., and Beckman, E.M. (2016). Towards a Determination of the Physiological Characteristics Distinguishing Successful Mixed Martial Arts Athletes: A Systematic Review of Combat Sport Literature. *Sports Medicine*, 46(10), 1525-1551.

Jetton, A., Lawrence, M., Meucci, M, Haines, T., Collier, S., Morris, D., and Utter, A. (2013) Dehydration and acute weight gain in mixed martial arts fighters before competition. *Journal of Strength and Conditioning Research* 27(5): 1322-1326.

Jidovtseff, B., Harris, N.K., Crielaard, J.M., and Cronin, J.B. (2011). Using the load-velocity relationship for 1RM prediction. *Journal of Strength and Conditioning Research*, 25(1), 267-270.

Johnson, B.L. and Nelson, J.K. (1979). *Practical Measurements for Evaluation in Physical Education.* 4th ed. Minneapolis: Burgess.

Kaminsky, L. ACSM's *Health-Related Physical Fitness Assessment Manual* (4th ed). Philadelphia, PA: Lippincott Williams and Wilkins, 2014.

Karlsson, J., Piehl, K., and Knuttgen, H. Performance and muscle metabolite changes in exercise with repeated maximal dynamic contractions. *International Journal of Sports Medicine*, v. 2, n. 2, p. 110-3, 1981.

Karpman, V.L., Belosorkovck, Z.B., and Gudkov, I.A. *Investigatsiirabotosposobnostisportmenov.* Moskva: Fizkulturai Sport, 1974. 96 p.

Karpman, V.L., Kruchov, S.V., and Boricova, I.A. *Tserdsairabotosposobnostisportmenov.* Moskva: Fizkulturai Sport, 1978. 120 p.

Katch, V.L., McArdle, W.D., and Katch, F.I. *Essentials of Exercise Physiology.* 4th ed. Philadelphia, PA: Lippincott, Williams and Wilkins, 2011.

Keller, K., and Schwarzkopf, R. Preexercise snacks may decrease exercise performance. *Physician and Sports Med*, v. 12, n. 4, p. 89-91, 1984.

Kotsa, A.M. *Fiziologiyamyshechnyyedeyatelnost.* Moskva: Fizkultura i Sport, 1982. p. 444.

_____. *Sportivniefiziologii.* Moskva: Fizkultura i Sport, 1986. p. 240.

Léger, L.A., Mercier, D., Gadoury, C., Lambert, J. The multistage 20 meter shuttle run test for aerobic fitness. *Journal of Sports Sciences*, v. 6, n. 2, p. 93-101, 1988.

Lemon, P.W., and Mullin, J.P. Effect of initial muscle glycogen levels on protein catabolism during exercise. *Journal of Applied Physiology: Respiratory, Environment and Exercise Physiology*, v. 48, n. 4, p. 624-9, 1980.

Lopez-Laval, I., Sitko, S., Muniz-Pardos, B., Cirer-Sastre, R., and Calleja-Gonzalez, J. (2020). Relationship between bench press strength and punch performance in male professional boxers. *Journal of Strength & Conditioning Research*, 34, 308-312.

Lusikov, V.N. *Regulirovaniyeformirovaniyamitokhondrii*: molekulyarnyyaspekt. Moskva: Nauka, 1980.

Maksimov, D.V., Seluianov, V.N., and Tabakov, S.E. Fizicheskaia Podgotovka Edinobortsiev. Moskva: TVT Division, 2011.

Marinho, B.F., Del Vecchio, F.B., and Franchini, E. Physical fitness and anthropometric profile of mixed martial arts athletes. *Revista de Artes Marciales Asiáticas*, v. 6, n. 2, p. 7-18, 2011.

Matsudo, V.K.R. *Testes em ciências do esporte*. 4. ed. São Caetano do Sul: Centro de Estudos do Laboratório de Aptidão Física de São Caetano, 1987.

Maughan, R., Gleeson, M., and Greenhaff, P.L. *Biochemistry of Exercise and Training*. Oxford: Oxford University, 1997.

McGuigan, M.R. Principles of test selection and administration. In *Essentials of Strength Training and Conditioning*. 4th ed. Haff, GG, and Triplett, NT, eds. Champaign, IL: Human Kinetics, 289, 2016.

McMurray, W.C. *Essentials of Human Metabolism*. 2nd ed. Philadelphia, PA: Lippincott Williams and Wilkins, 1983.

Meerson, F.Z. *Adaptatsii stress iprofiliatsii*. Moskva: Nauka, 1981. p. 278.

Meerson, F.Z. *Adaptatsiiserdtsa c nagruskoi*. Moskva: Nauka, 1975. p. 263.

_____. *Miokardprigiperfunktsii, gipertrofiiinedostatochnostiserdtsa*. Moskva: Meditsina, 1965. p. 119.

Miakinchenko, E.B., and Chestokov, M.P. *Aerobica*: teorii i metodologiizaniatii. Moscou: Division, 2006.

Morrow, J.R., Mood, D.P., Disch, J.G., and Kang, M. *Measurement and evaluation in human performance*, 5th ed. (Champaign, IL: Human Kinetics, 2016), 208.

Naka T., Kanno M., Shidochi S., Sakae K., and Shima N. Characteristics of upper-limb pull power and power endurance in Japanese female wrestlers. *Journal of Strength & Conditioning Research*. May 2021.

Nielsen, B. Diet, vitamins and fluids: intake before and after prolonged exercise. In: Shephard, R., Åstrand, P.O. *Endurance in Sport*. Oxford: Blackwell, 1992.

Nikityuk, B.A., and Talko, V.I. Adaptatsiisistemserdechnososudistoy c dolgonitelnoyuprazhneniye. *Teoriya i PraktikaFizicheskoyKultury*, v. 1, 1991. p. 23-5.

Nissen, S., Panton, L., Wilhelm, R., and Fuller, J. (1996). Effect of metabolite-hydroxy--methylbutyrate (HMB) supplementation on strength and body composition of trained and untrained males undergoing intense resistance training. *Federation of the American Society for Experimental Biology Journal* 10:287.

Norton, K. Standard for anthropometry assessment, In *Kinanthropometry and Exercise Physiology*, 4th ed. 68-137, 2018.

Paiva, L. *Pronto pra guerra*: preparação física para luta e superação. Manaus: OMP, 2009.

Panin, L.E. *Biochemical mechanism of stress*. Novosibirsk: Nauka, 1983.

Platonov, V.N. *Adaptatsia v sporte*. Kiev: Sdorovia, 1988.

_____. *Obshaiateoriyapodgotovkisportmenov v olimpiskomsporte*. Kiev: Olimpiskaia Literatura, 1997.

_____. *Podgotovkakvalitsitsirovannyjsportmenov*. Moskva: Fizkultura i Sport, 1986.

_____. *Teoria geral do treinamento desportivo olímpico*. Porto Alegre: Artmed, 2004.

Popov, D.B. *Factoriogranichivaioshieaerobniurabostposobnosti na urovnieotdelnoimuichtsie u liodei s raslijnimurovnemtrenirobanosti*. Moskva: Nauka, 2007.

Powers, S.K., and Howley, E.T. *Fisiologia do exercício*: teoria e aplicação ao condicionamento e ao desempenho. 3. ed. Barueri: Manole, 2000.

Powers, S.K., Dodd, S., and Garner, R. Precision of ventilatory and gas exchange alterations as a predictor of the anaerobic threshold. *European Journal of Applied Physiology and Occupational Physiology*, v. 52, p. 173-7, 1984.

Prilutski, B.I. Michejnieboli, biszvaniehepriviejnieuprajnenie. *Teoriyai Praktika Fizicheskoy Kultury*, v. 2, p. C16-22, 1989.

Salminen, A., Hongisto, K., and Vihko, V. Lysosomal changes related to exercise injuries and training-induced protection in mouse skeletal muscle. *Acta Physiologica Scandinavica*, v. 120, n. 1, p. 15-9, 1984.

Sanchez-Medina, L., Perez, C.E., and Gonzalez-Badillo, J.J. Importance of the propulsive phase in strength assessment. *Int J Sports Med*, v. 31, n. 2, p. 123-9, Feb 2010.

Santana, J.C. *The essence of Program Design*: The ultimate guide for trainers and coaches. Florida: [s.n.], 2007.

Sapega A.A. , Sokolow, D.P., Graham, T.J., and Chance, B. Phosphorus nuclear magnetic resonance: a non-invasive technique for the study of muscle bioenergetics during exercise. *Medicine and Science in Sports and Exercise*, v. 19, n. 4, p. 410-20, 1987.

Sarsania, S.K., and Seluianov, V.N. *Fizicheskayapodgotovka v sportivnykhigrakh.* Moskva: GTsOLIFK,1990. p. 97.

Sarsania, S.K., and Seluianov, V.N. *Analiza dinamiketrenirovoch noy gruskevsokokvalifikatsiisportsmenov v godichin-iesiclepodgotovki:* metodicheskaiarecomendatsii. Moskva: RGUFK, 1982. p. 32.

Sato, K., Beckham, G.K., Carroll, K., Bazyler, C., Zhanxin, S., and Haff, G. (2015) Validity of wireless device measuring velocity of resistance exercises. *Journal of Trainology.* 4:15-18.

Schantz, P.G. Plasticity of human skeletal muscle with special reference to effects of physical training on enzyme levels of the NADH shuttles and phenotypic expression of slow and fast myofibrillar proteins. *Acta Physiologica Scandinavica,* v. 558 (suppl.), p. 1-62, 1986.

Schick, M., Brown, L.E., Coburn, J.W., Beam, W.C., Schick, E.E., and Dabbs, N.C. Physiological profile of mixed martial artists. *Medicina Sportiva,* v. 14, n. 4, p. 182-7, 2010.

Schmeling, M.D. *Structuramichtsiiigipoksiinavisate.* Moskva: Nauka, 1985. p. 95.

Schuindt, V., and Vieira, F. (2020) International Society for the Advancement of Kinanthropometry (ISAK) Global: international accreditation scheme of the competent anthropometrist. *Revista Brasileira de Cinean-tropometria & Desempenho Humano, v22.*

Seluianov, V.N. *Isoton:* texnologiizdorovitelnomfizijeskoiculturii. *Teoriyai Praktika Fizicheskoy Kultury,* v. 8, p. C49-54, 2001.

Seluianov, V.N. *Teoriyaipraktikadidaktikerasvivaioshevoobujenia v podgotovkespesialistov po fisicheskomuvospitanio:* trudisotrudnikovproblemnoilaboratorii RGUFK. Moskva: Fizkultura Obrozavnie i Nauka, 1996.

Seluianov, V.N., Dias, B.C.D., and Andrade, S.L.F. *Musculação:* nova concepção russa de treinamento. Curitiba: Juruá, 2008.

Seluianov, V.N., and Sarsania, S.K. *Fiziologicheskiemcanism i metodiopredleniaaerobinie i anaerobnieparogi. Teoriyai Praktika Fizicheskoy Kultury,* v. 10, p. 10-18, 1991.

Shir Hamawie. *The beep test audio full.* https://www.youtube.com/watch?v=e0U_yQITBks&sns=em. Accessed March 13, 2017.

Signore, N. *Velocity-Based Training.* Champaign, IL: Human Kinetics, 2022.

Siqueido, A. *Physiological characteristics of competitive mixed martial arts fighters.* 2010. 87 f. Dissertação (Mestrado em Fisiologia do Movimento)-Universidade do Estado da Califórnia, Califórnia, 2010. http://gradworks.umi.com/14/86/1486711.html. Accessed October 23, 2014.

Stöggl, T., and Sperlich, B. (2014). Polarized training has greater impact on key endurance variables than threshold, high intensity, or high volume training. *Front. Physiol.* 5:33.

Stroeve, P. Myoglobin-facilitated oxygen transport in heterogeneous red muscle tissue. *Annals of Biomedical Engineering,* v. 10, n. 2, p. 49-70, 1982.

Suslov, F.P. *Teoriyaimetodicasporta:* uchebnoepocobiedliautchilicholimpiskovoreserva. Moskva: GKRFFKT, 1997.

Tarnopolsky, M.A., Atkinson, S.A., MacDougall, J.D., Chesley, A. Phillips, S., and Schwarcz, H.P. Evaluation of protein requirements for trained strength athletes. *Journal of Applied Physiology,* v. 73, n. 5, p. 1986-95, 1992.

Terjung, R.L. The turnover of cytochrome c in different skeletal-muscle fibre types of the rat. *Biochemistry Journal,* v. 178, n. 3, p. 569-74, 1979.

Thompson J., and Manore, M. *Nutrition for Life.* 3rd ed. London: Pearson, 2013.

Thorstensson, A., Sjödin, B., and Karlsson, J. Enzyme activities and muscle strength after "sprint training" in man. *Acta Physiologica Scandinavica,* v. 94, n. 3, p. 313-8, 1975.

Tritschler, K. *Medida e avaliação em educação física e esportes de Barrow e McGee.* Barueri: Manole, 2003.

UFC Performance Institute. *A Cross Sectional Performance Analysis and Projection of the UFC Athlete* (vol. 2), 2021.

Van Erp-Baart, A.M., Saris, W.H., Binkhorst, R.A., Vos, J.A., and Elvers, J.W. Nationwide survey on nutritional habits in elite athletes. Part I. Energy, carbohydrate, protein, and fat intake. *International Journal of Sports Medicine,* Supl. 1, p. S3-10, 1989.

Villani, R., Tomasso, A., and Angiari, P. Elaboration of a specific test to evaluate the execution time of the circular kick in full contact. *In: Annual Congress of the European College of Sport Science,* 9, 2004.

Volkov, V.I. *Bioenergeticanapriajoneimuichnoideatelnostichelovekaisposobipovicheniarabotasposobnostisportsmenov.* Moskva: Nauka, 1990.

_____. *Biojimiia.* Moskva: Fizkultura i Sport, 1986. 462 p.

Vorobiov, A.H. *Tiajoeliatleticheskii sport:* osherki po sportivnoi trenirovki. Moskva: Fizkultura I Sport, 1977.

Walker, J.B. Creatine: biosynthesis, regulation, and function. *Advances in Enzymology and Related Areas of Molecular Biology*, v. 50, p. 177-242, 1979.

Watson, A.W.S. *Physical Fitness and Athletic Performance: A Guide for Students, Athletes and Coaches*. Routledge, 2014.

Weider, J. *Joe Weider's Mr. Olympia Training Encyclopedia*. New York: McGraw-Hill, 1991.

Williams, M.H. *Nutrition for Fitness and Sport*. 3rd ed. Dubuque, IA: William C. Brown, 1992.

Zatsiorsky, V.M. *Fisicheskiekachestvasportsmena*. Moskva: Fizkultura i Sport, 1970a.

_____. *Fisicheskiekachestvasportsmena*. Moskva: Fizkulturai Sport, 1970b. p. 200.

Chapter 4

Bailey, S.J., Fulford, J., Vanhatalo, A., Winyard, P.G., Blackwell, J.R., DiMenna, F.J., and Jones, A.M. Dietary nitrate supplementation enhances muscle contractile efficiency during knee-extensor exercise in humans. *J Appl Physiol (1985)*, 109(1), 135-148, 2010.

Bailey, S.J., Varnham, R.L., DiMenna, F.J., Breese, B.C., Wylie, L.J., and Jones, A.M. Inorganic nitrate supplementation improves muscle oxygenation, O(2) uptake kinetics, and exercise tolerance at high but not low pedal rates. *J Appl Physiol*, 118(11), 1396-1405, 2015.

Bjorntorp, P. Importance of fat as a support nutrient for energy: metabolism of athletes. *Journal of Sport Sciences*, v. 9, n. special, p. 71-6, 1991.

Burke, L.M., Hawley, J.A., Wong, S.H., and Jeukendrup, A.E. Carbohydrates for training and competition. *J Sports Sci*, 29 Suppl 1, S17-27, 2011.

Burke, L.M. Caffeine and sports performance. *Applied Physiology, Nutrition, and Metabolism*, 33(6), 1319-1334, 2008.

Burke, L.M., and Kiens, B. "Fat adaptation" for athletic performance: the nail in the coffin? *J Appl Physiol*, 100(1), 7-8, 2006.

Campbell, B.I., La Bounty, P.M., and Wilborn, C.D. Dietary Supplements Used in Combat Sports. *Strength and Conditioning Journal*, 33(6), 50-59, 2011.

Cannell, J.J., Hollis, B.W., Sorenson, M.B., Taft, T.N., and Anderson, J.J. Athletic performance and vitamin D. *Med Sci Sports Exerc*, 41(5), 1102-1110, 2009.

Castell, L.M., Stear, S.J., and Burke, L. *Nutritional supplements in sport, exercise and health An A-Z guide.* (1st ed.). Routledge, 2015.

Christienssen, E. Zubervollarbeit und zubervolltraining. *International Zeitschrift fur Angewandte Physiologie Einschliesslich Arbeitsphysiologie*, v. 18, p. 345-96, 1960.

Clarkson, P.M. Minerals: exercise performance and supplementation in athletes. *Journal of Sports Sciences*, v. 9, p. 91-116, 1991.

De Andrade Kratz, C., De Salles Painelli, V., De Andrade Nemezio, K.M., Da Silva, R.P., Franchini, E., Zagatto, A.M., Gualano, B., Artioli, G.G. (2017). Beta-alanine supplementation enhances judo-related performance in highly trained athletes. *J Sci Med Sport*, 20(4), 403-408.

de Azevedo, A.P., Guerra, M.A., Jr., Caldas, L.C., and Guimaraes-Ferreira, L. (2019). Acute caffeine ingestion did not enhance punch performance in professional mixed martial arts athletes. *Nutrients*, 11(6), 1422.

De Vries, H.A., and Housh, T.J. *Physiology of Exercise.* 5th ed. Madison, WI: WCB Brown and Benchmark, 1994.

Dias, Stéfane B.C.D., Oliveira, E.B., Júnior, A.G.B. *Teoria e Prática do treinamento para o MMA /São Paulo*, SP: Phorte Editora, 2017.

Diaz-Lara, F.J., Del Coso, J., Portillo, J., Areces, F., Garcia, J.M., and Abian-Vicen, J. Enhancement of high-intensity actions and physical performance during a simulated Brazilian jiu-jitsu competition with a moderate dose of caffeine. *Int J Sports Physiol Perform*, 11(7), 861-867, 2016.

Donovan, T., Ballam, T., Morton, J.P., and Close, G.L. Beta-alanine improves punch force and frequency in amateur boxers during a simulated contest. *Int J Sport Nutr Exerc Metab*, 22(5), 331-337, 2012.

Duncan, C., Dougall, H., Johnston, P., Green, S., Brogan, R., Leifert, C., Smith, L., Golden, M., Benjamin, N. Chemical generation of nitric oxide in the mouth from the enterosalivary circulation of dietary nitrate. *Nat Med*, 1(6), 546-551, 1995.

Durkalec-Michalski, K., Jeszka, J., and Podgorski, T. The effect of a 12-week beta-hydroxy-beta-methylbutyrate (HMB) Supplementation on highly trained combat sports athletes: a randomised, double-blind, placebo-controlled crossover study. *Nutrients*, 9(7), 753, 2017.

Durkalec-Michalski, K., Zawieja, E.E., Podgorski, T., Zawieja, B.E., Michalowska, P., Loniewski, I., and Jeszka, J. The effect of a new sodium bicarbonate loading regimen on anaerobic capacity and wrestling performance. *Nutrients*, *10*(6), 697, 2018.

Farrokhyar, F., Sivakumar, G., Savage, K., Koziarz, A., Jamshidi, S., Ayeni, O.R., Peterson, D., and Bhandari, M. Effects of vitamin D supplementation on serum 25-hydroxyvitamin D concentrations and physical performance in athletes: A systematic review and meta-analysis of randomized controlled trials. *Sports Med*, *47*(11), 2323-2339, 2017.

Fredholm, B.B., Battig, K., Holmen, J., Nehlig, A., and Zvartau, E.E. Actions of caffeine in the brain with special reference to factors that contribute to its widespread use. *Pharmacol Rev*, *51*(1), 83-133, 1999.

Garlick, P.J. The role of leucine in the regulation of protein metabolism. *J Nutr*, *135*(6 Suppl), 1553s-1556s, 2005.

Garthe, I., and Maughan, R.J. Athletes and supplements: Prevalence and perspectives. *Int J Sport Nutr Exerc Metab*, *28*(2), 126-138, 2018.

Goldstein, E.R., Ziegenfuss, T., Kalman, D., Kreider, R., Campbell, B., Wilborn, C., Taylor, L., Willoughby, D., Stout, J., Graves, B.S., Wildman, R., Ivy, J.L., Spano, M., Smith, A.E., Antonio, J. International society of sports nutrition position stand: caffeine and performance. *J Int Soc Sports Nutr*, *7*(1), 5, 2010.

Gollnick, P.D. Metabolic regulation in skeletal muscle: Influence of endurance training as exerted by mitochondrial protein concentration. *Acta Physiologica Scandinavica*, v. 128, n. 556, Supplement, p. 53-66, 1986.

Gollnick, P.D., Piehl, K., and Saltin, B. Selective glycogen depletion pattern in human muscle fibers after exercise of varying intensity and at various pedaling rates. *Journal of Physiology*, v. 241, n. 1, p. 45-57, 1974.

Greenhaff, P.L. Creatine: its role in physical performance and fatigue and its application as a sports food supplement. *Insider*, v. 3, n. 1, p. 1-4, 1995.

Grossman, A., and Sutton, J.R. Endorphins: What are they? How are they measured? What is their role in exercise? *Med Sci Sports Exerc*, *17*(1), 74-81, 1985.

Hawley, J.A., Schabort, E.J., Noakes, T.D., and Dennis, S.C. Carbohydrate-loading and exercise performance. An update. *Sports Med*, *24*(2), 73-81, 1997.

Haytowitz, D.B., Ahuja, Jaspreet K.C., Wu, Xianli, Somanchi, M., Nickle, M., Nguyen, Quyen A., Roseland, J.M., Williams, J.R., Patterson, K.Y., Li, Y., and Pehrsson, P.R. *USDA National nutrient database for standard reference, legacy release.* Nutrient Data Laboratory, Beltsville Human Nutrition Research Center, ARS, USDA, 2019.

Hermansen, L. Effect of metabolic changes on force generation in skeletal muscle during maximal exercise. *Ciba Foundation Symposium*, v. 82, p. 75-88, 1981.

Hoon, M.W., Jones, A.M., Johnson, N.A., Blackwell, J.R., Broad, E.M., Lundy, B., Rice, A.J., and Burke, L.M. The effect of variable doses of inorganic nitrate-rich beetroot juice on simulated 2,000-m rowing performance in trained athletes. *Int J Sports Physiol Perform*, *9*(4), 615-620, 2014.

Jager, R., Kerksick, C.M., Campbell, B.I., Cribb, P.J., Wells, S.D., Skwiat, T.M., Purpura, M., Ziegenfuss, T.N., Ferrando, A., Arent, S.M., Smith-Ryan, A.E., Stout, J.R., Arciero, P.J., Ormsbee, M.J., Taylor, L.W., Wilborn, C.D., Kalman, D.S., Kreider, R.B., Willoughby, D.S., Hoffman, J.R., Krzykowski, J.L., and Antonio, J. International Society of Sports Nutrition position stand: Protein and exercise. *J Int Soc Sports Nutr*, *14*, 20, 2017.

Jones, A.M. Influence of dietary nitrate on the physiological determinants of exercise performance: a critical review. *Appl Physiol Nutr Metab*, *39*(9), 1019-1028, 2014.

Kalmar, J.M., and Cafarelli, E. Effects of caffeine on neuromuscular function. *J Appl Physiol (1985)*, *87*(2), 801-808, 1999.

Katch, V.L., McArdle, W.D., and Katch, F.I. *Essentials of Exercise Physiology.* 4th ed. Philadelphia, PA: Lippincott, Williams and Wilkins, 2011.

Kreider, R.B., Kalman, D.S., Antonio, J., Ziegenfuss, T.N., Wildman, R., Collins, R., Candow, D.G., Kleiner, S.M., Almada, A.L., and Lopez, H.L. International Society of Sports Nutrition position stand: Safety and efficacy of creatine supplementation in exercise, sport, and medicine. *J Int Soc Sports Nutr*, *14*, 18, 2017.

Lee, E.C., Fragala, M.S., Kavouras, S.A., Queen, R.M., Pryor, J.L., and Casa, D.J. Biomarkers in sports and exercise: Tracking health, performance, and recovery in athletes. *J Strength Cond Res*, *31*(10), 2920-2937, 2017.

Lemon, P.W., and Mullin, J.P. Effect of initial muscle glycogen levels on protein catabolism during exercise. *Journal of Applied Physiology: Respiratory, Environment and Exercise Physiology*, v. 48, n. 4, p. 624-9, 1980.

Lopes-Silva, J.P., Da Silva Santos, J.F., Artioli, G.G., Loturco, I., Abbiss, C., and Franchini, E. Sodium bicarbonate ingestion increases glycolytic contribution and improves performance during simulated taekwondo combat. *Eur J Sport Sci,* 18(3), 431-440, 2018.

López-González, L.M., Sánchez-Oliver, A.J., Mata, F., Jodra, P., Antonio, J., and Domínguez, R. Acute caffeine supplementation in combat sports: a systematic review. *Journal of the International Society of Sports Nutrition,* 15(1), 60, 2018.

Loucks, A.B. Energy balance and body composition in sports and exercise. *J Sports Sci,* 22(1), 1-14, 2004.

Mahan, L.K., Escott-Stump, S., and Krause, M.V. *Krause's Food and Nutrition Therapy.* 12th ed. Philadelphia, Pa., Edinburgh: Elsevier Saunders, 2008.

Martinez-Sanz, J.M., Sospedra, I., Ortiz, C.M., Baladia, E., Gil-Izquierdo, A., and Ortiz-Moncada, R. Intended or unintended doping? A review of the presence of doping substances in dietary supplements used in sports. *Nutrients,* 9(10), 1093, 2017.

Maughan, R.J., Burke, L.M., Dvorak, J., Larson-Meyer, D.E., Peeling, P., Phillips, S.M., Rawson, E.S., Walsh, N.P., Garthe, I., Geyer, H., Meeusen, R., van Loon, L., Shirreffs, S.M., Spriet, L.L., Stuart, M., Vernec, A., Currell, K., Ali, V.M., Budgett, R.G., Ljungqvist, A., Mountjoy, M., Pitsiladis, Y.P., Soligard, T., Erdener, U., and Engebretsen, L. IOC consensus statement: Dietary supplements and the high-performance athlete. *Br J Sports Med,* 52(7), 439-455, 2018.

Mountjoy, M., Sundgot-Borgen, J.K., Burke, L.M., Ackerman, K.E., Blauwet, C., Constantini, N., Lebrun, C., Lundy, B., Melin, A.K., Meyer, N.L., Sherman, R.T., Tenforde, A.S., Klungland Torstveit, M., and Budgett, R. IOC consensus statement on relative energy deficiency in sport (RED-S): 2018 update. *Br J Sports Med,* 52(11), 687-697, 2018.

Nielsen, B. Diet, vitamins and fluids: intake before and after prolonged exercise. In: Shephard, R., and Åstrand, P.O. *Endurance in Sport.* Oxford: Blackwell, 1992.

Platonov, V.N. *Adaptatsia v sporte.* Kiev: Sdorovia, 1988.

Platonov, V.N. *Obshaia teoriya podgotovki sportmenov v olimpiskom sporte.* Kiev: Olimpiskaia Literatura, 2007.

Platonov, V.N. Podgotovka kvalitsitsirovannyj sportmenov. Moskva: Fizkultura i Sport, 1986.

Platonov, V.N. *Teoria geral do treinamento desportivo olímpico.* Porto Alegre: Artmed, 2004.

Powers, S.K., Duarte, J., Kavazis, A.N., and Talbert, E.E. Reactive oxygen species are signaling molecules for skeletal muscle adaptation. *Exp Physiol,* 95(1), 1-9, 2010.

Powers, S.K., and Howley, E.T. *Fisiologia do exercício: teoria e aplicação ao condicionamento e ao desempenho.* 3. ed. Barueri: Manole, 2000.

Rawson, E.S., and Persky, A.M. Mechanisms of muscular adaptations to creatine supplementation: review article. *International SportMed Journal,* 8(2), 43-53. Retrieved from https://journals.co.za/content/ismj/8/2/EJC4861, 2007.

Santos, V.G., Santos, V.R., Felippe, L.J., Almeida, J.W., Jr., Bertuzzi, R., Kiss, M.A., and Lima-Silva, A.E. Caffeine reduces reaction time and improves performance in simulated contest of taekwondo. *Nutrients,* 6(2), 637-649, 2014.

Saunders, B., Elliott-Sale, K., Artioli, G.G., Swinton, P.A., Dolan, E., Roschel, H., Sale, C., and Gualano, B. Beta-alanine supplementation to improve exercise capacity and performance: A systematic review and meta-analysis. *Br J Sports Med,* 51(8), 658-669, 2017.

Seluianov, V.N., Sarsania S.K. *Fiziologicheskiemcanism i metodiopredleniaaerobinie i anaerobnieparogi. Teoriya i Praktika Fizicheskoy Kultury,* v. 10, p. 10-18, 1991.

Seluianov, V.N. *Isoton: texnologi izdorovitelnom fizijesko i culturii. Teoriya i Praktika Fizicheskoy Kultury,* v. 8, p. C49-54, 2001.

Seluianov, V.N. *Teoriya i praktika didaktike rasvivaioshevo obujenia v podgotovke spesialistov po fisicheskomu vospitanio: trudi sotrudnikov problemnoi laboratorii RGUFK.* Moskva: Fizkultura Obrozavnie i Nauka, 1996.

Seluianov, V.N., Dias, B.C.D., and Andrade, S.L.F. *Musculação:* nova concepção russa de treinamento. Curitiba: Juruá, 2008.

Siegler, J.C., and Hirscher, K. Sodium bicarbonate ingestion and boxing performance. *J Strength Cond Res,* 24(1), 103-108, 2010.

Sikora-Klak, J., Narvy, S.J., Yang, J., Makhni, E., Kharrazi, F.D., and Mehran, N. The Effect of Abnormal Vitamin D Levels in Athletes. *Perm J,* 22, 17-216, 2018.

Tarnopolsky, M. et al. Evaluation of protein requirements for trained strength athletes. *Journal of Applied Physiology,* v. 73, n. 5, p. 1986-95, 1992.

Thomas, D.T., Erdman, K.A., and Burke, L.M. Position of the Academy of Nutrition and Dietetics, Dietitians of Canada, and the American College of Sports Medicine: Nutrition and Athletic Performance. *J Acad Nutr Diet*, 116(3), 501-528, 2016.

Thompson J., and Manore, M. *Nutrition for Life*. 3rd ed. London: Pearson, 2013.

Trexler, E.T., Smith-Ryan, A.E., Stout, J.R., Hoffman, J.R., Wilborn, C.D., Sale, C., Kreider, R.B., Jäger, R., Earnest, C.P., Bannock, L., Campbell, B., Kalman, D., Ziegenfuss, T.N., and Antonio, J. International society of sports nutrition position stand: Beta-alanine. *J Int Soc Sports Nutr*, 12, 30, 2015.

Van Erp-Baart, A. M. J., Saris, W. H. M., Binkhorst, R. A., Vos, J. A., and Elvers, J. W. H. (1989). Nationwide survey on nutritional habits in elite athletes. Part II. Mineral and vitamin intake. Int J Sports Med, 10(suppl 1), S11-S16.

Walker, J.B. Creatine: biosynthesis, regulation, and function. *Advances in Enzymology and Related Areas of Molecular Biology*, v. 50, p. 177-242, 1979.

Williams, M.H. *Nutrition for Fitness and Sport*. 3rd ed. Dubuque, IA: William C. Brown, 1992.

Wilson, J.M., Fitschen, P.J., Campbell, B., Wilson, G.J., Zanchi, N., Taylor, L., Wilborn, C., Kalman, D.S., Stout, J.R., Hoffman, J.R., Ziegenfuss, T.N., Lopez, H.L., Kreider, R.B., Smith-Ryan, A.E., and Antonio, J. *International Society of Sports Nutrition* Position Stand: Beta-hydroxy-beta-methylbutyrate (HMB). *J Int Soc Sports Nutr*, 10(1), 6, 2013a.

Wilson, J.M., Lowery, R.P., Joy, J.M., Walters, J.A., Baier, S.M., Fuller, J.C., Jr., Stout, J.R., Norton, L.E., Sikorski, E.M., Wilson, S.M., Duncan, N.M., Zanchi, N.E., and Rathmacher, J. Beta-hydroxy-beta-methylbutyrate free acid reduces markers of exercise-induced muscle damage and improves recovery in resistance-trained men. *Br J Nutr*, 110(3), 538-544, 2013b.

Chapter 5

American College of Sports Medicine (ACSM). *ACSM's Guidelines for Exercise Testing and Prescription*. 9th ed. Baltimore (MD): Williams and Wilkins, 2014.

American College of Sports Medicine (ACSM). *ACSM's Resources for the Group Exercise Instructor*. Philadelphia, PA: Lippincott Williams and Wilkins, 2012.

Andrade, A., Flores Jr, M.A., Andreato, L.V., and Coimbra, D.R., 2019. Physical and training characteristics of mixed martial arts athletes: Systematic review. *Strength & Conditioning Journal*, 41(1), pp. 51-63.

Baechle, T. and Earle, R. (2020) *Weight Training: Steps to Success* (5th edition). Champaign, IL: Human Kinetics.

Baker, D. Acute effect of alternating heavy and light resistances on power output during upper-body complex power training. *J Strength Cond Res* 17: 493-497, 2003.

Baker, D. Selecting the appropriate exercises and loads for speed-strength development. *Strength Cond. Coach* 3:8-16. 1995.

Barley, O.R., Chapman, D.W., Guppy, S.N., and Abbiss, C.R. (2019). Considerations when assessing endurance in combat sport athletes. *Frontiers in Physiology*, 10, 205.

Bompa, T. (1999) *Periodization, Theory and Methodology of Training* 4th ed. Champaign, IL: Human Kinetics.

Bompa, T.O. *Treinamento Total para Jovens Campeões*. Tradução de Cássia Maria Nasser. Revisão Científica de Aylton J. Figueira Jr. Barueri: Manole, 2002.

Bompa, T.O. *Periodização Teoria e Metodologia do Treinamento*. São Paulo - SP: Phorte, 2002.

Bompa, T.O. *Treinamento de Atletas de Desporto Coletivo*. São Paulo - SP: Phorte, 2005.

Bompa, T.O. *Treinamento de Potência para o Esporte*. São Paulo - SP: Phorte, 2004.

Bondarchuk, A. *Transfer of Training in Sports. Vol 1*. Ultimate Athlete Concepts. 2007.

Boyle, M. *New Functional Training for Sports*. 2nd ed. Champaign, IL: Human Kinetics, 2016.

Brauer Junior, A.G.; Souza, R.M.; Andrade, S.L.F.; Dias, S.B.C.D.; Pimenta, T.F.F. *Esportes de Combate: a ciência no treinamento de atletas de MMA*. Curitiba: Editora Juruá, 2019.

Carter, J. and Greenwood, M., 2014. Complex training reexamined: Review and recommendations to improve strength and power. *Strength & Conditioning Journal*, 36(2), pp. 11-19.

Chaabène H., Tabben, M., Mkaouer, B., Franchini , N. Y., Hammami, M., Chaabène, RB, and Hachana, Y. (2015) Amateur boxing: physical and physiological attributes. *Sports Med.* 45(3):337-52.

Chebbi S., Chamari K., Van Dyk N., Gabbett T., and Tabben M. Hamstring injury prevention for elite soccer players: A real-world prevention program showing the effect of players' compliance on the outcome. *Journal of Strength & Conditioning Research*. 2020 Feb 14.

Chek, P. *Movement that Matters*. C.H.E.K Institute, 2001.

Clark, Michael, Lucett, Scott., McGill, Erin, Montel, Ian, and Sutton, Brian. (Eds.) *NASM Essentials of Personal Fitness Training* Burlington, MA: Jones and Bartlett Learning, 2018.

Cook, G., Burton L., Kiesel K., Rose G., and Bryant M.F. *Functional Training.* On Target Publications, 2011.

Cormie, P., McCaulley, G.O., Triplett, N.T., and McBride, J.M. Optimal loading for maximal power output during lower-body resistance exercises. *Medicine and Science in Sports and Exercise,* 39(2), 340-349, 2007.

Delavier, F. *Strength Training Anatomy (3rd edition).* Champaign, IL: Human Kinetics, 2010.

Delavier, F. and Gundill, M. (2013) *Mixed Martial Arts Anatomy.* Champaign, IL: Human Kinetics.

Dias S.B.C.D. and Oliveira E.B. Circuito para força e resistência. Tatame: a revista do lutador. ISSN 1414-3135. #203: (2013) 90-93.

Dias S.B.C.D. and Oliveira E.B. Força e resistência. Tatame: a revista do lutador. ISSN 1414-3135. #213: (2013) 92-98.

Dias S.B.C.D. and Oliveira E.B. Tratamento preventivo. Tatame: a revista do lutador. ISSN 1414-3135. #206: (2013) 74-77.

Dias S.B.C.D. and Oliveira E.B. Treinamento de MMA adaptado. Tatame: a revista do lutador. ISSN 1414-3135. #209: (2013) 68-72.

Dias S.B.C.D. and Oliveira E.B. Treinamento em grupo para lutadores. Tatame: a revista do lutador. ISSN 1414-3135. #211: (2013) 92-95.

Dias S.B.C.D. and Oliveira E.B. A ciência do alongamento. Tatame: a revista do lutador. ISSN 1414-3135. #214: (2013) 80-83.

Dias S.B.C.D. and Oliveira E.B. Circuito de força e velocidade. Tatame: a revista do lutador. ISSN 1414-3135. #205: (2013) 88-91.

Dias S.B.C.D. and Oliveira E.B. Circuito exclusivo para mulheres. Tatame: a revista do lutador. ISSN 1414-3135. #208: (2013) 74-77.

Dias, S. Seluianov, V., Lopes, L., and Viera, F. (2017) Isoton: Uma nova teoria e metodologia para o fitness. Curitiba, Brasil: Jurua Editora.

Dias, S., Oliveira E., and Everton, B. (2016) Velocidade no MMA. *Tatame: a revista do lutador,* v. 240: 60-63, 2016b.

Dias, Stéfane B.C.D., Oliveira, and Everton. B.A importância de treinar o Core. *Tatame: a revista do lutador,* v. 243, p. 58-61, 2016a.

Dias, Stéfane B.C.D., Oliveira, and Everton. B. Velocidade no MMA. *Tatame: a revista do lutador,* v. 240, p. 60-3, 2016b.

Dias, Stéfane B.C.D., Oliveira, and Everton. B., Júnior, André G.B. (2017) *Teoria e Prática do treinamento para o MMA /São Paulo,* SP: Phorte Editora.

Filin, V.P., Gomes, A.C., Gregorio da Silva, S. *Desporto Juvenil:teoria e motodologia.* Londrina: CID, 1996.

Filin, V., and Volkov, V. *Seleção de Talentos nos Desportos.* Londrina: Midiograf, 1998.

Fleck, S.J., and Kraemer, W.J. *Designing Resistance Training Programs.* 3rd ed. Champaign, IL: Human Kinetics, 2004.

Fleck, S.J., and Kraemer, W.J. *Fundamentos do Treinamento de Força Muscular.* 3. ed. Porto Alegre: Artmed, 2006.

Floyd, R.T. *Manual of Structural Kinesiology, (20th ed.)* New York, NY: McGraw-Hill Education, 2018.

Funato, K., Kanhisa, H., and Fajunada, T. Difference in muscle cross-sectional area and strength between elite senior and college Olympic weightlifters. *Journal of Sports Medicine and Physiology Fitness,* 40, 312-318, 2000.

Gago, P., Zoellner, A., Cezar Lima da Silva, J., and Ekblom, M. (2020). Post Activation Potentiation and Concentric Contraction Performance: Effects on Rate of Torque Development, Neuromuscular Efficiency, and Tensile Properties. Journal of Strength & Conditioning Research, 34, 1600-1608. https://doi.org/10.1519/JSC.0000000000002427

Haff, G., Triplett, N. *Essentials of Strength Training and Conditioning* (4th edition) Champaign, IL: Human Kinetics, 2016.

Henneman, E., Somjen, G., and Carpenter, D.O. Excitability and inhibitability of motoneurons of different sizes. J Neurophysiol 28: 599–620, 1965 (http://jn.physiology.org/cgi/reprint/28/3/599).

Hernández-Preciado, J.A., Baz, E., Balsalobre-Fernández, C., Marchante, D., and Santos-Concejero, J. Potentiation effects of the French contrast method on vertical jumping ability. *Journal of Strength and Conditioning Research,* 32(7), 1909-1914, 2018.

Hoeger, W.K., Hoeger, S.A. *Principles and Labs for Fitness and Wellness.* 13th ed. Boise, ID: Boise State University, 2014.

International Mixed Martial Arts Federation. *IMMAF Amateur MMA Eligibility to Compete.* Grono: Switzerland, 2021.

Iverson, V., Mork, P., Vasselien, O. Bergquist, R., and Fimland, M. Multiple-joint exercises using elastic resistance bands vs. conventional resistance-training equipment: A cross-over study. *European Journal of Sport Science,* 17(8), 2017.

Johnson, M., Baudin, P., Ley, A., and Collins, D. (2019). A Warm-Up Routine That Incorporates a Plyometric Protocol Potentiates the Force-Generating Capacity of the Quadriceps Muscles. *Journal of Strength & Conditioning Research,* 33, 380-389. https://doi.org/10.1519/JSC.0000000000002054

Jones M.T. Effect of compensatory acceleration training in combination with accommodating resistance on upper body strength in collegiate athletes. *Journal of Sports Medicine,* 5, 183-189, 2014.

Jones, K., Hunter, G., Fleisig, G., Escamilla, R., and Lemak, L. The effects of compensatory acceleration on upper-body strength and power in collegiate football players. *Journal of Strength and Conditioning Research,* 13(2), 99-105, 1999.

Júnior, A.G.B., Martins de Souza R., Andrade, S.L.F., Dias, S.B.C.D., Pimenta, T.F.F. *Esportes de combate: A ciência no treinamento de atletas de MMA.* Curitiba, PR: Jurua Editora, 2019.

Katch, V.L., McArdle, W.D., Katch, F.I. *Essentials of Exercise Physiology.* 4th ed. Philadelphia, PA: Lippincott, Williams and Wilkins, 2011.

Kibler, Ben., Press, Joel., Sciascia, Aaron. The role of core stability in athletic function: *Sports Med* 2006, 36 (3): 189-198.

Kostikiadis, I.N., Methenitis, S., Tsoukos, A., Veligekas, P., Terzis, G., and Bogdanis, G.C. The effect of short-term sport-specific strength and conditioning training on physical fitness of well-trained mixed martial arts athletes. *Journal of Sports Science and Medicine,* 17(3), 348-358, 2018.

Lee, S.S., de Boef Miara, M., Arnold, A.S., Biewener, A.A., and Wakeling, J.M. Recruitment of faster motor units is associated with greater rates of fascicle strain and rapid changes in muscle force during locomotion. *Journal of Experimental Biology,* 216 (Pt 2), 198-207, 2013.

Lopes, J., Machado, A.F., Micheletti, J.K., de Almeida, A.C., Cavina, A.P., and Pastre, C.M. Effects of training with elastic resistance versus conventional resistance on muscular strength: A systematic review and meta-analysis. *Sage Open Medicine,* 7, 2019.

Loturco, I., Nakamura, F.Y., Artioli, G.G., Kobal, R., Kitamura, K., Abad, C.C.C., Cruz, I.F., Romano, F., Pereira, L.A. and Franchini, E. Strength and power qualities are highly associated with punching impact in elite amateur boxers. *Journal of Strength and Conditioning Research,* 30(1), pp. 109-116, 2016.

Lowery, R., Duncan, N., Loenneke, J., Sikorski, E., Naimo, M., Brown, L., et al. (2012). The Effects of Potentiating Stimuli Intensity Under Varying Rest Periods on Vertical Jump Performance and Power. *Journal of Strength & Conditioning Research,* 26, 3320-3325. https://doi.org/10.1519/JSC.0b013e318270fc56

Maksimov D.V., Seluyanov V.N., Tabakov S.E. Physical training of martial artists (Sambo, judo). Moscow: TVT Division, 2011.

Malina, R.M.; Bouchard, C. Atividade física do atleta jovem: do crescimento à maturação. São Paulo: Roca, 2002.

Matveev, L.P. Fundamentos do Treino Desportivo. Livros Horizonte. Lisboa, 1991.

Matveev, L.P. Teoria i metodika fizicheskoi kulturiy. Moskvo Fizkultura i sport, 2001.

Matveev, L.P. Metodologia e treinamento. Treino desportivo. Guarulhos: Phorte editora, 1997.

Matveev, L.P. Teoria Geral do Treinamento Desportivo. Moscou, 1991.

Maughan, R.J., Watson, J.S., and Weir, J. Muscle strength and cross-sectional area in man: a comparison of strength-trained and untrained subjects. *British Journal of Sports Medicine,* 18(3), 149-157, 1984.

Maughan, R., Gleeson, M., Greenhaff, P., Bioquímica do exercício e do treinamento físico. São Paulo, Manole, 2000.

McArdle, W.D., Katch, F.I., and Katch, V.L. *Essentials of exercise physiology (5th ed).* Philadelphia, PA: Wolters Kluwer, 2016.

McArdle, W.D., Katch, F.I., Katch, V.L., Fisiologia do Exercício, Energia, Nutrição e Desempenho Humano, 4ª Edição. Ed. Guanabara Koogan S.A., Rio de Janeiro, 1998.

Newmire, D., Willoughby, D. Partial Compared with Full Range of Motion Resistance Training for Muscle Hypertrophy: A Brief Review and an Identification of Potential Mechanisms. *Journal of Strength and Conditioning Research* 32(9), 2018.

Platonov, V.N. Teoria do esporte - Kiev: Escola superior, 1987.

Platonov, V.N. Podgotovka kvalitsitsirovannyj sportmenov. (preparacion de los deportistas de alto nivel) Moscu, Fizkultura I sport, 1986.

Platonov, V.N. Teoria e metodologia do treinamento esportiva. Kiev: Escola Superior, 1984.

Platonov, V.N. Teoria geral do treinamento desportivo olímpico, trad. Ronei Silveira Pinto et al. Porto Alegre: Artmed, 2004.

Platonov, V.N., Vaitceksobski, S.M. Treinamento de nadadores de alto nível. M: Esporte e Cultura Física, 1985.

Potach, D.H., and Chu, D.A. Plyometric training. In: *Essentials of Strength Training and Conditioning*. Baechle, T.R. and Earle, R.W., eds. Champaign, IL: Human Kinetics, 2008. pp. 413-456.

Santana, J.C. *Functional Training*. 1st ed. Champaign, IL: Human Kinetics, 2015.

Sarsania S.K., Seluianov V.N. e co-autores., Análise da dinâmica das cargas de treinamento em atletas de alto nível no ciclo anual de preparação//Recomendação metódica. M: K para cultura física e esporte durante CM U.R.S.S, 1982. p. 32.

Sarsania S.K., Seluianov, V.N. Preparação física em jogos esportivos. M: Gtsolifk.,1990. p. 97.

Seluianov, V.N., Sabelev, I.A. Mecanismos internos de trabalho durante atividades na bicicleta ergométrica. *Fisiologia Humana*, 1982-8-2. p. 235-240.

Seluianov, V.N., Sarsania, S.K. Caminhos para o aumento da capacidade de trabalho esportivo: Recomendação metodológica. Gtsolifk.,1987. p. 22.

Seluianov, V.N., Sarsania, S.K. e co-autores. Classificação das cargas físicas na teoria da preparação física. Teoria e prática da cultura física. 1990, 12. p. 2-8.

Seluianov, V.N., Verkoshanski, Y.V. e co-autores. Mecanismos fisiológicos e métodos de determinação dos limiares anaeróbicos e aeróbicos. Teoria e prática da cultura física, 1991, 10. p. 10-18.

Seluianov, V.N. Isoton: texnologi izdorovitelnom fizijesko i culturii. *Teoriya i Praktika Fizicheskoy Kultury*, v. 8, p. C49-54, 2001.

Seluianov, V.N., Dias, S.B.C.D., Andrade, S.L.F. *Musculação: nova concepção russa de treinamento*. Curitiba: Editora Juruá, 2008.

Siff, M.C. *Supertraining*. Supertraining Institute: Denver, CO, 2003.

Soames, R., Palastnga, N. *Anatomy and Human Movement: Structure and Function* (7th ed). UK: Elsevier Ltd, Inc, BV, 2009.

Souza-Junior, T., Ide, B., Sasaki, J., Lima, F., Abad, C., Leite, R., Barros, M., and Utter, A. Mixed martial arts: history, physiology and training aspects. *Sports Science Journal*, 8/1-7, 2015.

Suchomel, T.J., Mumphius, S., and Stone, M.H. The importance of muscular strength in athletic performance. *Sports Medicine* (Auckland, NZ), 46(10), 1419-1449, 2016.

Sutton, B. (2022) *NASM's Essentials of Personal Fitness Training* (7th edition), Burlington, MA: Jones and Bartlett Learning.

UFC Performance Institute. *A Cross-Sectional Analysis and Projection of the UFC Athlete* (v. 2), 2021.

Van Hooren, B. and De Ste Croix, M.B. Sensitive periods to train general motor abilities in children and adolescents: do they exist? A critical appraisal. *Strength & Conditioning Journal*, 42(6), pp. 7-14, 2020.

Verkhoshansky Y., and Siff M. *Supertraining: Sixth Edition Expanded Version*. Verkhoshansky SSTM, Rome, 2009.

Verkhoshansky, Y.V. Treinamento Desportivo: teoria e metodologia. Porto Alegre: Artmed Editora, 2001.

Wilk, M., Zajac, A. and Tufano, J.J. The influence of movement tempo during resistance training on muscular strength and hypertrophy responses: A review. *Sports Medicine*, pp. 1-22, 2021.

Wilmore, J.H., Costill, D.L. Fisiologia do esporte e do exercício, Ed. Manole, São Paulo, 2008.

Zatsiorsky, V.M. *Science and Practice of Strength Training*. Champaign, IL: Human Kinetics, 1995.

Zatsiorsky, V.M., and Kraemer, W.J. *Science and Practice of Strength Training* (2nd ed). Champaign, IL: Human Kinetics, 2006.

Chapter 6

Al Attar, W.S.A., Soomro, N., Sinclair, P.J., Pappas, E., and Sanders, R.H. Effect of injury prevention programs that include the Nordic hamstring exercise on hamstring injury rates in soccer players: a systematic review and meta-analysis. *Sports Medicine*, (Vol. 47, pp. 907-916), 2017.

American College of Sports Medicine (ACSM). *ACSM's Resources For The Group Exercise Instructor.* Philadelphia, PA: Lippincott Williams and Wilkins, 2012.

American College of Sports Medicine (ACSM) position stand. Progression models in resistance training for healthy adults. *Medicine & Science in Sports & Exercise*, Madison, v. 41, n. 3, p. 687-708, 2009.

Aman, J.E., Elangovan, N., Yeh, I.L., and Konczak, J. (2015). The effectiveness of proprioceptive training for improving motor function: a systematic review. *Frontiers in Human Neuroscience*, 8, 1075.

Barber-Westin, S.D., and Noyes, F.R. Effect of Fatigue protocols on lower-limb neuromuscular function and implications for anterior cruciate ligament injury-prevention training: A systematic review. *Am J Sports Med*, 45, 3388-3396, 2017.

Barengo, N.C., Meneses-Echávez, J.F., Ramírez-Vélez, R., Cohen, D.D., Tovar, G., and Bautista, J.E.C. The impact of the FIFA 11+ training program on injury prevention in football players: a systematic review. *International Journal of Environmental Research and Public Health*, 11(11): 11986-12000, 2014.

Behm, D.G., and Chaouachi, A. A review of the acute effects of static and dynamic stretching on performance. *European Journal of Applied Physiology*, 111(11), 2633-51, 2011.

Bogdanis, G., Donti, O., Tsolakis, C. Smilios, I., Bishop, D. (2019). Intermittent but not continuous static stretching improves subsequent vertical jump performance in flexibility-trained athletes, *Journal of Strength and Conditioning Research*: 33, 203-210.

Bueno, J.C.A., Faro, H., Lenetsky, S., Gonçalves, A.F., Dias, S.B.C.D., Ribeiro, A.L.B., da Silva, B.V.C., Filho, C.A.C., de Vasconcelos, B.M., Serrão, J.C., Andrade, A., Souza-Junior, T.P., & Claudino, J.G. (2022). Exploratory systematic review of mixed martial arts: an overview of performance of importance factors with over 20,000 athletes. *Sports*, 10(6), 80.

Chaabene, H., Behm, D.G., Negra, Y., & Granacher, U. (2019). Acute effects of static stretching on muscle strength and power: an attempt to clarify previous caveats. *Front Physiol*, 10, 1468.

Chan, O., Del Buono, A., Best, T., and Maffulli, N. Acute muscle strain injuries: a proposed new classification system. *Knee Surgery, Sports Traumatology, Arthroscopy*, 20(11), 2356-2362, 2012.

da Silva Junior, J.N., Lima Kons, R., Dellagrana, R.A., and Detanico, D. Injury prevalence in Brazilian jiu-jitsu athletes: comparison between different competitive levels. / Prevalência de lesões em atletas de Brazilian jiu-jitsu: comparação entre diferentes níveis competitivos. *Brazilian Journal of Kineanthropometry and Human Performance*, 20(3), 280-289, 2018.

Dias, S.B.C.D. and Oliveira, E.B. Tratamento preventivo. Tatame: a revista do lutador. ISSN 1414-3135. #206: (2013) 74-77.

Dias, S.B.C.D.; Oliveira, E.B.; Júnior, A.G.B. *Teoria e Prática do treinamento para o MMA.* São Paulo, SP: Phorte Editora, 2017.

Drury, B.T., Lehman, T.P., and Rayan, G. Hand and wrist injuries in boxing and the martial arts. *Hand Clinics*, 33(1), 97-106, 2017.

e Lima, K.M., Carneiro, S.P., Alves Dde, S., Peixinho, C.C., & de Oliveira, L. F. (2015). Assessment of muscle architecture of the biceps femoris and vastus lateralis by ultrasound after a chronic stretching program. *Clinical Journal of Sport Medicine: Official Journal of the Canadian Academy of Sport Medicine*, 25(1), 55-60.

Eckner, J.T., Oh, Y.K., Joshi, M.S., Richardson, J.K., and Ashton-Miller, J.A. Effect of neck muscle strength and anticipatory cervical muscle activation on the kinematic response of the head to impulsive loads. *American Journal of Sports Medicine*, 42(3), 566-576, 2014.

Evans, L.J., and Clough, A. Prevention of ankle sprain: A systematic review. *International Musculoskeletal Medicine*, 34(4), 146, 2012.

Fernandes, J.R., Bello, F.D., De Brito Duarte, M.A., De Carvalho, P.H.B., Queiroz, A.C.C., Brito, C.J., and Miarka, B. Effect of rule changes on technical-tactical actions correlated with injury incidence in Professional Mixed Martial Arts. *Journal of Physical Education and Sport*, 18(3), 1713-1721, 2018.

Gabbe, B.J, Bennell K.L, Wajswelner H., & Finch C.F. (2004). Reliability of common lower extremity musculoskeletal screening tests. *Phys Ther Sport.*, 5(2):90-97.

Gibson, A., Wagner, D., and Heyward, V. (2019). Advanced fitness assessment and exercise prescription, 8th edition. Champaign, IL: Human Kinetics.

Gregory, H.B., Edbert, B.H., Jurek George, G., Justin, D.B., and Guohua, L. Incidence of injury in professional mixed martial arts competitions. *Journal of Sports Science and Medicine (Combat Sport)*, 136, 2006.

Haff, G., and Triplett, N.T. *Essentials of Strength Training and Conditioning.* Fourth edition. Champaign, IL: Human Kinetics, 2016.

Hammam, N., Hattabi, S., Salhi, A., Rezgui, T., Oueslati, M., and Bouassida, A. Combat sport injuries profile: A review (Profil des blessures en sports de combat: revue de la littérature). *Science and Sports* 33(2):73-79, 2018.

Han, J., Anson, J., Waddington, G., Adams, R., and Liu, Y. The role of ankle proprioception for balance control in relation to sports performance and injury. *BioMed Research International*, 2015, 842804, 2015.

Hutchison, M.G., Lawrence, D.W., Cusimano, M.D., and Schweizer, T.A. Head trauma in mixed martial arts. *American Journal of Sports Medicine*, 42(6):1352-1358, 2014.

Hynes, L.M., and Dickey, J.P. Is there a relationship between whiplash-associated disorders and concussion in hockey? A preliminary study. *Brain Injury*, 20(2), 179-188, 2006.

Jensen, A.R., Maciel, R.C., Petrigliano, F.A., Rodriguez, J.P., and Brooks, A.G. Injuries sustained by the mixed martial arts athlete. *Sports Health*, 9(1), 64-69, 2017.

Ji, M. Analysis of injury types for mixed martial arts athletes. *Journal of Physical Therapy Science*, 28(5), 1544-1546, 2016.

Kadakia, A.R., and Haddad, S.L. The role of ankle bracing and taping in the secondary prevention of ankle sprains in athletes. *International SportMed Journal*, 4(5), 1-10, 2003.

Kaminski, T.W., Needle, A.R., and Delahunt, E. Prevention of lateral ankle sprains. *Journal of Athletic Training*, 54(6), 650-661, 2019.

Karpman, S., Gross, D.P., Reid, P., Phillips, L., and Qin, Z. Combative sports injuries: An Edmonton retrospective. *Clinical Journal of Sport Medicine*, 26(4), 332-334, 2016.

Koh, J.O., Watkinson, E.J., and Cassidy, J.D. Incidence of concussion in contact sports: A systematic review of the evidence. *Brain Injury*, 17(10), 901-917, 2003.

Majewski, M., Susanne, H., and Klaus, S. (2006). Epidemiology of athletic knee injuries: a 10-year study. *The knee*, 13(3), 184-188.

McGill, S. Core training: Evidence translating to better performance and injury prevention. *Strength and Conditioning Journal*, 32(3), 33-46, 2010.

McKeown, I., Taylor-McKeown, K., Woods, C., & Ball, N. (2014). Athletic ability assessment: a movement assessment protocol for athletes. *International Journal of Sports Physical Therapy*, 9(7), 862-873.

McLean, S.G., and Samorezov, J.E. Fatigue-induced ACL injury risk stems from a degradation in central control. 41, 1661-1672. *Medicine and Science in Sports and Exercise*, 41, 1661-1672, 2009.

Monsma, E., Mensch, J., and Farroll, J. Keeping your head in the game: Sport-specific imagery and anxiety among injured athletes. *Journal of Athletic Training*, 44(4), 410-417, 2009.

Moreno Catalá, M., Schroll, A., Laube, G., and Arampatzis, A. Muscle strength and neuromuscular control in low-back pain: Elite athletes versus general population. *Frontiers in Neuroscience*, 12, 436, 2018.

Mujika, I., Halson, S., Burke, L.M., Balagué, G., and Farrow, D. An integrated, multifactorial approach to periodization for optimal performance in individual and team sports, *International Journal of Sports Physiology and Performance*, 13(5), 538-561, 2018.

Noh, J.W., Park, B.S., Kim, M.Y., Lee, L.K., Yang, S.M., Lee, W.D., Shin, Y.S., Kim, J.H., Lee, J.U., Kwak, T.Y., Lee, T.H., Kim, J.Y., Park, J., and Kim, J. Analysis of combat sports players' injuries according to playing style for sports physiotherapy research *Journal of Physical Therapy Science*, 27, 2425-2430, 2015.

Opplert, J., and Babault, N. Acute effects of dynamic stretching on mechanical properties result from both muscle–tendon stretching and muscle warm-up. *Journal of Sports Science and Medicine*, 18(2), 351-358, 2019.

Parsons, J. Exercises for injury prevention: Current practice among team sport coaches. *Physical Therapy in Sport*, 28, 2017.

Peeler, J.D., and Anderson, J.E. (2008). Reliability limits of the modified Thomas test for assessing rectus femoris muscle flexibility about the knee joint. *J Athl Train.*, 43(5), 470-476.

Prentice, W. (2020). *Essentials of athletic injury management* (11th ed.). Columbus, OH: McGraw Hill.

Rainey, C. Determining the prevalence and assessing the severity of injuries in mixed martial arts athletes. *Journal of Orthopaedic and Sports Physical Therapy*, 39(1), A115-116, 2009.

Ruan, M, Li, L, Chen, C, and Wu, X. Stretch could reduce hamstring injury risk during sprinting by right shifting the length torque curve. *J Strength Cond Res* 32(8): 2190-2198, 2018.

Ryan, L.M., and Warden, D.L. Post-concussion syndrome. *International Review of Psychiatry*, 15(4), 310-316, 2003.

Sherry, M.A., Best, T.M., Silder, A., Thelen, D.G., and Heiderscheit, B.C. Hamstring strains: Basic science and clinical research applications for preventing the recurrent injury. *Strength and Conditioning Journal*, 33(3), 56-71, 2011.

Sozbir, K., Willems, M., Tiryaki-Sonmez, G., and Ragauskas, P. (2016). Acute effects of contract-relax PNF and static stretching on flexibility, jump performance and EMG activities: A case study. *Journal Biology of Exercise*, 12, 33-55.

Strøm, M., Thorborg, K., Bandholm, T., Tang, L., Zebis, M., Nielsen, K., and Bencke, J. Ankle joint control during single-legged balance using common balance training devices-implications for rehabilitation strategies. *International Journal of Sports Physical Therapy*, 11(3), 388-399, 2016.

Stuber, K.J., Bruno, P., Sajko, S., and Hayden, J.A. Core stability exercises for low back pain in athletes: a systematic review of the literature. *Clinical Journal of Sport Medicine*, 24(6), 448-456, 2014.

Svoboda, Z., Janura, M., Kutilek, P., and Janurova, E. (2016). Relationships between movements of the lower limb joints and the pelvis in open and closed kinematic chains during a gait cycle. *Journal of human kinetics*, 51, 37 -43.

UFC Performance Institute. *A Cross-Sectional Performance Analysis and Projection of the UFC Athlete.* v. 2, 30-41, 2021.

van der Horst, N., Smits, D.-W., Petersen, J., Goedhart, E.A., and Backx, F.J.G. The preventive effect of the Nordic hamstring exercise on hamstring injuries in amateur soccer players: a randomized controlled trial. *American Journal of Sports Medicine*, 43(6), 1316-1323, 2015.

Vigotsky, A.D., Lehman, G.J., Beardsley, C., Contreras, B., Chung, B., and Feser, E.H. (2016). The modified Thomas test is not a valid measure of hip extension unless pelvic tilt is controlled. *PeerJ*, 4.

Wąsik, J. Kinematics and kinetics of taekwondo side kick. *Journal of Human Kinetics*, 30, 13-20, 2011.

Wheeler, R. Limiting lower back injuries with proper technique and strengthening. *Strength and Conditioning Journal*, 37(1), 18-23, 2015.

INDEX

ABOUT THE EDITORS

Stéfane Beloni Correa Dielle Dias, PhD, has a bachelor's degree in physical education from the Federal University of Paraná (Universidade Federal do Paraná) in Brazil and a PhD with honors in sports training and a master's degree with honors in sport and athlete preparation from Russian State University of Physical Education, Sport, Youth, and Tourism (SCOLIPE) in Moscow. In 2005, before starting his doctorate in sports training at the same university, Professor Victor Nikolaevich Seluyanov became his advisor, and he received the honor award for the best scientific research of the year at the Young Scientists Conference.

Dias worked for seven years as the head strength and conditioning coach of the best MMA team in the world, American Top Team, where he has trained and still advises some UFC athletes. He served as first secretary and counselor of the Regional Council of Physical Education–State of Paraná and has also worked as a guest professor in postgraduate programs at Pontifical Catholic University of Paraná, Faculdade Estadual de Educação Física de Jacarezinho, and Instituto Aleixo Educacao e Desporto, giving seminars and instructing courses in Brazil, the United States, Canada, Russia, and Portugal. In 2015, he began a full-time professorship at Keiser University–Orlando in their exercise and sport science program.

Dias trained Muay Thai for seven years at the legendary Noguchi Team in Curitiba, Brazil; earned his second-degree black belt in Brazilian jiu-jitsu; and since 2012 has been a regular columnist for *Tatame* magazine, where he writes about training programs and elite physical preparation. He has published six books in Brazil and Russia, and in 2019 he received the 15-Year Commemorative Medal from the Regional Council of Physical Education–State of Paraná for his contributions to the growth and strengthening of sport in the Brazilian state of Paraná.

Everton Bittar Oliveira holds a degree in physical education from Universidade Positivo in Brazil. He completed his specialization courses in sports training from Pontifical Catholic University of Paraná and is trained as a resistance training specialist (RST) and practitioner in neurolinguistic programming (NLP). In 2007, he earned his black belt in Brazilian jiu-jitsu after training with master Alexandre Penão.

With more than 15 years of experience in the field, Everton has trained several athletes and coached in several gyms in Brazil and the United States and has also worked as a guest speaker for several courses in sports training and personal training. In 2012, he moved to the United States, where he began working as a strength and conditioning coach for the best MMA team in the world, American Top Team, where he coached many champions, including Amanda Nunes (UFC champion in two divisions), Philipe Lins (PFL champion), Natan Schulte (PFL champion in 2018 and 2019), Adriano Moraes (ONE-FC world champion), Kyoji Horiguchi (Rizin champion), Rudson Caliocane (Titan FC champion), Raush Manfio (PFL and Titan FC champion), Victor Dias (Titan FC champion), Jessica Aguilar (WSOF champion), Thiago Moisés (LFA champion), Josh da Silveira (LFA champion in two divisions), and Thiago Alves (Bare Knuckle FC champion). Everton is also responsible for preparation of many professional racing car drivers and tennis players.

André Geraldo Brauer Júnior, PhD, holds a degree in physical education from Pontifical Catholic University of Paraná and has complemented his training with courses at the Brazilian Institute of Research and Extension; Russian State University of Physical Education, Sport, Youth, and Tourism (SCOLIPE); and Federal University of Paraná (Universidade Federal do Paraná). Since 2006, he has been teaching undergraduate and postgraduate studies in the discipline of sports training methodology. He works as a research professor at UniBrasil Centro Universitário and teaches courses in physical preparation for various sports. In addition to his academic work, he provides sports consultation for athletes of different modalities and various fitness facilities. Dr. Brauer is the author of books and scientific articles in specialized journals.

Pavel Vladimirovich Pashkin was born in Orenburg in the USSR. Pavel currently lives in Moscow, Russia. He started doing sports at the age of 10, in the same kind of sports as his father and first coach, Vladimir Alexandrovich Pashkin, who held the title of Master of Sports of the USSR in sambo wrestling and judo, and his uncle Valeriy Alexandrovich Pashkin, who was an honored Master of Sports of the USSR in sambo wrestling. At the age of 17, Pavel Pashkin became world champion in Slada Russian wrestling.

In 1998 Pavel entered Russian State University of Physical Education, Sport, Youth, and Tourism (SCOLIPE) in Moscow, where he continued his sambo wrestling classes under the guidance of Sergey Evgenyevich Tabakov and Sergey Vladimirovich Yeliseyev. Pavel took first prize in the Moscow Sambo Wrestling Student Games in 2000 and second prize in the Sambo Russian Championship in 2001. He fulfilled the standard for a Master of Sports of Russia in sambo wrestling, earned a diploma as a specialist in physical education and sports, and in 2006 defended his thesis to earn a master of physical education and sports degree. While studying for his master's degree, he studied under the guidance of the prominent Russian scientist and academician Lev Pavlovich Matveev, who instilled in him a love of science and gave real understanding of the essence of physical education and sports.

Since 2006 he has been working as a personal sambo and strength and conditioning coach with amateurs and with professional athletes. He was the organizer of fitness sambo and physical education tours for FitSambo Tour in Russia, Europe, Africa, and the United States. In 2009 Pavel held a seminar on sambo for the professional MMA fighters of American Top Team.

In 2016 Pavel together with his wife Olga Sergeyevna Pashkina, Master of Sports of Russia in rhythmic gymnastics, opened FitSambo LLS, a company providing personal coaching in the field of physical education and sports. In 2018 the FitSambo physical education and sports club opened in Moscow, with an emphasis on children's sports and fitness in the field of martial arts and rhythmic gymnastics.

ABOUT THE CONTRIBUTORS

Jeffrey Williams, PhD, NASM-CNC, CACWC, NASM-PES, NASM-CES, CrossFit Level 1, is an educator, coach, and nutritional specialist working both in and out of the classroom. He has taught in elementary and secondary physical education classrooms, and he is now the department chair in exercise and sport science at Keiser University. His research aims to find performance improvements through exercise and nutrition while continuing to determine how to decrease injury through better ways to find asymmetries. Outside the classroom, Dr. Williams has been providing strength and conditioning guidance to sports teams, CrossFit athletes, and weightlifters all over the country for more than 15 years.

Brian Binkley, MS, CSCS,*D, TSAC-F,*D, NASM-CES, NASM-PES, YES, has more than 18 years of experience in the strength and conditioning industry as a competitor, coach, and university instructor in exercise science as well as health and human performance. He holds the Certified Strength and Conditioning Specialist and Tactical Strength and Conditioning Facilitator certifications, both with distinction, from the National Strength and Conditioning Association. He is contracted as a brigade lead strength and conditioning coach with the military police working on the Holistic Health and Fitness (H2F) project for the U.S. Army. He holds a master's degree in exercise science and health promotion and a bachelor's degree in exercise science, and he is pursuing a PhD in health and human performance at Concordia University–Chicago.

Sérgio Luiz Ferreira Andrade, PhD, is a professor who teaches resistance training and kinesiology in both graduate and postgraduate programs of physical education. He also works as a fitness consultant at gyms where technical support is provided to trainers with the goal of improving the efficacy and efficiency of clients' training programs. He holds both a PhD and a master's degree in physical education from the Universidade Federal do Paraná in Brazil. His primary interests are methods of training for muscle hypertrophy and strength. He started lifting weights in 1994, which prompted his endless curiosity about exercise science.

Montverde Academy

Tim Crowley, BS, CSCS, RSSC, NASM-PES, has been the head strength and conditioning coach at Montverde Academy since 2012, overseeing the training of varsity sports and academies. During his tenure, his teams have won 14 national championships as well as multiple team and individual honors. Crowley is also the owner of TC2 Coaching LLC, where he coaches endurance athletes of all levels. His athletes have won professional and age-group national championships and world championships. He is an Olympic triathlon coach and has won USA Triathlon's National Coach of the Year and Development Coach of the Year awards. Crowley is a frequent presenter at national conferences and clinics, and he is the author of the book *The Powerful Triathlete*.

Diego de Castro e Silva Lacerda, MS, is a sports performance specialist and strength and conditioning coach for high-performance athletes (in various sports) and clients of all kinds. He holds a master's degree in sport science from the Russian State University of Physical Education, Sport, Youth, and Tourism and he is working toward his doctoral degree at UTAD in Portugal. He works with MMA and jiu-jitsu fighters, including Marcus "Buchecha" Almeida, Antônio "Shoeface" Carlos Jr., and Renato "Moicano" Carneiro. In addition, he has extensive experience as an athlete. He has a black belt in taekwondo, is a Brazilian national champion, and was on the national team of Brazil.

Vitaly Rybakov, PhD, is the laboratory head for the department of physical education and sports at National Research University in Moscow Institute of Physics and Technology. An expert in sport theory and practice, sports physiology, fitness, wellness, and physical education, he works with top Olympic and club teams in more than 50 sports, providing support in training program development, coaching during training camps and competition, assessment, education, and consulting. He has worked as a strength and conditioning coach for national teams. Dr. Rybakov is an instructor providing advanced training for coaches of elite sport and fitness. The author of more than 80 publications, scientific articles, and books, Dr. Rybakov is also the creator of several sports-related patents.

Ryan Fairall, PhD, CSCS, ACSM-CEP, NASM-CPT, NASM-CES, is originally from a small town outside Philadelphia. Dr. Fairall moved to Jacksonville, Florida, in May 2014 after living in New York City since 2002. Prior to entering higher education in 2015, Dr. Fairall worked in the field of exercise and sports for more than 15 years in roles such as youth and adult assistant sports director and coach, personal trainer, group fitness instructor, general manager, and occupational ergonomist. When not educating future health and fitness professionals, Dr. Fairall enjoys being active by playing softball, lifting weights, kayaking, and fishing as well as spending time with Bledsoe, his shih tzu dog.

João Carlos Alves Bueno, MS, has a bachelor's degree in physical education from Pontifical Catholic University of Paraná and a master's degree in sports performance from Universidade Federal do Paraná in Brazil. He is obtaining a doctorate in human movement sciences at Santa Catarina State University. His professional experience is as a sport scientist, exercise physiologist, and physical trainer in martial arts, soccer, stock car racing, and cheerleading. He is an instructor of combat sports, exercise physiology, sports training, and physical and technological assessment methods. He is a researcher at the Sport and Exercise Psychology Laboratory at Santa Catarina State University, doing research on the nutritional aspects of sports performance, methodological aspects of strength training, combat sports and sports physiotherapy, and the psychology of sport and exercise.

Montverde Academy

Guilherme Ferreira, MS, is originally from Brazil. Ferreira earned his master's degree in athlete preparation at the Russian State University of Physical Education, Sport, Youth, and Tourism in 2011. He then served as the head swim coach at Montverde Academy. Ferreira moved to the United States, where he coached swimmers who participated in the Olympic Games (London, Rio, and Tokyo), among many other international competitions. His swimmers won medals in world championships, Pan American Games, and national championships in 12 different countries. He is interested in studying the relationship between training and recovery.

Rokaya Mikhailenko, MS, CSCS, ACSM-CPfT, earned her master's degree in sport science and rehabilitation at Logan University in Chesterfield, Missouri. She has been working as a research and writing assistant to Dr. Stéfane Dias since 2016 while completing her undergraduate studies. She has a bachelor's degree in exercise science as well as a bachelor's degree in sports medicine and fitness technology from Keiser University–Orlando. Mikhailenko was a service combat medic with the U.S. Army. She is working as a coach at UFC Gym in Miami and also gives lectures virtually and in person. She teaches Brazilian jiu-jitsu and mixed martial arts at American Top Team in Fort Lauderdale.

Eduardo Poloni Silveira, MD, ACSM-CEP, IOC Dip Sp Phy, graduated with a degree in medicine from Universidade Federal do Paraná in 2000. Dr. Poloni Silveira is board certified in nutrology (nutritional medicine), an official medical specialty in Brazil. He works with professional and amateur athletes in sports ranging from triathlon to mixed martial arts. He got the Clinical Exercise Physiologist certification from ACSM, followed by the Certified Sports Nutritionist designation from the International Society of Sports Nutrition. He earned two degrees issued by the International Olympic Committee: the Sports Medicine Diploma and the Sports Nutrition Diploma. Dr. Poloni Silveira is the founder of Synergie, a private clinic focused on exercise performance and lifestyle medicine, and he is a fourth-degree black belt jiu-jitsu athlete.

Victoria Zaborova, MD, graduated with honors from the Moscow Medical Academy with a degree in medicine. From 2002 to 2005, she was enrolled in full-time postgraduate studies. In 2005 she earned her PhD in medical sciences. Dr. Zaborova works as an assistant professor in multiple departments at Sechenov Medical University. From 2009 to 2013, she worked as the head of the complex scientific group (CSG) of the Russian national team. During that period, their athletes repeatedly became winners in world championships and European championships. In 2016 she finished her postdoctoral dissertation and earned the position of associate professor in the department of physiotherapy and sports medicine, and she is the head of the Sports Adaptology Laboratory (ProSportLab) in Russia.

Fabio da Silva Ferreira Vieira, PhD, graduated from Universidade Estadual do Norte do Paraná (UENP) with a degree in physical education in 2001, did postgraduate studies in exercise physiology at UENP in 2009, earned a master's degree in physical education in human performance from Universidade Metodista de Piracicaba (UNIMEP) in 2011, and received his PhD in human movement sciences from UNIMEP in 2016. He has been a delegate of International Federation of Physical Education and Sports (FIEPS) since 2016. He was given an honorary degree in physical education by Logos University International (Unilogos) in 2021. A university professor since 2006, he has taught undergraduate courses in physical education, physiotherapy, nursing, law, and pedagogy. He is a postgraduate professor of public health at Unilogos in Miami.

Grigor Chilingaryan, BS, is the leading laboratory specialist in the department of physical education and sports at National Research University in Moscow Institute of Physics and Technology. He has a category C soccer coach license from the Russian Soccer Union. An expert in sports physiology, sport theory and practice, and physical education, he works with top athletes of Olympic and non-Olympic sports (Greco-Roman wrestling, freestyle wrestling, judo, sambo, boxing, mixed martial arts, soccer, hockey, etc.) in methodological support (training program development, coaching during training camps and competition, assessments, and education). He was a strength and conditioning coach for various sports' world champions and record holders in Russia and Europe.

Courtesy of Josephine C. Photography

Charla-Yvonne Girtman, DHSc(c), MBA, LAT, ATC, earned a bachelor of science degree in athletic training from the University of Central Florida; a master's degree in business administration, with a concentration in sports business management, from Saint Leo University; and a doctorate in health science from Nova Southeastern University. She is the owner and head athletic trainer of Girtman Athletic Group. She also serves as exercise and sport science program chair at the Orlando campus of Keiser University. She is licensed as an athletic trainer (Florida) and is certified as a Corrective Exercise Specialist with a focus on postrehabilitation.

Howard Gelb, MD, is a board-certified orthopedic surgeon and has been practicing for more than 25 years. He completed his undergraduate education at Cornell University in New York, where he graduated number one in his class with distinction. He then entered medical school at the University of Pennsylvania and was awarded the Botelho Prize in physiology and the Munns Memorial Prize for academic excellence. After graduating in 1989 he entered his orthopedic residency and was awarded the Philadelphia Orthopaedic Society's Research Award for academic excellence in 1993. Dr. Gelb has been certified in sports medicine since 2007 and has been a diplomat of the American Academy of Orthopaedic Surgeons since 1997. Dr. Gelb performs minimally invasive surgery, including joint replacements of the knee, shoulder, and hip, using state-of-the-art techniques. Combat sports have been a way of life for Dr. Gelb for decades. He began wrestling while in grade school, trained in taekwondo and achieved third-degree brown belt, and earned a black belt in jeet kune do in 2008. He also trained in Kali (arnis), kung fu, savate, and Muay Thai. He earned his BJJ black belt in 2019 at American Top Team, where he trained with Brazilian champion Jonatas "Tagarela" Gurgel. Dr. Gelb continues to work with athletes from UFC, Bellator, PFL, and other MMA organizations.

Tone Ricardo Benevides Panassollo, PT, MS, studied physiotherapy at the Pontifical Catholic University of Paraná in Brazil and earned his master's degree from the Russian State University of Physical Education, Sport, Youth, and Tourism (SCOLIPE). While in Russia, he worked as a musculoskeletal physiotherapist for Premier League soccer teams. Benevides Panassollo is obtaining his doctorate from Auckland University of Technology in New Zealand, where he is also working as a research officer and assistant. Tone's research interests include strength training, sports injury prevention, and high-intensity interval training.